John Hosack

On the Rise and Growth of the Law of Nations

John Hosack

On the Rise and Growth of the Law of Nations

ISBN/EAN: 9783337233082

Printed in Europe, USA, Canada, Australia, Japan

Cover: Foto ©Suzi / pixelio.de

More available books at **www.hansebooks.com**

ON

THE RISE AND GROWTH

OF THE

LAW OF NATIONS,

AS ESTABLISHED BY GENERAL USAGE AND
BY TREATIES,

FROM THE EARLIEST TIME TO THE TREATY OF UTRECHT.

BY

JOHN HOSACK,

OF THE MIDDLE TEMPLE, BARRISTER-AT-LAW.

LONDON:
JOHN MURRAY, ALBEMARLE STREET.
1882.

LONDON:
PRINTED BY JAS. WADE,
TAVISTOCK STREET, COVENT GARDEN.

PREFACE.

I HAVE attempted in the following pages to trace the progress of the Law of Nations from ancient down to modern times. As my object has been to describe generally the actual practice and usages of nations in their transactions with each other at different periods of history, I have not deemed it necessary to refer to the works of the many eminent writers who, in the course of the last three centuries, have sought to illustrate this extensive branch of jurisprudence and to lay down certain rules for the guidance of independent States as well in peace as in war. To enter upon this wide field would be entirely beyond the scope of this work. My present object is simply to deal, not with opinions but with results; and in these I venture to think there is much to interest the general reader as well as the professional student.

CONTENTS.

CHAPTER I.

THE LAW OF NATIONS AMONG THE ANCIENTS.

	PAGE
Ambassadors	3
Heralds	4
Spies	5
Treaties among the Ancients	5
Neutral States	6
Neutral Waters	7
The Right of Asylum	8
Blockade	9
Contraband of War	9
The Amphictyonic Council	10
Balance of Power	12
International Policy of the Greeks	15
Of the Romans	16
The Feciales	17
The Caudine Forks	18
The Second Punic War	20
Exchange of Prisoners	21

CHAPTER II.

THE LAW OF NATIONS IN THE MIDDLE AGES.

Influence of Christianity	23
On War	24

	PAGE
And Slavery	25
Age of Charlemagne	27
Alfred	28
The Papal Power	29
Hildebrand	31
Frederick Barbarossa	33
Alexander the Third	35
Prisoners of War	37
Richard the First	38
Innocent the Third	41
Frederick the Second	44
Council of Lyons	46
Frederick Deposed	48
The Pope Disposes of Sicily	50
Conradino is Beheaded	53
The Sicilian Vespers	54
Second Council of Lyons	56
Boniface the Eighth and Philip the Fair	57
Decline of the Papal Power	60

CHAPTER III.

OF THE BYZANTINE EMPIRE AND THE CRUSADES.

Revival of the Byzantine Empire	63
Leo the Third and the Pope	64
Haroun al Raschid	65
The Greek Church	65
Basil the Second	66
The Seljouk Turks	67
The Normans	67
The Crusaders in Palestine	68
Urban the Second	69
Constantinople taken by the French and the Venetians	71
The Ottoman Turks	73
Bajazet and Tamerlane	75
Constantine the Ninth	76
His Death	77

CHAPTER IV.

OF THE AGE OF CHIVALRY.

	PAGE
Richard the First at Chaluz	80
Edward the First in Wales	81
David Llewellyn	82
Question of the Scottish Succession	84
Edward chosen Arbitrator	87
War with Baliol	89
William Wallace	90
Intervention of the Pope	93
Letter of Edward	95
His Death	99
Treaty of Northampton	100
Edward the Third	101
He claims the Crown of France	102
Creci and Calais	104
King John of France	109
Taken Prisoner at Poitiers	110
Treaty of Bretigni	111
Bertrand du Guesclin	112
Limoges	114
Prisoners of War in the Fifteenth Century	115
Ransom	116
Travellers	117
Case of the Earl of Suffolk	118
Assassinations in France	119
Henry the Fifth at Harfleur	125
His Policy	126
The Maid of Orleans	129

CHAPTER V.

OF THE PRINCIPAL TREATIES OF THE SIXTEENTH CENTURY.

Louis the Eleventh	131
Charles the Eighth	132
The League of Cambray	135
Its Results	136

	PAGE
Charles the Fifth and Francis the First	139
Charles elected Emperor	140
Battle of Pavia	141
Sack of Rome	142
Treaty of Madrid	142
Peace of Cambray	143
League of Smalkalde	144
Fresh Rupture between France and Spain	145
Treaty between France and the Sultan	146
Assassination of Two French Envoys	147
War Declared against France by Henry the Eighth	148
Treaty of Crespy	148
The Reformation in Germany	149
Maurice of Saxony	150
Siege of Metz by Charles the Fifth	150
Treaty of Cateau Cambresis	151
Policy of Elizabeth	153
Her Treaty with the King of Scots	155
Case of the Bishop of Ross	156
The Queen of Scots	159
Political Changes and Political Morality in the Sixteenth Century	161

CHAPTER VI.

OF THE MARITIME LAW OF NATIONS FROM THE SIXTH TILL THE CLOSE OF THE SIXTEENTH CENTURY.

Piracy in the Middle Ages	163
The Consolato del Mare	164
The Hanseatic League	166
"Free Ships, Free Goods"	167
Right of Search	168
French Ordonnance of 1543	170
The African Slave Trade	171

CHAPTER VII.

OF THE THIRTY YEARS' WAR AND THE TREATY OF WESTPHALIA.

Causes of the War	173
The Duchy of Cleves	174

	PAGE
Policy of Henry the Fourth	175
Insurrection in Bohemia	178
Ferdinand the Second Emperor	181
The Elector Palatine King of Bohemia	181
His Defeat and Flight	182
Count Mansfeld and Christian of Brunswick	184
Diet of Ratisbon	185
Policy of Richelieu	186
Wallenstein	187
Siege of Stralsund	188
Wallenstein Dismissed	190
Gustavus Adolphus Lands in Germany	191
A Protestant Diet at Leipsic	194
Sack of Magdeburg	196
The Protestant Electors	198
Battle of Leipsic	199
Attitude of Ferdinand	201
France and Sweden	202
Wallenstein again in Command	203
Defeat and Death of Tilly	203
Wallenstein at Nuremberg	204
Gustavus to his Soldiers	205
Attempts at Negotiation	207
Lutzen	208
The Chancellor Oxenstiern	210
Wallenstein in Bohemia	211
His Pacific Views	212
He is Murdered	213
Imperial Victory at Nordlingen	214
French Intervention	215
John George of Saxony	215
Treaty of Prague	216
Ill Success of the French	217
A Spanish Fleet in the Downs	218
Victories of Condé and of Turenne	220
Diplomatic Disputes at Munster	221
Assembling of the Congress	223
Its Results	224

CHAPTER VIII.

FROM THE TREATY OF WESTPHALIA TO THE TREATY OF THE PYRENEES.

	PAGE
Mazarin and Cromwell	227
Case of Don Pantaleon Sa	229
He is Beheaded	231
Peace between France and Spain	233

CHAPTER IX.

FROM THE TREATY OF THE PYRENEES TO THE TREATY OF RYSWICK.

Death of Mazarin	236
Louis the Fourteenth and the United Provinces	236
War between England and Holland	237
Attitude of France	238
Treaty of Breda	239
Claim of Louis on the Spanish Netherlands	240
His Successes	241
The Triple Alliance	241
The Treaty of Aix-la-Chapelle	241
Secret Treaty between Louis and Charles the Second	242
Invasion of Holland by the French	244
The Demands of Louis	246
Treaty of Westminster	248
The Emperor declares War against France	249
Death of Turenne	250
The Prince of Orange	250
Treaty of Nimeguen	253
Sobieski	254
Louis the Fourteenth at the Height of his Power	255
His Attack upon Genoa	256
The Edict of Nantes	257
Affairs of the Palatinate	258
Laid Waste by the French	260
War in Ireland	262
Battle of the Boyne	263

	PAGE
And of Beachy Head	263
War in Flanders	264
Treaty of Ryswick	267
And of Carlowitz	269

CHAPTER X.

FROM THE TREATY OF RYSWICK TO THE TREATY OF UTRECHT.

Question of the Spanish Succession	270
The Partition Treaties	271
Intrigues at Madrid	273
Question referred to the Pope	273
His Decision	274
Will of the Spanish King	276
Duke of Anjou proclaimed King of Spain	276
The Emperor Refuses to Recognise him	277
Commences War against France	278
Death of James the Second	280
War between France and England	280
Death of William	281
Marlborough in the Netherlands	283
Questions of Ceremonial	284
Marlborough on the Danube	287
Blenheim	288
Gibraltar	289
Ramillies	289
Louis offers Terms	290
They are Rejected	290
Marlborough and Charles the Twelfth	291
The Earl of Peterborough	293
Battle of Almanza	294
Oudenarde	295
Union between England and Scotland	295
The Ambassador of the Czar	297
Fresh Overtures by Louis	299
Attempt to Bribe Marlborough	299
Malplaquet	302
The War in Spain	303

	PAGE
Change of Ministry in England	305
Marlborough Dismissed	306
Secret Negotiations	307
Debates in the British Parliament	311
Prince Eugene in London	311
Conferences Opened at Utrecht	314
An Armistice	315
Terms of the Treaty	316

APPENDICES.

I. The League of Cambray	321
II. Papers relating to the Thirty Years' War	323
III. Letter of the Emperor to the King of Sweden, and his Reply	327
IV. Proceedings of the Protestant Diet at Leipsic	336
V. Christina of Sweden	347
VI. Papers relating to the Russian Ambassador	348
VII. The "Assiento" Treaty	355

CHAPTER I.

THE LAW OF NATIONS AMONG THE ANCIENTS.

THROUGHOUT all periods of authentic history we find that certain international obligations have been regarded as binding upon mankind. From the time, indeed, when distinct political communities began to be formed, the establishment of some definite rules to be observed towards strangers would naturally suggest itself. The enterprising nature of man and his migratory habits would lead him frequently to wander beyond the limits of his birthplace, and an intercourse between neighbouring states, being once opened up, would, without some disturbing cause, be continued and extended on some footing of reciprocity. The law of nations may, therefore, be said to have its origin in the social nature and the necessities of man. Unless some acknowledged rules existed, by which the intercourse of different states was regulated, each separate community, except when engaged in the destructive work of war, would be compelled to remain entirely isolated from its neighbours.

International comity is a modern term, with a technical sense attached to it; but we are not, upon that account, to assume that, in its more comprehensive sense, it was unappreciated by the ancients. International hospitalities, it is well known, were regarded as sacred rights; and we have abundant proof that international courtesies of a more substantial kind were at times exchanged between the nations of antiquity. One of the earliest authenticated facts of profane history is the burning of the Temple of Delphi, B.C. 648. Herodotus informs us that, upon that occasion, the Amphictyonic council, having resolved that a sum of money should be raised for rebuilding it, Amasis, King of Egypt, sent large contributions for this purpose.[1] And we must bear in mind, with reference to this act of liberality, that his religion differed essentially from that of the Greeks. We have, from the same authority, another incident, similar in kind, in the life of this prince, who, during an illness of the great Cyrus, sent to attend upon him the most skilful physician in all Egypt. But probably the most remarkable instance of international sympathy of ancient or of modern times is related by Polybius. That most trustworthy of ancient historians informs us that the earthquake which happened at Rhodes, B.C. 224, which destroyed an immense amount of property, and overthrew the famous Colossus, was, in reality, of great advantage to that republic. At first the calamity appeared irreparable; but the states and princes, not only of Greece and Sicily, but of Egypt and Asia, sent to the Rhodians such large contributions of money, corn, timber for shipbuilding, and other commodities, that they far exceeded in value the amount of their losses.[2]

With regard to the positive law of nations, as it is understood and recognised in modern times, we are much more indebted to the ancients than is commonly supposed. Scattered throughout Herodotus we have numerous proofs of a recognition of international obligations, not only among the Greeks, but among the Egyptians, Persians, and Phœnicians. For example, although the narrative of the Father of History abounds with scenes of bloodshed, he furnishes us with only two instances in which violence was offered to the persons of ambassadors; and it is remarkable that these outrages were committed, not by Scythian or African barbarians,

---

[1] Herod., b. ii., 180. See also the remarks of Sir G. C. Lewis, "On the "Credibility of the Early Roman History," vol. ii., p. 513.
[2] Polyb., b. v., c. 9.

but by the people of the two most renowned commonwealths of Greece. Previous to the first Persian invasion, Darius sent ambassadors to Athens and Sparta to demand earth and water, in token of his supremacy, and in both cities they were ignominiously put to death. The Spartans, we may add, subsequently acknowledged that they had committed a heinous crime, and even made a formal offer of reparation to the successor of Darius. When Xerxes was on his march to the Hellespont, they sent to Susa two of their most distinguished citizens to expiate, by their death, the outrage that had been committed on the Persian ambassadors. The sole motive of the Spartans in taking this extraordinary step, the historian informs us, was to avert the Divine wrath, of which, ever since the incident in question, they conceived themselves to have been the especial objects. But upon this as upon other occasions, Xerxes evinced a magnanimity which, from his passionate and arbitrary temper, we should not have expected. When the Spartan envoys were introduced to his presence, he declared that he would not follow the example of their countrymen in violating "the usages of all mankind,"[1] and he allowed them accordingly to return to Greece. We may add that no offer of reparation was made by the Athenians, who, during the Peloponnesian War, were guilty of an outrage of a still graver kind. Thucydides informs us that, as ambassadors from Sparta were proceeding to Persia through the neutral territory of Thrace, the Athenians, by means of a stratagem, made them prisoners, and put them to death, without trial, on the very day of their arrival in the capital.[2]

The first war between the Romans and the Gauls, it is well known, arose from a dispute respecting the rights and duties of ambassadors. When Brennus, the Gaulish king, was besieging Clusium in Etruria in the year B.C. 390, ambassadors arrived from Rome for the purpose,

---

[1] "Τὰ πάντων ἀνθρώπων νομιμα."—Herod viii., 136.
[2] Thucyd., lib. ii., 67.

it was alleged, of mediating between the combatants. But instead of confining themselves to their proper duties they openly took part with the besieged, and Quintus Fabius, one of their number, in presence of both armies, challenged and slew a Gaulish chief. On witnessing this act of hostility, Brennus at once ordered a retreat to be sounded lest his countrymen should offend the gods by taking the life of an ambassador. He then despatched messengers to Rome to demand that the offender should be given up. The senate considered the demand to be just, and this was also the opinion of the Fecial College; but they were both overruled by the assembly of the people, and a peremptory refusal was given to the message of the Gaulish king. On receiving this reply, Brennus marched upon Rome, and it is said that during his march his followers were forbidden to pillage the country, as he declared he was at war only with the Romans.[1] On the banks of the Allia, some ten miles from the capital, the Roman army was totally defeated, the destruction of the city followed, and the Gauls were amply avenged.

The Persians were regarded as barbarians by the Greeks, as the Gauls were by the Romans; but we thus learn from the historians of Greece and Rome that in those remote ages both Persians and Gauls entertained juster notions of the rights and duties of ambassadors than either Greeks or Romans.

Heralds, like ambassadors, have at all times been invested with peculiar privileges. A violation of these, during the invasion of Egypt by Cambyses, appears to have met with signal retribution. While that prince was besieging Memphis, he despatched a herald to the city with an offer of terms. The Persian messenger approached the city by water, and both he and the entire crew of the galley in which he sailed, numbering 200 men, were murdered by the besieged. For every life

---

[1] Plutarch in vit. Camill.

thus sacrificed the Persian king, after the capture of the city, caused ten Egyptians to be put to death.¹

There is a third class of persons, regarding whom the same rules have been observed in all ages. As ambassadors and heralds have, at all times and in all countries, been regarded with peculiar favour, so have spies been invariably treated with peculiar severity. Their punishment in time of war has at all times been death.²

Treaties, when weighed in the scale with interest or ambition, have rarely, at any time, been observed with scrupulous fidelity. But the simplicity of ancient manners, and the religious character attached to international obligations, seem to have contributed materially to that result. During the period of which we now speak we have a striking example of the faithful observance of their engagements by a people who had, at the time, very strong motives for setting them aside. After the conquest of Egypt by Cambyses, he resolved to turn his arms against the rising power of Carthage.³ He applied accordingly to the Phœnicians—at that time the allies and the tributaries of Persia—to furnish him with ships for the expedition; but the people of Tyre, at the risk of provoking the hostility of the most powerful monarch in the world, refused to aid him in the enterprise. They alleged, as the reason of their refusal, their solemn treaties of amity, as well as their ties of blood, with the Carthaginians. The good faith of the Phœnicians obliged Cambyses to abandon his project; and thus, Herodotus remarks, Carthage escaped being made tributary to the Great King—an event, he might have added, which would have changed the history of the world.

In the year 480 B.C. a treaty was concluded between Gelon, Prince of Syracuse, and the Carthaginians, which

---

¹ Herod., b. iii., 14.
² But Xerxes dismissed unpunished the Athenian spies taken at Sardis — Herod., b. vii., 147.
³ Herod., b. iii., 19.

is deserving of attention from the singular nature of one of its provisions. It appears that, when Xerxes was about to invade Greece, he induced the Carthaginians to make a descent upon Sicily, with a view of preventing the Sicilian Greeks from sending aid to their kinsmen in the East. An immense armament accordingly sailed from Carthage for Sicily, and the total subjugation of the Hellenic race by the two most powerful states of Asia and Africa seemed at the time inevitable. But, on the very day on which the Persians were defeated at Salamis, the Prince of Syracuse gained a decisive victory over the Carthaginians; and of the mighty fleet which had sailed for Sicily, hardly a vessel escaped destruction. Prostrated by these disasters, Carthage sued humbly for peace. Having lost both her army and her fleet, she was wholly at the mercy of the conqueror. But if we admire the skill, and courage, and complete success of Gelon, we admire still more his moderation and humanity. Although the Carthaginians were prepared to submit to the most humiliating terms, the only conditions which he imposed were that they should pay a sum of money towards the expenses of the war, and that they should renounce their inhuman custom of sacrificing children to Saturn.[1] Montesquieu has pronounced this to be the noblest treaty of peace of which history makes mention.[2]

The privileges of ambassadors, and the sanctity of treaties, were, therefore, acknowledged from the remotest times to which authentic history can reach. The same may be said of neutral nations in time of war. Herodotus informs us that Cambyses, before his invasion of Egypt, asked and obtained permission from the Prince of Arabia to march through his territory. This proceeding, it is hardly necessary to say, accords exactly

---

[1] It appears, from Justin, lib. xix. 1, that Darius had, some time before, remonstrated with the Carthaginians as to this barbarous practice.
[2] "Glorious indeed! After having defeated three hundred thousand Carthaginians, he required a condition that was advantageous only to themselves."—"Spirit of Laws," b. x., c. 5.

with modern usage. A more arbitrary policy was adopted by Agesilaus on his return from his Asiatic expedition. As he approached any neutral state, he simply put the question, "whether they wished him to " pass as a friend or as an enemy?" and no one ventured to oppose his march. But we may remark that he had no option in putting this alternative. Several neutral states lay between him and the Spartan territory, and through these it was necessary for him to pass. In the opinion of Vattel,[1] he was justified, under the circumstances, in adopting the course he did, as upon it depended the safety of his army.

With regard to neutral waters and neutral harbours, the same rules applied. Of this an incident described by Livy, which took place during the Second Punic War, furnishes a strong example. It appears that, after Scipio had conquered Spain, he passed over to Africa, with the view of inducing Syphax, King of Numidia, who, at the time, took no part in the war, to abandon his neutrality. But, as he approached the Numidian port, the Roman general discovered that Hasdrubal, with a squadron of seven triremes, was already there before him. Scipio had with him only two ships; and, on perceiving them, the Carthaginians made all haste to put to sea. Resistance on the part of the Romans would have been hopeless against such numbers; but, fortunately for them, the wind was favourable, and, crowding all sail, they entered the port before the Carthaginians could get under way. Once in a neutral harbour, the Romans were secure from attack.[2] The historian adds that Scipio and the brother of Hannibal met the same evening at supper, at the table of the Numidian king.

The right of asylum is a necessary consequence of the inviolability of neutral territory; and we find that

[1] B. iii., c. 8.
[2] Livy, b. xxviii., 17 and 18. This incident can hardly fail to remind the reader of one that happened in Southampton Harbour during the late American War.

this right was claimed in ancient times by the most insignificant, and acknowledged by the most powerful, states. Herodotus informs us that when Pactyas the Lydian, who had excited a revolt against the great Cyrus, fled to Cyme, the Persians demanded that he should be delivered up to them. The Cymeans applied to the oracle, and the response was that the fugitive should be given up. Not satisfied with this reply they addressed the oracle a second time, in these significant words:—"To avoid a cruel death from the Persians, "Pactyas, a Lydian, fled to us for refuge; the Persians "required us to deliver him into their hands; much as "we fear their power, we fear still more to withdraw our "protection from a suppliant." The oracle, being, probably, under Persian influence, again replied that the fugitive should be given up. But it was disobeyed, notwithstanding; for, instead of handing him over to Cyrus, the Cymeans furnished him with the means of escaping to the Greek islands. Nor does their refusal to deliver up his rebellious subject appear to have been in any way resented by the Persian king. Pactyas was eventually surrendered to his enemies by the people of Chios, who were tempted by the bribe of a town in Asia Minor to violate the laws of hospitality. It is satisfactory to learn that they afterwards became painfully conscious of the baseness[1] of their conduct.

When the last king of Macedon was finally defeated by the Romans he fled for refuge to the island of Samothracia. A Roman fleet followed him to that asylum, but no force was employed or threatened to induce its inhabitants to give him up. Perseus at last surrendered of his own accord, after learning that his children were in the hands of his enemies.[2]

Of the practice of blockading an enemy's port, we

---

[1] "And, for a long time after this, none of the Chians would offer barley-meal "from Atarneus to any of the gods, or make any cakes of the fruit that came "from thence; but all the productions of that country were excluded from the "temples."—Herod., i., 160.

[2] Liv., b. xliv., 6.

have an example in the reign of Demetrius Poliorcetes. Plutarch[1] informs us that that prince put to death both the owner and the pilot of a merchant ship laden with corn, and bound for Athens, at a time when that city was invested and was suffering from scarcity of provisions. We learn from the same authority that this single act of severity had the effect of deterring other nations from sending supplies to the Athenians, and that they were in consequence speedily forced to surrender.

That some rules respecting "contraband of war" were recognised by the ancients appears from a passage of Polybius. On the conclusion of the First Punic War, a most formidable outbreak took place among the mercenary troops of Carthage. During the progress of this mutiny, which lasted upwards of three years, and which brought the Carthaginians at one time to the brink of ruin, he informs us that the Romans acted with strict good faith, and even with generosity. They not only refrained from taking advantage, in any way, of the distresses of their rivals, but they prohibited the export of provisions and other necessaries to the camp of the mutineers, while they allowed their merchants freely to supply all such articles to Carthage.[2]

The earliest definition extant of contraband of war is probably contained in the first treaty concluded between the Romans and the Jews in the time of Judas Maccabæus. By that treaty the contracting parties bound themselves not to supply to the enemies of each other, during war, *arms, ships, money,* or *provisions.*[3]

---

[1] In vit. Demet.
[2] Polyb., b. i., c. 6.
[3] The following is the treaty, as given in 1 Maccabees, c. 8:—"If there come "first any war upon the Romans or any of their confederates throughout all their "dominions, the people of the Jews shall help them, as the time shall be appointed, "with all their hearts; neither shall they give anything unto them that make war "upon them, or aid them with *victuals, weapons, money,* or *ships,* as it hath seemed "good unto the Romans; but they shall keep their covenants without taking "anything therefore. In the same manner also, if war come first upon the nation "of the Jews, the Romans shall help them with all their hearts, according as the "time shall be appointed them; neither shall *victuals* be given to them that take "part against them, or *weapons*, or *money*, or *ships*, as it hath seemed good to the "Romans; but they shall keep their covenants, and that without deceit." This treaty was concluded B.C. 161.

It has been, at times, assumed that the Amphictyonic council was invested with the power of settling disputes between the states of ancient Greece. But we have no proof that any such authority was ever practically recognised and enforced. That institution appears to have been, from the first, essentially of a religious character, and that character it maintained throughout the most brilliant period of Grecian history. It did not interfere, so far as we know, for the purpose either of preventing or of terminating the Peloponnesian War. Had it done so, we should certainly have known the fact from Thucydides. But the Amphictyonic council is not once mentioned either by that historian or by his contemporary Xenophon. The absolute silence of these authorities appears to furnish conclusive proof that it exercised no political authority in their day.[1]

At a later period, indeed, an attempt was made to convert the council of the Amphictyons into a court of international appeal. But we shall find, in the sequel, that this attempt not only failed, but that it brought upon Greece a long series of disasters Some time after their fatal defeat at Leuctra—the date cannot now be ascertained—a charge was preferred against the Spartans in the Amphictyonic council, to the effect that they had, in time of profound peace, treacherously seized the citadel of Thebes. The charge was notoriously true, but it was brought forward at least twenty years after the event, and in that interval the Cadmeia had not only been retaken, but its seizure had been amply avenged by the victories of Pelopidas and Epaminondas. It was not until after the death of both of those great men that Thebes first sought to invest the Amphictyonic council with political authority. She probably hoped, by this means, to maintain that ascendency in the Hellenic world which had been acquired by her two most illus-

---

[1] Herodotus says that the Amphictyons offered a reward for the traitor who betrayed the Spartans at Thermopylæ. But this might have been done on religious grounds, as Thermopylæ was one of the places of meeting of the council, Delphi being the other.—Herod., b. vii., 213.

trious sons. The charge thus made was entertained by the Amphictyonic council, and a fine of 500 talents was imposed upon the Lacedæmonians. This fine, probably, at the next half-yearly meeting of the Amphictyons, was doubled. Whether the Spartans disputed the jurisdiction of the council in the matter we are not informed, but they paid no portion of the fine, nor were any steps taken to compel them. In all probability, the chief motive of the Thebans was to inflict a fresh humiliation on their rivals; and thus far they were successful.

But an important precedent had been established, which, with less formidable enemies, might be turned to better account. We find, accordingly, that, in the year B.C. 357, the Thebans appeared a second time before the Amphictyons in the character of suitors for international justice. The defendants upon this occasion were the people of Phocis, the ancient enemies and rivals of Thebes, but the nature of the complaint made against them cannot now be ascertained; and we may, perhaps, infer, from this circumstance, that it was of a character as unsubstantial as that preferred against the Spartans.[1] Like the latter, however, the Phocians were condemned to pay a heavy fine. And the matter did not end here. The Phocians—relying on the example, and, probably, on the aid of Sparta—having refused to pay the fine, a resolution was passed, at the next half-yearly meeting of the council, and engraven on a column of the temple at Delphi, declaring that the whole of their territory was consecrated to the god. An army of execution was forthwith organised to carry into effect this terrible sentence; and the Phocians, perceiving that their enemies were bent upon their political extinction, wisely determined on resistance. A war accordingly ensued, in which all the principal states of Greece became eventually engaged, and in which excesses of an unprece-

---

[1] Various accounts are given by different historians. Pausanias, writing in the reign of Marcus Aurelius, says he had been unable to find out the true cause. Book x., c. 2.

dented kind were committed upon either side. After a continuous struggle of nine years, fortune seemed to turn against the Thebans, who, in an evil hour, sought the alliance of the King of Macedon. With Philip's aid they finally triumphed over the stubborn Phocians. But the Thebans paid dearly for their victory; for, from this time forward, Philip claimed, and obtained, the right of sending deputies to the Amphictyonic council, and Macedonian influence became paramount at Delphi, as it did soon afterwards throughout all Greece.

We have, therefore, no reason for believing that the Amphictyons, at any time, were recognised as independent arbitrators between the different Greek republics. We have no example of their interfering to protect a weak against a powerful state. They only assumed what may be called an international jurisdiction during the latter days of Grecian independence, and they did so at the instigation of a leading state, which sought to render the "Great Council" subservient to its own purposes of ambition or revenge. The history of these remote events is highly interesting, inasmuch as they furnish us with the first authentic example of an attempt on the part of civilised men to create a court of international appeal. The attempt was, no doubt, imperfect, and the motives which led to it unworthy; but its history may, perhaps, serve to convince us that there must always be two great, if not insuperable, obstacles to the formation of a tribunal of this kind. In the first place, it must ever be exposed to undue influences on the part of one or more powerful states; and, secondly, its decrees must either remain a dead letter, or, if attempted to be executed by force, are but too likely to provoke resistance on the part of all who are strong enough to set them at defiance.

It has been a question whether the notion of the balance of power, which, for upwards of two centuries, has been the guiding principle of European politics, was recognised by the ancients. So far as the Greeks are concerned, we may safely reply in the affirmative. Their whole history, indeed, from the time of the last Persian invasion until the days of Philip, consists of a series of attempts, on the part of one or other leading state, to acquire an undue ascendency, and of combinations formed for resistance by the weaker powers. Aristotle truly says, that the Greeks, united, would have ruled the world.[1] But, from causes to which we need not now refer, no such union ever was effected. The domineering and aggressive spirit of Athens, Sparta, or Thebes— each with a political organisation essentially distinct— led, in the little world of Greece, to a series of coalitions very similar in character to those which Europe has since witnessed on a grander scale, and which, in turn, have humbled the power of Spain, Austria, and France. Jealousy of Athens, Thucydides informs us,[2] led to the Peloponnesian war. After that disastrous contest the Athenians allied themselves at times with Thebes and at times with Sparta, but always with the object of opposing the stronger power. It was the policy of Athens, as declared by Demosthenes,[3] in reality to weaken both those states, and the alliances she made with, or against, them, had all this final aim. These incessant rivalries, as every one is aware, naturally paved the way to the fatal intervention of the Macedonian kings.

The breaking up of the Macedonian Monarchy, after the death of Alexander, afforded the Greeks a fresh opportunity of re-establishing their independence; but the only political result of the wars of the Achæan league was to place them once more at the feet of their former masters. Meanwhile, a contest had commenced in Italy, which fixed for the time the attention of all nations. The career of Hannibal was watched with eager interest both by Greeks and Macedonians, and Philip, the third

---

[1] Polit., b. iv.
[2] B. i.
[3] In his oration for the Megalopolitans.

of that name, prepared, in secret, to join the victorious side. When the news of the battle of Thrasymene reached him he still hesitated;[1] but, after Cannæ,[2] he no longer doubted that fortune had finally abandoned the Romans, and he sent ambassadors, accordingly, to make terms with the Carthaginian general. That he committed a grave error in taking this decisive step is sufficiently plain, and even at the time he was warned, in the most emphatic terms, of the consequences. He was told in the presence of deputies from all parts of Greece, that the time had at last come for all the states to lay aside their ancient rivalries, and to unite in defence of their common liberties against the threatened attack of foreign enemies. "For all," continued the speaker,[3] "who are possessed even of a moderate portion "of discernment in the affairs of policy must be able "clearly to perceive that the conquerors in this war, "whether the Carthaginians or the Romans, will never "rest contented with the sovereignty of Sicily and Italy, "but go on to spread wide their victories and extend "their conquests beyond all just and reasonable bounds." He conjured them, therefore, with the greatest earnestness, and Philip above all the rest, to secure themselves in time against the impending danger. "For if," he continued, "this cloud, which is now seen hovering in "the West, should, at last, settle and discharge itself "upon the provinces of Greece, how greatly do I fear "that an end will be put at once both to our wars and "treaties, and to all those childish contests in which we "are now so wantonly engaged!"

A line of policy is here suggested, which, if vigorously carried out, might have enabled Greece and Macedon to have set even the Romans for a long time at defiance. Its author clearly perceived the necessity of establishing a strong power in Eastern Europe as a counterpoise to

[1] Polyb., b. v., c. 9.
[2] Liv., b. xxiii.—xxxiii.
[3] Agelaus of Naupactus. See Polyb., b. v., c. 9.

the two great rivals then struggling for empire in the West. The notion of the balance of power, in short, has its origin in the instinct of self-preservation. History teaches us that it is the constant tendency of powerful states to render themselves still more powerful. It is no less the tendency of weaker states to watch with jealousy, and, if possible, to prevent, the aggrandisement of dangerous neighbours. Wherever, therefore, political communities are brought into contact with each other, we find these opposing principles more or less actively at work. They are perceptible alike, although in different degrees and under widely different circumstances, in ancient Greece, in Italy during the middle ages, and in modern Europe.

The indifference of the Greeks to human life, as exhibited in their frequent wars and revolutions, is a remarkable characteristic of that highly-cultivated people. We are shocked to find so much heroism and refined intelligence mingled with treachery and cruelty of the grossest kind. The judicial murder, by Spartan commissioners, of the prisoners at Platæa, who were artfully induced to surrender, in the belief that their lives would be spared; the barbarities committed by the Athenians at Melos, and the cruel treatment of the Athenian captives at Syracuse, after the defeat of Nicias, are incidents with which every reader of Thucydides is familiar. It would be easy to swell the catalogue from examples taken from the subsequent history of Greece. But it is sufficient for our purpose to admit—and the admission is a painful one—that in their international transactions the most enlightened people of antiquity appear to have been the most regardless of the rights of humanity.

Modern criticism has in vain attempted to penetrate the obscurity which envelops the early history of Rome. We are still at a loss to distinguish truth from fable throughout that most interesting period. But it seems to be universally admitted that the public morality of the early Romans was higher than that of any people of antiquity[1] with whom we are acquainted. Certain institutions, which we know they possessed, probably contributed to this result. The Latin league, unlike the council of the Amphictyons, partook more of a political than a religious character, and embracing in a federal compact the different states of Latium, it must necessarily have been governed by laws which were obeyed by all. But of the nature of these we have little, if any, positive knowledge. From the frequent wars which took place between the states of Latium we may assume that, like the states composing the Swiss and Germanic Confederations, the members of the league retained respectively their rights of independent sovereignty. A recent and learned historian of Rome[2] supposes that a court of arbitration was established by the league for the decision of disputes between its members. But this is a matter of conjecture, and so we fear it must remain.

The institution of the Fecial College was another important incident in the early history of Rome. It was in itself a recognition, to some extent, of international rights, and, consequently, a check upon military violence. All authorities agree that this order of priesthood was established in the days of the monarchy, but when its powers and privileges fell into abeyance we are not exactly informed. But that it exercised an important influence on the formation of Roman character and policy is highly probable. It was the duty of the Feciales, before declaring war, to make in person a formal demand of reparation from an offending state; and it is a striking proof of the estimation in which the Romans held their institutions that Coriolanus—if we are to credit Plutarch —insisted upon allowing the prescribed period of thirty days to elapse before he entered as an enemy the territory of his native city; and to this resolution he adhered,

---

[1] Polybius, even speaking of his own time—and his testimony as a stranger is of peculiar value—says, "As in other states a man is rarely to be found whose "hands are pure from public robbery, so among the Romans it is no less rare to "discover one that is tainted with this crime."—B. vi., Ex. 3.

[2] Mommsen, b. i., c. 3.

in spite of the warm remonstrances of his Volscian allies. Besides the duty of declaring war, the Feciales were invested with the peculiar rights and privileges of ambassadors, and in that capacity they concluded treaties of peace and alliance. They also exercised judicial functions of a certain kind. If any state in alliance with Rome had reason to complain of the conduct of a Roman citizen, it was their duty to inquire into the matter, and, if satisfied that the charge was true, they had power to hand over the guilty party to the complainants.[1]

We are not aware that this species of extradition was practised by other states, but we cannot believe that the Romans would have sanctioned it without reciprocity. Livy informs us that Ancus Martius borrowed the institution of Feciales from a neighbouring people of Latium; and, as no trace of anything like it is to be found in Greece or elsewhere, we may assume that its origin was Italian, and that perhaps establishments similar, if not identical, in character, prevailed among the various states composing the Latin confederacy. However that may be, not only those states, but their neighbours and rivals, seem to have entertained notions of international justice and international courtesy decidedly superior to those of any contemporary people. The chivalrous character of the Etruscan hero, Lars Porsenna, and of Pontius, the Samnite chief who spared the Roman army at the Caudine Forks, and whose generosity was afterwards so ill-requited, may well bear comparison with the more familiar portraits of Fabricius and Camillus.

The affair of the "Caudine Forks," which has given rise to much discussion both in ancient and in modern times, occurred during the early struggles between the Romans and the Samnites. A Roman army commanded by the two consuls, and consisting of no less than four legions, was compelled to surrender at discretion to the Samnite leader Caius Pontius. He was advised to put them all to death, but he resolved to take another

[1] Dionys. Halicarn., l. ii, 72.

course, in the fallacious hope that by a generous use of his victory he would establish a lasting peace with the Romans. "Restore to us," he said to the consuls, "the " towns and the territory which you have taken from us ; " call home your colonists whom you have unjustly settled " upon our soil; and conclude with us a treaty which " shall acknowledge each nation to be alike independent " of the other. If ye will swear to do this I will spare " your lives and let you go without ransom, each man of " you giving up his arms merely, and keeping his clothes " untouched ; and you shall pass in sight of our army as " prisoners whom we had in our power and whom we set " free of our own free will, when we might have killed " them, or sold them, or held them to ransom."[1]

To these terms the two consuls agreed, and took a solemn oath in presence of both armies to observe them faithfully. They also agreed to leave in the Samnite camp six hundred knights as hostages for the due performance of the treaty. They were then, after surrendering their arms and passing under the yoke,[2] permitted to return to Rome. Pontius not only supplied them with provisions for the journey, but provided carriages for the conveyance of the sick and wounded.

The Samnite chief knew well that the senate and the people of Rome were no parties to this treaty ; but considering his moderate demands, and considering the number and the rank of the hostages whom he held as surety for its fulfilment, he, no doubt, concluded that it would be cheerfully accepted, and that a lasting peace would be established between the two republics. But he had taken no account of the intense patriotism or the insatiable ambition of the Romans, which led them, when the national interest was concerned, to disregard not only the ties of blood, but every other consideration.

---

[1] Arnold, Hist. of Rome, vol. ii., 216.

[2] "Two spears were set upright, and a third was fastened across them at the " top, and through this gateway the vanquished army marched out, as a token that " they had been conquered in war, and owed their lives to the enemy's mercy."— Arnold, vol. ii., p. 220.

The treaty which the consuls had concluded was indignantly repudiated, and both they and the six hundred hostages were abandoned to the vengeance of the Samnites. The two consuls returned to the Samnite camp accompanied by the Feciales, in whose presence they declared that the treaty was cancelled, as it had been concluded without the authority of the Roman people. They and their countrymen who were held as hostages had, therefore, forfeited their liberty and their lives in atonement for their breach of faith. One of the consuls, Sp. Postumius, then violently struck one of the Feciales with his knee, his hands and feet being fettered, and at the same time cried out, "I now belong to the "Samnites, and I have done violence to the sacred "person of a Roman Fecialis and ambassador. Ye will "rightfully wage war with the Romans to avenge this "affront."

But the Samnite chief refused the proffered victims. "They were not," he said, "the guilty parties, nor "would he by punishing them acquit their country. The "Roman people had reaped all the advantages of the "treaty of Caudium, but refused to fulfil its conditions. "Either the legions should be replaced in the desperate "position from which nothing but that treaty could "have delivered them, or the stipulated price of their "deliverance should be paid. The gods would not be "mocked with a piece of childish trickery which invoked "their holy names in support of perfidy and injustice." So saying he allowed them to depart unhurt. The Roman historian who describes this extraordinary scene has not a word to say in extenuation of the conduct of his countrymen, and not a word in commendation of the noble Samnite.[1]

It was certainly contrary to the law of nations, as practised by the early Romans, to put their prisoners of war to death. The custom seems to have been to deliver them up on payment of a ransom, and, if that were not

---

[1] Liv., lib. ix.

paid within a stated time, to sell them as slaves.[1] Livy informs us that, during the First Punic War, the practice of exchanging prisoners was introduced, a fixed sum per man—namely, two pounds and a half of silver[2]—being paid for any number in excess on either side. During the Second Punic War the same practice prevailed. Nor do the courtesies of warfare appear to have been forgotten by the Carthaginians, notwithstanding the desperate nature of that ever-memorable contest. Although the Roman historian loses no opportunity of blackening the character of Hannibal, he informs us that the Carthaginian general caused diligent search to be made on the field of Thrasymene for the body of the consul Flaminius, in order that it might receive the rites of burial.[3] We learn from the same source that he ordered his soldiers to spare the farm of Fabius, while they laid waste the surrounding country;[4] and, at a later period of the war, we find that he honoured Marcellus, the most successful opponent whom, up to that time, he had encountered, with a splendid funeral, and sent his ashes to his son.[5]

After the Punic Wars, the political as well as the social morality of Rome underwent a gradual change. Continued success produced its natural results, until at

---

[1] Niebuhr upon this point says, "The prisoners would have been kept, "according to the Italian law of nations, until they were ransomed; and they "would only have been sold as slaves if this could not have been agreed upon; "they would not have been treated like the Athenian prisoners at Syracuse."—Vol. iii., p. 438.

[2] £8 1s. 5d.

[3] Livy, xxii., c. 7.

[4] Livy, xxii., c. 23. We may observe that Livy gives Hannibal no credit for this act of clemency. On the contrary, he says that his motive in sparing the farm of Fabius was to induce the belief that there was a secret understanding between him and the Dictator, and thus to destroy the credit of the latter with his countrymen, who were impatient of his dilatory tactics. The remark proves nothing except the strong prejudice of the writer. The subsequent history of this farm is singular. The balance of account on the exchange of prisoners was at this time against the Romans, who had received 247 men more than they had given up. The senate having demurred to paying the required amount (viz., two pounds and a half of silver per man) Fabius sold the farm which had been spared by the Carthaginians, and, with the proceeds, paid the debt and maintained the public credit.

[5] Plutarch, vol. iii., p. 130. Livy, l. xxvii., c. 28.

length the ungovernable ambition of her leading citizens, and the no less unruly passions of the multitude, rendered the maintenance of the republic impossible. If it is difficult for individuals to acquire rapid wealth by honest means, it is still more so for states to advance from conquest to conquest unstained by crime. We need not, therefore, be surprised that, after Rome aimed openly at universal dominion, innumerable breaches of the law of nations, as she once had recognised it, were committed. When Marius put to death the unresisting inhabitants of a Numidian town,[1] when Sylla gave orders for the wholesale slaughter of the Samnites, and when Julius Cæsar committed similar acts of violence in Gaul, they each offended against the *jus gentium* recognised from time immemorial by their ancestors. But an adherence to ancient maxims was incompatible with the policy and objects of those aspirants to universal rule.

It would appear, from the examples we have cited, that many of the leading principles of the modern law of nations have come down to us from a period of remote antiquity. It is hardly necessary to add that, in the lapse of time, the usages of warfare have undergone a marked improvement. Two circumstances, it is believed, have mainly contributed to this result—the spirit of Christianity and the progress of commerce. The one has powerfully tended to soften the rigours of war; the other, to render wars less frequent and less protracted. The modern maritime laws of warfare, although they long have been, and still are, open to doubt and controversy, have been framed with the view of interrupting as little as possible the ordinary intercourse of nations in time of hostilities. But, in drawing comparisons of this kind, we ought not to forget that modern civilisation has its dark as well as its bright spots. If we

---

[1] Sallust, notwithstanding his connection with Cæsar, and through him with the Marian faction, does not hesitate to denounce this act as "*contra jus belli.*"--Jugurth., c. 91.

can boast of our superior humanity in war, we are forced to confess that we have sanctioned atrocities in time of peace to which ancient history affords no parallel. Slavery, in one form or in another, has existed in every age; but the African slave-trade, with all its attendant horrors, is of modern growth, and is no offence against the modern law of nations.[1] Until this fertile source of misery and crime, past, present, and to come, be effectually stopped, we must upon one point be content to suffer in comparison with the civilised nations of antiquity.

[1] Madrazo v. Willis, 3 Barn. and Ald. 353. See, also, the American law—the Antelope, 10 Wheaton Rep. 66.

CHAPTER II.

THE LAW OF NATIONS IN THE MIDDLE AGES.

The introduction of Christianity exercised at first but little influence upon the law of nations. Centuries elapsed before its benign doctrines had any perceptible effect in restraining violence and in mitigating the miseries of war. The breaking up of the Roman empire and the rise of innumerable new states upon its ruins led necessarily to ages of confusion. The growth of feudalism which followed, although an improvement upon the anarchy which preceded it, was by no means favourable to the development of international amity. It was not, indeed, until the feudal system was on the decline that the modern public law of Europe may be said to have fairly taken root.

But that Christianity had begun to exercise an important influence upon the rulers of mankind, long before this period, we have abundant proofs. From the time, at least, of Constantine the Great this influence may be readily traced; and during the century in which he lived we have a striking instance of the power of the new faith over the greatest of his successors. Theodosius, the last of the Roman emperors, who maintained in undiminished splendour the vast inheritance of the Cæsars, was in the year 387 publicly rebuked by Ambrose, Archbishop of Milan, on account of a most barbarous massacre which had been committed by the imperial troops,[1]

---

[1] The governor of Thessalonica had been murdered by the populace, and as he was a favourite with the emperor he determined to inflict a signal punishment on the rebellious city. The result is thus described by Gibbon:—"The people of "Thessalonica were treacherously invited in the name of their sovereign to the "games of the circus; and such was their insatiable avidity for those amusements "that every consideration of fear or suspicion was disregarded by the numerous "spectators. As soon as the assembly was complete, the soldiers, who had been "secretly posted round the circus, received the signal, not of the races, but of a "general massacre. The promiscuous carnage continued three hours without dis-

and instead of resenting the conduct of that virtuous and courageous prelate, the master of the world melted into tears before him.¹ Even upon the barbarian conquerors of the empire Christianity appears to have worked a speedy change. At the siege and sack of Rome, in the year 410, Alaric strictly enjoined his followers to respect the Christian churches, and to spare the lives of unresisting citizens; and the greatest of English historians does not hesitate to assert that the capital of Italy was more ruthlessly pillaged by a Christian army in the sixteenth century than by the victorious King of the Goths.² We may add that the most distinguished of the successors of Alaric was alike conspicuous for his humanity and for his strict fidelity to his engagements.³

Half a century after the death of Alaric, when Rome was besieged by the Vandals, Pope Leo the Great sought an audience of their chief, and obtained from him a promise, which was at least in part fulfilled, that he would spare the defenceless multitude, protect the city from fire, and exempt his captives from torture.

If in the sixth century we compare the campaigns of Belisarius and Narses with those of Sylla and Cæsar, we cannot but conclude that the two Christian commanders were much more sparing of bloodshed than their heathen predecessors in the art of war. Belisarius, whose life was one long series of heroic achievements, who reconquered Carthage from the Vandals and Rome from the Goths, and who, even in old age and unmerited disgrace, drove the enemies of his country from the gates

"crimination of strangers or natives, of age or sex, of innocence or guilt; the most moderate accounts state the number of the slain at seven thousand, and it is affirmed by some writers that more than fifteen thousand victims were sacrificed to the manes of Botheric."—Gibbon, vol. v., p. 66.

¹ Ibid., p. 71.

² Gibbon, vol. v., p. 323, describing the sack of Rome by the army of the Constable Bourbon.

³ "The virtues of Totila are equally laudable whether they proceeded from true policy, religious principle, or the instinct of humanity; he often harangued his troops, and it was his constant theme that national vice and ruin are inseparably connected, that victory is the fruit of moral as well as military virtue, and that the prince, and even the people, are responsible for the crimes which they neglect to punish."—Gibbon, vol. vii., p. 359.

of Constantinople, was ever merciful as he was ever modest in the hour of victory.[1] The triumphs of Narses, the first exarch of Ravenna, were hardly less glorious, and they were won with quite as much regard to the rights of humanity.[2]

To the influence of Christianity, too, must be attributed the first systematic efforts that were made to extinguish slavery. The philosophers of Greece, it is true, had not failed to perceive that slavery, being founded upon violence, was necessarily inconsistent with natural justice. Aristotle, in part at least, adopted this doctrine when he distinguished between domestic servitude, of which he approved, and slavery the result of war, which he no less plainly condemned. A state of servitude, he says, may be beneficial both to master and slave, for some men are fitted by nature to command and others to obey; but a captive and his conqueror must ever regard each other with feelings of mutual hostility.[3] It was reserved for the teachers of Christianity to sweep away all such nice distinctions, and to condemn slavery under every aspect. Pope Gregory the Great, by liberating his own slaves, and publishing his reasons[4] for this humane act, furnished an example of the highest importance to succeeding ages. The benevolence of this Pontiff led him even to attempt to mitigate the evils of slavery in countries beyond the Alps. In the year 596 he directed his representative in France to purchase any Anglo-Saxon slaves under the

[1] His treatment of the vanquished at Carthage, at Naples, and at Rome is described by Gibbon (Hist., chap. xli.) with his accustomed eloquence. There appears to have been only one act in the public life of Belisarius which in the practice of modern warfare would be condemned—namely, his poisoning the aqueducts which supplied Ravenna at the siege of that city in the year 539. But he had the high authority of Solon for this proceeding.—Pausanias, L. x., c. xxxvii.

[2] Gibbon, vol. vii., p 381, et seq.

[3] Arist. Polit., B. i.

[4] The following were the reasons given by Gregory for liberating his slaves:—
"Cum redemptor noster, totius conditor naturæ ad hoc propitiatus humanam
"carnem voluerit assumere, ut divinitatis suæ gratia dirempto (quo tenebamur
"captivi) vinculo, pristinæ restitueret libertati, salubriter agitur, si homines quos
"*ab initio liberos natura prolulit* et jus gentium jugo substituit servitutis, in
"eâ quâ nati fuerant, manumittentes beneficio libertati reddantur."

age of eighteen that were exposed for sale, that they might be sent to Rome for their education and instruction in the true faith. The humane example of Gregory was followed by various of his successors. We find that in the year 701 John the Sixth purchased the freedom of a number of Lombard prisoners who had been taken by the Duke of Benevento.[1] About half a century later Pope Zachary induced the King of the Lombards to set free, without ransom, all the prisoners he had taken from the Romans.[2]

Finally, at the third Lateran Council, held in the year 1167, Alexander the Third took a step in advance of all his predecessors by declaring that "all Christian " men ought to be exempt from slavery." The most inveterate enemy of ecclesiastical authority who ever lived has said that this act of Alexander ought alone to render his memory dear to all mankind.[3]

To the influence and the example of the Popes we may attribute the fact that slavery became extinct in Italy much sooner than in any other country in Europe. Even during the eleventh and twelfth centuries the number of slaves in Italy greatly diminished; and in the beginning of the fifteenth century we learn from Muratori that they had entirely disappeared.[4] In England, under the later Anglo-Saxon kings, although slavery existed, we find that the traffic in slaves was positively prohibited.[5] But at the period of the Norman Conquest this humane law had apparently become obsolete. We find that during the reign of the Conqueror there was a large export trade of slaves from Bristol to the Continent. But Wulfstan, Bishop of Worcester, a prelate highly esteemed throughout the nation, inveighed so

[1] Bower's Popes, vol. iii., p. 159.
[2] Ibid., 313.
[3] Voltaire. Essais sur les mœurs.
[4] Muratori. Antich. dissert. 14, Dei servi.
[5] The following is an ordinance of King Ethelred in the tenth century:—" And " the ordinance of our Lord and His Witan is that Christian men and uncondemned " be not sold, and of the country especially, unto a heathen nation; and be it " jealously guarded against that those souls perish not that Christ bought with " His own life."—See Stubbs's Select Charters, p. 72.

earnestly against the traffic that the citizens were finally induced to abandon it.¹ And it is, perhaps, worthy of note that a city which had furnished so early an example of humanity should, seven centuries later, have become conspicuous for the ardour with which it engaged in a slave traffic of a far more odious kind than that which, through the pious exhortations of Wulfstan, it had suppressed. Prædial servitude existed in England until the reign of James the First, and in France and Germany until a much later period. The serfs of Hungary were only liberated in the year 1849, and those of Russia in 1861.²

The long and prosperous reign of Charlemagne forms a distinct epoch in the history of the middle ages. From this period we trace the rise of Christianity in Germany and of modern civilisation in France. Although both were for a time obscured, they were never afterwards effaced. But we must not, in our admiration of this enlightened conqueror, lose sight of the means by which he rose to greatness. That he usurped the inheritance of his brother's children is undisputed, and that he extended his religion as well as his dominions by the sword is as true of Charlemagne as of Mahomet. Although the wanton effusion of blood is expressly forbidden by the written laws which bear his name,³ he caused to be beheaded in one day four thousand five hundred Saxons for no other crime than that of resolutely opposing the invaders of their country.⁴ And as this act of barbarity served only to exasperate instead of subduing the spirit of a warlike people, we find that fourteen years later he laid waste with fire and sword

---

[1] Freeman's History of the Norman Conquest, chap. xxi. The Conqueror in his latter days, whether moved by the eloquence of Wulfstan or stung by remorse for his past deeds, prohibited the slave trade under heavy penalties as follows:— " Ego prohibio ut nullus vendat, hominem extra patriam super plenam foris factu-" ram meam."—Stubbs's Select Charters, p. 81.

[2] See the imperial manifesto issued by the late Emperor Alexander the Second on the 3rd March, 1861.—Annual Register, p. 207. Twenty years afterwards—namely, on the 13th March, 1881—this monarch was barbarously murdered in the streets of Saint Petersburg.

[3] Capit. Carol., lib. v., cap. clxxx.

[4] Hallam, Middle Ages, vol. i.

the whole of that extensive tract of country which lies between the Weser and the Elbe. Nor did he finally reduce the Saxons to subjection until after a continuous struggle of three-and-thirty years.

No such acts of wanton violence tarnish the glory of the great Alfred; for among his many claims upon the veneration of his country and of mankind must be numbered his efforts to ameliorate by his example the sanguinary rules of warfare that were practised in his time. No hero of antiquity treated his enemies with greater generosity than the restorer of the English monarchy. After his first great victory over the Danes he not only spared the lives of his prisoners, but he allowed their chief and his followers to settle in England on condition of their embracing Christianity. The wisdom of this policy was proved by the event, for Guthrum remained ever afterwards faithful to the king.[1] Towards a still more formidable adversary Alfred displayed a similar spirit. He twice made prisoners of the wife and children of the famous Hastings,[2] and upon both occasions he sent them back without ransom to the Danish camp. Yet Alfred could be severe when severity was necessary and just. Among the Scandinavian nations in the ninth century piracy was reckoned the most honourable of all pursuits, but he determined that the Danes who had settled in England should not follow the savage habits of their forefathers. He accordingly caused a band of Northumbrian pirates who had committed great ravages on the Southern coasts to be executed at Winchester, to the great relief of his subjects and of the infant commerce of the age.[3]

Among the results of Christianity, as it affected the progress of the law of nations, the rise of the Papal power is deserving of especial attention. The successors of Saint Peter, it is well known, claimed for a time a paramount authority over all temporal princes, and as a consequence

---

[1] Asser and Chron. Sax.
[2] Chron. Sax., p. 108.
[3] Ibid, p. 115.

of that authority the right of adjudicating upon all international disputes. To trace step by step the growth of this extraordinary jurisdiction would be a task far beyond the scope of this treatise, but it is necessary with reference to the present inquiry shortly to consider how the temporal powers of the Papacy were acquired, how they were exercised, and how they were eventually lost.

The Bishops of Rome, notwithstanding the removal of the seat of empire to the East, continued to be subject to Constantine and his successors. The citizens, as well as the ecclesiastics, had the privilege of electing their spiritual chief, but the election required the confirmation of the emperor, or his delegate, the Exarch of Italy. And although this connection was interrupted by the invasion of the Goths, it was fully restored in the sixth century by the victories of Belisarius. That victorious general indeed, after he had made himself master of Rome, of his own authority deposed and sent into exile the Pope Sylverius upon proof that he was carrying on a treasonable correspondence with the enemy;[1] and in due time the Emperor Justinian issued orders for the election of a new Pope. Gregory the Great, who lived at the close of the same century, acknowledged in the plainest terms[2] his subjection to the emperor; and about fifty years later Martin the First was not only carried off a prisoner to Constantinople by the imperial authorities, but he was tried and condemned to death for heresy and treason, and but for the intercession of the Patriarch it appears that the sentence would have been carried into effect.[3] In the following century we find a marked change in the political situation of Europe. A new race of conquerors had appeared upon the scene, who threatened to wrest from the Northern invaders the spoils of the

---

[1] "Accused by credible witnesses, and the evidence of his own subscription, "the successor of Saint Peter was despoiled of his Pontifical ornaments, clad in "the mean habit of a monk, and embarked without delay for a distant exile "in the East. At the emperor's command the clergy of Rome proceeded to the "choice of a new bishop."—Gibbon, vol. vii., chap. xli.

[2] "Ego equidem jussioni subjectus" are the words he uses in a letter to the emperor.

[3] Bower, vol. iii., p. 44. History of the Western Empire, by Sir R. Comyn, vol. i., p. 105.

Western Empire. The Saracens, after overrunning Sicily and Spain, had carried their victorious arms into the heart of France. Threatened by these new enemies, the Popes naturally looked for the alliance and protection of some power more able to support and defend them than the successors of Constantine. We find accordingly that after Charles Martel had, by his decisive victory at Tours, effectually stopped the progress of the Saracens in the West, Pope Gregory the Second sought the friendship of that triumphant champion of Christianity.[1] This appeal to the leader of the Franks was afterwards attended by very important consequences. Pepin, the son of Charles Martel, who a few years later usurped[2] the crown of France, obtained the sanction of Pope Zachary to his assumption of the royal dignity; and the founder of the Carlovingian dynasty repaid the obligation by bestowing upon the Church a valuable portion of Central Italy which he had wrested from the Lombards, and which until the year 1859 formed a portion of the Papal territory. Under the all-powerful favour and protection of Charlemagne the temporal authority of Rome was consolidated and extended, and from the time that he assumed the imperial crown in the year 800 the allegiance of the Popes was transferred to the emperors of the West. The breaking up of the immense empire of Charlemagne, which fell piecemeal from the nerveless grasp of his successors, was the prelude to the darkest period of mediæval history, and especially dark when we turn to the annals of the Church. The scandals and the crimes which disgraced her in the course of the tenth century far surpass those of any later age, not even excepting the era of the Borgias.[3] It was not until after these monstrous abuses had been corrected by an iron hand that the Papal power reached its meridian height.

[1] See the letter of the Pope at length.—Daniel, Hist. de France, vol i., p. 485. Charles Martel was at the time nominally Mayor of the Palace, but virtually ruler of France.

[2] Pepin set aside Childeric the Second, the last of the Merovingian kings.—Daniel, vol. i, p. 511.

[3] Gibbon, vol. ix., p. 196. Comyn, vol. i., p. 109.

Of the political changes which followed the breaking up of the Carlovingian empire the permanent separation of France and Germany was the most important. Up to that time the election of the Popes had been generally, but not invariably, confirmed by the descendants of Charlemagne, as it formerly had been by the emperors of the East. But from the time of Otho the Great this privilege was transferred to the German emperors, who were ever ambitious of extending their influence in Italy, and who in process of time became in turn the masters, the rivals, and the vassals of the Roman Pontiffs. In the latter part of his reign Otho published an ordinance prohibiting the election of any Pope without the express sanction of the emperor, and for upwards of a century this mandate seems to have been implicitly obeyed. But during the reign of the Emperor Henry the Fourth its validity was contested under circum-stances which attracted the attention of the whole of Europe.

In the history of the middle ages there are two names which occupy a pre-eminently distinguished place. Foremost in the military and political annals of the time stands that of Charlemagne. In its ecclesiastical and social history the name of Hildebrand is no less conspicuous. Widely different, indeed, was the situation in which fortune originally placed those celebrated men, for the greatest of the Roman Pontiffs was the son of a Tuscan peasant. Yet he, too, laid the foundation of a new and mighty empire, and one far more extensive and enduring than that of Charlemagne. While the latter hardly outlived its founder, the monuments of Hildebrand's creative genius have survived the revolutions, political and religious, of eight hundred years. The most important changes which he effected in the discipline and in the constitution of the Church have been steadfastly maintained by his successors. By prohibiting absolutely the marriage of the clergy he increased enormously, in an age of ignorance and credulity, their spiritual influence. By investing the College of Cardinals with the sole privilege of electing the Popes he rendered his successors independent of all temporal authority, and eventually placed them for a time above all temporal princes.

It was not without a long and desperate struggle that he achieved these mighty changes. There were difficulties innumerable to be overcome, but nothing could daunt the courage or shake the inflexible will of Hildebrand. To reform ecclesiastical abuses and to emancipate the Papal authority from the state of vassalage in which, from the time of Otho, the German emperors had held it, were at first the objects, and the legitimate objects, of his ambition. During four successive Pontificates[1] before he ascended the Papal throne under the name of Gregory the Seventh he may be said to have alone directed the councils of the Church, and throughout this eventful period of its history we follow, always with interest and generally with approval, his arduous career as the great reformer of the age. It is only when he seeks as Pope to establish a tyranny more absolute than that which he had overthrown that he ceases to command our sympathies.

The long minority of the Emperor Henry the Fourth, who inherited the crown of his ancestors at four years of age, contributed essentially to the success of Hildebrand. The character of that prince, after he arrived at manhood, encouraged the Pope to pursue, and enabled him in a great measure to realise, his long-cherished schemes of aggrandisement. Although by no means deficient in good qualities, Henry was headstrong in temper and capricious in policy and conduct. We need not, therefore, be surprised to find that in his first struggles for supremacy with Hildebrand he should have been defeated. But the abject humiliation to which he afterwards submitted in order to regain the favour of

---

[1] Namely, those of Leo the Ninth, Victor the Second, Nicolas the Second, and Alexander the Second.

the Pope may well astonish us.[1] Moderation was not one of the virtues of Hildebrand, and the abuse which he made of his victory created a reaction in favour of the emperor which proved all but fatal to the pretensions of his adversary. The contest broke out afresh with greater violence than ever, and the Pope was eventually besieged in his capital by the imperial armies. But although then advanced in years and declining in health, his lofty spirit never quailed. He opposed to his adversaries the wealth and the resources of the devout Countess Matilda and the arms of Robert Guiscard. And although he was eventually driven from Rome and died in exile, his purpose was in the main accomplished. The foremost in rank of all the Christian princes had approached him in the guise of the humblest of suppliants, and in so doing had publicly acknowledged the subjection of the temporal to the spiritual power. It was an incident never to be forgotten in the annals of the Church or of the empire.

In the course of the following century the struggle between the popes and the emperors was renewed, first under the Emperor Henry the Fifth, and again under Frederick the First, better known by his surname of Barbarossa, and the wars of the last-named prince have supplied the materials for one of the most remarkable chapters of Italian history. To restore and to extend the imperial authority in Italy, Barbarossa, in the course of two-and-twenty years, led across the Alps no less than seven formidable armies. The circumstances under which the first of these expeditions was undertaken furnish us with an interesting insight into the manners of the age.

In the year 1153, while Frederick was holding a Diet of the empire at Constance, there appeared before him two merchants of Lodi, who, after complaining of

---

[1] For three whole days, in the midst of a winter of unusual severity, the emperor was compelled to stand bareheaded and barefooted at the gates of the castle of Canossa before he was admitted to the presence of the Pontiff. This was in February, 1077.—Mosheim, B. iii., Part 2.

the grievous tyranny exercised by the people of Milan upon their countrymen, earnestly besought his interference in their behalf. Frederick, without inquiring whether the suppliants had authority from their fellow-citizens to seek redress at his hands, eagerly availed himself of an opportunity of asserting his feudal supremacy in Lombardy. He not only lent a willing ear to their complaints, but forthwith despatched an envoy to Milan to remonstrate with the rulers of that city on their conduct. The two consuls—for the chief magistrates of the Lombard republics assumed in this age the titles and dignities of ancient Rome—treated the imperial envoy with defiance and contempt. They not only threatened him with violence if he did not immediately leave the city, but they even had the audacity to trample under foot in his presence the letters of the emperor. Frederick was only too glad to accept the challenge thus recklessly thrown down to him by his rebellious vassals, and a sanguinary war ensued, in the course of which he caused Milan to be levelled with the ground. This unparalleled act of high-handed violence was committed on the 25th March, 1161. It was not the mere insolence of conquest which induced Barbarossa to destroy the most populous and flourishing city of Italy. The aggressive and domineering spirit of the Milanese had rendered them hateful to most of their neighbours, and the people of Lodi, Cremona, Pavia, and Como not only urged the emperor to execute summary vengeance on their ancient enemies, but they bribed him with large sums of money to induce him to gratify their wishes. Barbarossa not only accepted their gifts, but by a refinement of tyranny he employed Italians only in the work of destruction, well knowing that it would be much more effectually performed by the hereditary enemies of the Milanese than by his German followers. The latter, it is said, regarded with amazement, and even with horror, the savage delight with which Italians levelled to the dust the fairest of Italian cities. By this terrible example Frederick hoped to crush for ever the spirit of the Lombards. But, happily for mankind, excessive severity is always dangerous and often fatal to those who practise it. The jealousy entertained of the Milanese was soon converted into sympathy even among those who had been the instruments of Frederick's vengeance, while among the other states of Northern Italy indignation at his barbarity and inextinguishable hatred of German rule led to the rise and growth of the famous Lombard League.[1] That League, as similar combinations of freemen have done both before and since, finally triumphed over every obstacle.[2] On the decisive field of Legnano, within fifteen miles of Milan, the Xerxes of the middle ages was completely routed by the militia of the Lombard towns, and at the peace of Constance,[3] concluded shortly afterwards at Venice, he was forced to acknowledge their independence.

The Papal power was materially strengthened by the result of this long struggle. Throughout a considerable portion of it the cause of the Lombards and of Italian independence was steadily supported by Alexander the Third, under whose able and enlightened rule the influence of the Church was generally exercised in the most becoming manner. Alexander was a liberal patron of learning, a reformer of ecclesiastical abuses, and an enemy of strife in every shape. If Thomas à Becket had listened to his prudent

[1] That League was composed of Venice, Verona, Vicenza, Padua, Treviso, Ferrara, Breschia, Bergamo, Cremona, Milan, Lodi, Piacenza, Parma, Modena, Mantua, and Bologna. Deputies from all these cities, on the 1st December, 1167, took a solemn oath that they would "share in common the good and evil of the "coming struggle," and that none of them "should make any peace or truce with "the emperor without the consent of the rest," &c.—Testa, Liv. ix.

[2] This famous battle was fought on the 29th May, 1176. At first the Germans were successful, but in leading his troops against the *Caroccio*, or sacred carriage of the Milanese, which was placed in the centre of their line, Barbarossa had his horse killed under him, upon which it was rumoured that he himself was slain. A panic and a complete defeat ensued. The emperor escaped on foot, and after wandering about for two or three days in constant danger of capture, arrived, with a few followers haggard and hungry like himself, at Pavia, which was held by the imperialists.—Testa, L. xi.

[3] On 1 August, 1177.

counsels that ambitious prelate might have lived and died in peace.[1] Of Alexander's declaration concerning slavery at the third Lateran Council we have already spoken.

Although the destruction of Milan by Barbarossa furnishes a striking proof of the harsh rules of warfare practised in the twelfth century, we can discover symptoms of improvement even in that age. Certain regulations issued by that monarch to his troops while serving in Italy are still preserved, and they exhibit a greater regard for justice and humanity than his arbitrary temper would lead us to expect. Commerce, it appears, was even then regarded with especial favour, for the emperor declares that if a soldier robs a merchant he shall be compelled to restore double the value of the property taken. Whoever set fire to a house was to be scourged, and afterwards shaven and branded on the cheek. Whoever found any wine was entitled to drink it, but not to injure the vessel or cask in which it was contained. When a castle was taken by storm the besiegers were entitled to everything which it contained, but they were not permitted to set it on fire without express orders to that effect.[2]

It must be further mentioned to the credit of Barbarossa that, although he regarded the people of Lombardy as vassals of the empire, no one was put to death by judicial process as a rebel or a traitor. He treated them ever as open enemies, and after he had once acknowledged their independence he never sought to recede from his engagements. But it must be admitted that he was at times guilty of acts of great cruelty, and even of deliberate treachery. At the siege of Crema in the

---

[1] The Pope, writing to Thomas à Becket in the year 1168, says, "Where you are certain that justice and the liberty of the Church are *greatly* injured do not endeavour to make your peace with the king to the depression and diminution of the ecclesiastical dignity; but nevertheless, as far as it can be done, saving the honour of your office and the liberty of the Church, *humble yourself to him,* and strive to recover his favour and affection; neither be too much afraid of him, nor require greater securities than you need."—See Lord Lyttelton's Hist. of Henry the Second, vol. ii., p. 476.

[2] Sismondi, Histoire des républiques Italiennes, cap. viii.

year 1159, being exasperated by the obstinacy of the defence, he caused a number of his prisoners to be fastened to the engines employed in the siege that they might be killed or wounded by the missiles discharged by their own fellow-citizens.[1] And at the siege of Alessandria in 1175, having proclaimed a truce during Easter week, he made a night attack upon the town when the besieged were wholly unprepared, but who, notwithstanding, succeeded in completely defeating their assailants.[2]

Although the treatment of prisoners of war in this age seems to have varied with the temper of the conqueror, and the barbarous custom of blinding and mutilation still continued to be practised, they were rarely put to death in cold blood. But it is well known that Richard the First sullied the lustre of his great achievements in Palestine by the slaughter of some thousands of unarmed Saracens.[3] Of the international morality of the age the subsequent history of Richard furnishes an instructive picture. When Philip Augustus, jealous of the fame acquired by the King of England, took leave of him in Palestine, he made a solemn promise that he would commit no act of hostility against his dominions on his return to Europe, yet the French monarch forthwith applied to Pope Celestine the Third to release him from his vow. This audacious application having been peremptorily refused, he next proceeded, in concert with Prince John, to take measures for depriving Richard of his kingdom. They made tempting offers to the King of Scotland, William the Lion, to induce him to join their perfidious scheme, but that prince being on terms of friendship with Richard—a friendship which was steadily maintained during their respective lives—refused to listen to their proposals.[4] On being apprised

[1] History of the Western Empire, by Sir Robert Comyn, vol. i., p. 241.
[2] Sismondi, tom. ii., p. 200.
[3] Hoveden, p. 697.
[4] Hoveden, ibid.

of the bad faith of Philip and the treachery of his brother, Richard resolved to return to his dominions, but the vessel in which he sailed was wrecked on the coast of Istria, and in attempting to pass in disguise through the dominions of the Duke of Austria he was seized by that prince, and by him handed over to the Emperor Henry the Sixth. Neither the duke nor the emperor was at that time at war with the King of England, yet he was kept in close confinement, and an enormous sum was demanded for his ransom. After having been detained in prison for several months, his keepers even ventured to arraign him before the Diet of the empire and to accuse him of the most heinous crimes; but the intrepid bearing of the royal captive and the manly eloquence with which he defended himself against these scandalous charges so won the sympathies of the German princes that they with one accord entreated the emperor to set him free. Philip and John meanwhile were using all their influence to induce Henry to detain him in captivity. They even at length offered a larger sum for his detention than was offered for his release, the bearer of this remarkable proposal being the Bishop of Beauvais, cousin-german of the French king. Thus doubly tempted the emperor resolved to avail himself of the liberality both of the friends and of the enemies of Richard. He allowed him to depart after having received the immense ransom stipulated to be paid by England, but fully intending to retake him before he reached the sea-coast, and then to come to terms with Philip and Prince John. It was only by the speed of his movements that Richard, who had been secretly apprised of his danger, defeated their nefarious scheme.[1] Such in the twelfth century was the public morality of the leading potentates of Christendom.

During the captivity of Richard, which lasted about fifteen months, his mother, Eleanor, the queen-dowager, made frequent appeals to the Pope to interfere on his

[1] Hoveden, p. 740.

behalf. Modern historians[1] have generally assumed that these appeals were fruitless, and that Celestine made no efforts to obtain the liberation of the English king, but a contemporary writer of undoubted credit has furnished us with evidence to the contrary. We find from Hoveden that in the year 1193 Celestine wrote to the prelates of England informing them that the emperor and the whole of his dominions would be laid under an interdict unless Richard was speedily set at liberty; and we learn from the same authority, not only that this penalty was inflicted, but that on the death of the emperor, which occurred at Messina in the year 1197, the Pope refused to allow his body the rites of Christian burial except with the consent of the King of England, and unless the ransom paid by him to Henry should be repaid. We learn further that while Richard was a prisoner Celestine warned the King of France that his kingdom would be laid under an interdict unless he desisted from attacking the English dominions. Finally, the Duke of Austria, having been fatally injured by a fall from his horse, made a will in which he expressed deep penitence and sorrow for having unjustly made a prisoner of the King of England, declaring at the same time that he could not in conscience receive a ransom for his deliverance, and desiring that the hostages whom he held as security for its payment should be released. His son and successor, nevertheless, refused to obey these injunctions until he was threatened by Celestine with excommunication. He then reluctantly gave up the hostages. The portion of the ransom, however, which his father had received was not repaid at this time. We

---

[1] Rapin says, alluding to the letters of Eleanor to the Pope, "But all these "instances were to no purpose. The Pope did not think fit to concern himself "about an unfortunate prince for fear of displeasing the King of France, who "pressed him, on the other hand, not to interpose."—Rapin, vol. iii., p. 129. Hume only remarks, "The zeal of Celestine corresponded not to the impatience of the "queen-mother."—Chap. x. Hallam makes a remarkable mistake, for he accuses, not Celestine but Innocent the Third, of indifference to the fate of Richard, the fact being that Innocent did not become Pope until five years after Richard had left his German prison.—See Hallam, Middle Ages, vol. i., p. 552, note.

learn this from the fact that the successor of Celestine, the celebrated Innocent the Third, subsequently applied in peremptory terms to the brother of the emperor[1] and to the young Duke of Austria for the sum in question, and from what we know of the character of Innocent it is highly probable that these just demands were eventually complied with.

Although Richard had the generosity to forgive his brother's baseness, he did not always treat his enemies with the like forbearance. Having made a prisoner of the Bishop of Beauvais in his subsequent wars in Normandy, he ordered that prelate, who was taken fighting at the head of his retainers, to be put in irons and confined in a dungeon at Rouen. Two retainers of the bishop having thrown themselves at the feet of the king and asked permission to share the captivity of their master, Richard sternly refused their request. "You "shall yourselves judge," he said, "whether I am justified "in my treatment of the Bishop of Beauvais. I count as "nothing many of the injuries he has done me, but there "is one I cannot forget. When I was a prisoner in "Germany I was at first treated reasonably well. But "one day the Bishop of Beauvais arrived at court and had "a private audience of the emperor, and next morning "they chained me like a slave, and covered me with more "iron than a horse could carry. If I treat your master "in the same fashion what have you to say?"[2] Pope Celestine afterwards interceded with the king on behalf of the captive bishop, but with no better success;[3] nor did he regain his liberty until after Richard's death.[4]

---

[1] The letter is addressed to the Archbishop of Magdeburg, whom he instructs to apply to the brother of the late emperor, and who, Innocent says, "vel hæres "sit vel tutor hæredis."—Rymer, Fœdera, vol. i.

[2] Daniel, Hist. de France, tom. iii., p. 464.

[3] Celestine in his letter to the king said he interceded for the bishop as a father would for his son. Richard, in reply, sent to the Pope the coat of mail in which the bishop had been taken, and which was stained with blood, and asking in the language addressed by the sons of Jacob to the patriarch, "Dost thou know thy "son's coat?"—Hoveden, 438.

[4] He was subsequently released by John for a ransom of 2,000 marks.—Hoveden, 452.

It was under the Pontificate of Innocent the Third that the power of Rome reached its meridian height. Of noble birth, and in the prime of manhood when he ascended the Papal throne, equal in ambition and hardly inferior in ability to Hildebrand, he aspired still more openly to universal dominion, and his efforts were crowned with still more signal success. No Pope before his time ever exercised an authority so absolute and so extensive: no prince, however powerful, successfully resisted his authority. Peter the Second of Aragon acknowledged himself his vassal, and the most worthless king who ever wore the English crown submitted to the like degrading terms.[1] Over Philip Augustus of France, a monarch of a very different stamp, the Pope obtained a triumph still more remarkable. Philip had divorced without cause his wife Isemburga, a Danish princess, and had contracted another marriage. This step was strongly disapproved as well in Denmark as in France, in both of which countries the repudiated queen was deservedly esteemed. By the operation of a Papal interdict, which brought his subjects to the verge of rebellion, Philip was at length compelled to annul his existing marriage, and to receive back the wife he had unjustly divorced.[2] There was, indeed, hardly a prince in Christendom who did not feel the weight of Innocent's authority. At a time when war appeared imminent between the kings of Portugal and Castile we find him directing his legate to threaten both with excommunication in case the peace was broken.[3] Complaints having been made against his vassal, the King of

---

[1] On the 15th of May, 1213, John did homage to the Pope's legate at Dover in presence of a number of the nobility and people. He engaged to pay to the Pontiff a yearly tribute of a thousand marks—namely, seven hundred for England and three hundred for Ireland—and he stipulated that if he or any of his successors should fail to fulfil his engagements the crown of England should be forfeited to the Pope. After he had thus solemnly acknowledged himself a vassal of the Pope, John delivered up to the legate his crown and sceptre, who retained them in his possession for five whole days before he restored them to the king.—Rapin, vol. iii., p. 209.

[2] Hallam pronounces this "the proudest trophy in the scutcheon of Rome."— Middle Ages, vol. i., chap. vii.

[3] Innocent, Opera, p. 146.

Aragon, for debasing his coin, he commands him to restore it to the proper standard.[1] At the fourth Lateran Council he absolutely deprived Raymond, Count of Thoulouse, of his dominions on account of his alleged complicity with the Albigenses, and at the same council he declared, after hearing the ambassadors of both the competitors, that Frederick the Second, grandson of Barbarossa, had made good his claim to the imperial crown. Otho the Fourth, who had formerly been crowned by Innocent, was at the same time declared to be no longer emperor. The true reasons for this decision are well known. Otho had solemnly promised[2] at his coronation to restore to the Church certain territories in his possession, and he had wholly disregarded his engagements.

Innocent the Third freely exercised the privilege of creating as well as deposing kings. He gave one king to the Armenians and another to the Bulgarians, and in the year 1200 he transmuted the ducal coronet of Bohemia into a regal crown.[3] Nor did he confine his attention to affairs of state alone. We find him at times assuming jurisdiction in private disputes and exercising the functions of a supreme court of equity.[4] Heretical

---

[1] Innocent, Opera, p. 378.

[2] The following was the oath taken by Otho the Fourth at his coronation:— "I promise to honour and obey Pope Innocent as my predecessors have honoured and obeyed his. The election of bishops shall be free, and the vacant sees shall be filled by such as shall have been elected by the whole chapter or by a majority. Appeals to Rome shall be made freely and freely pursued. I promise to suppress and abolish the abuse that has obtained of seizing the effects of deceased bishops and the revenues of vacant sees. I promise to extirpate all heresies, to restore to the Church all her possessions, whether granted to her by my predecessors or by others, particularly the march of Ancona, the duchy of Spoleto, and the territories of the Countess Matilda, and to maintain inviolate all the rights and privileges enjoyed by the Apostolic See in the kingdom of Sicily." Otho not only refused to restore the territories of the Countess Matilda, but he took possession of Apulia, which was then under the suzerainty of the Pope.

[3] Acta, Jun. and Epist., 14, 15.

[4] He writes to the Chapter of Pisa that one Rubens, a citizen of that town, had complained to him that having mortgaged a house and garden for a sum which was to be repaid on a certain day, by which time he had been unavoidably prevented from raising the money, and the creditor had since refused to receive it, but kept possession of the property. He therefore desires the chapter to inquire into the facts of the case; and if they find the allegations true to compel the creditor by spiritual censures to restore the property upon payment of his debt, *minus* the rent of the premises during the time he had wrongfully occupied them.—Opera, ii., p. 17.

opinions he suppressed by a new and terrible engine of ecclesiastical authority, for inquisitors were first employed in the so-called crusade against the unhappy Albigenses. It was under the Pontificate of Innocent, too, that Constantinople was besieged and taken by the Venetians and the French,[1] and the Patriarch at length acknowledged the supremacy of Rome. From the Bosphorus to the western shores of Ireland, and from Sicily to Lapland, the Pope now reigned supreme. After a hundred and fifty years of incessant toil and strife the dream of Hildebrand was realised, and Rome became a second time the mistress of the world.

The last incident in the life of Innocent is creditable to his memory. In the year 1216, a war having broken out between Genoa and Pisa, the Pope undertook a journey to the latter city with the view of restoring peace. But he was seized with fever while he was on the journey, and died before he reached his destination. The character of this great Pontiff is best portrayed in the voluminous correspondence which he has left behind him. That he was eminently despotic, as well from temperament as policy, is abundantly clear; and it is equally plain that where the interests or the pretensions of the Church were concerned his ambition knew no bounds. But in purely temporal affairs he displayed an amount of industry and sagacity and an inherent love of justice which have been extolled alike by Catholic and Protestant biographers.[2]

The amity which subsisted between the Emperor

---

[1] Constantinople was taken by a joint expedition of the Venetians and the French on the 12th of April, 1204, when Alexius Ducas, who had usurped the crown, was deposed, and Baldwin, Earl of Flanders, was elected in his stead. The Patriarch, therefore, repaired to Rome and was confirmed in his dignity by the Pope, whom he thus acknowledged as his spiritual superior.—Acta, Jun., 92, 93.

[2] A Protestant biographer of Innocent observes:—"He is said to have been "the best civilian as well as the best divine of his time; and it is observed of him "by the author of his life that in all disputes he so faithfully recapitulated the "reasons upon both sides, and urged them with such force, that nobody could "tell what side he inclined to till he gave sentence, and that his sentence was "ever agreeable to the strictest rules of justice and equity."—Bower, Hist. of the Popes, vol. vi., p. 215.

Frederick the Second and Innocent the Third during their respective lives was destined to be rudely broken during the reign of Innocent's successors. The distracted state of Italy during the greater part of this century furnished Frederick with abundant opportunities for interfering in her affairs, and the ancient rivalry between the Empire and the Church once more divided the whole peninsula. The independence of the Lombard republics, it is true, had been solemnly acknowledged by Barbarossa, and after peace was finally established he had scrupulously observed his promise. But those states had no sooner defeated their great transalpine enemy than discord broke out among themselves; and regardless alike of the engagements of his grandfather and of the censures of the Church, Frederick resolved to restore the imperial authority in Italy. We may add that in his mode of conducting war he showed himself to be quite as indifferent to human life as he was to the faith of treaties.

At the battle of Cortanuova, in the year 1237, where the Milanese were totally defeated, he caused their commander, Pietro Tiepolo,[1] a son of the reigning Doge of Venice, to be publicly hanged—an act of barbarity through which he incurred the implacable hatred of that proud Republic. At the siege of Brescia, in the following year, he imitated the evil example of his grandfather by exposing his prisoners on his battering-engines, that they might be destroyed by their fellow-countrymen. And in his attack upon Parma some years afterwards he was guilty of an act of cruelty of which it would be difficult to find a parallel in any age. He made search for natives of Parma in all the adjacent cities, and caused a certain number of them to be butchered daily outside the walls in sight of the besieged.[2] To kill prisoners of war was an act which in this age might still be justified; but to put to death

[1] Muratori, Annal. 1237.
[2] Ibid., Annal. 1247. Sismondi, tom. iii., p. 87.

those who had taken no part in the conflict, and who were not even present at the scene of operations, was an atrocity without example.

But the reign of Frederick is chiefly memorable from his great struggle with the Church, which attracted the attention of the whole of Europe, and eventually brought ruin as well upon himself as his descendants. Frederick, on receiving the imperial crown at Rome, had solemnly promised to Pope Honorius, the successor of Innocent, to lead a crusade to the Holy Land, and in consequence of the violation of his vow had been excommunicated. He subsequently did fulfil his pledge of leading an expedition to Palestine, but at such a time that it was regarded by the Pontiff as an aggravation of his offence, and a second sentence of excommunication was passed upon him. Frederick affected to treat the censures of the Church with ridicule and contempt, but he lived to find that in his estimate of the Papal power he had been grievously mistaken.

During the Pontificate of Gregory the Ninth, who was the successor of Honorius, peace was for a short time restored, but the old quarrel soon broke out afresh with greater bitterness than ever. Frederick invaded the Papal States, where he did not hesitate to plunder the churches and other holy places, but he even made prisoners on the high seas of certain cardinals and prelates who were on a voyage from Genoa to Rome, whither they had been summoned to attend a council by the Pope. This last act was regarded at the Vatican as an unpardonable crime; and Innocent the Fourth, who then filled the Papal throne, determined that the only adequate punishment was the loss of that imperial crown which another Innocent had placed upon the head of Frederick. But to summon a general council in Italy for the purpose was at this time impracticable. Many of the Papal cities were occupied by imperial troops, and even Rome was not secure from attack. Under these circumstances the Pope resolved to hold a council beyond the Alps, and having quitted Rome before Frederick was aware of his intention, he proceeded by sea to Genoa, and from thence to Lyons, where the emperor and the other princes of Christendom were summoned to attend.

About Midsummer, 1245, accordingly, the council was opened with great pomp by the Pope in person. On his right hand sat the Emperor of the East, Baldwin the Second. In addition to the ecclesiastical dignitaries there were present representatives of the leading European States, and to testify their loyalty to the Church and their readiness to shed their blood in her defence the cardinals appeared for the first time in their scarlet hats,[1] a distinction which they have ever since retained. After some days had been spent in preliminary matters, the Pope in person opened his accusation against the emperor, charging him with heresy, sacrilege, and perjury—of heresy because he associated with Saracens and Pagans, of sacrilege because he had pillaged churches and other sacred places, and of perjury because he had never kept faith with him or with any of his predecessors. The Bishop of Carniola then proceeded to detail more circumstantially the crimes with which Frederick was charged. He said that the emperor believed neither in God nor in the saints; that he showed more favour to infidels than to Christians; that he lived in notorious adultery with Saracen concubines after the manner of the Soldan of Babylon, whose friendship he had sought, and whose manners he had adopted; that he was restrained by no laws human or divine; and that he had been frequently heard to say that the whole world had been deceived by three impostors—namely, the Jews by Moses, the Christians by Jesus Christ, and the Mohammedans by Mahomet.[2] The bishop concluded his

---

[1] "Primieramente ornò del cappello rosso i cardinali volendo dimostrar con tal colore, che doveano esser pronti sino allo sporgere del sangue in servigio della chiesa."—Gianonne, lib. xvii.

[2] It seems there was also a rumour that Frederick was the author of a book entitled *De tribus impostoribus*, but it is doubtful whether any such book ever existed.

speech by asserting that Frederick was wont to say that the riches and revenues of the Church were exorbitant, and that he had often boasted he would one day reduce ecclesiastics of every grade to that state of poverty in which they had been content to live in the early days of Christianity. It seems highly probable, not only that the latter charge was well founded, but that, although preferred last of all, it was in truth regarded by his accusers as the gravest they had to make against him.[1]

One of the representatives of the emperor, Thaddeus de Suessa, then rose and solemnly denied the truth of all the charges made against him, and as Frederick was at the time at Turin, he earnestly besought the council to give him an opportunity of replying to them in person. As the emperor had been summoned to the council and had not thought fit to appear, the Pope at first refused to listen to this application, but on the intercession of the ambassadors of France and England he agreed to adjourn the consideration of the matter for a fortnight to allow the emperor an opportunity of replying in person to his accusers.

On being made acquainted with the decision of the council[2] Frederick flatly refused to attend, and he refused, moreover, in very offensive terms. He said, alluding to the capture of the cardinals, that Innocent was acting solely from motives of revenge because he had seized and imprisoned certain Genoese pirates who happened to be kinsmen of the Pontiff.[3] Exasperated by the defiant attitude and still more by the reckless language of Frederick, the Pope no longer hesitated, and although not a single witness had been produced against him, proceeded to depose the most powerful monarch of the age. In vain did the representatives of the emperor,

---

[1] M. Paris in 1245.

[2] Gibbon has not displayed his proverbial accuracy in alluding to this council. "Never," he says, "did any court of justice less deserve the name. *It heard neither the accusation nor the defence,* and refused to grant to the person accused *the smallest delay,* although his ministers, entrusted with full powers, "hastened to Lyons," &c.—Gibbon, Miscellaneous Works, p. 402.

[3] Innocent was a member of the noble Genoese family the Sinibaldi.

who seemed to have formed a truer estimate of the peril in which he stood than Frederick himself, bewail with tears and lamentations the decision of the council. The dreaded sentence was thundered forth with all those imposing solemnities which in a rude and superstitious age were so well calculated to strike the imagination and to move the pity or the terror of the beholder.[1]

Frederick treated the sentence of the council with defiance and derision, and he addressed a letter to his brother-in-law, the King of England,[2] which affords strong confirmation of the truth of at least one of the charges made against him by the Bishop of Carniola—namely, that he intended to strip the bishops of their superfluous wealth. "We beg you," he said, "not to
" consider that the majesty of our high station is in any
" degree lowered by the sentence pronounced against us
" by the Pope, for we are pure in conscience, and conse-
" quently have God with us." "It has always been our
" intention and wish to induce the clerks of every order,
" and chiefly those of the highest rank, to lead such lives
" as their predecessors did in the days of the primitive
" Church, and to imitate our Lord's humility. They used
" to heal the sick, to bring the dead to life, and to reduce
" kings and princes to submission, not by arms but by
" holiness; but these men, devoted to the world and to its
" pleasures, put away the Lord, and by the super-
" abundance of their riches and possessions all religion
" is choked. To take away from such persons the super-
" fluous wealth with which they are burdened to their
" damnation would be a work of charity. For this pur-
" pose, therefore, you and all other princes ought to unite
" with us," &c.

---

[1] "Magistri igitur Thaddeus de Suessa et Walterus de Ocra et alii procuratores, " imperatoris, et qui cum ipsis erant, emisso ejulatu flebili, hic femur hic pectus in " indicium doloris percutientes vix a profluxio lachrymarum sese continuerunt. Et " ait magister Thaddeus memoratus. 'Dies ista, dies iræ, calamitatis et miseriæ.' " Dominus igitur Papa, et prelati assidentes concilio, candelis accensis, in dictum " imperatorem Fredericum, qui jam jam imperator non est nominandus terribiliter, " recedentibus et confusis ejus procuratoribus, fulgurarunt."—M. Paris, p. 672.

[2] Frederick was married to Isabella, sister of Henry the Third.

In a subsequent letter, addressed to the prelates and barons of England, Frederick emphatically denied the temporal jurisdiction of the Popes. He said, " Although " we with all good Catholics most distinctly acknowledge " our belief that full power in spiritual matters was " conferred by the Lord on the high priest of the Holy " Roman See, however great a sinner (which God forbid) " he might be, and also that whatever he should bind on " earth should be bound also in heaven, and that whatever " he loosed should also be loosed, yet nowhere do we read " that power was given to him, either by Divine or human " law, to transfer empires at his pleasure, or to decide on " the temporal punishment of kings and princes."[1]

To these appeals the king and the barons of England turned a deaf ear. Henry the Third was even weak enough to publish the sentence of deposition throughout the kingdom, alleging that he was a vassal of the Pope, and therefore bound to obey his commands.[2] That sentence declared that the thrones both of Germany and Sicily were vacant. The electors of the empire were invited to choose a successor to the deposed monarch, and the Pope reserved to himself the right of disposing of the Sicilian crown.[3] The result was a destructive civil war in Germany, during which first the Landgrave of Thuringia and afterwards the Count of Holland claimed the imperial throne. In Italy the prospects of Frederick were not more promising. The sanguinary tactics to which he had resorted at Parma failed to shake the resolution of its defenders. He was finally compelled to abandon

[1] M. Paris, anno 1245.
[2] Rymer, vol. i., p. 383.
[3] The sentence of deposition was in the following terms :—" We do hereby " sentence and deprive him, and all who are in any way bound to him by an oath " of allegiance we for ever absolve and release them from that oath, and by the " apostolic authority strictly forbid any one from obeying him, or in any way " whatever attempting to obey him, as an emperor or king ; and we decree that " any one who shall henceforth give him assistance or advice, or show favour to " him as an emperor or king, shall be *ipso facto* excommunicated ; and those in " the empire on whom the election of an emperor devolves may freely elect a " successor in his place. With respect to the aforesaid kingdom of Sicily, we, with " the advice of our brother cardinals, will make such provision as may seem " expedient to us. Given at Lyons, &c."—M. Paris, A.D. 1245.

the siege, and shortly afterwards he received intelligence of the total defeat of his forces in Lombardy. With the remnant of his followers he retired to Apulia, where he died in the year 1250;[1] and his enemies did not fail to discern the righteous hand of an avenging Providence in the succession of misfortunes which clouded his latter days.

The deposition of Frederick the Second may be regarded as the most extraordinary stretch of authority ever exercised by the Church of Rome. History records no such signal triumph of spiritual over temporal power. The victories won by Hildebrand over Henry the Fourth and by Innocent over Philip Augustus, although events highly interesting and instructive, established no precedent of such transcendent importance as the deposition of Frederick. No act even of Innocent the Third can be compared with it. Not only was Frederick the most conspicuous personage of the age in which he lived, but sentence of deposition was passed upon him within his own dominions. It was in the imperial city of Lyons that the Pope assumed the right of depriving the emperor of his crown.

And if his memorable feud with Rome brought defeat and ruin upon Frederick, it proved still more disastrous to his descendants. As he was declared to have forfeited the crown of Sicily as well as that of Germany, it became, for obvious reasons, a fixed maxim of Papal policy from this time forward that those two dignities should never be again united in the same person. Frederick left behind him one legitimate and one illegitimate son. The former died at the early age of twenty-five, leaving in Germany an infant named Conradino.[2] Manfred, the illegitimate son of Frederick, was at first appointed guardian of the child, but was subsequently, in the year 1258, crowned King of Sicily in consequence of a rumour having got abroad that his nephew Conra-

---

[1] Comyn's Western Empire, vol. i., p. 318.
[2] So named by the Italians to distinguish him from his father, Conrad.

dino was dead. But the title of Manfred was never acknowledged by the Pope, and after the kingdom had been offered to various princes as a fief of the Church, it was finally granted by Clement the Fourth, who was himself a Frenchman, to Charles of Anjou, brother of Louis the Ninth. The bull which invested Charles with this dignity was dated the 25th February, 1265, and the territories conferred upon Charles embraced, in addition to the island of Sicily, the whole of the South of Italy, from the Straits of Messina to the boundary of the Papal States. The kingdom was to be held as a fief of the Church in consideration of a tribute of 8,000 ounces of gold, to be paid annually under pain of forfeiture and excommunication; and every third year a white palfrey was to be presented to the Pope. Charles was, moreover, strictly prohibited from aspiring to the empire or to the sovereignty of any other state in Italy, was bound to leave all ecclesiastical causes to the exclusive jurisdiction of the tribunals of the Church, and to exempt all ecclesiastics from the payment of taxes.[1]

With an army of thirty thousand adventurers, collected from every part of Europe, but raised principally in France and Flanders, Charles set out for Rome, where, after swearing allegiance to the Pope, he was, on the 6th of January, 1266, solemnly crowned King of Sicily. But Manfred, a brave and ambitious prince, was still in possession of his kingdom, and, in spite of Papal bulls and interdicts, prepared to defend it to the last. With a singularly-assorted army, composed of Sicilians, Saracens, and Germans, he encountered Charles at Benevento. The combat was long and doubtful, but French discipline and valour finally prevailed; and unwilling to survive defeat, Manfred plunged into the ranks of the enemy and died desperately fighting at the head of a few devoted followers. The conquerors, in admiration of his valour, raised a rude monument of stones over the fallen

---

[1] See Amari, the War of the Sicilian Vespers, by Lord Ellesmere, vol. i., chap ii.

king. But generosity to a vanquished enemy was never a virtue of the Church, and by the orders of the Papal legate the body of the gallant bastard was thrown to the dogs on the banks of the Volturno. Manfred left behind him an only daughter Constantia, who was married to the eldest son of the King of Aragon, through which marriage the princes of that house afterwards laid claim to the Sicilian crown.

Only one legitimate descendant of Frederick the Second now remained. Conradino, the grandson of that prince, was the undoubted heir of the Sicilian crown; and to him the Ghibelline faction, jealous of the growing strength of their opponents, now naturally turned. Conradino, though just emerging from boyhood, was of a singularly enterprising temper, and, stimulated by his young kinsman the Duke of Austria, who was no less ambitious of military fame, listened eagerly to the tempting offers of his partisans in Italy. His mother, Elizabeth of Bavaria, trembled for the safety of her only son; but he determined at all hazards to strike a blow for the recovery of his lost inheritance, and, accompanied by the Duke of Austria and a few thousand horse, he crossed the Alps in the spring of 1267. As he advanced through Lombardy and Tuscany the number of his followers rapidly increased, and, heedless of the Pope's anathemas, he entered Rome, without striking a blow, at the head of an army of not less than twenty thousand men. Charles awaited the approach of his youthful antagonist at Tagliacozzo, and on the 23rd of August, 1268, was fought the battle which decided the fate of Sicily. Although greatly superior in numbers, the army of Conradino was totally defeated, and his victorious rival was guilty of the atrocious cruelty of first mutilating and then burning alive a number of Roman prisoners who had been taken in the battle.[1] For Conradino himself another fate was reserved. Charles summoned a Parliament of barons, syndics, and burgesses of the cities of

[1] Amari, vol. i., p. 66.

Apulia, and by this tribunal, and with all the solemnities
of law, the last male descendant of the imperial house of
Suabia was condemned to die by the hands of the
common executioner. One of the deputies only, Guidone
da Suzara, a civilian of high repute, had the courage to
protest against the iniquitous sentence.[1] But Charles
was inexorable.[2] On the 29th of October, 1268, a
scaffold, covered with scarlet cloth to denote the high
rank of the victim, was erected in the market-place of
Naples, and Conradino—who was only sixteen years old—
was led to execution. As an aggravation of his punishment he was compelled to witness the death of his comrade the Duke of Austria, who was beheaded before his
eyes. Turning then to the people, it is said that Conradino, after solemnly protesting against the injustice of his
sentence, flung his glove among the crowd who thronged
the market-place, and desired him who found it to carry
it to his cousin Constantia of Aragon, to whom he
bequeathed his right to the crown of Sicily. He then
patiently submitted to his doom. The extreme youth,
the exalted rank, and the undaunted demeanour of
Conradino excited the warmest sympathy of the spectators, and created, even in that ruthless age, a profound
sensation throughout Europe. For such an act of
violence no precedent could be found, at least in the
history of Christendom, and many of the followers of
Charles regarded it with horror. But the murder of
Conradino was only a prelude to further atrocities, for
never was a conquered nation treated with more systematic brutality than were the unhappy Sicilians by
their French masters. It was in vain that Pope Clement
the Tenth interfered again and again on behalf of that
oppressed people. Charles[3] and his satellites held on

[1] Amari, vol. i., p. 67.
[2] It is asserted by some writers, but denied by others, that Charles put Conradino to death at the instigation of the Pope. We can only remark upon this
point that the execution of Conradino was an act of tyranny and cruelty quite
consistent with the character and policy of Charles.
[3] "Two letters of Clement the Tenth addressed to him," says Amari, "are
"still preserved to us. They are models of political prudence and humanity; but

their reckless course, and private as well as public outrages continued to exasperate a people at once keenly sensitive of wrong and passionately vindictive until a day of terrible retribution came, and fourteen years of intolerable tyranny were avenged by the massacre of the Sicilian Vespers.[1]

That celebrated insurrection deprived the French for ever of the island of Sicily, and brought back the line of Manfred in the person of his daughter Constantia, whose husband was now King of Aragon. Charles made desperate efforts to recover his lost dominions, but all his attempts failed, and in a great sea-fight which took place in the Bay of Naples in June, 1284, his eldest son, the Prince of Salerno, was defeated and taken prisoner.[2] Constantia, at that time Regent of Sicily, into whose hands he had fallen, was urged by her subjects to avenge by his death the murder of her cousin Conradino. But she magnanimously refused to follow the evil example of her enemies; and the Prince of Salerno, although detained in captivity, was treated with all attention and respect. Previous to the capture of

"Charles treated them with the contempt which despots generally show for good "advice. These letters touch upon every part of the administration of the State, "and concerning the taxes levied, the Pope writes thus :—'Son, we advise thee "'that, calling together the barons, prelates, and principal burgesses of the towns, "'thou shouldst expose to them thy wants, and that with their consent thou "'shouldst determine the subsidy due to thee. Be thou then content with it and "'with thy rights; leave thy subjects free,'" &c.—Amari, vol. i., p. 88, who quotes from Raynald, Ann. Eccles., Ann. 1267.

[1] It is a question whether the revolution which deprived Charles of Sicily was the result of a deep-laid conspiracy to transfer the island to the house of Aragon, or was a spontaneous outburst of popular vengeance provoked by the brutality of his countrymen in Palermo. The former theory is adopted by many historians, but when we consider the character of the Sicilians and the conduct of their French masters the latter seems the more probable of the two. The notion of a conspiracy has apparently been adopted—for there is no direct evidence on the subject—from the fact that it was in consequence of "the Sicilian Vespers" that the house of Aragon acquired Sicily.—See remarks on this subject, Amari, vol. i., p. 220.

[2] After the defeat of the French fleet, Loria, the Sicilian admiral, demanded the immediate liberation of Beatrice, a daughter of Manfred, who ever since the death of that prince had been kept a close prisoner by Charles. Loria added that if she was not given up he would immediately order the head of the Prince of Salerno to be cut off. Upon this Beatrice was sent on board the Sicilian fleet and conveyed to Messina, where her sister Constantia was then residing.—Amari, vol. ii., p. 108.

his son Charles had offered to decide the quarrel between him and the King of Aragon by a personal encounter. The challenge was accepted, and it was agreed that the crown of Sicily should belong to the victor. The combatants were to meet at Bordeaux, each attended by a hundred knights, and Edward the First of England, as Lord of Guienne, was to act as umpire. On the one side it was maintained by Charles, who sent the challenge, "that the King of Aragon had entered the kingdom of "Sicily treacherously and against right, without first "declaring war;" while the King of Aragon declared in reply "that the occupation of Sicily and everything "else done by him against Charles was neither a stain "upon his honour nor any cause of shame before any "tribunal whatsoever, or before the eyes of honest "men."[1] Pope Martin the Fourth, who now reigned at the Vatican, strongly disapproved of the projected duel, and denounced in most emphatic terms this unchristian mode of settling disputes. "Religion," he said, addressing Charles, "forbade these single combats even "to private individuals, much more to the rulers of "nations. As Vicar of Christ he would absolve him "from the oaths by which he had bound himself; but "in case of disobedience he menaced him with every "punishment which it was in the power of the Church "to inflict."[2] To Edward the First[3] and to the King of France, in case they sanctioned the proposed meeting by their presence, the Pope addressed language of an equally menacing kind. Charles and his antagonist did notwithstanding repair to Bordeaux at the appointed time; but from causes to which it is unnecessary here to advert the project of the duel was finally abandoned.

Charles died in the year 1285 most justly execrated by his Sicilian subjects, and after that event another attempt, of a kind not unusual in that age, was made to

---

[1] Amari, vol. ii., p. 17.
[2] Raynaldi, Ann. Eccles. 1283.
[3] See Rymer, vol. ii., pp. 242, 244.

adjust the disputes of the houses of Aragon and Anjou. Edward the First was chosen arbitrator to decide upon their rival claims to the crown of Sicily; but the result, as too often happens in transactions of this kind, was by no means commensurate with the time and labour bestowed upon it. Eventually, by a kind of tacit agreement, the descendants of Charles continued in possession of their territories on the mainland of Italy, while the Kings of Aragon continued to reign over Sicily.[1]

In the year 1274, during the Pontificate of Gregory the First, a second general council was held at Lyons, and upon this occasion the election of Count Rudolph of Hapsburg to the imperial throne was confirmed by the Pope.[2] At this council, among a variety of other matters, a question of a purely international character was discussed and determined. The inhabitants of Ancona complained that the Venetians levied tolls and exercised other rights of exclusive sovereignty in the Adriatic. The Venetians, on the other hand, asserted their right from ancient usage to make such exactions, and the final judgment of the Pope was in favour of the latter and against his own temporal subjects. None of the princes or ambassadors present seem to have taken exception to the decision, which we may, therefore, conclude was regarded by the parties as absolutely final.[3]

It was towards the close of this century that a contest, remarkable alike for its violence and its important consequences, arose between Pope Boniface the Eighth and Philip the Fair of France. Surpassing in the loftiness of his pretensions even the most ambitious of his predecessors, and blind to the spirit of political independence which about this period began to manifest itself in various parts of Europe, Boniface rashly embarked in a struggle of life and death with a prince

---

[1] Rapin, vol. iv., p. 20, says that a treaty was signed by the Princes of Aragon and Anjou to this effect; but he gives no authority for this statement. Edward, having vainly attempted to mediate between the rival princes, appears to have finally given up the office of arbitrator.
[2] Comyn's Western Empire.
[3] Selden's Mare Clausum.

who was no less imperious and headstrong than himself. Shortly after his elevation to the Papal throne Boniface had issued a bull prohibiting any prince from levying taxes on the clergy without his express sanction. This mandate was disobeyed in England by Edward the First, whose frequent wars obliged him to augment the public revenue by every possible means, nor did Boniface seem inclined to enforce the obedience of that politic and powerful monarch. In France Philip replied to the Papal bull by prohibiting the export of all gold and silver from the kingdom. Then followed a correspondence in which the king asserted in the broadest terms that the government of his kingdom, in so far as all temporal matters were concerned, belonged to him alone, and that with regard to these he acknowledged no earthly superior. To this Boniface, after some delay and some vain attempts at a reconciliation, replied that the King of France, like all other Christian princes, held his temporal sovereignty from the Pope. The bearer of this imperious message further informed the king that if he refused to acknowledge the Pope's authority sentence of excommunication would forthwith be pronounced against him. Philip, after reading the letter of Boniface, handed it to the Count d'Artois, who was present at the time, and who, before the eyes of the astonished legate, consigned it to the flames. The latter immediately returned to Rome, and after acquainting Boniface with the result of his mission the King of France was excommunicated in due form.

Philip, determined on resisting to the utmost the pretensions of the Pope, now took an extraordinary and decisive step. He called together the States-General of the kingdom, and on this occasion, for the first time in the history of France, he summoned the representatives of the commons to the National Council. Some of the higher dignitaries of the Church, under various pretexts, failed to attend, but the great body of the clergy, the nobles, and the commons espoused the cause of the king. Philip, assured of such support, instructed Nogaret, his Advocate-General, not only to denounce Boniface before the States as a false Pope, but to accuse him of the most infamous crimes.

A letter was then addressed by the nobles of the kingdom, including the princes of the blood, to the College of Cardinals at Rome, complaining of the attempt of Boniface to interfere with the temporal rights of the Crown, and of the serious evils to which his unjust pretensions had given rise. This letter further declared that it was the firm determination of the nobles of France to support the king in resisting all such encroachments, and that from this resolution nothing would induce them to depart. Two other letters, couched in similar terms, were addressed to the College of Cardinals, the one by the clergy and the other by the commons, and the unanimity thus displayed by all orders of men in the State appears at first to have somewhat disconcerted the Pope. The cardinals, in their replies to the nobles and the commons, even went so far as to say that it had never been the intention of his Holiness to claim superiority over the king in temporal affairs; but Boniface, who replied to the prelates and clergy himself, used very different language. He reproached them with their cowardice in not maintaining the spiritual supremacy of the Church. He complained of the scandalous charges which they had allowed to be made against him before the States-General, and he finally asserted, although in terms less explicit than formerly, his claim to authority even in temporal concerns.

At the Council of Rome, held in the year 1303, this claim was put forward more openly and boldly than ever. In the famous bull issued upon that occasion, and commencing with the words "*Unam sanctam,*" it was declared that all mankind were subject to the Pope, and that none could escape damnation who rejected this article of faith. A legate was thereafter sent to the

King of France with certain fresh proposals; but these having been peremptorily rejected, a second sentence of excommunication was pronounced against Philip. The Pope further determined at this stage of the controversy to have recourse to carnal as well as spiritual weapons. He supported the Count of Flanders in a revolt in which he had engaged against the French king, and he urged Albert of Austria, though without effect, to take part in the war. Perceiving the fresh dangers to which he was exposed, Philip determined that he too would have recourse to temporal weapons, and he employed them to better purpose than his antagonist. He commissioned Nogaret and Sciarra Colonna, a mortal enemy of Boniface, to seize the person of the Pope—an act of violence which had never been attempted since the days of Martin the First. While on a visit to Agnani his palace was surrounded in the middle of the night, and he was treated with such indignity, more especially by Colonna, who is said to have struck him with his mailed gauntlet in the face, that he never recovered its effects. The combined results of indignation, grief, and physical suffering brought on a fever, of which he died a few weeks afterwards.

The signal defeat of Boniface the Eighth by Philip the Fair terminates the most ambitious era of Papal history. It was by a King of France that the Roman Pontiffs were first raised to the rank of temporal princes, and it was from a King of France that their authority received a blow from which it never afterwards recovered. The successor of Boniface did not venture to renew the struggle with Philip, and the great schism which divided the Church throughout a large portion of the fourteenth century materially weakened its influence. The Popes were still destined to play a leading part in Europe both as spiritual and temporal sovereigns, but they never again acquired the transcendent powers which they exercised from the age of Hildebrand till that of Boniface the Eighth.

The extent and the abuses of the Papal power during that long interval have furnished a fruitful theme for speculation and invective; but notwithstanding the evils inseparable from the exercise of an authority so vast and irresponsible, the impartial historian must allow that these were far outweighed by its attendant advantages. We must bear in mind that while that power was at its height the whole of Europe, with the exception of the Italian republics and a few free cities in Spain and Germany, was subjected to feudal tyranny. The people at large were without either privileges or opinions. Even in England the right of the commons to send representatives to Parliament was not acknowledged, at least under her Norman kings, until the middle of the thirteenth century. In those rude times the ecclesiastical authority was the only check upon the licence of the great, and that it was frequently, if not generally, interposed in behalf of humanity and justice we have abundant proofs. Even the rivalry which from time to time grew up between the Church and the more powerful of the European princes contributed materially to this result. It is to this spirit that we may, perhaps, ascribe the general tendency of the Popes in the days of their greatness to side with the weak against the strong. We have seen that they consistently supported the Lombard republics against the emperors, and that Innocent the Third on a memorable occasion took the side of Denmark against a very powerful King of France. Against a still more powerful King of England Boniface the Eighth took part in the course of the same century, for during the wars of Edward the First with Scotland the Pope warmly espoused the weaker and the juster side,[1] and this is the more remarkable from the fact that

---

[1] In the year 1298 the Pope remonstrated with Edward in very strong terms as to his proceedings in Scotland. The following is a passage from a letter to that prince :—" Nam qualiter in die judicii respondebis, aut quam excusationis causam " pretendere poteris coram tremendo judice qui scrutator est cordium quique " retribuit singulis juxta suorum operum qualitatem?"—Rymer, ii., p. 884. In the following year—1299—the Pope addressed another letter, styled " Bulla " Monitoria," to Edward on the same subject, and on this occasion he laid claim,

no country in Europe appears to have more energetically and more successfully opposed the ambitious pretensions of the Church.[1]

In enumerating the causes which led to the growth of the Papal power the character of the men under whom it was acquired ought not to be omitted. Throughout the period of which we speak there were some Popes distinguished for their great abilities and learning, there were some esteemed for their private virtues, there were none conspicuous for their vices. When we consider the dissolute lives of many of their contemporary princes and the criminal enterprises in which they too frequently engaged, we cannot but conclude that the remarkable ascendency acquired by the Popes over the minds of men was not due to spiritual influences alone, and that if the moral element had been wanting that degree of ascendency would never have been attained. The odious spirit of persecution for which the Church of Rome afterwards became so conspicuous had not yet been displayed except by the suppression of the Albigenses by Innocent the Third. It was in after ages, when half Europe had risen in revolt against her, and she was desperately struggling to regain her lost dominion, that the Church of Rome inflicted the most serious evils upon humanity.

The extraordinary jurisdiction exercised by the Popes in the twelfth and thirteenth centuries constituted the nearest approach to a court of international appeal of which history makes mention. The Amphictyonic Council of Greece, we have already shown, only assumed powers of this description for a very short period, and it

doubtless at the instigation of Scottish ecclesiastics then in Rome, to the kingdom of Scotland as a fief of the Church. It had belonged to her, he asserted, "pleno " jure et ab antiquis temporibus." He further commands Edward to set at liberty all the Scottish prelates who were then in prison, and to send ambassadors to Rome within six months to justify his pretensions to the feudal superiority of Scotland.—Rymer, ibid. Edward did not reply to this summons until the year 1301, when he set forth his claims at great length in his famous letter to the Pope.

[1] See remarks of Hallam, Middle Ages, vol. i.

was, moreover, wholly without the means of enforcing its decrees. But the Popes, by means of their spiritual censures, were enabled to compel the obedience of the most powerful monarchs. By a sentence of excommunication, or by the still more dreaded process of an interdict, the proudest of thrones of Christendom might be shaken to their base. But powers of so extensive a kind, it is obvious, could only be exercised at a time when the head of the Church was an object of superstitious veneration. Such a state of things was wholly incompatible with the progress of knowledge and the dignity of independent states. It is, therefore, with surprise that we find the learned Leibnitz proposing, even in the eighteenth century, the establishment of a tribunal of international appeal over which the Pope and the Emperor of Germany should jointly preside.[1] But this scheme of perpetual peace does not appear to be more impracticable than others that have since found distinguished advocates.

[1] Opera, iv., pp. 330, 331.

CHAPTER III.

OF THE BYZANTINE EMPIRE AND THE CRUSADES.

In the history of the Byzantine Empire we have an example, and probably a solitary example, of a state which, after exhibiting every symptom of decay, and even of approaching dissolution, was suddenly restored to a lengthened period of prosperity and independence. During the greater part of the sixth and seventh centuries its decline was continuous and rapid. During the eighth a succession of able and energetic rulers raised it to a pitch of opulence and power wholly unexampled in that age. Its very existence was threatened at that time by two formidable assailants. The Saracens in the South and the Slavonians in the North both regarded the city of Constantine as their destined prey, but both were triumphantly repelled. Seven centuries had yet to elapse before a new race of conquerors appeared on the Bosphorus, and after a long and desperate struggle finally won the prize which Slavonians and Saracens had coveted in vain, and which, we may add, seems destined through all time to excite the ambition and cupidity of surrounding states.

The Emperor Leo the Third, under whose vigorous rule the Byzantine Empire was restored to prosperity and power, was an enlightened reformer as well as a successful warrior; and a learned modern historian seems to be justified in asserting that it owed its stability in succeeding ages less to the prowess of its fleets and armies than to the excellence of its laws.[1] The comprehensive codes of Justinian, embodying as they did the soundest maxims of municipal and commercial jurispru-

---

[1] Finlay's Byzantine Empire, vol. i., p. 27.

dence, were generally obeyed throughout the empire; and, confiding in the administration of equal laws, the people lived in comparative security at a time when by far the greater portion of Europe was the scene of perpetual wars and revolutions.

During the reign of Leo Gregory the Third was elected to the Papal throne, and for the last time in the history of the Latin Church the Roman Pontiff solicited and obtained the confirmation of his election by the Emperor of the East. But the war soon afterwards declared by Leo against images and image-worship led to a fatal breach with Rome. Gregory despatched three legates in succession to Constantinople to remonstrate with the emperor on the subject, but Leo refused to receive them. The Pontiff was no less resolute than his imperial adversary. He summoned a council,[1] which was attended by ninety-three bishops and by the nobles and the people of Rome, at which sentence of excommunication was passed upon all "who should thenceforth "presume to pull down, destroy, profane, or blaspheme "the sacred images—namely, the images of our Lord "God Jesus Christ, of His ever immaculate and glorious "Mother the Virgin Mary, of the holy apostles and "other saints." On hearing of the proceedings of the council Leo took prompt measures to assert the imperial authority. He determined to seize the Pope in person, and to arraign him at Constantinople on a charge of treason. A powerful fleet was despatched to Italy for this purpose, but it was scattered by a storm in the Adriatic, and such of the imperial troops as effected a landing were completely routed by the men of Ravenna. A danger which threatened the very existence of the Latin Church was thus averted. But the breach between Rome and Constantinople was irreparable. The Popes henceforth sought and obtained in the West allies and protectors more orthodox, if not more potent, than the iconoclast Emperors of the East.

---

[1] In the year 732.—Bower, vol. iii., p. 298.

Towards the close of the eighth century we find that in the wars between the Greeks and the Mohammedans the custom of exchanging prisoners was regulated by treaty. At that time the Caliph Haroun Al Raschid, the hero of Arabian fiction, reigned at Bagdad, and the no less celebrated Empress Irene at Constantinople. The Caliph, unlike his contemporaries in general, seems to have regarded war merely as a commercial speculation. His chief object was the acquisition, not of territory but of prisoners, whom he sold as slaves. The Romans, as they still styled themselves, treated their enemies in the same manner until a convention was finally agreed upon between the Caliph and the empress as to the exchange of prisoners.[1] It does not appear that any such humane practice existed at this time among the Western nations.

From the commencement of the ninth century until the first crusade the history of the Byzantine Empire is interesting only in one point of view. The monotonous record of intrigues, conspiracies, and assassinations of which it is made up is wearisome in the extreme, even though the narrative is at times relieved by the appearance of a prince who, like Basil the First, or Alexius Comnenus, or John the Handsome, left an enduring mark on the age in which he lived. But the literature of Greece was still taught in the schools; the laws, and, to some extent, the military discipline of Rome, were still preserved, and in intellectual culture and even, perhaps, in social morality, the Byzantines far excelled the nations of the West.

Under a despotism so thorough as that which prevailed at Constantinople it could not be expected that the Greek Church should acquire a degree of influence at all approaching to that of Rome. Occasionally, indeed, we find some virtuous prelate denouncing in

---

[1] This was in 797. The treaty concluded in that year bound the contracting parties to release all captives in excess on the payment of a fixed sum for each. A similar treaty was concluded between Haroun and the Emperor Nicephorus in 805.—Finlay's Byzantine Empire, p. 106.

becoming terms the vices of the great, but the habitual attitude of the Greek Church was one of servile obedience to the imperial authorities. It produced no commanding spirits who, like Hildebrand or Innocent the Third, curbed the ambition and even punished the crimes of the greatest princes. Nor did the Patriarchs ever arrogate to themselves the privilege of deciding international disputes. This marked diversity in the character and history of the two Churches is only to be explained by the totally different circumstances in which they were placed. It was not until the Roman Pontiffs had risen to the rank of temporal princes that they acquired their commanding influence in Christendom. The Greek Church always remained dependent on the temporal power.

The Byzantine Empire reached its culminating point of greatness during the long reign of Basil the Second. For fifty years this monarch not only succeeded in maintaining his authority at home but he extended the limits of his dominions in nearly every direction. From the Danube to the Euphrates his legions were everywhere victorious, but he too often sullied his triumphs by frightful acts of cruelty. In the year 1014, having defeated the King of the Bulgarians in a great and decisive battle, he ordered 15,000 prisoners to lose their eyes—an act of barbarity unparalleled in that or perhaps in any age.[1] Basil the Second died in the year 1025, when about to lead an expedition against the Saracens in Sicily.

In the course of this century the Byzantine Empire was assailed with fatal success by two new and very formidable enemies. The Seljouk Turks overran the greater part of Asia Minor, while a body of Normans, under Robert and Roger Guiscard, invaded Southern Italy, besieged and captured in succession Otranto, Brindisi, and Bari, and for ever deprived the Greeks of their Italian dominions. In the year 1071 the Emperor

---

[1] Finlay, p. 445.

Romanus the Third, who at that time reigned at Constantinople, led a powerful army into Asia Minor against the Turks, but he was defeated and taken prisoner in a decisive battle by Alp Arslan, the celebrated Sultan of the Seljouks. The generous treatment which Romanus received at the hands of his Mohammedan conqueror has been immortalised by Gibbon.[1] The sultan entertained his royal captive at his own table, imposed upon him a moderate ransom, and bestowed rich presents upon him when he left the Turkish camp. We look in vain for a similar display of generosity among the Normans, although they professed to obey the laws of chivalry, which the Turks did not. Five years before the defeat and capture of Romanus, the last Saxon King of England was defeated at Hastings, and as he lay mortally wounded on that fatal field four Norman *knights*[2] deliberately hacked his body in pieces, so that, to use the words of the contemporary chronicle, his own mother could not have recognised him.[3] In accordance with the barbarous maxims of the feudal law even the rites of Christian burial were denied to him.

Of all the warrior tribes of the Middle Ages none appear to have been so savage and rapacious as the Normans, nor is there anything in Turkish history to compare with the systematic atrocities practised in England by the Norman barons during the long and troubled reign of Stephen.[4]

The ferocious spirit displayed by the Crusaders in Palestine is unhappily characteristic of all religious

---

[1] Gibbon, vol. x., p. 359 et seq.
[2] "Four knights rushed upon him and despatched him with various wounds. "One thrust pierced through the shield of the dying king and stabbed him in the "breast. Another assailant finished the work by striking off his head with his "sword. But even this vengeance was not enough. A third pierced the dead "body and scattered about the entrails; the fourth, coming, it would seem, too "late for any more efficient share in the deed, cut off the king's leg as he lay "dead."—Freeman, vol. iii., p. 500, and the authorities there cited. "Christian "burial was refused, and the body of Harold was buried beneath a heap of stones "upon the rocks of Sussex."—Freeman, Hist. of the Conquest, vol. iii., p. 500.
[3] William of Malmesbury, anno 1066.
[4] Hoveden, Rapin, Lingard, and Lappenberg.

wars, but probably no parallel can be found to the treatment which Jerusalem received at the hands of its Christian conquerors on the 15th of July, 1099. The following appalling description of the capture of that city I shall venture to give in the words of an eminent modern historian, whom no one will accuse of exaggeration:—

"No barbarian, no infidel, no Saracen ever perpetrated such wanton and cold-blooded atrocities of cruelty as the wearers of the cross of Christ on the capture of that city. Murder was mercy, rape tenderness, simple plunder the mere assertion of the conqueror's right, children were seized by their legs, some of them were plucked from their mothers' breasts and dashed against the walls or whirled from the battlements. Others were obliged to leap from the walls; some tortured or roasted by slow fires. They ripped up prisoners to see if they had swallowed gold. Of 70,000 Saracens there were not left enough to bury the dead; poor Christians were hired to perform the office. Every one surprised in the temple was slaughtered, till the reek from the dead bodies drove away the slayers. The Jews were burned alive in their synagogues. Even the day after, all who had taken refuge on the roofs, notwithstanding Tancred's resistance, were hewn to pieces. Still later the few Saracens who had escaped, not excepting babes of a year old, were put to death to avoid the danger from the Egyptian army and to avenge the insults to the dead. Bishop Adhemar de Puy, the legate, was seen in his sacerdotal habit partaking in the triumph, and, it appears, not checking the carnage."[1]

Eighty-eight years afterwards—namely, in the year 1187—Jerusalem was retaken by Saladin, the renowned Sultan of Egypt, and the remarkable generosity with which he treated the captive Christians has been often contrasted with the unparalleled brutality of the Crusaders. The

---

[1] Milman, Hist. of Latin Christianity, vol. iii., p. 238.

circumstances, indeed, were different, for the Crusaders took Jerusalem by storm, whereas the Christian garrison capitulated to Saladin after a siege of five months. But that celebrated warrior was a very singular compound of fanaticism and philanthropy. Although reputed a saint from his extreme devotion to his faith, he was tolerant and charitable alike to all religions. Saladin did on certain occasions put his prisoners to death, but he was never guilty of such an act of barbarity as his great adversary Richard of England, who at the siege of Acre, in 1192, put to death, almost in sight of the sultan, three thousand unarmed men. Upon the whole, the remark of Hume seems to be fully justified, that during the Crusades "the advantage of science, moderation, and "humanity was entirely on the side of the Saracens."[1]

The Popes had cordially approved of the First Crusade. The speech of Urban the Second at the Council of Clermont, in the year 1094, is still extant, and we learn that the fiery eloquence with which he proclaimed the cause of the Crusaders to be the cause of God was hailed with rapture, not only in France, but throughout Western Europe.[2] Urban did not live to hear even of the capture of Jerusalem, but his policy was faithfully, though somewhat less zealously, followed by his successors. One motive of the Popes in thus warmly espousing the cause of the Crusades was the belief or the hope that the recovery of the Holy Sepulchre would be the means of re-uniting the Greek and Latin Churches. But these anticipations proved utterly fallacious, for the effect of the Crusades was seriously to widen, instead of healing up, the breach. The intercourse between the Western warriors and the Greeks was little calculated to promote friendly relations between the two. The Greeks soon began to regard the Franks as barbarians and robbers, while the Franks

[1] Hist. of England, cap. x.
[2] "Never, perhaps, did a single speech of man work such extraordinary and "lasting results as that of Urban the Second at the Council of Clermont."—Milman, vol. iii., p. 232.

despised the Greeks as little better than Oriental serfs. There were besides more serious causes of misunderstanding than mere personal antipathies. The Crusaders and their followers were in the habit of committing innumerable outrages in the Byzantine territories, while the Byzantine emperors were suspected, not without reason, of making secret treaties with the Mohammedans to the disadvantage of their Latin allies. These mutual jealousies and hatreds led eventually to an open breach between the two nationalities, and to the combined attack upon Constantinople by the French and the Venetians in the year 1204.

It was under the pretext of deposing a usurper and restoring a legitimate monarch to his throne that a formidable armament of French and Venetians, instead of steering for the Holy Land, appeared in that year before Constantinople. The capital of the Byzantine Empire was at that time beyond doubt the richest city in the world. It had for centuries monopolised the trade of the East, and the commercial jealousy of Venice and the military ambition of France were alike stimulated by the prospect of sharing the plunder of so tempting a prize. The most distinguished nobles of France took part in the siege, and the Venetians were led by Henry Dandolo, the Doge of the Republic. It is confidently asserted, but it is hard to believe, that Dandolo, who was at this time ninety-seven years old and totally blind, acted a conspicuous part in the final assault. The Greeks, whose knowledge of the arts of destruction was superior to that of their assailants, made a stubborn defence, but the gallantry of the French and the naval skill of the Venetians finally prevailed. The usurper fled, the so-called legitimate monarch, Isaac the Second, was restored, but, like many monarchs who have been indebted for their crowns to foreign aid, he soon found the insolence of his protectors insupportable. A rupture and a second siege of Constantinople were the result. The city was taken by storm and the usual scenes of violence and outrage followed. The Crusaders of the West displayed their hatred of their fellow-Christians by plundering the churches amid scenes of the wildest debauchery. In the cathedral of Saint Sophia a prostitute was seated on the throne of the Patriarch, and sang ribald songs for the amusement of the infuriated soldiers. But the religious frenzy of the French and Venetians was not shared by their spiritual chief.[1] Innocent the Third, who at that time occupied the Papal throne, seems to have regarded their conduct with unmixed abhorrence. He saw, no doubt, that it destroyed for the time all hope of reconciliation between the Greek and Latin Churches.

Previous to the final assault of Constantinople a treaty for the partition, not only of the spoils of the city, but of the Byzantine Empire itself, had been signed by Dandolo on the part of the Venetians, and by Boniface Marquis of Monserrat, Baldwin Count of Flanders, Louis Count of Blois, and Henry Count of St. Pol on the part of the French. The Venetians, who had fitted out the fleet for the expedition, were to receive the larger share of the plunder of the city, and they were also to name six electors, who, along with six to be named by the French, were to choose a new emperor. In accordance with this treaty Baldwin Count of Flanders was elected emperor on the 9th of May, 1204, and the Eastern Empire was at an end.

A line of Latin emperors reigned at Constantinople until the year 1261, when the Greek dynasty was revived in the person of Michael Paleologus. But neither he nor any one of his successors was possessed of the qualities requisite for restoring a sinking empire. A Leo the Third or a Basil the First might have given it a new lease of life, but no such ruler appeared. The

[1] "Illudque longe gravius reputantur quod quidam nec religioni nec ætati "nec sexui pepercerent, sed fornicationes, adulteria et incestus in oculis omnium "exercentes, non solum maritatas et viduas, sed et matronas et virgines Deoque "dicatas exposuerent spurcitus garcionum," &c., &c.—Gesta Innocenti III., p. 57, ed. Beluze.

empire had received its death-wound, not from Slavonians or Saracens, but from the French and Venetian marauders. Its commerce had passed into other channels, and its laws had fallen into decay under the barbarous feudal customs introduced by the Latins. The discipline of its armies, too, was gone; and its rulers were fain to avail themselves of the services of mercenary soldiers—French, English, Italian, and Catalan, whose insolence and avarice knew no bounds. It was remarkable, not that an empire reduced to this condition should have fallen, but that it should have endured so long.

The stupendous folly of the Crusades has been denounced by every historian worthy of the name. To wrest the Holy Land from the infidel and to stem the tide of Mohammedan conquest were the purposes for which they were undertaken, but in both they signally failed. After two hundred years of war and the sacrifice of millions of lives the Holy Land remained in the hands of the Mohammedans. And this was not all. The Crusaders themselves, by their attack on the Byzantine Empire, rendered a Mohammedan invasion of Europe inevitable. Until the commencement of the thirteenth century Constantinople had triumphantly repelled both Saracens and Turks. The subversion of the empire by the French and the Venetians paved the way to its final subjugation. There has been much ingenious speculation as to the supposed advantages which mankind have derived from the Crusades. It has been said that they promoted commerce and spread a knowledge of the arts throughout Europe. But it may well be asked if in the natural progress of events those results might not have followed, and to a still greater extent, if the world had remained at peace. In one point of view only the Crusades may be said to have proved positively beneficial to mankind. The fitting out of so many costly expeditions must have seriously impoverished the resources and diminished the exorbitant power of the feudal aristocracy; and we may attribute, partly at least, to this cause the general advance in social and political progress which is perceptible throughout Western Europe in the thirteenth and fourteenth centuries.

The Byzantine Empire had been reduced to a state of comparative dependence before the Ottoman Turks, so named from Othman, their acknowledged chief, appeared upon the scene. Their progress under a succession of able and warlike chiefs was singularly rapid. In the course of the fourteenth century they not only invaded the European provinces of the Eastern Empire, but in the year 1361 they captured Adrianople, which they have ever since retained. The great-grandson of Othman was the famous Bajazet, who first assumed the title of sultan, and was surnamed the "Thunderbolt" from the rapidity of his conquests both in Asia and in Europe. After subduing Servia and Bulgaria Bajazet led his victorious army against Sigismund, the King of Hungary. The Hungarian monarch appealed for help to the Western Powers, and a host of French and Burgundian nobles hastened to the banks of the Danube, confident of success against the infidel, and impiously boasting that if the sky were to fall they would uphold it on the point of their lances. The Turkish sultan, upon his part, threatened that, after subduing Hungary and Germany, he would march upon Rome and stable his charger in the cathedral of Saint Peter. Neither boast was realised; but at Nicopolis, on the 28th September, 1396, the Hungarians and their allies were totally defeated. Before the battle commenced the latter had put their Turkish prisoners to death, and the sultan signalised his victory by a terrible act of retaliation. On the day following the battle he caused, it is said, ten thousand Christian prisoners to be beheaded in his presence. The slaughter commenced at sunrise and continued until late in the afternoon. The French and Burgundian nobles were admitted to ransom, according to the custom of the Western nations. As the price of their liberty Bajazet agreed to accept two hundred thousand ducats, and it is significant of the growing importance of commerce in this age that he was content that certain Genoese merchants should become surety for the amount.[1] Among the prisoners ransomed was the Count of Nevers, the eldest son and heir of the Duke of Burgundy, and he was prepared, according to the custom on such occasions, to take a solemn pledge never again to bear arms against the sultan. But with a characteristic mixture of barbarian arrogance and magnanimity Bajazet declined to receive the proffered pledge. "I might exact it," he said, "according to the "laws of war which you profess to obey, but I despise "alike your oaths and your arms."[2]

Bajazet next resolved on the conquest of Constantinople, which with its adjacent territory, measuring some fifty miles in length by thirty in breadth, was all that now remained of the Eastern Empire. But he was induced to consent to a truce for two years on the Greeks undertaking to pay him an annual tribute of thirty thousand ducats. They agreed at the same time to allow a Turkish cadi to reside in Constantinople to administer justice to the Turkish inhabitants, and also that a mosque should be built for their convenience. But this truce was of short duration. The sultan grew impatient to seize the prize he had so long coveted, and under the pretext, very common in Oriental history, of dethroning a usurper and restoring a legitimate prince, he laid formal siege to Constantinople. But the approach of an enemy more formidable than any he had yet encountered induced him hastily to raise the siege, and prolonged for another half-century the flickering existence of the Eastern Empire. Tamerlane, the descendant and reputed heir of Gengis Khan, after having shed even more human blood than his mighty ancestor, and wasted with fire and sword the richest kingdoms of Asia, was

[1] Hammer Purgstall Geschichte des Osmanischen Reiches, b. vi.
[2] Ibid.

approaching the shores of the Mediterranean and threatening the conquest of the world. A collision between the Tartar and the Turk became inevitable, and after some slight attempt at negotiation the rival armies, numbering together probably not less than a million of men, met at Angora. In this great battle, the most sanguinary of all mediæval history, the Turks were totally defeated and Bajazet remained a prisoner in the hands of his Tartar conqueror. Whether or not the latter confined him in an iron cage is a question which has been much debated; but the fact is undisputed that Bajazet died in captivity a few months after his defeat. Had Tamerlane possessed the means of transporting his victorious hordes into Europe he might with ease have extended his conquests to the Danube. But although omnipotent on land he was powerless on the sea, and to the immense relief of Christendom he turned once more to the East, resolving to add China to his huge dominions. It is but too probable that he would have accomplished his purpose had not death overtaken him on his march to Pekin. This ruthless conqueror, who was in the habit of erecting as trophies of his victories, not pyramids of stone but pyramids of human heads, has found admirers even among the learned. That among his other great qualities he was " strictly observant of the law of nations" is emphatically stated by Voltaire.[1] But the only proof adduced of this remarkable assertion is the fact that before declaring war against Bajazet the Tartar chief summoned him to raise the siege of Constantinople.

After the retreat of Tamerlane the Turks rapidly recovered the Asiatic provinces of which they had been temporarily deprived. The descendants of Bajazet continued to reign at Adrianople, and the successors of Constantine were content to pay them tribute. At length Mahomet the Second, a young and enterprising prince, who succeeded his father, Murad the Second, in

[1] Essais sur les Mœurs.

the year 1451, determined as soon as he ascended the throne that he would realise the design of Bajazet and add Constantinople to his dominions.

Constantine the Ninth, the last of the Byzantine emperors, had given mortal offence to the Greeks by becoming a convert to the Latin Church and acknowledging the supremacy of the Pope. The more fanatical of his subjects were wont to declare that they would rather see the turban of the sultan in Constantinople than the hat of a cardinal.[1] The emperor, who was sincere in his conversion, was well aware of the peril in which he stood. With a disaffected population within and a young and warlike adversary without, he was compelled to place his chief reliance on his foreign mercenaries. He had appealed for help in vain to the European Powers, and he could not but feel that with the slender resources at his command the days of his empire were numbered. But in the face of impending ruin he displayed a calm and intrepid spirit worthy of the most distinguished of his ancestors. If he could not save his empire, he was at least resolved not to survive its fall.

In the spring of 1453 the preparations of the sultan were complete, and Constantinople was closely invested both by land and sea. For seven weeks the city was vigorously and successfully defended, but a breach was at length made near the main gate, and the emperor was summoned to surrender. The terms offered by the sultan were indignantly refused, and at daybreak on the morning of the 29th of May, 1453, the city was assaulted on every side. The defence had been entrusted to Justiniani, a Genoese soldier of fortune, and, accompanied by the emperor on horseback, he took his post at the main breach, where for several hours the storming parties, including a band of thirty janissaries, who, with characteristic daring, contrived to climb the wall, were successfully repelled. At this critical time Justiniani received

[1] Hammer Purgstall, b. xii.

a wound in the arm which obliged him to leave his post. The emperor in vain called on him to remain as the wound was slight, but the mercenary soldier was not bound to die for a cause not his own, and he retired on board ship, to the great discouragement of the besieged. Two or three faithful followers, one of whom was a gallant Spaniard, still remained with Constantine, who soon afterwards fell fighting in the breach, as well became the last of his imperial race, and thus redeemed by an heroic death an age of national humiliation. Alas for the degenerate Greeks! No outburst of patriotic spirit was heard within the walls of the beleaguered city at this supreme crisis of its history. No band of gallant youths followed their sovereign to the breach, pledged, by the memory of Thermopylæ, to share his fate. The path of duty and of honour was trod by the emperor alone. It was eleven hundred and twenty-five years after his great namesake had laid the foundations of the city that the last of the Constantines fell gloriously in its defence.[1]

On the day following the assault the youthful conqueror entered the city amid scenes of misery and desolation which touched even his stern and unrelenting nature. He traversed the deserted streets in silence, and, on witnessing the havoc that had been made in the imperial palace, where only the bare walls remained, he repeated, like Scipio at Carthage, the words of a favourite poet expressive of the vanity of human greatness. But these passing sentiments were soon effaced by schemes of ambition and revenge. The body of Constantine had been with difficulty discovered among the heaps of slain, and, unmoved by his heroic death, the sultan forthwith ordered his head to be struck off[2] and exhibited to the people. Various Greek nobles of the highest rank he subsequently caused to be put to death in cold blood, not because they had taken part in the defence of the

[1] Hammer Purgstall, b. xiii
[2] Gibbon, vol. xii., cap. 68.

city, but lest their disaffection might prove a source of future danger. Yet with the barbarity of a savage the sultan united some of the qualities of a sage. No sooner was he master of Constantinople than he proclaimed freedom of religious worship, and even declared himself the protector of the Greek Church. Within two days of the assault a new Patriarch was installed with all the accustomed solemnities, who accepted the pastoral staff from the hands of the sultan.

CHAPTER IV.

OF THE AGE OF CHIVALRY.

THE institution of chivalry exercised a very peculiar influence on the history and character of the Middle Ages. We are still in the dark as to its origin, notwithstanding all the ingenuity and research that have been expended on the subject. Some writers would trace it from the Homeric age; others from the early history of Rome; others, again, from the forests of ancient Germany. The most eloquent of the Roman historians has left us a striking picture of a people rude and simple in their habits, but whose reverence for valour was only equalled by their strict regard for truth and their respect for women, and we know that these were maxims especially inculcated by mediæval chivalry. A more probable conjecture appears to be that the institution grew up amid the general anarchy which followed the death of Charlemagne. In those dark ages Europe became the prey of innumerable petty tyrants, who lived in a state of perpetual war, and against whose avarice or lust the weak and defenceless were wholly without protection. The unarmed traveller, the merchant, the humbler class of ecclesiastics, and women of all except the highest rank were thus so frequently exposed to injury and insult that a natural desire must have arisen in every generous breast to afford some protection to those who were unable to protect themselves. Hence, it is said, by slow degrees grew up the institution of chivalry, which flourished in full vigour until the close of the fifteenth century, and the effects of which are still abundantly perceptible in the manners of modern Europe.

That the institution of chivalry tended to some extent to soften the rigours of war may be readily allowed, but its influence has been probably much over-rated. We naturally take a more lively interest in the heroes of the Middle Ages than in those of more remote times, and partial chroniclers have thrown around the former a charm which it is difficult to break; but if we carefully examine the history of those times we are driven to the conclusion that the spirit of chivalry, however strongly it might operate at times upon individuals, had but little real effect upon the policy of princes and the general condition of mankind.

We should naturally expect to find that the military virtues of fidelity and courage would be especially honoured in an age of chivalry, and in a vassal or a subject such might be the case. But in an enemy these qualities were commonly regarded as unpardonable crimes. Richard the First could be generous at times, as in the case of his brother John, even to those who had deeply wronged him; but at the siege of Chaluz, in the year 1199, the garrison having offered to surrender, he replied that as they had given him the trouble to invest the place, he would take it by force and hang the whole of them: a threat which he afterwards fulfilled, although at the cost of his life.[1]

Edward the First, too, lived in the days of chivalry, and no monarch of the Middle Ages has been more highly commended by historians for his wisdom and magnanimity; and that he was a very able, and, in a certain sense, a patriotic prince, is not to be disputed. It was natural that a monarch so famous as a warrior and a legislator should find both in his own day and in succeeding ages abundance of admirers. But clemency to his enemies and courtesy to women were not among the virtues of Edward. The cruel persecutor of the Jews,[2] whom he first mercilessly plundered and then drove out of the kingdom, the

---

[1] Hoveden, p. 791.
[2] Two hundred and eighty of them were hanged in London alone in 1275.— See Hume, c. xiii. See also Pearson, History of England during the Early Middle Ages, vol. ii., p. 320.

ruthless conqueror of Wales, and the mortal enemy of Scotland, notwithstanding an occasional display of liberality and moderation, was essentially, and more especially during his latter days, a crafty and unscrupulous tyrant.

It was certainly not in accordance with the maxims of chivalry that he made a prisoner on the high seas of the affianced bride[1] of Llewellyn, and detained her for upwards of two years for the sole purpose of inducing the last of the British princes to acknowledge his feudal supremacy. In the treaty which was eventually concluded with Edward in 1277, the Welsh historians assert that it was stipulated that Llewellyn should be the last prince of Wales.[2] This does not appear from the text of the treaty printed in Rymer. But there is a provision in that treaty which reserves to Llewellyn and his heirs for ever the island of Anglesea.[3] It is difficult to see what could be the object of this provision unless it was to limit the sovereignty of the princes of Wales, after the death of Llewellyn, to that island. It could not be expected that a treaty of this nature could be of long duration, but it furnished Edward with a plausible pretext for denouncing Llewellyn as a traitor when he made a final effort to recover the independence of his country. Llewellyn was fortunate enough to die on the field of battle, and his head, by the orders of the king, was placed on the Tower of London. A fate more terrible awaited his brother David, who soon afterwards was made a prisoner and carried in chains to Shrewsbury.

Edward had some reason to be incensed at the conduct of David Llewellyn. When his brother had refused to perform the accustomed homage he had not only sworn

---

[1] She was a daughter of Simon de Montfort, and was detained from 1276 until 1278, when, after Llewellyn had signed away the independence of his country, she was allowed to marry him.—Rapin, iv., p. 8.

[2] Powell, History of Wales, p. 284. Dr. Pauli is of the same opinion.—See Geschichte von England, vol. iv., p. 23.

[3] "Concedit et confirmat Dominus Rex quod dictus Llewellinus et hæredes sui "de corpore suo legitime procreandi habeant et teneant Angleisam eo modo quo "prius eam tenuit," &c.—Rymer, vol. ii., p. 89.

allegiance to the English king, but he had received substantial favours at his hands.[1] But no amount of provocation could justify the treatment of this unfortunate prince. Edward was very careful of appearances, and his most tyrannical acts were generally committed with all the formalities of law. He summoned a Parliament at Shrewsbury[2] to decide on the fate of Llewellyn, and by that tribunal the last prince of the British race was condemned to die as a traitor; and he was condemned, moreover, to die by a new and horrible process, unknown before in England, but only too well known in after ages as the punishment of treason. He was sentenced to be dragged naked along the ground at a horse's tail to the scaffold; he was then to be half-strangled, and while still alive to be disembowelled, and finally, before life was quite extinct, to have his entrails burnt before his eyes.[3] To this fate in an age of chivalry did Edward condemn a prince of at least as ancient lineage as his own. Through the extraordinary partiality of his biographers Edward has escaped that just measure of execration which the inventors of new and terrible punishments rarely fail to incur. It is certain that if he did not invent the punishment to which David Llewellyn was condemned it was inflicted by his sanction, and he thereby furnished a precedent as well to his own as to succeeding ages for the infliction of an incalculable amount of human suffering. In enumerating the various alterations and amendments of the law effected during the reign of Edward the introduction of a new and terrible punishment for treason ought not to be omitted.[4]

Some twenty years later Robert Bruce, like Llewel-

---

[1] He was knighted by Edward, and he also obtained grants of land in Denbighshire, and was married to a daughter of Ferrers, Earl of Derby.—Pearson, Middle Ages, vol. ii., p. 320.

[2] This was the first Parliament, apparently, to which the Commons were *legally* summoned.—See Hist. of Shrewsbury, by Owen and Blakeway, vol. i., p. 149.

[3] Matthew of Westminster, anno 1283. Trivet, anno 1283.—History of Shrewsbury, by Oliver and Blakeway, vol. i., p 149.

[4] David Llewellyn left two sons and seven daughters.—Matt. of Westminster, anno 1283. What became of them the historian does not say.

lyn, raised the standard of revolt or rebellion against Edward the First Like the Welsh prince, Bruce had sworn fealty to the English king, and had received favours at his hands; yet such is the influence of success, even among the learned, that Bruce has been universally extolled as a hero, while Llewellyn has been denounced as an ungrateful traitor who well deserved his fate.[1]

"Ille crucem pretium sceleris tulit, hic diadema."

In this age, as has been already stated, a custom had grown up of referring national disputes to arbitration; but in no instance, apparently, was this mode of settlement attended with success. The quarrel between Henry the Third and his rebellious barons had in the year 1264 been referred, by the full and formal consent of the parties, to Louis the Ninth of France. Louis, after ample deliberation, published his award, which appears to have been framed with a due regard to the rights and interests of both; but it was at once repudiated by Simon de Montfort and his confederates as being too favourable to the king, and the war was renewed with greater fury than ever. We have seen that the attempt of Edward the First to mediate between the King of Aragon and Charles of Anjou was attended with no better success; and Edward subsequently became engaged as arbitrator in a dispute which he not only failed to settle, but which eventually involved him in a war of which he did not live to see the end.

This was the disputed succession to the crown of Scotland, which, on the failure of lineal heirs by the death of Margaret, granddaughter of Alexander the Third and grand-niece of Edward the First, was claimed by no less than thirteen competitors. Practically the contest lay between three of the claimants—namely, John Baliol, Robert Bruce, and John de Hastings.

These three barons all claimed to be descended from three daughters of David, Earl of Huntingdon, a brother of William the Lion. Baliol was the grandson

[1] Pearson, Middle Ages, vol. ii., p. 330. See also Lingard, chap. vii.

of the eldest daughter, and claimed the crown on the ground of primogeniture. Bruce was the son of the second daughter, and maintained that, being one degree nearer, his claim was preferable to that of Baliol; and Hastings contended that there having been a failure of heirs male, the representatives of the three sisters had equal claims to the kingdom, and that it was equally divisible among their three descendants.

The circumstances under which Edward undertook to decide this weighty cause were peculiar and unprecedented. It is not pretended that he was invited by the States of Scotland,[1] or even by the different competitors, to adjudicate upon their respective claims. He simply took upon himself this onerous duty as a matter of right. When the different claimants assembled by his invitation at Norham[2] he informed them by the mouth of his chief justiciary that he was prepared, as Lord Paramount of Scotland, to hear and adjudicate upon their claims, but that before so doing they must each and all acknowledge his feudal sovereignty.[3] Edward meanwhile had summoned the crown vassals of the five northern counties of England to join him, and, taken by surprise by the unexpected declaration of the king, and overawed by the imposing force he was gathering around him, the different claimants, after a delay of three weeks, consented that he should adjudicate between them on the conditions he had proposed.[4]

It is to be observed that not only the three claimants we have named, but all the others, with one or two exceptions, were, like Edward himself, of Norman descent, and therefore naturally inclined to regard him

---

[1] Edward does not hesitate to say so in his celebrated letter to Pope Boniface the Eighth, but there is no evidence of this. The only document in the shape of an invitation of which we have any proof is a letter from the Bishop of Saint Andrews, who was an adherent of Baliol, and written before the death of the young Queen Margaret.—Hailes, Annals of Scotland, vol. i., p. 239.

[2] This was in the parish church of Norham, which still exists in excellent preservation.

[3] Hemingford, vol. ii., p. 32, et seq.   [4] Ibid., p. 34.

as their feudal chief. After some hesitation on the part of Baliol, they one and all took a formal oath of allegiance to the English king as Lord Paramount of Scotland.

Volumes have been written, and still continue to be written, about this claim of superiority, but, antiquarian speculations apart, the historical evidence on the subject lies in a very small compass. Let us admit that before the establishment of the feudal system some kind of superiority was claimed by the more powerful Anglo-Saxon and Anglo-Danish kings over the whole of Britain. Without authentic proofs that such supremacy was acknowledged the vague unverified assertions of partial chroniclers are absolutely worthless. We have, in fact, no historical evidence upon the subject until after the Norman dynasty had been firmly established in England. During the reign of Henry the Second William the Lion was made a prisoner during a skirmish in Northumberland, which county he at that time claimed as a portion of the kingdom of Scotland. The royal captive was conveyed to Falaise, in Normandy, and there, while still a prisoner, he, with all feudal solemnities, acknowledged himself to be the vassal of the King of England.[1]

There are two reflections naturally suggested by this treaty. In the first place, if William had already been the vassal of the English king it was superfluous; and secondly, if he was an independent prince no renunciation of his independence extorted from him while in captivity could be valid. This, in fact, was expressly admitted by the immediate successor of Henry. Richard the First, before setting out to the Holy Land in the year 1189, made a formal renunciation of the treaty of Falaise. "We have restored," he says, "to our dearest cousin "William, King of Scotland, his castles of Roxburgh "and Berwick, as his own by hereditary right, to be by "him and his heirs possessed for ever. Moreover we

[1] Lord Lyttelton's Henry the Second, vol. iii., p. 168.

"have quitted him of all the pactions which our good father Henry King of England by new charters *and by his capture extorted.*"[1] The language of this instrument, unlike many others of the feudal ages, is perfectly clear and unambiguous; and for a whole century afterwards, until, in fact, the claim of superiority was revived by Edward, the two countries remained happily at peace.

That Edward himself was by no means confident as to the validity of his claim we may conclude from the fact that after its acknowledgment by the Scottish barons he applied to the Pope to confirm it. Two envoys[2] whom he sent to Rome for this purpose were courteously received by Nicholas the Fourth; but after discussing the matter with his council the Pontiff positively refused to acknowledge the English king as Lord Paramount of Scotland. It was probably known at Rome that in the course of the preceding century this claim had been formally raised by one king and no less formally renounced by another. To revive a pretension of this kind when Scotland was practically defenceless might serve the purpose of King Edward, but to aid him in the prosecution of his ambitious schemes was neither the duty nor the interest of the Church. It was clearly the policy of Rome to remain free and unfettered on a question of such delicacy, and which was only too likely to lead to dangerous complications.

There were, and are, in fact, three distinct theories maintained regarding this question of supremacy. The Scottish historians have generally contended that whatever homage the kings of Scotland rendered was for lands which they held in England. One of the best informed but least known of English historians maintains with equal plausibility that the Scottish kings did homage, in addition, for Lothian and Strathclyde—that is, the

---

[1] This instrument is printed at length among the fac-similes of the national manuscripts of Scotland now in course of publication.

[2] John of St. John and Roger L'Estrange were the envoys sent to Rome.—Raynald ii., p. 456.

lowland district of Scotland lying between the Solway and the Firths of Forth and Clyde.[1] Lastly, Edward claimed to be Lord Paramount of the whole kingdom, and he asserted his claim with all the audacity and all the subtlety for which the Norman race was pre-eminently conspicuous.

Having been duly chosen arbitrator by the various claimants, Edward proceeded through his chief justiciary to lay down rules for the trial of the cause. And that which strikes us throughout is what we may perhaps venture to call the unnational character of the whole proceedings. The only claimants were Normans; the pleadings were carried on in Norman-French, and exhibited all the ingenuity and elaboration for which the Norman lawyers were proverbial; the addresses of the chief justiciary were in Norman-French, and King Edward himself seems to have spoken no other language. To all appearance the extension of the Norman conquest over Scotland seemed to be inevitable, and it even promised to be peaceful. Edward had taken all his measures with so much skill and foresight that he was apparently absolute master of the situation; but he made one important oversight which proved fatal to all his schemes. By means of bribes and

---

[1] The following is the opinion of Carte upon the subject:—"Upon the whole it seems very clear that the kings of Scotland derive their possessions, as well of Lothian as of the kingdom of Strathclyde, from grants of the kings of England before the Conquest; that these grants were confirmed after it by our kings of the Norman race; that they were made on the condition of their doing homage and fealty to the Crown of England; and that such homage and fealty were regularly done for these territories by the Scottish kings from the time of the first grants to the reign of Edward, who now took upon him to judge of the right of the several pretenders to the Crown of Scotland. As to Scotland itself, which is spoken of by ancient writers as a distinct country from either Lothian or Cambria and Galloway, the Scottish kings enjoyed it in their own right, and not from any grant of those of England, who never were possessed of any part thereof, nor is there sufficient reason to think that they ever held it of the Crown of England, or ever did any homage for it, before William's captivity. The treaty made for this king's liberty obliged him, indeed, to do such homage; but as things may be dissolved the same way they are created, this obligation was rescinded by a posterior treaty with Richard, releasing him and all his barons of all the engagements they had entered into," &c.—Carte, Hist. of England, book viii. This theory would be unanswerable if it could be shown that "Lothian and Strathclyde" were originally granted by the kings of England to the kings of Scotland, but no evidence of this exists.

promises[1] and threats[2] he had either gained or silenced the great majority of the nobles and the clergy of Scotland, but the people he left entirely out of his calculation, as princes in the thirteenth century were wont to do. The Scots were in this age unused to war, but the event proved that a century of peace had not extinguished their intense love of independence and their jealousy of foreign laws and foreign rulers.

On the 17th November, 1292, Edward finally pronounced judgment in favour of Baliol in the hall of the castle of Berwick-upon-Tweed, and on the 20th of the same month Baliol swore fealty in due form to the English king.[3]

Baliol soon began to feel the weight of his newly-forged feudal fetters. He was summoned again and again[4] to appear personally in the courts at Westminster at the suit of his own subjects; and it cannot be denied that this was an unprecedented exercise of authority on the part of the English Crown.[5] When war broke out between France and England in 1294 Baliol was ordered to lay an embargo on all French shipping in Scotland, and he was also summoned to send an auxiliary force to aid in a projected expedition to Gascony.[6] Whether Edward adopted this course of policy from his lofty notions of his prerogative, or whether his object was to provoke resistance and rebellion on the part of Baliol, it is needless to inquire. Suffice it to say that the latter was the inevitable result. The position of the Scottish king became intolerable, and he secretly concluded a treaty offensive and defensive with Philip the Fair.[7] In consequence of this treaty

---

[1] See the remission of large sums due by Baliol to the Crown.—Palgrave's Documents illustrating the History of Scotland, p. 117; also remissions to Bruce, p. 232.

[2] As to the threats uttered by Edward when the competitors for the crown hesitated to acknowledge his supremacy, see Hemingford ii., p. 34.

[3] Lord Hailes' Annals of Scotland, vol. i., p. 269.

[4] Ibid, p. 270. et seq.

[5] See note and references in Lingard, chap. vii., anno 1293.

[6] No number of troops is specified. The words of the order are, "Vos "requirimus et rogamus in fide et homagis, &c., *quod de hominibus vestris ad nos* "*mittatis.*"—Rymer, ii., p. 643.

[7] In October, 1295.

John Comyn, Earl of Buchan, invaded Cumberland with a large force, and the country was plundered and laid waste in a fashion that had not been witnessed for upwards of a century. Even the religious houses were not spared, and it is said that at some place, which, however, has not been specified, two hundred young scholars were burnt alive.[1] The gauntlet thus recklessly thrown down to Edward was promptly taken up. He marched northwards at the head of a formidable army, and laid siege to Berwick, at that time the chief commercial town in Scotland. In consequence of the peace that had so long subsisted between the two kingdoms the fortifications had fallen into such disrepair that it is said that Edward on his charger leaped over the town wall. The resistance seems to have been of the feeblest kind, but there was notwithstanding an indiscriminate massacre of the inhabitants.[2] The number of the slain has been ridiculously exaggerated, but it is certain that Berwick never afterwards recovered the effects of this disastrous siege. It was no doubt the purpose of Edward by this terrible example of severity to stamp out the so-called rebellion of the Scots. It had the opposite effect.

Baliol was wholly unfitted for the troubled times in which he lived. He was incapable of any consistent course of action. He had rashly commenced hostilities against Edward, no doubt in expectation of aid from France; and a few months later we find him abdicating his crown in favour of Edward, and making over to him the kingdom "and *the whole people of Scotland.*"[3] This instrument is dated the 4th of July, 1296. After five years of anxious toil and not a little bloodshed, Edward had at length attained his object. He was as far as

[1] See the letter of Edward to Pope Boniface the Eighth.—Rymer, anno 1301.
[2] Matthew of Westminster sets down the number at 60,000. Rishanger says the king was roused to fury by the conduct of the Scots, and ordered that none should be spared.—P. 374.
[3] The instrument is in Norman-French: "Nous esteant en nostre plein poer e " nostre fraunche volunte lui avons rendu la terre d'Escoce *e tout la gent.*"— Hemingford, ii., p. 108.

feudal law could make him no longer the Lord Paramount but the Sovereign Lord of Scotland and all its inhabitants.

Edward now proceeded to make arrangements for the settlement of his new conquest. He appointed his kinsman, John Plantagenet, Earl of Warenne and Surrey, governor; he sent from England a chief justiciary and a treasurer, and he removed from Scone to Westminster the stone of destiny upon which, from time immemorial, the kings of Scotland had been crowned. Before his return to England he held a parliament at Berwick, at which a number of the nobles, the clergy, and the laity swore fealty to their new ruler. Among these was Robert Bruce the younger, Earl of Carrick, the grandson of the competitor and the future King of Scots.[1] To all appearance the conquest of the kingdom was complete; but in the course of a very few months Edward found all his work undone.

Surrey, the governor, appears to have been of a conciliatory temper, and well adapted for the difficult post he occupied; but his subordinates exasperated the people, who were already profoundly disaffected, by their rapacity and insolence. It was in this critical state of affairs that William Wallace appeared as the champion of national independence.

It is much to be regretted that so little is known of this remarkable personage, and that little we know only from his enemies. But that he was not only a born leader of men but a commander of rare ability are facts beyond dispute. Without any previous experience of war we find him within a twelvemonth of Baliol's submission at the head of an army with which he attacked and totally defeated the Earl of Surrey at Stirling. It is on this occasion that we have the only reported speech of Wallace. Before the battle Surrey sent two ecclesiastics to the Scottish chief with an offer of terms. "Go back to those who sent you," was the reply, "and tell them that we are here prepared not to

[1] Hailes' Annals, i., p. 295.

"treat but to fight; to liberate our country and avenge "her wrongs." The event proved that these were no idle words, for the victory which followed was decisive and complete. Surrey fled with the remnant of his army to Berwick, and Wallace having freed Scotland for the time invaded Cumberland and Northumberland, where his followers are accused, no doubt justly, of ravaging the country in the most barbarous manner. The English historians in general charge the Scottish leader with encouraging his followers to commit all kinds of atrocities. They invariably speak of the avowed enemy of the "magnificent King Edward" as a robber and a murderer. But their language is vague and indefinite, and Hemingford, who was better acquainted with the affairs of Scotland than any of his contemporaries, relates some incidents respecting Wallace which throw a very different light on his conduct. He informs us that the Scottish leader not only saved the monks of Hexham from being plundered by his followers, but that he gave them a written protection, a copy of which that historian has preserved.[1] It also appears that Wallace saved a monastery at Alnwick from the flames, although the monks could not pay the stipulated ransom.[2] Hemingford further relates that two ecclesiastics arrived from Scotland at the priory in Yorkshire where he resided, and informed him that they had been brought before Wallace at Perth expecting instant death; but that he dismissed them simply on their promise that they would not return to Scotland. These incidents, related by an avowed enemy, are wholly inconsistent with the

---

[1] Hemingford, who was a canon of Gisborough, in the East Riding of Yorkshire, has given a verbatim copy of this curious document. The protection is by Andrew Moray and William Wallace, who describe themselves as "duces exercitus "Scotorum nomine Principis domini Johannis," &c. They still regarded Baliol as their lawful king, although that unfortunate prince was at the time a prisoner in the Tower. It is worthy of note that Hemingford, who in the previous part of his narrative invariably styles Wallace "*ille latro*," drops that and similar epithets after relating the incident of the protection, and calls him simply "ille Wilhelmus." —Hemingford, t. i, p. 135. It does not appear from Hemingford, nor from any of his contemporaries, that any similar protection was granted by any of Edward's generals in Scotland.

[2] Pearson, vol. ii., p. 411.

charges of savage cruelty brought against Wallace, on mere hearsay, by Trivet, Matthew of Westminster, and even Hemingford himself.

The position of Wallace at this time was wholly unprecedented. None of the magnates of the land had as yet joined him. Not a single noble shared with him the glory of his victory at Stirling; and there was apparently present on his side only one knight, Sir Andrew Moray, who was slain in the battle, and whose son accompanied Wallace in his expedition into England. The "pro-"tection" to the monks at Hexham is granted in the name of John Baliol. But it is certain that Wallace and Moray had no commission from Baliol, who was at that time, and for long afterwards, a prisoner in the Tower.[1] Edward himself was in Flanders, and he learned with surprise and indignation, not only that Scotland was still unsubdued, but that his own dominions had been invaded and plundered by the Scots. And it was, no doubt, in his eyes, a most serious aggravation that an unknown adventurer had dared to defeat his armies and defy his power. Wallace on his return to Scotland was chosen guardian of the kingdom, by what means is unknown, but that he retained this high office until he was defeated by Edward in person at the great battle of Falkirk in 1298 is certain.[2] After that defeat, which he suffered, according to Hemingford, through the treachery of two Scoto-Norman nobles,[3] he seems to have resigned his office and retired to France. But although defeated he had rendered inestimable service, not only to his country but to the cause of European freedom. He had shown that the ironclad men-at-arms, who up to that time, at least in Western Europe, had been deemed invincible, might be successfully resisted. It was a lesson which was never afterwards forgotten by the

---

[1] He was eventually released in 1299 on the intercession of the Pope, and he spent the remainder of his days in France, where he possessed extensive estates.—Burton's History of Scotland, vol. ii., cap. xxi.

[2] See Burton's History of Scotland, vol. ii., cap. xxi.

[3] Hemingford ii., p. 176.

Scots, and which was subsequently practised with decisive effect both in Flanders and in Switzerland, at Courtrais and Morgarten.

But the prize for which Edward so strenuously toiled and fought still remained to be won. The example of Wallace had roused to action a large section of the nobles. New guardians were appointed for the defence of the kingdom, and to add to Edward's troubles a new and unexpected rival came forward to claim the Scottish crown. When Edward was on the banks of the Solway preparing fresh plans of operations against his so-called rebels he was surprised by a visit from Winchelsea, the Archbishop of Canterbury, who at much personal inconvenience and no inconsiderable risk had sought out the king in those remote regions with a letter from Pope Boniface, which he was specially desired to deliver into the king's own hands.[1] Certain Scottish emissaries at Rome—and it is possible that Wallace[2] may have been among the number—in order to thwart the designs of Edward, had induced the Pope to lay claim to Scotland as a fief of the Holy See. "Your Highness," said the Pontiff, "may have heard, and we doubt not " that the truth is locked in the book of your memory, " that of old the kingdom of Scotland did and doth still " belong in full right to the Church of Rome, and that " neither your ancestors the kings of England nor " yourself enjoyed over it any feudal superiority. Your " father, Henry, King of England, of glorious memory, " when in the wars between him and Simon de Montfort " he requested the assistance of Alexander the Third, " King of Scotland, did by his letters patent acknow- " ledge that he received such assistance, not as a matter " of right but of special favour. When you yourself

[1] Prynne, Ed. 1st, p. 882.
[2] Among the papers relating to Wallace in the Tower there was discovered by Sir F. Palgrave a safe-conduct granted by Philip the Fair to the Scottish leader, with a recommendation to the Pope. We may conclude from this document that he intended to proceed to Rome; but we have no evidence that this intention was carried out.—Palgrave's Documents relating to the History of Scotland.

"requested the presence of the same King Alexander at
"the solemnity of your coronation, you in like manner,
"by your letters patent, invited him as a matter of
"favour and not of right. Moreover, when the King of
"Scotland did homage to you for his lands in Tynedale
"and Penrith he publicly protested that his homage
"was paid, not for his kingdom of Scotland, but for his
"lands in England: that as King of Scotland he was
"independent, and owed no fealty, which homage so
"restricted you did accordingly receive. Again, when
"Alexander the Third died, leaving as heiress to the
"crown a granddaughter in her minority, the wardship
"of this infant was not conferred upon you, which it
"would have been had you been Lord Superior, but was
"given to certain nobles of the kingdom chosen for that
"office."

After alluding to various other matters the Pope earnestly exhorted Edward to release the Bishop of Glasgow, the Bishop of Sodor, and several other ecclesiastics who were then in prison, "and in chains;" and he concluded as follows:—" If you assert that you have
"any right over this same kingdom of Scotland, or any
"part thereof, then we will that you do not forbear to
"send your procurators and ambassadors specially ap-
"pointed for this object, with all laws and documents in
"your possession which bear upon this subject, within
"six months, to be counted from your receipt of these
"present letters, as we are ready to render you full
"justice on the above subject as our beloved son, and in-
"violably to uphold your rights if any such you have."[1]

Although indignant in the extreme at the interference of the Pope, Edward thought fit, after a delay of many months, to cause an elaborate reply to be prepared

---

[1] Rymer, vol. i., p. 92. The bull is dated 5th July, 1299. Edward received it when at or near Carlaverock Castle, on the north bank of the Solway; and it is said that on hearing it read he broke into a paroxysm of rage, and declared with a great oath that he would "defend his rights as long as there was breath in his "nostrils."—Walsingham, p. 78. We learn from the archbishop that he had the letter translated into French for the use of Edward and his nobles.—Matthew of Westminster, edit. by Bohn, p. 546.

to his letter. The result, as has been truly remarked, was one of the most extraordinary state papers in existence.[1] It was the work, we may presume, of the most learned lawyers and scholars of the day, for both universities had been invited to furnish materials to confute the claims of the Pope, and to establish once for all the feudal supremacy of the English kings over Scotland.

The Pope in his letter alluded only to recent examples in proof of his allegation that Scotland was independent of the kings of England; if false they could, therefore, be easily disproved. But for obvious reasons Edward and his advisers in their reply adopted a totally different line of argument. They went back to the days of Brutus, the Trojan, who cleared Britain of its giants, and who in consequence became the progenitor of a line of kings. They then described the victories of King Arthur and the miracles of King Athelstan, and furnished numerous extracts, some genuine, some forged from ancient chronicles, and gave a full account of the homage extorted by Henry the Second from William the Lion, but not a word of its renunciation by Richard the First. It may well be asked if Edward could seriously hope to impose on the astute ecclesiastics of the Vatican by repeating to them a series of fairy tales collected or invented by Geoffrey of Monmouth? The reply is that this extraordinary production was never sent, and most probably was never intended to be sent, to Pope Boniface. It was, no doubt, intended only to impose on King Edward's own subjects. How far it answered that purpose we have now no means of knowing.[2]

Towards the close of this famous letter Edward refers to the conduct of Baliol in renouncing his allegiance, and to the invasion of Cumberland by Comyn, Earl of Buchan, in the same year. He describes the

[1] Burton's History of Scotland, vol. ii., cap. xxi.
[2] See Documents relating to the History of Scotland by Sir F. Palgrave, vol. i, Introduction, p. 131. Speaking of the fact that the letter was not sent, he says, amongst "other conjectures to which this fact may give rise it is difficult to resist "the inference that Edward intended this manifesto at least as much as an appeal "to the public mind at home as an appeal from the apostolic authority."

many atrocities committed upon this occasion, and in particular the destruction of a building in which two hundred young scholars were burnt to death. This outrage was afterwards attributed by the chroniclers to Wallace, who were ever ready to credit any charge, however terrible[1] or improbable, that could be made against the hated enemy of the great king.

Although Pope Boniface had thus warmly espoused the cause of the Scots, he was subsequently induced by some unknown means to change his tone and express approval of the policy of Edward. As the Pontiff had by this time become involved in his memorable contest with the King of France, he probably deemed that it would be unadvisable to make enemies at the same time of the two most powerful monarchs of the age. Philip at the same time abandoned the cause of the Scots, who, left entirely to their own resources, were wholly unable to meet in the field the overwhelming forces which Edward again and again led against them; and he is accused in one of his campaigns of having destroyed Dunfermline Abbey, the finest in Scotland. It was of such extent, says Matthew of Westminster,[2] "that three " illustrious kings could be at the same time, and all " together, entertained within its walls with all their " followers, without their inconveniencing one another. " Therefore," he adds, " on account of the great magni- " tude of the place the chief nobles of the kingdom of " Scotland were accustomed to meet there and arrange " their designs against the King of England. Therefore " the army of the king, seeing that the temple of the " Lord was not a church but a den of thieves, and as it " were a beam in the eyes of the people of England, sent " forth a torch of conflagration and utterly destroyed it."

But it was only in appearance that Scotland was subdued; so long as Wallace lived Edward felt that his conquest was insecure. Large rewards were offered for his capture; he was taken prisoner, most probably by

---

[1] See Matthew of Westminster, p. 578. [2] Anno 1303.

treachery, and sent to London with a powerful escort. His fate had no doubt been decided on beforehand. After some kind of trial, no record of which remains, the indomitable hero, who had never sworn allegiance to the English king, and who had saved his country from the fate of Ireland and of Wales, was butchered at Smithfield[1] with all the circumstances of ignominy and horror which attended the execution of Llewellyn. With the overweening notions that he entertained of his sovereign rights, Edward no doubt persuaded himself that he had justly punished an inveterate traitor; but when he sent the mangled limbs of his hapless victim to be exhibited in the principal towns of Scotland he little dreamed of the future he was preparing for himself and for his son. Wallace had not been dead six months before another hero, more fortunate but not more illustrious, challenged Edward's title to the crown of Scotland, and rendered fruitless the labours and the bloodshed of fifteen years.

Edward in his latter days had become remarkably devout. But bigotry and cruelty are often found united, and, exasperated beyond measure by this fresh revolt, he took summary vengeance upon every adherent of Bruce upon whom he could lay his hands. " One by " one," says a recent learned historian of this reign, " the noble company of Scotch patriots passed away from " a short captivity to the scaffold or the gallows. The " queen and the English nobles interceded for the Earl " of Athol, who claimed kindred with royalty through " descent from an uncle of Edward's. 'His only pri- " ' vilege,' said the king, 'shall be to be hanged on a " ' higher gallows than the rest, as his treasons have " ' been more flagrant and numerous.' The earl was " further suffered to ride to the place of execution; but " it was his only privilege, and he was disembowelled " while yet alive. The same miserable fate was inflicted " on Sir Simon Fraser,[2] on Sir Herbert Norham and his

---

[1] Burton, vol. ii., cap. xxii.
[2] One of the chief companions of Wallace.

"squire, on Nigel, Thomas and Alexander Bruce,[1] and on Christopher Seton and his two brothers Six others of less note, including Bruce's marshal, standard-bearer, and chaplain, suffered in the blood-bath of Berwick, where the prisoners taken at Methuen were tried and sentenced. But, in fact, one reliable English chronicler tells us that Edward's justiciaries went through Scotland burning the Scotch, dragging them at horses' tails, and hanging them;[2] and another, writing from the borders, records with horror that not only peasants were hanged but knights and clergymen.[3] An ordinance of the English council put the whole kingdom at the mercy of foreign officials by proscribing not only all who had taken part in Comyn's murder, but all who had borne arms against the king, or who had sheltered rebels."[4]

The vindictive spirit of Edward at this time displayed itself even towards the weaker sex. Tamerlane, it is said, confined his vanquished adversary in a cage, but Edward anticipated him by inflicting this punishment upon a woman. He ordered the Countess of Buchan, who had placed the crown on the head of Bruce at Scone, not only to be shut up in a wooden cage on the walls of Berwick, but to be exposed in that situation to the gaze of the populace.[5] A sister of Bruce was confined in a cage at Roxburgh, and a daughter of the Scottish king, who could only have been a child at the time,[6] was ordered to be shut up in a cage in the Tower; but this latter outrageous order seems to have been subsequently cancelled.[7]

---

[1] These were the three brothers of Robert Bruce, and Christopher Seton was his brother-in-law.

[2] Hemingford, vol. ii., p. 265. These things were done, says the historian, "secundum legem Anglicanam," and he naïvely adds that many were induced to follow Bruce, "volentes potius mori quam Anglicanis legibus judicari."

[3] Chron. de Lanercost, p. 204.

[4] Pearson's England during the Early Middle Ages, vol. ii., p. 444.

[5] Jusset eam poni supra murum castri de Berwyk in tristega lignea pixa, ut sic a transeuntibus videri posset et cognosci.—Hemingford, vol. ii., p. 247. See also Rishanger, p. 229.

[6] Bruce at this time was only thirty-three.

[7] Palgrave, i., p. 188.

When a prince of Edward's vigorous intellect condescended to such acts of petty tyranny, we may form some notion of the state of exasperation into which he had been thrown by the revolt of Bruce. He moved northwards once more at the head of a great army, mingling with his frequent devotions no less frequent vows of deadly vengeance against the Scots. But he never more set foot in Scotland.[1] He breathed his last within sight of the rebellious land, bequeathing to his successor the work of vengeance, and commanding that his unburied[2] body should be carried in the van of his army until it was accomplished. The savage mandate was disobeyed, for Edward was laid in Westminster by the side of his faithful queen, and near to the stone of Destiny, the only trophy that remained to him of all his Scottish wars.

The question may be asked whether, assuming Edward to have been suzerain of Scotland, his proceedings could be justified by the law and custom of Christendom. The German emperors, from the time of Otho the Great, were undoubtedly suzerains of Lombardy, but in their frequent wars in that country they treated the people as enemies and not as rebel subjects; and we have seen that the execution of Tiepolo by Frederick the Second was an exception to the rules of warfare practised in that country.[3] The kings of France were for centuries the feudal sovereigns of Burgundy and Flanders, but their wars with those countries were carried on in the same manner as their wars with other foreign states. Nor does it appear that the contemporary of Edward, Philip the Fair, a tyrannical and cruel prince, during his wars in Flanders put his Flemish prisoners to death. But it is plain that from the first Edward aimed at something more than the assertion of his feudal sovereignty. His design, beyond a doubt, was to make himself abso-

---

[1] He died at Burgh-on-the-Sands, near Carlisle, in July, 1307.
[2] Matthew of Westminster, anno 1307. See also Froissart.
[3] Ante, p. 44.

lute master of Britain, and it must be reckoned a most fortunate circumstance for its inhabitants at large that he failed in the attempt; for he was essentially a despot, and the significant fact that although he had with all solemnity sworn to maintain the great Charter he obtained a short time before his death a secret dispensation from the Pope to release him from his vow,[1] may convince us that Edward was in reality as regardless of the rights of his own subjects as he was of those of his neighbours.

It reflects the highest credit upon Bruce that notwithstanding the grievous amount of provocation he had received he did not retaliate upon his enemies, and he is universally admitted to have treated his prisoners with humanity after Bannockburn.[2] That victory secured the independence of Scotland, which was fully and formally acknowledged by Edward the Third by the treaty of Northampton on the 4th of May, 1328.

I have been induced to dwell at some length on the Scottish war of independence, as no period of mediæval history more forcibly illustrates the true character and consequences of the feudal system. No scheme of polity, in short, could have been better adapted for the oppression of mankind. In theory the superior and his vassal were bound by reciprocal ties of protection and allegiance. In reality the feudal law was so full of subtleties and contradictions that the strong and the powerful never found any difficulty in evading their obligations or in oppressing the defenceless. What, for example, could be more absurd than that Edward should first declare that Baliol had forfeited his crown and then accept from Baliol a title to the very crown that he was said to have forfeited, and to all the people of

---

[1] See the Bull of Pope Clement the Fifth, Rymer, ii., 170.

[2] Of one curious piece of retaliation Bruce was guilty on this occasion. Among his numerous prisoners was a certain Carmelite friar who had accompanied Edward the Second to Scotland for the purpose of celebrating his victory over the Scots in a heroic poem. Bruce obliged him to celebrate, as best he might, the defeat instead of the triumph of his royal patron.—See Fordun, b. xii., 22.

Scotland besides? The feudal law, however, such as it was, furnished Edward and his Norman counsellors with an opportunity and a pretext for attempting the subjugation of a kindred people with whom he had no quarrel, and which led to a series of wars that lasted, with only occasional intermissions, for three hundred years. To the weaker country the result of this protracted struggle proved injurious to the last degree; for Scotland appears to have been in a more prosperous condition, commercially and socially, previous to the wars of Edward the First, than at any time during the long interval that elapsed between the reign of that prince and the union of the two crowns under James the First.[1]

The two first Edwards had failed to annex Scotland to their dominions, but undeterred by their example their successor embarked in an enterprise of far greater magnitude—namely, the invasion and the conquest of France. The circumstances under which this memorable enterprise was undertaken were as follows:—

Philip the Fair died in 1314, leaving three sons and one daughter. All these sons became successively kings of France under the names of Louis the Tenth, Philip the Fifth, and Charles the Fourth, but in the short space of thirteen years all these monarchs died without leaving male heirs. Thus ended the male line of the house of Capet. The only daughter of Philip the Fair was Isabella, the profligate queen of Edward the Second and the mother of Edward the Third, through whom he eventually claimed the French crown.

The claim was unquestionably bad, for not only did the Salic law which prevailed in France exclude females from the succession, but if females were to be admitted Louis the Tenth had left a daughter married to the Count of Evreux whose pretensions were preferable to those of Edward. Nothing, in fact, was said publicly

---

[1] See upon this point the remarks of Cosmo Innes' Scotland in the Middle Ages, p. 296.

about this claim until some years after the death of Charles the Fourth. Philip of Valois, the first of that house who succeeded to the French crown, was, as the nearest male heir of Charles, universally acknowledged king; and Edward,[1] being at that time only seventeen years old, on the 29th of May, 1329, did homage to him in person in the cathedral of Amiens for the territories which he held in France.

Five years after this event there arrived in England a fugitive and an outlaw, at whose instigation Edward appears to have first seriously entertained the notion of claiming the crown of France. The person in question was Robert, Count d'Artois, who had been convicted of a gross act of forgery, and had fled to England to escape the punishment due to his crimes. Partly through the influence of this nobleman, who was animated by the most deadly hatred of the French king, and partly at the instigation of the famous brewer of Ghent, Jacques d'Arteveld, who at this time exercised unbounded sway over his countrymen, Edward was finally induced to break with Philip and to attempt to deprive him of his crown.

Pope Benedict the Twelfth had from the first made every effort to prevent the outbreak of hostilities between the two monarchs; and on learning that Edward had assumed the title of King of France he addressed to him a very friendly and sensible remonstrance. He said that he much feared that his own unbridled ambition, and that of his allies, was leading him into unknown difficulties and dangers; that it was utter folly to rely on the fidelity of the men of Flanders, who had always been noted for their disloyalty to their native princes; that even admitting the justice of his claim he had acted with extraordinary rashness in proclaiming himself

---

[1] Edward, in a letter to the Pope, says that he was not at this time of age—that is, eighteen—nor his own master, being under the control of certain persons in England; and that he made a protestation saving all his rights.—Lingard, vol. iii., p. 65, note. Edward may have meant a protestation to his own council, for no public protestation was made to Philip at Amiens.

King of France before he was possessed of a single place of strength in that kingdom; that unless it could be shown that the heirs of females were capable by law of inheriting the crown his claim was worthless; and even if such heirs were capable of inheriting, there were persons living who had a better claim; that by doing homage to Philip of Valois he had publicly acknowledged the title of that prince, and that to wrest the sceptre from him against the wishes of his own subjects was, in the judgment of all impartial men, an enterprise wholly impracticable.[1]

Edward found by experience that the Pope had not overrated the difficulties and dangers of the enterprise in which he had embarked. The first few years of the war were productive of no decisive result, and both monarchs seemed disposed to come to terms when another question of a disputed succession offered to Edward additional facilities for attacking his adversary, and rendered hopeless all prospects of a permanent peace. In 1341, John III., Duke of Brittany, died without male heirs, but leaving a granddaughter who was married to Charles of Blois, a nephew of the French king. Philip maintained that the Salic law applied only to the succession of the crown itself, and not to that of fiefs dependent on the crown; but this was disputed by the Count de Montfort, the nearest collateral male heir of the late duke. Montfort, moreover, not only seized the treasures of his kinsman and took possession of the chief fortresses of the duchy, but he came to England and did homage to Edward as sovereign of France. By consenting to receive his homage Edward involved himself in one of those singular contradictions with which the history of the feudal law abounds. By claiming the crown of France he maintained that females were not excluded from the succession; by recognising the claim of Montfort to the duchy of Brittany he in effect maintained that they were excluded even from inheriting a royal fief.

[1] Rymer, vol. v., p. 173.

It is to the war which now ensued that we must look for the most brilliant records of chivalry. To support the claim of Montfort, Edward, accompanied by the Prince of Wales, landed in Normandy and advanced unopposed to the gates of Paris. The utmost licence appears to have been permitted to the troops on their march, for both French and English historians agree that the country through which they passed was ravaged in the most merciless manner. But want of provisions and the approach of Philip at the head of an army far outnumbering the English obliged the latter to retreat. They were closely followed by the French king, who was confident that they must either fight at a disadvantage or surrender at discretion; but on the fatal field of Creci he was defeated with enormous loss. This was the first great victory achieved by the English on the Continent, and it proved to be the prelude to many more. One historian[1] attributes their victory to the use of cannon. But this seems to be a mistake. The artillery which mowed down the chivalry of France at Creci was the long bow of the English yeoman.

Of the siege of Calais which followed the victory of Creci we have a detailed and animated narrative from Froissart. That town was captured, not by assault, as was the usual practice of the age, but by the slow process of a blockade. It was closely invested both by sea and land for eleven months, and Froissart informs us that at the commencement of the siege Edward generously allowed seventeen hundred of the inhabitants to pass through his lines, and even made each of them a present of a small sum of money. A second appeal that was made to his clemency proved less successful,[2] but the incident related by Froissart

---

[1] See Villani, 947. He says of the cannon, "Che facieno si grande tremuoto "e romore, che parea che Iddio tonasse, con grande uccisione di gente e sfonda- "mente di cavalli."—See also Pauli, Geschichte von England, vol. iv., p. 404, note.

[2] "Eodem tempore ejecti sunt de Calesia circiter quingenti viri qui venerunt "ad regem Angliæ quærentes gratiam, *quos rex jussit redire in villam* verun- "tamen qui in villæ cræcit introitum ipsis negæverunt. Et sic moram traxerunt

affords a striking proof of the humanity of Edward, for even in the present age it does not appear that such an act of indulgence would be shown to the inhabitants of a closely-invested town.

On the final surrender of Calais we are told that Edward insisted that six of the principal citizens should be delivered into his hands to be dealt with as he might think fit; that accordingly Eustace de St. Pierre and five others surrendered themselves to Sir Walter Manny, one of the most distinguished of the English knights; that on being presented to the king Manny made an earnest appeal on their behalf, but that Edward remained unmoved, and ordered them to be forthwith put to death; that thereupon Queen Philippa threw herself at his feet and finally prevailed upon him to relent, and that thereafter she invited them into her own tent, entertained them sumptuously, and presented each of them with six gold nobles on their departure from the camp. This dramatic scene is not referred to by any other writer, and on that account some historians[1] have treated it as a pure fiction, but there are innumerable incidents described in the narrative of Froissart which are not corroborated by contemporary authorities, and if we rejected all these we should deprive his work of half its charm. It is much easier to exaggerate and embellish than to invent, and the story of the citizens of Calais is told so circumstantially from first to last that we can more readily believe that it was founded in fact than that it is an entire fiction. But admitting the incident to be substantially true, it may be asked whether Edward was sincere in his expressed determination to sacrifice the

---

" inter exercitum et villam et fame et frigore pereuntes spissim de die in diem " mortui sunt."—Knyghton, p. 2593. With respect to the practice in modern warfare we may mention that at the siege of Metz in 1870 an order was issued by the Prussian commander to cut off all communication "and prevent the escape of " the inhabitants, who are to be driven back by firing on them if necessary."— Orders issued by Prince Frederick Charles, 2nd September, 1870. See "Operations of the 1st Army Corps under General Steinmetz," by Major A. V. Schell, p. 227.

[1] Pauli, vol. iv., p. 413.

lives of Eustace de St. Pierre and his companions, or was the whole scene so graphically described by Froissart prearranged beforehand? There seems to be little doubt that the latter was the case. We cannot believe from Edward's subsequent conduct that he had any real intention of taking the lives of these brave men, whose devoted patriotism he could not but admire. When we turn to the text of Froissart we find that he represents the king as "winking"[1] to Sir Walter Manny when he ordered the executioner to be sent for. The queen then appeared upon the scene, and after having obtained their pardon she invited them to a repast which had, no doubt, been already prepared. But the most conclusive proof of Edward's real intentions was the fact that he not only restored to Eustace de St. Pierre all his property in Calais, but bestowed upon him a pension, as well as various other marks of royal favour.[2] Edward, no doubt, desired to attach to his interest a citizen of his high character and influence. As long as the kings of England entertained projects of conquest in France the possession of Calais, which they regarded as the key of that kingdom, was obviously a matter of the first importance, and in order to secure his conquest Edward obliged all the inhabitants who refused to take the oath of fealty to leave the town, which henceforth became peopled chiefly by English subjects. It was to this harsh but sagacious policy that his successors were probably indebted for the undisturbed possession of Calais for upwards of two hundred years.

It was during a subsequent attempt of the French to recover Calais that Edward fought as a simple knight under the banner of Sir Walter Manny, and encountered hand to hand Eustace de Ribeaumont, described by Froissart as "a strong and hardy knight. He fought a "long time marvellously well with the king, so that it "was a pleasure to see them." He adds that many of

---

[1] Adonc guygna le roy y dist soit fait venir le couppe teste. C. cxlv.
[2] La France sous les cinque Premiers Valois, par M. Levesque, p. 518.

the French knights distinguished themselves on that day, "but they were all surpassed by Eustace de "Ribeaumont, who struck the king twice down on his "knees. At last, however, he was obliged to surrender "his sword to the king, saying, 'Sir knight, I surrender "'myself your prisoner, for the honour of the day must "'fall to the English.'" The scene that followed we shall give in the words of the historian:—

"When the engagement was over the king returned "to the castle of Calais and ordered all the prisoners to "be brought before him. The French then knew for "the first time that the King of England had been "there in person under the banner of Sir Walter "Manny. The king said he would this evening of the "new year entertain them all at supper in the castle. "When the hour for supper was come, the tables spread, "and the king and his knights dressed in new robes, as "well as the French, who, notwithstanding they were "prisoners, made good cheer (for the king wished it to "be so), the king seated himself at table, and made "those knights do the same around him, in a most "honourable manner. The gallant Prince of Wales and "the knights of England served up the first course and "waited on their guests. At the second course they "went and seated themselves at another table, where "they were served and attended on very quietly.

"When supper was over, and the tables removed, "the king remained in the hall among the English and "French knights bareheaded, except a chaplet of fine "pearls which was round his head. When he came "to Sir Eustace de Ribeaumont he assumed a cheerful "look, and said with a smile, 'Sir Eustace, you are the "'most valiant knight in Christendom that I ever saw "'attack his enemy or defend himself. I never yet "'found any one in battle who body to body had given "'me so much to do as you have done this day. I "'adjudge to you the prize of valour above all the "'knights of my court as what is justly due to you.'

"The king then took off the chaplet, which was very rich and handsome, and placing it on the head of Sir Eustace said, 'Sir Eustace, I present you with this chaplet[1] as being the best combatant this day; and I beg of you to wear it this year for the love of me. I know that you are lively and amorous, and love the company of ladies and damsels; therefore say wherever you go that I gave it to you. I also give you your liberty free of ransom, and you may set out to-morrow, if you please, and go whither you will.'"

The war of succession in Brittany was meanwhile carried on, amid scenes of violence and treachery unsurpassed in that age,[2] but without any marked success on either side. In the year 1351 a proposal was made, whether by the French or English commander does not appear, that a battle should take place with thirty combatants on each side with a view of settling the dispute. The meeting actually took place without the knowledge or assent of the kings of France and England. The choice of weapons was left entirely to the combatants, each arming himself as he thought fit, and some fighting on foot and some on horseback. The struggle was long and bloody, and eventually the death of the English commander seems to have put a stop to the contest, and enabled the Bretons to claim the victory. This incident had no effect on the progress of the war, which continued to desolate Brittany until the rival claimants of the duchy met at Auray in 1364. The celebrated Breton warrior, Bertrand du Guesclin, commanded on this occasion for Charles of Blois, and Sir John Chandos for De Montfort. The contest for the duchy had now lasted upwards of twenty years, and it appears to have been tacitly understood on both sides that as both claimants were on the field the dispute should at length be finally determined. The battle was well contested on both sides, but Charles of Blois was eventually defeated and

---

[1] Froissart, cap. cli.
[2] Histoire de Bretagne, vol. i., p. 280.

slain, and his conqueror De Montfort was invested in the disputed fief.¹

Philip the Sixth died in the year 1350, and was succeeded by his son John. At this time there was a fair prospect of the restoration of peace. Edward was prepared to renounce his claim to the crown of France provided he was invested with the sovereignty of the provinces which he held as a vassal of the French king, and John professed his willingness to negotiate a peace on these terms. This proposal was cordially approved of by Pope Innocent the Sixth, in whose presence it was agreed that the two monarchs should make the necessary renunciations. But it seems doubtful whether John, a prince of a violent and volatile temper, was sincere in his desire for peace; at all events he was guilty of an outrage during the progress of the negotiations which gave serious offence to Edward, and was not improbably intended as a signal for a fresh breach of the peace. The Constable d'Eu had been taken prisoner by the English, and had been allowed to return to France for the purpose of collecting his ransom. John accused him of treason, and apparently without any kind of trial caused him to be beheaded.² Edward was thus deprived of the ransom which the Constable had undertaken to pay. John soon afterwards made a prisoner of the King of Navarre, the ally of Edward; so that we cannot but conclude that, instead of desiring peace, the French monarch, in the hope of repairing the disaster of Creci, was bent on a renewal of the war.

Edward was not slow in accepting the challenge. Personally generous and humane, it is admitted by all the authorities that on this march he allowed unbounded licence to his followers. In his campaign in Normandy in 1355 the country was ravaged in the most ruthless manner, but being compelled to retire for want of provisions before he reached Amiens the extent of damage

---

¹ Froissart, cap. ccxxviii.
² Bonnechose, Hist. de France, t. i., p. 256.

was comparatively small. Very different results followed the expedition of the Black Prince, who in this year left Bordeaux at the head of sixty thousand men, and who, without meeting an enemy, laid waste with fire and sword the whole of the rich and fertile country which lies between that city and Toulouse. The orders issued to the soldiers were not only to plunder but "to burn "and destroy," and with the purpose of extending the ravages over as wide a field as possible the army was divided into several "battles" or divisions, with directions to keep at a certain distance from each other. It is said the prince could boast that in the short space of seven weeks he had laid in ashes more than five hundred towns and villages[1] in one of the most populous districts of France. Let us hope that his flatterers exaggerated the havoc he had wrought.

In his march to the North, before the battle of Poitiers, the same scenes of indiscriminate pillage and destruction were repeated. Military success has ever exercised so irresistible a fascination over mankind that we need not be surprised if contemporary historians, dazzled by his wonderful achievements, have closed their eyes to the dark spots in his character; but there can be no doubt that the Black Prince, although a perfect model of knighthood in time of peace, displayed in war a much more relentless spirit than his illustrious father.

There is not to be found in the annals of chivalry a more pleasing picture than the conduct of the Black Prince to King John of France after his terrible defeat at Poitiers. But the extraordinary courtesy exhibited to the royal captive—both on the field of battle and in London—was strangely at variance with the hard terms afterwards imposed upon him. By the 14th article of the treaty of Bretigni he became bound to pay the exorbitant sum of three millions of gold crowns[2]—a sum which France, impoverished by a disastrous war, was wholly

---

[1] Avesbury, 210.

[2] In addition to this great sum, it is stated by M. Michelet that he had to pay the sum of 10,000 rials per month for the expenses of his table while he was a prisoner in England.—T. iii., p. 361.

unable to supply. The humiliation to which the French monarch was subjected in his sincere but fruitless efforts to obtain the required amount were of the most painful kind. Before he could raise even a portion of the required ransom he was compelled to stoop to an alliance with the Visconti, the wealthy tyrants of Milan,[1] and he was compelled to allow the Jews, who had been banished in the days of Philip Augustus, to return to France. But he died, notwithstanding, before a third of the amount was paid. The great Alfred, who did not live in the days of chivalry, treated his prisoners of distinction in a very different manner.

On his arrival in England King John found a companion in misfortune in David the Second of Scotland. That prince, the son and heir of Robert Bruce, had during the siege of Calais entered England with a powerful army, but he was defeated and taken prisoner at Nevil's Cross by Earl Percy.[2] His ransom, which was fixed at ninety thousand marks, was eventually paid, although not during his lifetime. The last instalment was paid by Robert the Second, the first of the family of Stewart who succeeded to the Scottish crown.

Some years before his death King John acquired by right of succession the duchy of Burgundy; but instead of annexing that important province to his dominions, which prudence should have suggested, he bestowed it, as a fief of the crown, upon his fourth son Philip. Thus was created the first Duke of Burgundy of the house of Valois, whose descendants in the following century proved so formidable to France.

By the treaty of Bretigni, concluded in 1360, Edward the Third renounced his claim to the crown of France; and he also renounced his claim to Normandy, Maine, Touraine, and Anjou. But, in addition to Calais, he obtained the absolute sovereignty of the duchy of

---

[1] His third daughter, Isabella, was betrothed to a son of John Galeazzo Visconti, who, instead of receiving a dowry with his daughter-in-law, paid three hundred thousand florins for the honour of the alliance.—Michelet, iii., p. 361.

[2] Froissart says that Queen Philippa was present at this battle; but this is a mistake.

Guienne with its dependent provinces. He entrusted the government of these to the Prince of Wales, whose heroic achievements were the theme of universal admiration, and which, in short, had rendered England, for the time, the first military power in Europe.

But at Bordeaux the prince soon found occupation more attractive than the government of a peaceful province. In the year 1365 Pedro the Cruel, who most justly deserved that epithet, having been expelled from Castile, sought the aid of the English to restore him to his throne. The Prince of Wales, ever eager for action, lent a too ready ear to the Castilian monarch, and without regard to the character of the suppliant and the difficulty of replacing on his throne a tyrant abhorred by his subjects, he resolved to undertake in person an expedition on his behalf. He entered Spain accordingly at the head of a veteran army, and the good fortune which had attended him at Creci and Poitiers did not desert him on the equally decisive field of Najarra, where he defeated, with enormous loss, the pretender to the Castilian crown.

Among the prisoners taken at this battle was the celebrated Bertrand du Guesclin, and the story of his captivity and his release furnishes a picture characteristic alike of the age and of the two most distinguished warriors which it produced. On the return of the Prince of Wales to Bordeaux, Bertrand applied to him through a friend to be admitted to ransom. The prince, after consulting with his council, sent word to his prisoner that they were of opinion that he ought not to be released. " You may tell the prince," replied Bertrand, " that I take their refusal as the greatest compliment " that could be paid to me, for if they did not fear my " lance they would not deny me my liberty." This message having been duly reported to the prince, he immediately answered, without referring to his council, that he would admit Bertrand to ransom at once ; and further, that whatever sum he chose to name he would accept.¹ Not to be outdone by the generosity of the prince, Du Guesclin named a hundred thousand golden francs. As he was notoriously poor, every one was astonished that he should have offered such a sum. But it was soon raised in Brittany, his native province; and it was afterwards repaid by Charles the Fifth, who had formed a just estimate of the value of that eminent soldier.

Although the expedition of Edward into Spain was attended with his accustomed glory and success, it eventually proved fatal, at least for a time, to English influence in France. Adversity, the best teacher of princes, wrought no change in the character of the tyrant of Castile. Restored once more to his throne, Pedro kept faith neither with friend nor foe. The troops that had been raised for his service remained unpaid, and to meet their demands a hearth-tax was imposed by the Prince of Wales for five years on Guienne and Gascony. The brave Chandos, whose prudence equalled his valour, in vain opposed this rash measure, which soon led to a formidable insurrection, and eventually to a rupture of the treaty of Bretigni and a renewal of the war.² In this fresh struggle nearly all the conquests that had been made by the two Edwards were lost, and, what is much more to be regretted, the reputation of the most distinguished commander of the age sustained irreparable injury.

In the year 1370 the Black Prince besieged Limoges, which had fallen into the hands of his enemies. After he had been about a month before the place it was taken

---

¹ "La entencion del principe era esta, que si Mosen Beltran dijese que por "cinco francos queria salir di prision que mas non le demandose."—Cron. de Ayala, lib. xx., cap. xviii. The above account of the liberation of Du Guesclin is taken from Ayala, who was himself made a prisoner at the battle of Najarra. The version given by Froissart is much shorter and somewhat different.

² The imposition of a direct tax has led to many important revolutions and insurrections. The hearth-tax led to the loss of Guienne and Gascony; the poll-tax, in the following reign, led to the formidable insurrection of Wat Tyler; Spain lost the Netherlands, not through her religious persecutions, but by the imposition of the twelfth penny; and the imposition of ship-money cost Charles the First his crown.

I

by surprise, a part of the wall having been blown down by a mine and a space thus cleared for the entrance of the assailants. There was no further attempt at resistance, and the prince was carried into the town in a litter at the head of his troops, for he was unable at this time, from declining health, to mount his horse. There was then an indiscriminate massacre of the defenceless inhabitants, and, according to Froissart, "three thousand " men, women, and children"[1] were butchered before his eyes. This was the last military enterprise in which the Black Prince was engaged, and we would fain reject the incident of the massacre as a fiction did it not rest on the authority of one who loses no opportunity of extolling the clemency as well as the valour of the Prince of Wales.

The people of Limoges were doubtless put to death as rebels, but it is worthy of note that, three years before, on the field of Najarra, the prince had prevented the tyrant of Castile from treating in a similar manner certain prisoners taken in the battle. And they were not an unarmed multitude, but soldiers fighting openly against their sovereign. So much easier is it to give than to follow good advice, and to be virtuous at the expense of others than at our own.[2]

It would be easy to multiply examples of the barbarous treatment of prisoners of war in the days of

---

[1] Froissart, cap. ccxc.

[2] The following dialogue, according to Froissart, passed between the prince and the King of Castile on the subject:—"Don Pedro, having saluted him, said : " ' Dear lord and fair cousin, I entreat and beseech you, as a mark of your friend- " ' ship, that you will have the kindness to deliver up to me the traitors of " ' my country, especially my brother Sancho, the bastard, and the others, that I " ' may cut off their heads,' &c.

"The Prince of Wales, having considered for a moment the request which " Don Pedro had just made him, answered :—' Sir king, I have also a request to " ' ask of you; and I beg of you, in the name of our friendship, that you will not " ' deny it to me.' Don Pedro, who could refuse him nothing, most cheerfully " assented, saying :—' My lord and fair cousin, whatever I have is yours!' Upon " which the prince replied:—' Sir king, I entreat and beg of you to pardon all " ' the ill which your rebellious subjects have done against you. You will do an " ' act of kindness and generosity, and will by this means remain in peace in your " ' kingdom,' &c. The king, Don Pedro, granted this favour, though much against " his inclination."—Froissart, c. ccxlii.

chivalry. In the year 1414 Beurnanville, an officer of the Duke of Burgundy, who had most gallantly defended Soissons, was, upon the surrender of the place, immediately beheaded by order of Charles the Sixth of France, surnamed *bien aimé* by his subjects on account of his amiable temper.[1]

In the year 1476, when Charles the Bold of Burgundy was besieging Nanci, several gentlemen of Lorraine attempted to make their way into the town; and one of them, having been taken prisoner, was immediately hanged by order of the duke. Philip de Comines expresses his disapproval of this act, but he says that under similar circumstances the prisoner would have met the like fate in Italy or Spain.[2] In the year 1479 Maximilian of Austria put to death the commandant of a fortress who had surrendered on the faith that his life would be spared; and in retaliation for this act of perfidy Louis the Eleventh of France caused fifty prisoners that were in his hands to be executed.[3] In the year 1509 Louis the Twelfth, having taken the town of Caravos, in the Venetian territory, ordered all the soldiers that were found in the place to be hanged.[4] The Venetians in the same year, having captured Padua by surprise, put the whole of the garrison, consisting of eight hundred Germans, to the sword.[5] Even in the seventeenth century these barbarous customs had not entirely disappeared. During the thirty years' war the imperial general Wallenstein caused to be executed, in the year 1633, the commandant of a fortress who had refused to surrender on the first summons a place that was untenable.[6]

Although the custom of exacting ransom from prisoners of war would appear, at first sight, conducive

---

[1] Chron. de St. Denis, i., 278.
[2] Book iv., cap. vi.
[3] Daniel, Hist. de France, vol. vi., p. 540.
[4] Vie du Cardinal d'Amboise, p. 288.
[5] Vie d'Amboise, p. 299.
[6] Schiller, Hist., b. iv., 175.

to the interests of humanity, a more careful consideration of its results will probably lead us to the opposite conclusion. It furnished, no doubt, a strong motive for sparing the lives of prisoners of rank, and hence, in the great battles of the Middle Ages, we often find that a large proportion of such fell into the hands of the victors. But this very circumstance was apt to lead to a more indiscriminate slaughter of meaner combatants. Of the cruel treatment of prisoners of war who were unable to pay a ransom we have a striking example in the reign of Charles the Seventh of France. That prince having, in the year 1441, taken Pontoise by assault, the English found in the town were exposed in chains to the gaze and insults of the populace. Those who could pay a ransom were afterwards set free, while those who could not—by far the greater number—were bound hand and foot and cast into the Seine.[1]

We must bear in mind, moreover, that the payment of a ransom, when it could be paid, fell generally upon those who could but ill afford the burthen. The feudal lord in captivity compelled his vassals and tenants to raise the sum necessary for his release, and they were frequently obliged to part with their cattle, their horses, and even their implements of husbandry, to raise the required sum. An immense amount of suffering was thus at times inflicted. The sums required for the ransom of the French nobles taken at Poitiers were so great that whole districts were impoverished by the exactions made on their behalf, and from this as well as other causes the distress of the inhabitants became so intolerable that a sanguinary social war, unequal for its horrors in mediæval history, was the result. But the combatants were unequally matched, and the feudal fetters were riveted on the hapless people more firmly than before.[2]

At times an agreement was come to between the

---

[1] Monstrelet, an. 1441.
[2] Sismondi, Hist. des Français, t. vii., p. 102. Michelet, iii., p. 332.

commanders of contending armies as to whether prisoners should be spared or not. At the battle of Verneuil, in the year 1423, which terminated so fatally for the French and their Scottish auxiliaries, the Duke of Bedford, then Regent of France, sent a herald to the Earl of Douglas to inquire upon what terms they should engage. Douglas, who commanded the French and Scots, replied that he should neither give nor take quarter, and he himself was slain, with nearly all his countrymen who were present in the battle.[1]

The treatment of travellers in the days of chivalry was inhospitable to the last degree. Without a safe-conduct from the prince whose territory they entered they were liable to be seized and imprisoned for any length of time. No distinction of rank exempted them from this harsh treatment; indeed, the higher the rank the harder were the terms imposed. The imprisonment of Richard the First in Germany is not a solitary example of this kind. In the year 1405 Robert the Third of Scotland determined to send his son and heir to the court of France for his education. The vessel in which the young prince sailed was captured by an English armed ship off Flamborough Head, and he was carried as a prisoner to London, and although peace then subsisted between the two kingdoms, the royal captive was detained in England for the space of eighteen years, and he was then only released upon payment of a heavy ransom.[2] Henry the Fourth did, however, make some amends for his ungracious conduct by bestowing on the young prince an excellent education, the fruits of which he exhibited in a very striking manner when he afterwards became King of Scotland under the name of James the First.

A century later we have another example of a similar kind. In the year 1506 Philip, King of Castile, the father of the Emperor Charles the Fifth, while on a

[1] Michel, Les Écossais en France, anno 1423.
[2] Burton, Hist. of Scotland, vol. iii., p. 89; Tytler, vol. iii., p. 133.

voyage from Flanders to Spain, was compelled by a storm to take refuge in Weymouth. Henry the Seventh treated the royal stranger with all courtesy, but demanded as the price of his hospitality that the Earl of Suffolk, nephew of Edward the Fourth, who had taken refuge in Philip's dominions, and who, being of a turbulent and enterprising temper, might have revived the claims of the House of York, should be given up to him. The King of Castile at first refused his assent to this demand, alleging that the transaction would be equally dishonourable to him and to Henry; but he was in the end induced to comply, after having exacted from Henry a solemn promise that he would at least spare Suffolk's life.[1] Nor was Philip allowed to depart until the earl was a prisoner in the Tower.[2]

The subsequent history of Suffolk forcibly reminds us of a highly-characteristic incident in the life of King David. Henry had promised to spare the life of Suffolk, as David had promised to spare the life of Shimei after his rebellion. We do not know whether, like the Hebrew king, he impressed upon his son that he, at all events, was not bound by the promise. But we do know that Suffolk was subsequently put to death by Henry the Eighth, as Shimei was by Solomon in obedience to the dying injunction of his father.[3]

Any stranger, in short, who in the Middle Ages ventured without a safe-conduct into a foreign country was practically at the mercy of its rulers. And even at

---

[1] Lord Bacon, in his history of the reign of Henry the Seventh, relates the conversation which took place between the two kings on the subject as follows:—
"'Sir,' said Henry, 'you have been saved upon my coast. I hope you will not suffer me to wreck upon yours.' The King of Castile asked him what he meant by that speech. 'I mean,' saith the king, 'by that same harebrain wild fellow, my subject, the Earl of Suffolk, who is protected in your country, and begins to play the fool when all others are weary of it.' Upon this Philip undertook to banish him, but Henry insisted that he should be given up to him. Philip, after some hesitation, said, 'Sir, you give law to me, but so will I to you. You shall have him, but upon your honour you shall not take his life.' The king, embracing him, said, 'Agreed.'"—P. 224.

[2] Rapin, b. xiv.

[3] Edward de la Pole, Earl of Suffolk, was attainted 19 Henry the Seventh (1493).—See Rot. Parl. vi., 545. Beheaded 30th April, 1513. See 1 Kings, chap. ii.

times, as in the memorable instance of John Huss, a safe-conduct did not suffice to protect him from violence. The Bohemian reformer, relying on the word of the Emperor Sigismund, was induced to attend the Council of Constance in the year 1415. The safe-conduct of Huss was addressed by the emperor to "all his loving " subjects to let him pass, stop, stay, and *return* freely " without any hindrance whatever.' Yet notwithstanding Huss was first imprisoned and then sent to the stake by orders of the Council. When he was first arrested several Bohemian nobles strenuously protested against the proceeding. But Sigismund not only refused to interfere, but he apparently approved of the tragedy which followed; for when Huss was at the stake the Elector Palatine exhorted him, in the name of the emperor, to save his life[1] by renouncing his heretical opinions.

Nothing could be more repugnant to the spirit of chivalry than the practice of secret assassination. Yet never were political murders more frequent in Europe than during the fifteenth century. Never before, at all events, do we find the perpetrators of such crimes openly avowing and seriously attempting to justify them. It is in France herself, the country of all others in which the influence of chivalry most prevailed, where we find these detestable doctrines expressed in the most public manner in justification of an atrocious murder.

The reign of Charles the Sixth was marked by a long series of calamities. The king, though beloved by his people, from time to time was subject to fits of mental derangement, and during these intervals Louis, Duke of Orleans, his only brother, naturally aspired to the chief direction of affairs. But he found a formidable opponent in his cousin, John, Duke of Burgundy, whose extensive dominions, augmented by the acquisition of Flanders, which he inherited in right of his mother, rendered him by far the most powerful vassal of the

---

[1] Histoire du Concile de Constance, par Lenfant, p. 410.

Crown. In the year 1407, however, a reconciliation was brought about between those rival candidates for power. In the most public and solemn manner they renounced their mutual jealousies, and pledged themselves in future to act in concert for the national welfare. Within three days after this event, and on the eve of a great banquet by which it was intended to celebrate the happy reconciliation of the rival princes, the Duke of Orleans was waylaid in the streets of Paris and barbarously murdered. At first not the slightest suspicion attached to the Duke of Burgundy. He attended the funeral of his cousin with every outward sign of sorrow; and their reconciliation had been so recent, and apparently so sincere, that no one dreamed of accusing him of so horrible a crime. The authorities of Paris meanwhile made every effort to discover the assassins, but in vain. At length, acting apparently on some secret information, they requested permission of the king to search the palaces of the princes of the blood. The application was granted, and the Duke of Burgundy, perceiving that concealment was no longer possible, fled from Paris after having avowed his guilt to several of his friends. He thereafter repaired to Lille, where he convoked the States of Flanders, and issued a proclamation, in which he openly justified the murder of the Duke of Orleans. Such were the notions of equity and loyalty in the fifteenth century that in reply to this extraordinary document the States did not hesitate to assure him of their sincere attachment, and that they would freely risk their lives and fortunes in his service in case the King of France should seek by force of arms to avenge his brother's murder.

The subsequent proceedings of the Duke of Burgundy were still more remarkable. Within three months of the assassination of his cousin he returned to Paris at the head of a thousand men-at-arms, and was received by the citizens with the utmost enthusiasm. Presuming on his popularity and power, he now not only refused to ask pardon of the king for his crime, but he resolved to justify it in the most public manner. In presence of the dauphin, the princes of the blood, the principal officers of state, and a large number of the clergy and citizens of Paris, John Petit, a learned professor of theology, pronounced an elaborate harangue, in which he maintained, on the authority of examples drawn both from sacred and profane history, that the murder of the Duke of Orleans was not only a lawful but a meritorious act. This singular composition has been preserved by a contemporary historian, and a more perfect specimen of perverse reasoning is not to be found in the annals of mankind.[1]

The doctrine of assassination has been unhappily both preached and practised in modern times, and the attempts made so persistently, and in too many instances so successfully, against the lives of distinguished individuals, constitute perhaps the darkest feature of the present age. But the apostles of this atrocious creed are content to work in secret. They do not venture to outrage the common sense of mankind by making a public display of their doctrines. They are content to disseminate them through the vilest channels, for they can only hope to make converts of the most depraved or the most desperate of men. But the advocate of the Duke of Burgundy had the inconceivable effrontery not only to justify but to eulogise his patron in the presence of the most distinguished audience that France could furnish; and what is more extraordinary still, not a voice in that august assembly was raised against the monstrous doctrine of premeditated murder.

But all the devices of successful guilt failed to stifle the instincts of humanity. Valentine Visconti,[2] the widow of the murdered duke, never ceased during the

---

[1] Barnnte, Hist. de ducs de Bourgogne, t. iii., p. 108. The proposition which Petit undertook to maintain was the following:—" It is lawful and even meri-" torious for any private man, subject or vassal, to kill a tyrant by lying in " ambush for him, or by any other method whatsoever, without order from " any one whomsoever, or any form of law, and notwithstanding any preceding " reconciliation or oath to the contrary." This proposition was condemned by the Council of Constance in the year 1415.—Acta Concil., Sess. 15.

[2] She was the daughter of John Galeazzo Visconti, the first Duke of Milan.

remainder of her life, in spite of the power and the menaces of the Burgundian faction, to demand that justice should be done on the assassins of her husband. Her son, the young Duke of Orleans, combined with the other princes of the blood to oppose the Duke of Burgundy, and the whole kingdom was once more divided between the partisans of the rival houses. A sanguinary and protracted civil war was the result, during which the royal authority fell altogether into abeyance. Whichever of the two contending factions happened for the time to be the stronger usurped the prerogatives and ruled in the name of the unhappy king. At length, in the year 1415, the Duke of Burgundy was driven from France by the combined efforts of his enemies. But, though defeated for the time, he did not scruple to seek the aid and alliance of Henry the Fifth of England against his lawful sovereign. Henry, without committing himself to any engagement with the duke, was not unwilling to avail himself of so favourable an opportunity for reviving the pretensions of his ancestors, and at Agincourt he inflicted upon France a blow more terrible than she had ever before sustained from any English invader. That disastrous defeat revived the hopes of the Duke of Burgundy, who forthwith resumed the offensive, and, assailed at once by her rebellious vassal and the most formidable public enemy she had yet encountered, France became again the prey of civil war. In the year 1418 the Burgundian faction once more became dominant in Paris, and the scenes of violence and bloodshed which were then enacted bear a painfully close resemblance to those which at different epochs in the subsequent history of that capital have filled the neighbouring nations with horror and alarm.[1] The frightful massacre of the Orleanist faction in the streets of Paris on the 12th of June, 1418, may well bear comparison with that of Saint Bartholomew or with that of September, 1792.

[1] Daniel, t. v, p. 568.

The uninterrupted success of the English arms at length induced the warring factions, with a view to their mutual safety, to come to terms. During the progress of this civil war the king had lost his two eldest sons. The third, who afterwards inherited the crown under the name of Charles the Seventh, was now dauphin, and between this prince and the Duke of Burgundy conditions of peace were finally agreed upon in June, 1419. It was further stipulated that the two princes should meet in person in order the better to concert measures against the common enemy.

Twelve years had now elapsed since the murder of the Duke of Orleans, and in the interval his rival had not risen in the estimation of mankind. On the contrary, the attempt of the Duke of Burgundy to justify his crime and the massacres subsequently perpetrated in Paris by his adherents rendered him an object of general detestation. Great precautions were, therefore, taken to secure the safety of the dauphin during the projected interview. The duke, on the other hand, was warned against putting himself in the power of a prince whose sympathies were believed to be entirely on the side of the House of Orleans. In consequence of these mutual suspicions it was at length arranged that the interview should take place upon ground where a surprise was hardly possible. It was agreed that the two princes should meet on a bridge which crossed the river Yonne, near Montereau, and that each should be attended by not more than ten followers. The dauphin first reached the appointed place. The duke soon afterwards arrived, but as he knelt down to do homage to the son of his sovereign he was instantly attacked and slain. His attendants either shared his fate or were made prisoners on the spot. The principal actors in this tragedy were well-known adherents of the House of Orleans, and there is every reason to believe that the dauphin was accessory to the plot. The extreme youth of that prince, the scenes of perpetual violence amid which he had passed his days, and the character of the Duke of Burgundy may serve to extenuate but they cannot efface his share of guilt in this act of perfidy.

The murder of the Duke of Burgundy was followed by consequences most disastrous to France. His son Philip, never doubting that the dauphin was the author of the crime, forthwith renounced the alliance which his father had so recently concluded, and sought that of the King of England. Henry was not slow to profit by this unexpected incident, and by the combined efforts of the English and the Burgundians province after province was wrested from the dauphin. Blind with resentment against the reputed assassin of his father, the Duke of Burgundy was even induced to become a party to the treaty of Troyes, concluded in 1420, by which the reversion of the crown of France after the death of Charles the Sixth was settled on the King of England. But the premature death of that warlike monarch proved fatal to his cherished scheme of uniting the two kingdoms, and it was fortunate alike for both that that ambitious project was never realised.

Henry had, in fact, no pretension to the crown of France excepting that of conquest. He did, indeed, reassert the claim of Edward the Third, which was notoriously bad. But the Earl of March,[1] as Henry well knew, was the true heir of Edward the Third, and to him were transmitted whatever rights Edward possessed. Like many distinguished warriors, however, Henry was a zealot in his religion, and it is easy for an ambitious monarch of this stamp to persuade himself that he can do no wrong. We may add that it was apparently the religious element in Henry's character which induced him, at least at the commencement of his career, to conduct his military operations in a much more systematic and orderly manner than his predecessors. On his arrival in Normandy on the 13th of August,

---

[1] The Earl of March was the lineal descendant of Lionel, Duke of Clarence, third son of Edward the Third.

1415, he issued a proclamation forbidding the burning of houses or the desecration of churches and other sacred places under pain of death, and declaring that all acts of violence committed on women and unarmed priests would be visited by the like penalty.[1]

Before commencing operations against Harfleur he summoned the inhabitants to surrender in terms of the twenty-ninth chapter of Deuteronomy.[2] During the siege he twice warned them from the same authority of the consequences that would follow if the place were taken by storm. But Harfleur surrendered before the time had arrived for a general assault, and although the inhabitants were treated with severity, no life was taken after hostilities had ceased.

Before setting out, in spite of the remonstrances of his wisest counsellors,[3] on his memorable march from Harfleur to Calais, Henry issued an order to his troops[4] similar in its terms to that which he had made on his arrival in France; and in conformity therewith we find that he caused one of his soldiers to be hanged in presence of the whole army for stealing from a church. Owing to the discipline thus maintained he was able to obtain provisions on his march with comparatively little difficulty. We have seen that Edward the Third during his last expedition to France laid waste with fire and sword the whole country which he traversed, and the army of the Black Prince committed similar ravages previous to the battle of Poitiers. Here, then, was an improvement, and one of vast importance, in the mode of conducting war; but it must be admitted that in his subsequent campaigns Henry did not always

---

[1] History of the Battle of Agincourt, by Sir Harris Nicolas, p. 52.

[2] "And the anger of the Lord was kindled against this land, to bring upon it "all the curses that are written in this book. And the Lord rooted them out of "their land in anger, and in wrath, and in great indignation, and cast them into "another land."—Deut. xxix., 27, 28.

[3] To all such remonstrances Henry replied that he was anxious to view the territories which by right were his own; that his trust was in God, and that he was resolved at all hazards to proceed.—Nicolas, p. 79.

[4] Ibid.

adhere to the enlightened maxims which marked the commencement of his great career.

On arriving in front of the French army, which he found posted in overwhelming force at Agincourt, he dismissed the prisoners he had taken at Harfleur. "If "your masters survive," he said, "you will meet them "at Calais." It is unfortunately true that during the progress of the battle Henry gave orders that the prisoners who had been there taken should be put to death. But it was in consequence of a piece of false intelligence having reached him that this barbarous order was issued, and as soon as the truth was known it was revoked.[1]

But although Henry carried on war much more upon a system than his predecessors, we perceive in him little of that chivalrous spirit which, in spite of many blemishes, is conspicuous in Edward the Third and in his famous son. Henry did, indeed, challenge the dauphin to single combat, but it would have been no equal match, for Henry was in the prime of manhood and the dauphin was a youth of nineteen.[2] But another act of Henry has been much and justly commended—namely, his treatment of the Earl of March, whose title to the English crown was better than his own, and whom, notwithstanding, he restored to liberty before setting sail for France. But we ought, perhaps, to attribute this act of clemency more to the excellence of his judgment than the goodness of his heart. Henry sought by this means to disarm a dangerous enemy, and he succeeded. It was a hazardous experiment at best, but one quite consistent with his fearless and self-reliant nature, and his decision was justified by the result. We are led to these reflections from the fact that other prisoners of rank were treated by Henry in a very different manner. The young King of Scots, who had been captured on the high seas in time of peace, was

---

[1] The circumstances are described by Monstrelet, chap. cxlvi.
[2] Lingard, chap. v.

detained in England during the whole of Henry's reign. The Duke of Orleans, who was made a prisoner at Agincourt, was refused his liberty on any terms, and Henry, while on his deathbed, charged his ministers upon no account to release him during the minority of the Prince of Wales. The harsh injunctions of Henry were faithfully obeyed. The Duke of Orleans remained a prisoner in England for twenty-five years, and was only released on payment of a ransom of 100,000 nobles. The Duke of Bourbon, Marshal Boucicault, and various other prisoners of rank died in confinement, being unable to pay the exorbitant ransoms demanded for their release.

The warfare of the Middle Ages seems to have invariably exercised a pernicious influence on all who practised it. The sudden transformation of Henry from the wild, unmanageable youth into the sagacious ruler and the triumphant warrior has been portrayed in immortal colours by the greatest of all artists, but the darker shades of the picture have been omitted. Although not without an innate sense of justice and perfectly sincere in his religion, Henry as king and ruler was enormously ambitious, and as he proceeded on his victorious career he abandoned by degrees the humane rules of warfare which he had proclaimed on his arrival in France, and became more and more reckless of human life. When irritated by the obstinacy or by the successes of his enemies this disposition became painfully apparent. At the siege of Rouen in 1418, forgetting the generous example of Edward the Third at Calais, he refused to allow the non-combatants to pass his lines, and they perished by thousands of cold and hunger in the presence of his army. And when the town at length surrendered he caused its most distinguished citizen, Alain Blanchard, who had made heroic efforts in its defence, to be publicly executed as a traitor.[1] At the siege of Montereau in 1420 he caused eleven

[1] Lingard, chap. vi.

gentlemen who had been made prisoners during the assault to be hanged; and after the surrender of Melun, which stood a siege of several months, a number of the principal inhabitants were put to death in cold blood.[1]

While Henry was in England in 1421 the Duke of Clarence, whom he had appointed Regent of France during his absence, was defeated and killed at Beaugé by an army of French and Scots commanded by the Earl of Buchan. That Henry was highly exasperated by this disaster, the first that had befallen his army in France, we may assume from his subsequent treatment both of the French and Scots. "He had noticed," says Monstrelet, "that for some days fifty or sixty Dauphinois, "very well mounted, had followed his army to observe "his motions. On their one day coming nearer to "him than usual he ordered them to be pursued, when "they fled to the castle of Rougemont, which the "king commanded to be instantly attacked, and this "was attended with such success that it was won and "all within taken, with the loss of only one English- "man. King Henry, however, caused them all to be "drowned in the Loire."[2]

In this expedition Henry was accompanied to France by the young King of Scots, who consented to serve as a volunteer on condition of his being restored to liberty on his return to England. He was also induced by Henry to issue an order to the Earl of Buchan and the Scots under his command to abandon the service of the dauphin. But Buchan, who on account of his victory had been created Constable of France, replied that he declined to obey the orders of his sovereign so long as he remained a prisoner. Henry was not thus to be balked in his design. He was enabled from the presence of King James in his camp and the refusal of his subjects to obey him to declare that the Scots were rebels, and as

---

[1] Monstrelet, ccxxix.
[2] Ibid., cap. cclix.

such he did not hesitate to treat them whenever they fell into his hands. On the surrender of Meaux, which was defended with great obstinacy for several months, he caused all the Scots in the place, as well as its commandant the bastard of Vaurus, to be hanged.[1]

The premature death of Henry put a stop to all his ambitious projects; but this event wrought no material change in the condition of France. His brother the Duke of Bedford, who continued to administer the affairs of the kingdom as regent, was a prince of great ability, and in the year 1424 he gained at Verneuil a victory over the army of the dauphin and his Scottish allies which was hardly less decisive than that of Agincourt. But at the siege of Orleans in 1429 he received an unexpected check which turned the tide of fortune, and eventually proved fatal to English influence in France. Nothing in history approaches so nearly to the miraculous as the story of the simple peasant girl who, when king and nobles had despaired of the salvation of their country, stepped forth for its deliverance. Nothing in history, or even in fiction, surpasses in tragic horror the dismal details of her captivity and death; for of all the innumerable atrocities committed in the days of chivalry the burning of this incomparable heroine was, beyond all doubt, the worst. Two nations must be content to share between them the infamy of the deed, for we cannot but regard with equal abhorrence the criminal indifference of her countrymen and the unrelenting malice of her murderers. It is no exaggeration to say that to her Charles the Seventh was indebted for his crown. Yet although she was for upwards of twelve months a prisoner, first in the hands of the Burgundians and subsequently in those of the English, he made not an effort, by word or deed, to effect her deliverance. He might, according to the usage of the age, have offered a ransom for her person, and in case of a refusal he might have threatened reprisals upon the prisoners in his hands. The

[1] Monstrelet, cap. cclix.

Duke of Bedford may have believed that his victim was a sorceress; indeed, we have some evidence to this effect.[1] But even this poor plea cannot avail Charles, who, with his nobles, ever treated the Maid of Orleans in the days of her success with the regard due to her sex and her transcendent services, but who in her hour of need raised not a finger to avert or to avenge her dreadful doom.[2]

[1] In a letter to his nephew, King Henry the Sixth, the Duke of Bedford, after informing him that the siege of Orleans had been raised, expresses himself as follows:—"Your troops, who were very numerous at this siege, have received a "terrible blow. This has happened partly, as we believe, by the confidence the "enemy have placed in a hell-born woman, a limb of Satan called La Pucelle, who "has made use of enchantments and witchcraft. This defeat has not only di-"minished your troops, but withal has bereaved the rest of courage in an extraor-"dinary manner," &c. See Rapin, book xii.

[2] " Les coupable ne sont pas seulement ceux qui ont fait ou ordonné le procès ; "les Bedford, les Winchester, les Warwick et leurs pareils; ce sont encore ceux qui "l'ont laissé faire. Rien dans cette histoire si remplie de prodiges et si souillée "d'infamies, rien de plus surprenant et de plus révoltant que la conduite de la "cour de France envers la Pucelle."—Jeanne d'Arc, par H. Wallon, p. 353, edition of 1876.

CHAPTER V.

OF THE PRINCIPAL TREATIES OF THE SIXTEENTH CENTURY.

During the latter half of the fifteenth century France recovered with astonishing rapidity from the deplorable condition to which domestic anarchy and foreign war had reduced her in the long reign of Charles the Sixth. His son and successor, Charles the Seventh, lived to see the English deprived of all their French dominions excepting Calais, and after him there came a sovereign, famed alike for his talents and his crimes, who not only extended in nearly every direction the limits of the monarchy, but reduced to permanent obedience the great vassals of the Crown. The abuses of the feudal system had grown to an intolerable height when Louis the Eleventh ascended the throne, and the iron despotism which he succeeded in establishing in its place was in many respects preferable to the chronic anarchy which preceded it. While the policy of this sagacious tyrant depressed the nobles, it tended materially to improve the condition of the people and to develop the national resources, and he bequeathed to his son in 1483 the most peaceful and prosperous kingdom in Christendom. And while tranquillity was maintained at home, the condition of the neighbouring states secured it from all danger from without. Fortunately for France, England was at this time still convulsed by the wars of the Roses. In Spain the Moors still bade defiance to Ferdinand and Isabella. Charles the Bold of Burgundy was dead, and an extensive portion of his dominions had been annexed to France; and the house of Austria, destined soon to become so formidable, was as yet comparatively powerless. France, moreover, was not only at this time secure from attack; she possessed, in addition, a weapon of offence peculiar to herself, at least on this side of the Alps.[1] Charles the Seventh, in the course of his deadly struggle with the English, had succeeded in establishing a standing army insignificant in point of numbers when compared with modern armaments, but very formidable when compared with the undisciplined feudal militia of neighbouring states. This force was increased and consolidated by Louis the Eleventh, to whom it rendered essential service in his numerous wars and negotiations; and Charles the Eighth, on arriving at manhood, found himself the master of forty thousand trained soldiers. Through the excessive jealousy of his father this prince had been brought up in total ignorance of public affairs. His youth had been chiefly spent in the reading of romances and books of chivalry, and ambitious of military fame, though wholly unfitted to achieve it, he resolved, like Charlemagne and Barbarossa, to lead an expedition into Italy. This event, from the important consequences to which it led, has been justly considered the commencement of modern history.

Charles had no quarrel with any of the Italian states, but princes who are resolved on war are never at a loss for a pretext. As representing, or assuming to represent, the house of Anjou, he revived its claim to the crown of Naples, which was now worn by a prince of Aragon, and, crossing the Alps in the summer of 1494, he marched unopposed through Italy. Pisa, Florence, and Rome successively opened their gates to the invader. As he approached Naples his rival fled, and Charles quietly took possession of the vacant throne. His progress had resembled more a triumphal procession than the invasion of a hostile country. But the threatening attitude of the Milanese and the Venetians, who began to assemble their forces with the view of cutting off his communi-

---

[1] Several of the Italian princes and republics had in the fourteenth century introduced the practice of paying regular troops. — Sismondi, Républiques Italiennes, chap. ix. The first Duke of Milan, it is said, kept on foot an army of 20,000 men.

cations with France, soon obliged him to retrace his steps. With them, the only enemies he encountered in Italy, he fought one successful battle, and regained his kingdom in safety. But the garrison he had left behind at Naples was forced, in the course of a few months, to surrender to Gonsalvo di Cordova, the famous captain of Ferdinand and Isabella, and the Angevin dynasty of Naples was at an end.

Although the expedition of Charles the Eighth failed, it had demonstrated to all the world the inherent weakness of the Italian states, and for ages afterwards they became the battlefield and the prey of their more warlike neighbours. The formation of the League of Cambray was one of the first results of the expedition of Charles. To trace the history of this famous treaty it is necessary to glance at the condition of the Papacy at the commencement of the sixteenth century.

The extension of the Papal dominions had ever been a favourite project of Alexander the Sixth, who was at this time Pontiff, and the perfidious arts by which he and his terrible son sought to accomplish their purpose have rendered the name of Borgia the most odious in Italian history. Julius the Second adopted with equal zeal, but with more regard to humanity, the ambitious policy of his predecessor. But Venice, monopolising as she still did the commerce of the East, was now in the zenith of her power, and seemed to offer an insuperable barrier to all his schemes of aggrandisement. Until that proud republic was humbled he could never hope to render the Papacy the leading state in Italy. But Julius was not to be turned from his purpose by any amount of difficulty or danger. Although he could not venture to cope with Venice singlehanded, he conceived the daring project of uniting all the powers of Christendom against her, and by holding out to each a share in the plunder of her dominions, sanctioned as it would be by Papal approbation, a willing ear was lent to his proposals.

Charles the Eighth was now dead, and his nearest kinsman had succeeded him under the name of Louis the Twelfth. The chief minister of Louis, the Cardinal d'Amboise, entered eagerly into the ambitious projects of the Pontiff, and the French king was easily persuaded to lay claim to Venetian Lombardy in right of his grandmother, Valentine Visconti, who was a daughter of the first Duke of Milan. The Emperor Maximilian, with equal readiness, revived the pretensions of his ancestors to the provinces bordering the Adriatic—pretensions which were now advanced after the lapse of three hundred years. Ferdinand the Fifth of Spain, as representing the house of Aragon, claimed all the seaports in Apulia and Calabria belonging to the republic. Julius reserved for himself, in the first instance, the principality of Romagna, which was then a portion of the Venetian dominions, and the Duke of Savoy claimed the island of Cyprus, which had been granted by Richard the First to Guy de Lusignan during the crusades, and one of whose descendants had married an ancestor of the duke. Even the petty princes of Este and Mantua laid claim to portions of the Venetian dominions; and other distant powers, such as Hungary and England—which had no direct interest in the spoliation of the republic— were by the terms of the treaty allowed to become parties at any time within three months after its ratification.[1]

There are frequent examples in later ages of different European states combining against an ambitious and aggressive neighbour; but it is a notable fact that on the first occasion in modern times on which we find a coalition of this description, they were banded together, not for the purpose of defence, but solely for purposes of plunder. In the treaties formed during the last century for the partition of Poland we have probably the nearest historical parallel to the League of Cambray. The

---

[1] See the treaty in Dumont and Append. No. 1, Letter of the Council of Ten to Henry the Seventh.

enemies of Poland, however, could allege, and perhaps with some show of reason, as a pretext for their intervention, that her constitution was not only incurably bad, but that it was, moreover, a source of constant danger to her neighbours. But the only crime of Venice was her unrivalled wealth and prosperity. Had she not been the best governed as well as the richest state in Christendom, she never could have outlived the storm which at this time threatened her from every quarter in the horizon.

It is a remarkable circumstance that at this crisis in her history, while her most formidable assailants experienced the greatest difficulty in obtaining money for the purpose of the war, her commercial credit remained unshaken.[1] But assailed at once by the fleets of Spain and the armies of France and Germany, she was forced to act strictly on the defensive, and her territories on the mainland were quickly overrun. But her rulers calculated, not without reason, that the confederacy formed against them contained too many elements of discord to prove of long duration; and in these hopes they were not disappointed.

The first in point of rank of the three sovereigns who now aimed at supremacy in Italy was the Emperor Maximilian. This prince, by his marriage with Mary of Burgundy, the daughter and sole heiress of Charles the Bold, had added many rich and extensive provinces to his dominions, and this important accession of territory gave increased weight to his pretensions. But Maximilian, although eager for distinction and ambitious of conquest, was essentially irresolute and weak. He had none of the qualities of a leader except personal valour, of which he was wont to make too ostentatious a display. But of any consistent course of action, either in policy or war, he was wholly incapable. Italy had more to dread from the character of Louis the Twelfth,

---

[1] Venice was able to borrow what money she required at five per cent.—Hist. de la ligue fait à Cambray, par M. l'Abbé du Bos, lib. v.

whose private virtues endeared him to his subjects, and who counted among his nobles some of the most distinguished warriors of the age. The character of the third of the triumvirate differed essentially from that of either of his confederates. Ferdinand, surnamed the Catholic, was, in short, by far the most remarkable monarch of the age. He had inherited from his father only the barren kingdom of Aragon; but in the course of his reign he acquired Castile by marriage, Grenada by conquest, and Navarre and Naples, Sicily and Sardinia, either by force or fraud. He subjugated, besides, a large African province, and the genius of Columbus had literally added a new world to his vast dominions. Prosperity is fatal to the common run of conquerors; but although his ambition was inordinate, his native strength of mind enabled him to bear all his astonishing good fortune with moderation; nor would any prospect, however dazzling, tempt him to undertake an enterprise beyond his means. And although his faithlessness was proverbial, and it was truly said of him that he had made and broken more treaties than any prince in Christendom, he was, on the whole, no less successful in negotiation than in war.

It was not to be expected that three such monarchs should long continue to act in concert. The intrigues of Ferdinand, who from the first had designed to add Naples to his dominions, soon brought about a rupture between him and the French king, and the League of Cambray came prematurely to an end. Pope Julius had discovered when too late his fatal error of inviting so many warlike neighbours into Italy, and now that they were about to turn their arms against each other for the possession of the prize, he was forced in self-defence to take part in the struggle. The address and the superior resources of Ferdinand induced him, after some hesitation, to side with Spain. Venice, though despoiled of many of her fairest provinces, was once more received into Papal favour. The sentence of excommunication which had been pronounced against her was recalled, and was now levelled with all its accompanying terrors against the King of France. Maximilian, though still professing to adhere to the League, took no active part in the war, and Louis was left to contend alone against the Spaniards, the Venetians, and the Pope. In the brief but bloody struggle which ensued, the career of his celebrated nephew, Gaston de Foix, was marked by a series of brilliant achievements. But the death of that youthful hero at the great battle of Ravenna, where he gained a decisive victory over the Spanish and Papal armies, wrought a rapid change in the aspect of affairs, and, indeed, proved fatal for the time to French influence in Italy.[1]

Louis meanwhile had been confronted by another enemy. England now for the first time began to take an active part in the general politics of Europe, and Henry the Eighth, who, thanks to the prudence of his father, had succeeded to an overflowing treasury and an undisputed throne, readily consented to join the coalition against the French king. Henry was induced to take this step partly through the flattery of the Pope,[2] but more through the persuasion of his father-in-law, Ferdinand of Aragon, who held out to him the alluring prospect of regaining the French dominions which were formerly possessed by the kings of England. Henry, who delighted in all martial exercises and was ambitious at this time of following in the footsteps of his victorious ancestors, projected a campaign in Normandy, but Ferdinand, for reasons of his own, persuaded him instead to send an expedition to Guienne. His real design was not to employ this force for the recovery of that province for his son-in-law, but for the conquest of Navarre for himself. On discovering his intention, the English commanders refused to aid him in his scheme. But the presence of an English army in the adjacent territory

[1] The battle of Ravenna was fought on Easter Sunday of the year 1512.
[2] Julius sent him "the golden roses," with a letter in which he saluted Henry as the head of the Italian League.—Wilkins' Concilia, vol. iii., p. 652.

answered his purpose as well. He succeeded in adding Navarre to his dominions, and for the first time since the days of the Goths united Spain under one sceptre.

Henry now carried out his original intention of invading France in person. He was accompanied by a powerful army, and he was joined by the Emperor Maximilian, who, with characteristic inconstancy, deserted his ally Louis in the hour of danger. But the invaders effected nothing in this expedition at all commensurate with the means at their disposal. The famous skirmish at Guinegate, better known as the "Battle of Spurs," and the capture of Tournay, were its only results. But Henry, who displayed none of the military qualities of his great namesake, made no use either of his victory or of his conquest. He neglected to follow up the one at a time when Louis was surrounded by enemies on every side, and he gave up the other without any equivalent, after retaining it only four years. In the course of these transactions Henry had discovered ample proofs of the duplicity as well of his new ally Maximilian as of Ferdinand, and this discovery induced him to listen willingly to overtures of peace on the part of the French king. In the year 1514 a treaty was concluded between the two monarchs, in which it was agreed that Louis should marry the Princess Mary, the youngest sister of Henry, with whom he was to receive a nominal dowry of four hundred thousand crowns. But this money was not actually paid; for by a separate treaty Louis acknowledged that he was indebted to Henry in the sum of one million of crowns, being for various debts owing by the kings of France to the kings of England.[1] It was stipulated that the dowry of the Princess Mary should be deducted from the sum thus owing from the King of France. As to the claims of the kings of England to Normandy and Guienne the treaty was silent.

[1] Dumont.

Louis died a few months after the execution of this treaty, and his successor, Francis the First, had no sooner ascended the throne than he resolved to follow the ambitious policy of his two predecessors. Like them he crossed the Alps at the head of a gallant army, and the sanguinary victory which he won at Marignano[1] once more turned the tide against the imperialists, and led to new complications on both sides of the Alps.

The rivalry which henceforth sprang up between the monarchs of France and Austria, and which led to results so calamitous to Europe, had its origin in the marriage of Mary of Burgundy with Maximilian. Louis the Eleventh had done his utmost to prevent a union which promised to bring so large an accession of wealth and power to the house of Austria. But the results proved infinitely more important than the most sagacious politician could have anticipated. Philip, the son of this marriage, married Joanna, the Infanta of Spain, daughter of Ferdinand the Fifth and Isabella of Castile. Two sons were born of this marriage—namely, Charles, afterwards Emperor of Germany, and Ferdinand, to whom were assigned the hereditary estates of Austria, and who subsequently acquired by marriage the crowns of Hungary and Bohemia, both of which he transmitted to his descendants.

In the year 1516, Charles, who was then only sixteen years old, succeeded to the vast inheritance of his maternal grandfather Ferdinand, and three years later the death of his paternal grandfather Maximilian opened up another and an apparently boundless field for his ambition. He forthwith announced himself a candidate for the imperial crown. But his pretensions to that dignity were opposed by a formidable rival. Francis the First, justly dreading the prospect of a union of the Spanish and the imperial crowns, made a vigorous

---

[1] In the year 1515.

effort to obtain the coveted prize for himself; and appealing to the patriotism of the German princes and to the fears and jealousies of the smaller European states, he was supported throughout the contest by partisans quite as numerous, though, as the event proved, less influential than those of his opponent. The privilege of nominating the emperor had long been vested in seven electors, and at this time they consisted of the King of Bohemia, the Elector of Saxony, the Margrave of Brandenburg, the Count Palatine of the Rhine, and the three Archbishops of Mentz, Cologne, and Trèves. For upwards of five months every species of influence was brought to bear upon those princes and prelates by the rival candidates. Bribes, promises, and threats were lavishly employed by both in the most open and shameless manner, and Europe watched with intense anxiety the progress of a contest which, however it might terminate, could hardly fail to be attended with momentous consequences. That Henry the Eighth, at that time in the vigour of youth, should have remained an inactive spectator of this exciting struggle may somewhat surprise us. But Henry had at one time proposed to enter the lists himself against both competitors, and had only abandoned his design on ascertaining that he had not the smallest prospect of success. Favouring the claims neither of Charles nor of Francis, and unwilling to see either acquire so great an accession of dignity and power, Henry stood entirely aloof, while nearly all the other European states had espoused the cause of one or other of the candidates. The contest was finally decided at Frankfort on the 28th of June, 1519, when by the unanimous vote of the electors Charles was raised to the imperial throne.

Although the defeat of Francis did not lead to an immediate rupture between the two monarchs, it may be said to have rendered peace impossible. Their conflicting claims and interests in Navarre, in Naples, and in Lombardy could only have been adjusted by a far greater amount of equity and moderation than was possessed by either. The spirit of rivalry so natural in two young and ambitious princes was henceforth aggravated by a sense of humiliation on the one side and of triumph on the other, and the war which broke out in Navarre in the year 1521 was the commencement of a struggle in which nearly every state in Europe was destined to take a part, and which, indeed, from the death of Maximilian might have been regarded as inevitable.

The war begun in Navarre in 1521 soon extended to Italy and Flanders, and continued without intermission until the defeat of Francis at the battle of Pavia.[1] Francis not only lost his army but his liberty on this disastrous day. He was made prisoner on the field of battle, and was detained in close captivity until the 14th of January, 1526, when he consented to sign the treaty of Madrid. We may learn from the history of all wars that the vanquished have little to hope from the generosity of a conqueror; and we may add that this is one, and probably the main cause why treaties are so often broken. The terms now imposed upon Francis by his victorious rival were hard in the extreme. The treaty contained a great variety of articles, but the most important related to Burgundy, to the duchy of Milan, and to Flanders. Francis engaged to restore the first of those provinces to the emperor, and to renounce all claim of sovereignty over the two latter. He further agreed—and this was probably the hardest condition of all—to restore to his rank and dignities in France the Constable Bourbon. There are few more romantic histories than that of this celebrated character. Persecuted first by the love and then by the hatred of Louise of Savoy, the mother of Francis, the Constable had been induced to renounce his allegiance, and by his skill and valour had contributed essentially to the defeat of his sovereign at Pavia. Francis now engaged to reinstate

[1] Fought on 25th February, 1525.

this distinguished rebel in all his vast possessions. As hostages for the due execution of the treaty the dauphin and his brother the Duke of Orleans were delivered up to the emperor. It was agreed that they should reside in Spain until all its stipulations were fulfilled.[1]

The treaty was executed with all due formality, but Francis had not only no intention of observing it, but he expressed that intention on the same day in an instrument no less formal than the treaty itself. He signed a secret but solemn protest in the presence of notaries to the effect that as he was still a prisoner, and had, moreover, been treated with extreme harshness during his captivity, he did not consider himself bound by the conditions imposed upon him.[2] And on his return to France he not only repudiated the treaty but obtained the sanction of Pope Clement the Seventh to this flagrant breach of faith. Naturally alarmed at the progress of the imperial arms in Italy, Clement saw no means of curbing the ambition of Charles but by the arms of France. But the Pontiff soon found occasion to repent of his decision. The Constable Bourbon, who at this time commanded the imperial forces in Lombardy, being in want of money to pay his troops, formed the daring resolution of marching upon Rome with the double object of punishing the Pope, and of enriching his followers with the plunder of a city which for centuries had escaped the calamities of war. The expedition proved successful. Rome was taken by assault on the 5th of May, 1527, and although Bourbon himself was killed while in the act of scaling the wall, his army, strangely composed as it was of Spanish Papists and German Lutherans, took possession of the city amid scenes of violence and horror which never, even during the invasions of the Goths and Vandals, had been equalled. The Pope, with his guards, took refuge in

---

[1] Dumont. [2] Ibid.

the castle of Saint Angelo, and for many weeks the defenceless citizens were subjected to every conceivable and inconceivable kind of outrage. Clement was finally compelled to surrender himself a prisoner to the imperial commander, who fixed his ransom at the sum of four hundred thousand ducats, and he was detained in captivity until a considerable portion of the money had been paid and he had found ample security for the remainder. With an affectation of solicitude which deceived nobody, the emperor appeared to be profoundly moved on hearing that the Pope was a prisoner. He even went through the solemn farce of causing prayers to be offered up for his deliverance, although a word to his generals would have sufficed to set him free. It is said that in treating the Pope as a prisoner Charles was guided by the advice of the Duke of Alva. It is said that his opinion having been asked on the subject, he replied that if the Pope had not taken upon himself the functions of a temporal prince, and not only carried on war but placed himself at the head of a league against the emperor, he would have recommended that he should be at once set at liberty; but that having assumed the character, he ought not to be allowed to evade the responsibilities, of a temporal prince.[1]

The rivalry between the emperor and the King of France may be said to have culminated with the sack of Rome and the captivity of the Pope. It was at this time that, exasperated by the reproaches of Charles, who accused him of falsehood and of breach of faith unworthy of a gentleman, Francis challenged the emperor to single combat. Charles accepted the challenge, and various messages passed to and fro respecting a place of meeting. But on reflection both monarchs appear to have been at last convinced of the absurdity of resorting to such a method of settling their disputes, and the subject was quietly dropped. Terms of peace were once more concluded at Cambray. Francis once more renounced his claims to

[1] Bower's Popes, Clement the Seventh.

all territories beyond the Alps, as well as to Flanders and Artois. He agreed, moreover, to pay two millions of crowns for the ransom of his two sons, who were still detained as hostages in Spain for the due performance of the treaty of Madrid.

While the arms of Charles were thus victorious in Italy, his brother the Archduke Ferdinand had by a piece of mere good fortune achieved in another quarter of Europe a success of a far more important kind. In the summer of 1526 Louis the Second, King of Hungary and Bohemia, was defeated and slain at the fatal battle of Mohacz, when Solyman the Magnificent, one of the most renowned of the Ottoman princes, gained a decisive victory over the Hungarian king. As Louis was the last male heir of the royal race of Jagellon, the crowns both of Hungary and Bohemia were claimed by Ferdinand, partly in right of his wife, who was a sister of Louis, and partly in virtue of certain treaties subsisting between his predecessors and the kings of Hungary.[1] After some opposition on the part of a rival pretender to the Hungarian crown, the claims of Ferdinand were finally recognised by the states both of Hungary and Bohemia, and a vast extent of territory was thus added to the Austrian dominions.

Amidst these incessant wars and negotiations the Reformation in Germany had been making steady progress. The rivalry between Charles and Francis contributed materially to this result, and prevented them for a time from appreciating the importance of that great religious revolution.

The formation of the league of Smalkalde in the year 1534 at length awakened both monarchs to its true character and objects. The leaders of that confederacy were the Elector of Saxony and the Landgrave of Hesse, who, along with the other Protestant princes of Germany, had formed an alliance offensive and defensive for the maintenance of their religious liberties. With them

[1] Koch, Révolutions de Europe, vol. i., p. 402.

Francis now entered into a secret treaty, which was eventually attended by very remarkable results. From this time until the days of Richelieu we find that the kings of France, while suppressing Protestantism with an iron hand at home, systematically supported it in Germany, at times by secret intrigues, at times by negotiation, and at times by open war. Jealousy of Austria was the motive for a policy apparently so inconsistent. Religious prejudice in this instance gave way to state expediency. It is perhaps too much to say that Germany was indebted for the establishment of her religious liberty to the despotic kings of France, but it cannot be denied, and it is one of the most extraordinary anomalies of history that they should have powerfully contributed to this result.

Although by the peace of Cambray Francis had renounced all claim to Milan and to Naples, he was prepared to repudiate this treaty, as he had that of Madrid, on the first opportunity; and to strengthen his influence in Italy he proposed a marriage between his second son, the Duke of Orleans, and Catherine de Medici, a niece of the Pope. Dazzled with the prospect of so brilliant an alliance for his kinswoman, Clement gave his cordial consent to a match which was destined to prove a source of numberless calamities to France. With the view of a speedy rupture with the emperor, Francis also sought an alliance with Henry the Eighth. But the immediate cause of a fresh war between the rival monarchs was the execution of an envoy of the French king at the court of Francis Sforza, who had been invested by the emperor with the duchy of Milan. The Frenchman had happened in a quarrel to kill his antagonist, and for this offence, notwithstanding his character of an ambassador, had been immediately afterwards tried, condemned to death, and beheaded. Francis complained loudly of this breach of the law of nations both to the Duke of Milan and to the emperor, at whose instigation it was said that the execution had taken place, and as no reparation was made, the French king entered Savoy at the head of a powerful army, while Charles retaliated by an invasion of Provence. In the spring of 1536 he entered that territory accompanied by a numerous and well-appointed army. The Constable Montmorency, to whom Francis had entrusted the defence of the kingdom, laid waste the country far and wide as the invaders advanced, and he finally entrenched himself so skilfully at Avignon that they found his position impregnable. The Fabian tactics of Montmorency proved fatal to the invaders. Want of provisions soon forced the emperor to retreat, and with difficulty he reached the frontiers of Spain, after losing half his army. Francis now formed a new alliance still more remarkable than that which he had made with the Protestant princes of Germany. He entered into a treaty with Solyman the Magnificent, whose fleets ravaged the coasts of Naples, and whose soldiers at the siege of Nice in 1543 fought side by side with those of France. Much indignation was excited throughout Europe at the unholy alliance between the King of France and the avowed enemy of his faith. But it is to be observed that throughout these transactions Solyman proved much more faithful to his engagements than his Christian ally, who, though capable of the most generous actions, regarded treaties as binding only so long as it served his interest to observe them.

To put an end to this alliance, Paul the Third, who was now Pope, made strenuous efforts to bring about a peace between the two rival monarchs of Western Europe. With this purpose he repaired to France, and through his mediation a truce for ten years was concluded at Nice between them.[1] Shortly afterwards Charles, being desirous of visiting his native city of Ghent, where an insurrection had broken out among the people, applied to Francis for permission to pass through his dominions. Francis not only com-

[1] In 1538.

plied with his request but received him in Paris with every mark of esteem; and Europe witnessed the strange spectacle of two monarchs who had not only spent their lives in incessant war but had accused each other of the most atrocious crimes, now vying with each other in demonstrations of mutual affection. It is a fact worthy of note as illustrating the political morality of the age that Francis was advised by his ministers to make a prisoner of the emperor, who, relying on the pledge of the French king, had thus placed himself in his power. But Francis, wholly deceived by the friendly professions of the emperor, who artfully led him to believe that he was about to invest the Duke of Orleans with the duchy of Milan, but without the remotest intention of keeping his word, refused to listen to their advice.[1] It is well for his reputation that he did so, but we may well doubt whether he would have adhered so loyally to his pledge had he been aware of the deliberate deception which his guest was practising upon him respecting the duchy of Milan, on the possession of which Francis had all his life set his heart, and for which he had sacrificed so much of the best blood of France.

As Charles after quitting France wholly refused to fulfil his promise, war became again inevitable. But the immediate cause of the rupture was the assassination of two French envoys who were proceeding through Lombardy in 1541 on a secret mission to Constantinople. The imperial general, Guasto, desiring to obtain their papers, caused them to be waylaid and murdered. There is no reason to suppose that the emperor was in any way privy to this outrage, but as no reparation was offered hostilities recommenced with greater animosity than ever. France was now threatened with another enemy

---

[1] The following conversation is said to have taken place between Tribaulet, the king's jester, and Francis on the subject of the detention of Charles:—Tribaulet told the king that on hearing that the emperor had arrived in Provence he had placed his name in his list of fools. "If I allow him to pass," said Francis, "what "will you say?" "In that case," replied Tribaulet, "I will strike out his name "and insert yours in its place."—Bonnechose, Hist. de France, t. i., p. 391.

no less formidable than the emperor. Henry the Eighth having resolved against the wishes of the Scots to marry his son to their infant queen, had sought to accomplish his purpose by laying waste their country with fire and sword,[1] and the invasion of Scotland led necessarily to war with France. During his long and troubled reign Francis was never in greater peril than at this time. The emperor and the King of England engaged to invade France simultaneously from the South and from the West, and after joining their forces to march upon Paris. But a brilliant victory gained over the imperialists in Piedmont[2] by the Count d'Enghein, a youthful scion of the house of Bourbon, revived the memories of Ravenna and Marignano, and convinced the emperor that France, although assailed by two such formidable enemies, was still capable of a vigorous resistance, and finally induced him, without consulting his ally, to come to terms with Francis. The treaty of Crespy, signed on the 18th of September, 1544, brought to a close the rivalry between the two monarchs which for a quarter of a century had brought innumerable calamities upon Europe, and which, we may add, resulted in no permanent advantage to either. By this treaty Francis renounced all claim to Milan and to Naples as well as to Flanders and to Artois, while the emperor on his part abandoned all claim to Burgundy. The war was continued with the English, who captured Boulogne, but which was restored to France by the treaty of Guisnes for the sum of two millions of golden crowns. This was the last public transaction in which Henry and Francis

---

[1] The Earl of Hertford, who commanded the expedition, was instructed "to burn Edinburgh, so that it may remain for ever a perpetual memory of the vengeance of God." The general is then ordered to sack Leith, "putting man, woman, and child to fire and sword *without exception*." Hertford is then to cross over to Fife "to spoil and turn upside down the cardinal's (Beaton) town of Saint Andrews, sparing no creature alive within the same," &c. During this invasion the English borderers, having apparently rules of warfare of their own, refused to burn the standing corn in Scotland.—Record Office, Hertford to the King, 18th September, 1545. Hertford says that in consequence Irish troops were employed for the purpose.—Ibid.

[2] At Cerisoles in 1544.

were engaged. They both died a few months after the execution of the treaty.

Hitherto the Reformation in Germany had led to no actual hostilities between the rival sects. But the assembling of the Council of Trent in 1546 brought matters to a crisis. The measures which, at the instigation of the Papal Court, were taken for the suppression of Protestantism[1] induced the Elector of Saxony, the Landgrave of Hesse, and other princes who had embraced the doctrines of Luther, to take up arms for the defence of their religious liberties. Charles not only accepted the challenge, but without summoning a Diet of the empire took upon himself to proclaim the Elector and his confederates as rebels, and at the battle of Muhlberg he totally defeated them, and made a prisoner of their chief. The Elector was forthwith brought before a military tribunal of which the Duke of Alva was president, and was by that court condemned to die as a traitor. It is probable that Charles had no intention of carrying into effect this most arbitrary and illegal sentence. But although he spared the Elector's life he deprived him of his dominions. His youthful kinsman Maurice, who by a long course of dissimulation had won the favour of the emperor, was invested with the electorate in his stead. The Landgrave of Hesse, the father-in-law of Prince Maurice, was detained a prisoner, and the despotic measures promulgated at the Diet of Augsburg in 1548 convinced the Protestants of Germany that the emperor had resolved upon the overthrow of their civil as well as their religious liberties. It says little for the sagacity of that monarch that he should have been foiled in his purpose by a man in whose fidelity he placed unbounded confidence, and on whose co-operation he mainly relied for the accomplishment of his designs.

It was in vain that the emperor and his ministers received repeated warnings as to the schemes of Maurice of Saxony. Such was the address of that prince, and

[1] Father Paul, Lib. ii.

with such secrecy did he lay his plans, that he had concluded an alliance as well with the Protestant princes of Germany as with Henry the Second of France before the emperor even entertained a suspicion of his design. It must be admitted that Maurice took all his measures with consummate skill, and on the outbreak of hostilities he advanced so rapidly upon Innspruck, where the emperor at the time resided, that it was only by a hasty flight across the Alps that he escaped being made a prisoner. At the same time the King of France advanced into Lorraine with a powerful army. He everywhere proclaimed himself " Protector of the liberties of Germany," and captured in succession the cities of Toul, Verdun, and Metz, all of which he annexed to France, and which continued to form a portion of the French dominions until the year 1871. Exasperated alike by the defection of Prince Maurice and the loss of Lorraine, Charles collected a veteran army of 50,000 men and advanced by rapid marches upon Metz. He was warned, as winter was approaching, that it would be hazardous to attempt the capture of that place, which was held by Francis, Duke of Guise, and an ample garrison. But he refused to listen to the advice of his most experienced officers, and after a siege of sixty days he was compelled to retreat with the loss of more than half his army. By his successful defence of Metz the Duke of Guise became the idol of his countrymen; and we may add that he won the no less hearty admiration of his enemies by his humane and generous treatment of their sick and wounded,[1] thousands of whom they were compelled to leave behind them on their retreat. At a period when wars were carried on with a reckless disregard of human life, this conduct of the Duke of Guise is especially deserving of notice. It seemed to mark the commencement of a new era in military history. But the outbreak of the religious wars in France and Flanders, by stimulating the worst of human passions, proved fatal for a time to

[1] Record Office. Correspondence, 1552.

all moral progress, and amid the din of clashing creeds the voice of humanity was well-nigh stifled in Western Europe for half a century.

The emperor meanwhile had been induced, through the mediation of his brother Ferdinand, to come to terms with Prince Maurice. By the treaty of Passau, which was signed on the second of August, 1552, Charles consented, although with extreme reluctance, to abandon his project of overturning the liberties of Germany, and agreed to accord to Lutheran and Catholic alike the free exercise of their religion. Three years later—namely, on the 25th September, 1555—this treaty was confirmed by the Diet of Augsburg, which, for a time at least, put an end to the strife between the rival sects. So many defeats and disappointments, together with rapidly-failing health, induced the emperor shortly afterwards to resign his crown and retire into private life. The war with France was continued by his son and successor Philip the Second until the year 1559, when the treaty of Cateau Cambresis brought the long and bloody struggle between the rival monarchies to a close.

To this treaty, the most important of the sixteenth century, nearly all the princes and states of Christendom were parties. France now finally renounced all claims to Milan and to Naples, and restored the Duke of Savoy to his dominions; but she retained the important fortresses of Toul, Verdun, and Metz. Henry the Second further stipulated that he should retain Calais[1] for a period of eight years, and in case it were not restored to England at the expiration of that period he should forfeit a sum of five hundred thousand crowns. The kings of France and Spain further bound themselves to take effective means for checking the progress of heresy and restoring unity to the Church. The Pope, the emperor, the kings of Poland, Denmark, Sweden, and Portugal, the King and Queen of Scots—namely, the dauphin and Mary Stewart—and various other princes

---

[1] Calais had been captured by the Duke of Guise in 1558.

and states, were comprehended as the allies either of France or Spain in this famous treaty of peace.

The French historians of the sixteenth century affect to regard this treaty as humiliating for France, apparently on the ground that after a struggle of upwards of sixty years she finally abandoned her claims to Italy. But at the present distance of time we may probably arrive at a different conclusion. The opposition of the kings of France to the ambitious schemes of Charles the Fifth, notwithstanding the immense resources of their antagonist, proved successful in the end. Although they failed to establish a permanent footing in Italy, they had not only defeated, or at least contributed effectually to the defeat of, his schemes in Germany, but by annexing the Lorraine fortresses to their dominions they obtained a new and most important line of defence on their eastern frontier. On the west the possession of Calais promised to secure them in all time coming from the dangers of an English invasion. Although the King of Spain was still the most powerful monarch in Christendom, his vast but unwieldy dominions, inhabited as they were by races differing in blood, in religion, and in laws, presented many more points of attack to an enterprising assailant than the compact territories of the French king, whose authority at this time was absolute over his people, and whose nobles delighted in war. France had never before been rendered so secure against foreign invasion as she was by the treaty of Cateau Cambresis.

But although thus secured apparently against external dangers, France was now on the eve of a national convulsion more terrible in its consequences than any foreign invasion could ever be. The Huguenot conspiracy of Amboise in 1560 proved to be the commencement of a series of wars and massacres which desolated the kingdom for nearly forty years. Three sons of Catherine de Medici[1] successively misgoverned France

---

[1] Francis the Second, Charles the Ninth, and Henry the Third.

during this disastrous period of her history. But fortunately the last and worst of them was succeeded by a prince who most justly earned the epithet of "great," bestowed on him by his admiring countrymen. Henry the Fourth, in whom we know not whether we more admire his unrivalled qualities as a ruler or his amiable qualities as a man, at length gave peace to France, and the Edict of Nantes, which he promulgated in 1598, promised to Protestant and Catholic alike the free exercise of their religion. It was designed, like the treaty of Passau, to effect a permanent peace between the rival sects. It was no fault of those who planned those solemn compacts that both were eventually broken.

While France was convulsed with civil war the people of the Netherlands revolted against the tyranny of Spain, and a succession of viceroys, distinguished alike in war and politics—namely, the Duke of Alva, Don John of Austria, and Alexander Farnese, Prince of Parma—all failed to reduce the people to subjection. Religious sympathy as well as policy induced Queen Elizabeth and her ministers to take part with the Huguenots of France and the insurgents of the Netherlands, but the foreign policy of this celebrated princess differed essentially from that of her predecessors. Hitherto the kings of England when they engaged in foreign wars had done so in the most open and public manner. But Elizabeth conducted her operations on an entirely new plan. She professed to be on terms of perfect amity with the kings of France and Spain, while she was secretly aiding to the utmost of her power their disaffected subjects in their rebellion. She permitted and encouraged her sailors to prey on the commerce of Spain, and did not scruple, in consideration of the licence she allowed them, to accept a large share of the plunder. The troubled condition of France and the Netherlands enabled her to carry on this piratical kind of warfare with impunity for upwards of twenty years. Philip meanwhile never ceased to meditate on schemes of retaliation and revenge, and after due deliberation he determined that his purpose would be best effected by the murder of the English queen. The fact that this nefarious project was not only openly discussed by his ministers, but that a report of their discussions should have been preserved,[1] furnishes a striking proof of the state of public morality in this age. The scheme of assassination was, however, abandoned, not from any scruples on the part of Philip and his council, but from the obstacles which stood in the way of its execution. A more legitimate project was the invasion of England, and in the year 1583 it was agreed between Philip and Henry of Guise, the celebrated leader of the League, that the latter should sail with a sufficient force for a quarter where an invasion was least expected—namely, Morecambe Bay, in Lancashire—that with the aid of the disaffected in that part of the kingdom, with whom he was in close correspondence, he should advance rapidly on Tutbury, where his cousin the Queen of Scots was at that time confined, and proclaim her Queen of England.[2] But this scheme fell to the ground through the ambition or the obstinacy of Philip, who vainly imagined that he would make a conquest of England for himself.[3] With this avowed object the Armada finally sailed in the summer of 1588. It was designed to destroy the English fleet, or at least to drive it from the Channel, while the Prince of Parma with a veteran army of thirty thousand men should pass securely over from the Netherlands and march through Kent or Essex upon London. Elizabeth and her ministers were singularly ill-informed as to the perils which at this time threatened the kingdom; for when the Armada appeared off the coast of Devonshire the land defences of the kingdom were practically worthless. England was saved at this time from the dangers and the miseries of an invasion partly through the

---

[1] See Froude, vol. x., p. 251, et seq.
[2] See Teulet, v., pp. 309 and 312.
[3] See "Instruccion para Inglaterra," Teulet, v., pp. 312, and the passage marked with Philip's hand as to the Queen of Scots.

obstinacy of Philip, who gave strict orders that his fleet should steer straight for Calais Roads, partly through the heroic conduct of Drake and his companions, aided as they were by unusually boisterous weather, and, last, not least, by the loyal and energetic co-operation of the Dutch, who held the army of the Prince of Parma closely blockaded in the ports of the Netherlands until the Armada had been driven from the Channel.

Elizabeth adopted exactly the same policy towards Scotland which she had pursued in France and in the Netherlands. She secretly supported the Earl of Murray in his rebellion against the Queen of Scots, and when the attempt failed she publicly denounced him as a traitor. It was, in short, the policy of this princess systematically to foment wars and insurrections among her neighbours as the best means of preserving tranquillity in her own dominions; and it cannot be denied that she was, upon the whole, remarkably successful. But that she never ventured openly to justify this insidious policy must be taken as a clear proof that even in that age it was regarded as indefensible.

There never was a more disgraceful treaty[1] than that by which King James of Scotland agreed with Elizabeth, for a pension of five thousand pounds a year and the promise of an English dukedom, which he never obtained, to abandon the cause of his mother, who, in defiance of all law, had been detained a prisoner in England for upwards of eighteen years. The ministers of Elizabeth had long desired to bring Mary to the scaffold. They regarded with alarm the possible accession to the crown of a princess whom they had so deeply wronged. But, to do her justice, Elizabeth was to the last opposed to this fatal step. She knew that by taking the life of her rival she would violate not only the law of nations, but the still more sacred laws of hospitality. She knew that it was by her invitation that Mary had sought a

---

[1] The treaty was signed on the 5th July, 1586, at Berwick.—See Record Office.

refuge in her dominions. Nor is there any reason to believe, as the enemies of the English queen have often alleged, that she sought by false professions of friendship and affection to induce her rival to place herself in her power. On the contrary, we have abundant proof that Elizabeth[1] displayed extreme indignation on hearing of the treatment of the Queen of Scots by her rebellious subjects. She even had the candour to reproach herself with having been, in part at least, the cause of Mary's misfortunes; and it was with difficulty that she was prevented by Cecil from sending an army into Scotland to effect her deliverance.[2] The change in her conduct after Mary's arrival in England must be attributed to the influence of Elizabeth's ministers, who knew so well how to work on the fears, the prejudices, and the follies of their mistress.

During the captivity of Mary there arose a novel question regarding the rights and privileges of an ambassador. John Leslie, Bishop of Ross, after Mary's arrival in England, had been received at the English court as her representative. He had carried on an active correspondence with the Earl of Northumberland, the Duke of Norfolk, and others of her partisans in England, and was no doubt cognisant of the various plots that were formed from time to time for the deliverance of his mistress. After the arrest of the Duke of Norfolk in 1571 the bishop was taken into custody, and it was proposed to examine him as to his knowledge of Norfolk's designs. But the bishop pleaded his privilege of an ambassador, alleging that he had come to England with a safe-conduct from Queen Elizabeth, that by the law and usage of Christendom the person of an ambassador was inviolable, and that even if he had been guilty of conspiring against her, which he emphatically denied, the only punishment to which he was liable was banish-

---

[1] On the 6th of August, 1567, Leicester writes to Sir H. Throgmorton that their mistress " will spend anything to redeem the Queen of Scots out of captivity."—Letter in Record Office. See also Thomas Heneage to Cecil, 8th July.
[2] Ibid.

ment from the kingdom. These elementary rules of the law of nations were perfectly well understood by Lord Burghley and his colleagues, but being satisfied that the bishop was the depositary of many important secrets, and being resolved apparently not to allow him to avail himself of his privilege, they went through the ceremony of submitting the following question to certain learned civilians, both English and foreign, with the view of justifying their conduct:—"Whether an ambassador "which raiseth rebellion against the prince to whom he "is sent may enjoy the privileges of an ambassador, "and be not subject to punishment as an enemy."

The reply of the foreign civilians was probably unfavourable to the views of Lord Burghley, for it has not been preserved. The reply of the English civilians, five in number, and described by Camden as "most learned "civil lawyers," was as follows:—"That such an am- "bassador, both by the law of nations and by the civil "law of the Romans, forfeited all the privileges of an "ambassador, and is to be subjected to punishment." No reference was made to any precedent in support of this opinion, and in the subsequent case of the Spanish ambassador Mendoza, Lord Burghley did not think fit to act upon it. There was the clearest proof that Mendoza was conspiring against the life of Elizabeth, but without being subjected to any examination he was simply ordered to leave the kingdom.[1] But Mendoza was the ambassador of Philip the Second, the most powerful monarch in Christendom; the Bishop of Ross was the ambassador of a princess who had been deposed by her rebellious subjects, and who at the time was a helpless prisoner in Sheffield Castle. The opinion of the civilians was also taken on the latter point—namely, whether the ambassador of a sovereign who had been deposed was privileged from arrest and punishment.

To this query it was answered:—"We think that "the solicitor of a prince lawfully deposed, and another

[1] Froude, vol. xi., p. 623.

"being invested in his place, cannot have the privilege
"of an ambassador; for that none but princes and such
"others as have sovereignty may have ambassadors."

In accordance with these opinions the Bishop of Ross was informed that he could no longer be acknowledged as an ambassador, and that he was liable to be interrogated and punished like any private person. To this he replied that he was the ambassador of an independent queen who had been unjustly deposed, and that according to his duty he had earnestly sought to obtain her deliverance and restoration with a view to the welfare of both kingdoms; that he had come into England with full powers as an ambassador, and with a formal safe-conduct which he had exhibited, and that by all nations the privileges of an ambassador were held sacred. Lord Burghley upon this observed that no safe-conduct could protect an ambassador from the consequences of any act committed by him against the public peace, for in such a case he was liable to arrest and punishment like any private person. But the bishop had a ready answer to this proposition of the Lord Treasurer. He reminded him of two recent incidents which had occurred, the one in France and the other in Scotland, with reference to the point in question. The English ambassador in France, Sir Nicolas Throgmorton, had not only taken an active part in promoting the Huguenot rebellion, but at the battle of Dreux, in 1562, he was actually taken prisoner in the Huguenot camp. Yet no proceedings were taken against him; he was allowed at once to return to England. Subsequently to this two English ambassadors in Scotland—namely, Randolph and Tamworth—were sent out of the country for notoriously and persistently aiding and abetting the rebellions of the Earl of Murray and his confederates. With these discreditable proceedings, both in France and Scotland, Lord Burghley was well acquainted. Indeed, whatever was done in those countries by the representatives of his mistress was done with his knowledge and assent. He was, therefore, little beholden to the bishop for reminding him of those past transactions, and hastened to cut the controversy short by informing him that his alleged privilege would not avail him, and that he would be compelled to disclose all he knew. He was forthwith committed to close custody in the Tower, and subjected for several days to a rigorous examination. After an imprisonment of many months he was eventually liberated through the intervention of the French Government,[1] and retired to France.

The treatment of the Bishop of Ross appears from first to last to have been wholly unjustifiable. The question, indeed, whether the ambassador of a sovereign in captivity could plead his privilege was a novel one. But Elizabeth and her ministers were precluded from raising this point because Mary was a prisoner when he came to England as her ambassador. He was formally acknowledged as such at the conferences both at York and Westminster, and it was not until they were in want of evidence against the Duke of Norfolk, whom they had resolved to sacrifice, that they ventured to dispute the legality of his commission.

The proceedings by which the Queen of Scots was eventually brought to the scaffold were alike anomalous and unprecedented. The Crown lawyers, indeed, at one time considered that they had found a precedent for the execution in the tragedy of Conradino.[2] But on reflection this notion was abandoned. It was only in one point of view that the history of Conradino resembled that of the Queen of Scots. The grandson of Frederick the Second was regarded by his adherents as the rightful sovereign of Naples, as Mary was regarded by her partisans as the lawful Queen of England. But here the parallel ended. Conradino sought to recover his kingdom by force of arms, and was defeated, made a prisoner, and put to death. Mary came to England a helpless fugitive,

---

[1] See Camden, p. 141; Murdin, vol. ii., p. 18, et seq.
[2] Strype's Annals, vol. iii. Append.

and, after having been detained in captivity for nineteen years, under one pretext or another, was finally put to death by virtue of a statute which had been expressly passed for the purpose of bringing her to the scaffold. To justify these proceedings, even if all that her enemies alleged against her were true, was plainly impossible; and, making every allowance for the character of the age and for the spirit of religious rivalry with which it was imbued, the execution of the Queen of Scots will ever remain perhaps the darkest incident in the history of the sixteenth century.

The great event of this age was the establishment of the Reformation throughout an extensive portion of Northern and Western Europe. Its success or failure appeared, in fact, to be chiefly a question of race. By the nations of Teutonic and Scandinavian origin the new doctrines found a comparatively ready acceptance, while the Latin, Celtic, and Slavonic races, generally speaking, adhered to their ancient creed. In Sweden the establishment of Protestantism was the result of a political revolution. Christian the Second of Denmark, the most odious tyrant of the age, had so cruelly oppressed the Swedes that Gustavus Vasa, one of those extraordinary men who from time to time appear in the world as deliverers of their country and benefactors of mankind, freed Sweden from the Danish yoke and founded a dynasty which was destined to play a most important part in the general politics of Europe. Gustavus Vasa, who had embraced the Lutheran religion, was crowned King of Sweden in 1520.[1] But a succession of wars followed, and it was not until the peace of Stettin in 1570 that Denmark formally and finally acknowledged the independence of Sweden.[2]

Christian the Second, whose tyranny had led to the revolt and the independence of Sweden, was eventually deposed by his own subjects, and Frederick, Duke of Holstein, was elected King of Denmark in his stead.

---

[1] Koch, tom. i., p. 382. [2] Dumont.

Under this prince and his successor, Christian the Third, the Lutheran religion was finally established in Denmark in the year 1535.[1]

The political changes which took place in the sixteenth century were not less important than the religious. We find that in the course of this century many of the European states assumed the dimensions which they have since maintained. We find that in this period wars and negotiations were carried on on a much more extensive scale than formerly; that there was more order and regularity in the conduct of public affairs, and that in consequence of the growing increase of the executive authority in nearly every country private feuds and popular tumults were much more easily suppressed. But if in the sixteenth century we find less brutal violence than in that which preceded it, we find more artifice and more duplicity; and this result we may probably attribute, in part at least, to the influence of a man of extraordinary talents, whose system of political philosophy proved only too attractive to the rulers of mankind. It has, indeed, been all along maintained by the admirers and apologists of Machiavelli that in composing his famous treatise he sought, not to teach the arts of tyranny, but to expose and hold them up to execration. But however that may be, there is no doubt of the fact, not only that his maxims were taken in their literal sense by the mass of mankind, but that they were regarded as the perfection of wisdom by the most unscrupulous politicians of this age. Few more ambitious monarchs have ever lived than the Emperor Charles the Fifth; France was never afflicted with a more vicious ruler than Catherine de Medici; and a worse king than Philip the Second never reigned in Spain. With all these potentates the "Prince" of Machiavelli was a household word. It has been further said that there is nothing contained in that work which is not to be found in Aristotle, and this may be true. But in

---

[1] Koch, tom. i., p. 382.

delineating with his accustomed accuracy the various arts of tyranny Aristotle never fails to denounce them as alike mischievous and dangerous. We find no such healthy sentiment in the work of the great Florentine, which stands alone a matchless monument of prostituted genius, that must ever be regarded with mingled feelings of pain and admiration.

[1] Aristotle, Polit. There are in Shakespeare's dramas two references to Machiavelli, and both made by persons who could not possibly have been aware of his existence. The first is in the first part of Henry the Sixth, where, upon Joan of Arc boasting that Alençon had been her lover, the Duke of York exclaims—

"Alençon, that notorious Machiavel."

Act v., scene 4.

A curious anachronism, for the Maid of Orleans was put to death in 1431, many years before Machiavelli was born. The next reference is in the third part of Henry the Sixth, in the famous soliloquy of the Duke of Gloucester—

"And set the murtherous Machiavel to school."

We may infer from these references that the name of Machiavel had become proverbial in Shakespeare's day.

According to Hudibras we derive the well-known term "Old Nick" from Niccolo Machiavelli :—

"Nick Machiavel had ne'er a trick
(He gave his name to our Old Nick.")

Part iii., canto 1.

CHAPTER VI.

OF THE MARITIME LAW OF NATIONS FROM THE SIXTH TILL THE CLOSE OF THE SIXTEENTH CENTURY.

PIRACY was so universally practised during the early Middle Ages that we find no record in those rude times of any acknowledged rules of international usages at sea. The Scandinavians in the North and the Saracens in the South of Europe regarded all commerce as lawful prey, and it was not until long after the devastations committed by those conquering races both by land and sea had ceased that we find any distinct recognition on the part of maritime states of international rights and duties. The laws of Oleron, compiled in the reign of King Richard the First after his return from Palestine, form the earliest maritime code extant. But, like the laws of the ancient Rhodians, an important fragment of which has been preserved in the Digest, the laws of Oleron contain no rules for the decision of international disputes. The only exception appears to be certain humane provisions for the protection of shipwrecked property and the treatment of shipwrecked mariners.[1]

[1] By the 26th article of the laws of Oleron it was provided that if a vessel was lost with all its crew, but that a portion of the cargo was saved, the lord of the place where it was cast ashore was bound to see that the goods so saved should be securely kept until they could be delivered to the owners or their representatives. And in case no claim was made within a year he was directed to sell them to the highest bidder, and with the proceeds "procure prayers to be "made for the remission of the sins of the deceased, or provide marriages for poor "maids, and to do therewith such other works of piety and charity as are con- "sonant to reason and a good conscience. But if he assumes the said goods either "in whole or in part unto himself he shall incur the curse and malediction of Our "Mother the Holy Church, with the aforesaid pains and penalties, without ever "obtaining remission, unless he make satisfaction."
With respect to shipwrecked mariners :—"If a ship or other vessel happens to "be lost by striking on some rock or elsewhere upon the coast, and the mariners, "thinking to escape and save their lives, attempt to come near the shore in hope "of help, and instead thereof it happens, as it often does, that in many places

It is to another quarter that we must look for the first germs of international maritime law. We find that from the remotest ages an active intercourse was carried on between the various nations inhabiting the coasts of the Mediterranean Sea. During the darkest periods of European history that intercourse never ceased, and the Crusades from first to last brought an immense increase of wealth to the commercial cities of Spain and Italy. But commercial rivalry has ever been a fruitful source of strife, and the hostilities in which the Mediterranean republics so frequently engaged led them of necessity to adopt some fixed rules for the protection of their commerce in time of war. All maritime states had a common interest in the establishment of such rules, and hence there grew up in the course of the fourteenth century that celebrated collection of laws which under the name of *costumbres maritimos*, or the *consolato del mare*, were gradually adopted, and for centuries held to be binding by the general consent of European nations.

In this famous code we find laid down for the first time a set of clear and definite rules applicable alike to belligerent and neutral shipping in time of war. Some of these rules have from time to time led to warm disputes, and even to sanguinary wars; but the significant fact that they continued to be observed, with only occasional interruptions, for the space of five centuries, furnishes strong proof that they were framed in accordance with the general interest and convenience of maritime nations. And it by no means follows that because some of the most important of those rules have now been altered by an agreement among the leading European Powers,[1] the new doctrines when tested by experience will find universal acceptance, and finally supersede the

---

" they meet with people more barbarous, cruel, and inhuman than mad dogs, who
" to gain their moneys, apparel, and other goods do sometimes murder and destroy
" these poor mariners—in this case the lord of that country ought to execute death
" on such wretches, to plunge them in the sea till they be half-dead, and then to
" have them drawn forth out of the sea and stoned to death."

[1] By the Treaty of Paris of 1856.

old. It is well to bear in mind, while speculating on
the future, that in times past more than one strenuous
attempt has been made by a coalition of powerful states
to alter by force of arms the established rules of maritime
law, and that those attempts invariably failed.[1]

It is assumed in the *Consolato* as a fundamental rule
of maritime law that the commerce of an enemy at sea
may at all times be lawfully captured.[2] If both ship
and cargo belonged to an enemy both were regarded as
lawful prizes, and this latter rule is still followed both
in Europe and in America.

The *Consolato* next proceeds to the case of a ship
belonging to a friendly or a neutral state, but carrying
the property of an enemy. In that case the cargo only
was declared to be lawful prize. The ship was restored
to the owner, and he also received from the captor the
whole freight which he would have earned if the cargo
had reached its destination. This rule as to the capture
of an enemy's goods in a neutral ship was consistently
observed by the Admiralty Courts of Great Britain[3]
down to the year 1856. By a declaration attached to
the Treaty of Paris in that year the chief maritime
Powers of the world, with the exception of the United
States of America, agreed to adopt in future the rule
that the flag should cover the cargo. This unprecedented concession to the interests of neutral commerce
was at the time, and still continues to be, a subject of
much controversy.

The *Consolato* next provides for the case of a ship
which is the property of an enemy while the cargo is the

[1] By the Armed Neutrality of 1780 and 1800.—See Manning, p. 257.
[2] Consolato del Mare, cap. cclxxiii.
[3] In the year 1327, when England was at war with Scotland, a Flemish ship
was captured and brought to Yarmouth. On the petition of the Flemish owner
the ship was restored, while the goods belonging to the enemy were detained as
lawful prize. "Proviso quod bona et mercimenta, quae fuerunt hominum Scotiae
" et quae in ea occasione fuerant arrestata salvo, sicure abique distractione aliquâ
" custodiantur."—Rymer, vol. iv., p. 328. A similar order was made in the year
1373, when England was at war with Spain, as to the restitution of a Portuguese
ship and the detention of enemy's goods which were found on board.—Rymer,
vol. vii., p. 3.

property of a friend. In this case the ship was deemed lawful prize, while the cargo was restored to the owner; and if any undue violence was employed by the captor through which the cargo suffered injury, he was bound to compensate the owner to the full amount of the damage done.

Provision is also made for a ship which has been captured by an enemy and subsequently recaptured by a friendly Power. In that case the vessel was to be restored to the original owner on the payment by him to the recaptor of an adequate compensation for his risk and trouble.

Such were the general rules of maritime capture and restitution which we find established in Southern and in Western Europe in the fourteenth century. In the North, meanwhile, the progress of commerce had not been less rapid than in the Mediterranean. The cities of Bremen and Amsterdam formed an alliance for the mutual advancement and protection of their trade. This was the foundation of the Hanseatic League, a confederacy which eventually embraced not only all the most important cities in the North of Europe, but also many of those of France, Spain, and Italy.[1] As the security of their commerce was the main object of the Hanseatic League, they naturally sought to preserve it from interruption while their neighbours were at war—a circumstance of very frequent occurrence among the Baltic states in the thirteenth and fourteenth centuries; and it is to the Hanse Towns that we must look for the first attempt to alter the maritime law of capture laid down in the *Consolato del Mare*. The Hanseatic traders did not fail to perceive the immense advantage they would derive provided they were allowed to carry on their traffic without interruption while their neighbours were at war. Hence they sought to establish the rule that the goods of an enemy on

[1] In the year 1200 there were no less than seventy-two towns in the Hanseatic League, London being one of them.

board a neutral ship ought to be exempt from capture—in other words, that the flag ought to protect the cargo. At first sight the doctrine seems founded in equity, for it is hard that a nation at peace should suffer through the quarrels of its neighbours. But it unfortunately happens that in this case there is a direct conflict of interest between the belligerent and the neutral. It is the interest of the former to weaken the resources of his antagonist by destroying his foreign commerce; it is the interest of the latter to carry on his trade without interruption. To reconcile these interests is obviously impossible; the one must of necessity give way to the other, and hence the interminable disputes to which this question has given rise. We shall have to refer more particularly to these in a subsequent part of this work. Suffice it to say for the present that the rule of " free ships " free goods," which was formally adopted by the leading European Powers in the year 1856, was first sought to be established by the Hanseatic League.

But it is worthy of note that the authors of the doctrine of "free ships free goods," although eager on all occasions to apply it to their neighbours, invariably resisted its application to themselves. They found it extremely advantageous so long as they remained at peace to monopolise the trade of their belligerent neighbours, but as soon as they themselves were engaged in war they reverted without scruple to the ancient rule.

" The Hanseatic merchants," says the learned historian of the League, " were too knowing not to be " aware of the advantages which would accrue from the " maintenance of such an unlimited freedom of trade " during war as would allow them to supply both belligerents " without risk, and in fact to carry on, in a great " measure, the maritime traffic of both. The Hanse " Towns," continues the same author, " as neutrals demanded " freedom for their merchandise, even for what " might be found on board of hostile vessels; freedom

"for their neutral flag to trade to the countries of the
"belligerent states, to carry to those countries their own
"native Hanseatic and also foreign goods, as well as to
"export from the countries involved in war all and
"sundry goods and wares, and to carry them thence to
"any places whatever; at most, perhaps, they promise
"to abstain from the conveyance of ammunition or war-
"like stores to the countries engaged in war." "But
"these very liberal principles," continues Sartorius,
"the Hanseatic states did not follow or observe in
"relation to neutral nations when they were themselves
"involved in war."[1] And he adds that in the days of
their decline they generally looked to their own immediate profit regardless of any treaty engagements which
subsisted between them and their neighbours. We may
observe that both in the last and the present century the
example of the Hanse Towns has been closely followed by
other maritime nations—in other words, the doctrines
which they strenuously upheld while they remained at
peace were tacitly abandoned when they themselves
became engaged in war.[2]

That the right of visitation and search was an
acknowledged incident of naval warfare in the early part
of the sixteenth century we may learn from the instructions of Henry the Eighth to the admiral of the fleet
which sailed in the expedition to Guienne in the year
1512.[3] We may perhaps assume that this had long
been an acknowledged right, for its exercise was abso-

[1] Reddie, Maritime International Law, vol. i., p. 62.
[2] "Not fifteen years from the date of the Armed Neutrality, the wars with
"France had involved almost every European state, and the principle which
"obtained such general prevalence was abandoned by nearly all the members of
"the Northern Confederacy, the great leader in that alliance, Russia, being the
"chief instigator of the unusual severities which were adopted towards neutrals."
—Manning, p. 271.
[3] "If any shippe or shippes of the flete mete any other shippes or vessels on
"the see or in porte or portes, making rebellion, resistance, or defence against
"theym, then it is lawfull for them to assemble and take theym with strong hand
"to bring them holy and entirely to the said admirall without despoylling, or
"embeselying of the goods, or doing harme to the parties ther to abyde the
"ordinance of the lawe as the said admirall shall awarde."—Rymer, Fœdera,
vol. xiii., p. 829.

lutely necessary to determine the nationality and the character of any suspected ship. With regard to contraband we find a variety of provisions in the treaties of the fifteenth and sixteenth centuries.[1] In the year 1589 a question arose between Queen Elizabeth and the Hanse Towns on this subject. The latter complained that their ships freighted with corn were captured by English cruisers on the high seas. The vessels in question, sixty in number, were taken by Sir Francis Drake at the mouth of the Tagus, laden with provisions, which it was alleged were intended for a second Armada which the King of Spain was preparing for an invasion of England. To avoid the risk of capture these vessels had sailed round the Orkney Islands and the West Coast of Ireland, and their owners maintained that the provisions which they carried, not being munitions of war, were not liable to seizure as contraband. To these complaints Queen Elizabeth, according to Camden,[2] replied that she had warned the men of the Hanse Towns not to supply her enemies with provisions; that to supply such to an enemy was not only a breach of the law of nations, but that the Hanseatic League, in their treaty with her predecessor King Edward the First, had expressly stipulated not to furnish any such articles to the enemies of England; that it was notorious that their ships had often been captured while carrying provisions to the French, and that such supplies had been treated as contraband, not by the English alone, but by the Emperor Charles the Fifth, by the Kings of Sweden, Poland, and Denmark, and more recently by the Prince of Orange in his contest with the King of Spain. It would appear that in this case both the ships and their cargoes were detained as lawful prize.

In the course of the sixteenth century an important innovation was attempted to be introduced into the law of maritime capture by France. By the ordonnance of

---

[1] Manning, p. 284, note.   [2] L. iv.

1543,[1] and also by that of 1584, the property of a friend in an enemy's ship, and also the ship of a friend having the property of an enemy on board, were both declared to be lawful prize. This was a clear departure from the rules laid down in the *Consolato*, nor does any other country appear to have followed the example of France in subjecting commerce to fresh perils in time of war.

We cannot close these remarks on the maritime history of the sixteenth century without adverting to the rise and growth of a traffic which has since been the subject of much negotiation and of many treaties, and which, notwithstanding the strenuous efforts made for its suppression, is by no means yet extinct. We allude to the African slave trade. It has been very generally supposed that the first promoters of this disgraceful traffic were men imbued with the purest spirit of philanthropy. The exportation of negroes to America commenced at a time when the Indian population of the Spanish colonies was fast disappearing under the merciless tyranny of their European taskmasters, and it is said that to save the aborigines from extermination the virtuous Las Casas conceived the project of introducing Africans from the coast of Guinea. The Indians, who delighted only in war and in the chase, were averse to regular labour of every kind. The negro was of a much more peaceful and docile nature, and in a climate far superior to his own and under the protection of equal laws would make a happy exchange from his native swamps to the gorgeous islands of the West. Such, it is said, were the dreams of Las Casas[2] and his companions, and such was the commencement of a traffic which has desolated, and still continues to desolate, the

---

[1] See the Ordonnances in Pardessus.

[2] Las Casas Breve relacion de la destruccion de las Indias Occidentales, London, 1812. Relation des Voyages et des Découvertes des Espagnols dans les Indes Occidentales, Amst., 1698.

African continent, and which, we may add, has corrupted and debased both the Old World and the New. War and pestilence are mighty evils, but it may well be doubted whether both combined have in the course of three thousand years—to take the extreme limit of the world's history—produced so vast an amount of misery and crime as has this inhuman traffic in the comparatively short space of three centuries. We know that slavery existed among all the most celebrated nations of antiquity, but there is nothing in history to compare with this wholesale commerce in human beings, which was, and still is, the peculiar characteristic of the African slave trade. Another peculiarity, and one which at its commencement contributed essentially to its rapid extension, was the remarkably lucrative nature of the traffic. Persons of the highest rank in Spain eagerly embarked in it, and in England Queen Elizabeth was not only content to share its profits with the celebrated John Hawkins, who earned the unenviable reputation of being the first Englishman who carried a cargo of negroes to America, but even supplied him with ships for the purpose.[1] During the greater part of the sixteenth century the traffic flourished unimpeded, and to swell the gains of Spanish, Portuguese, and English adventurers, myriads of unhappy wretches were torn from their homes to perish in the pestilential hold of a slave-ship, or to spend the brief remainder of their lives in the mines or in the burning fields of tropical America. It does not appear that a voice was raised in any quarter against this new and murderous traffic. The Popes, who in former ages had so nobly stood forth as the champions of humanity, and denounced slavery in every shape, now that it had assumed an aspect more hideous than ever looked on in silence. Nay, those who embarked most largely in the trade professed to believe that they were the chosen instruments of Providence in carrying

[1] Lingard vi., p. 235.

out a great and beneficent work. "Almighty God[1] never "suffers his elect to perish," was the pious ejaculation of Hawkins after having weathered a dangerous tempest in a vessel expressly provided for the slave traffic by his royal mistress.

[1] Froude, History of England, vol. viii., p. 475.

CHAPTER VII.

OF THE THIRTY YEARS' WAR AND THE TREATY OF WESTPHALIA.

THE treaty of Passau, for which Germany was indebted to Prince Maurice of Saxony, put a stop for a time to the armed struggle between the old religion and the new. But it was more in the nature of a truce than of a permanent peace. The treaty was, in fact, so partial in its operation, and it left so many material points open to dispute, that we may well feel surprised, not that the contest was renewed, but that it was so long delayed.

Of the various sects of Reformers the Lutherans only were recognised by the treaty of Passau, and this circumstance alone was sufficient to create deep dissatisfaction among all other Protestants. The exclusion of the Calvinists was from the first felt to be especially galling by the professors of that gloomy creed, and in the beginning of the seventeenth century Calvinism was professed by millions of Germans. At their head were two princes of the highest rank—Christian of Anhalt and the Elector Palatine, the one distinguished for his political talents, the other formidable from the situation and the extent of his dominions. Another and a still more fertile source of trouble was the perpetual struggle between the rival creeds for the possession of the Church lands. The provisions of the treaty of Passau upon this essential point were vague and ambiguous, and the intrigues of the Jesuits on the one hand, and the rapacity of the Protestant princes on the other, kept alive the spirit of discord, and led eventually to serious acts of violence. In consequence of a religious riot which took place in the year 1607 the Protestant town of Donauwerth in Suabia was laid under the ban of the empire, and the place itself annexed to the territories of the Catholic Elector of Bavaria.

The Protestants were naturally indignant at this arbitrary proceeding. They asserted that the sentence was illegal, as it had been pronounced by the Aulic Council, a purely Catholic tribunal, and they forthwith proceeded, under the guidance of Christian of Anhalt, to concert measures for the maintenance of their liberties. But the Emperor Rudolf, to whom they applied for protection and redress, was at this time powerless. He had been deprived of the crown of Hungary by his brother Matthias, and he had been threatened with a rebellion in Bohemia, which he only averted by proclaiming, much against his will, religious toleration[1] in that kingdom; and, to add to the general complication, an event occurred which placed the Catholic and Protestant powers in direct antagonism, and threatened to involve Europe in a general war.

This was the disputed succession to the duchy of Cleves, which became vacant in the year 1609. The acquisition of this territory, situated as it was between the Austrian dominions and the Netherlands, became an object of immediate interest to all the neighbouring Powers. It was of the utmost importance to Austria to strengthen her position on the Lower Rhine; while, on the other hand, the men of the Netherlands, who had concluded a twelve years' truce with Spain, saw in the extension of the imperial dominions in that direction a menace and a danger which they were prepared, if necessary, to avert by force.

The last Duke of Cleves was a lunatic, and he died childless and without collateral male heirs. But he had four sisters, all of whom were married. The eldest of the four, Maria Eleonora, was married, in the year 1572,[2] to Albert Frederick of Brandenburg, Duke of Prussia,

---

[1] See the Royal Letter in Dumont.
[2] Sully, Mem., vol. i., p. 179.

and in the articles of marriage the entire succession of Cleves was settled upon her and her descendants in case of the failure of the male line. Two years later—namely, in 1574—the second sister, Anna, married Philip Louis, Count Palatine of Neuburg, with a like stipulation as to the rights of her descendants. Similar provisions were made on the marriage of the two younger sisters as to the rights of succession of them and their posterity.

How there could have been any serious question between the representative of the eldest sister[1] and that of any other sister it is difficult at the present day to explain. But it is certain that between the claims of Brandenburg and Neuburg the lawyers and diplomatists of the day were hopelessly puzzled. After an infinite amount of argument and negotiation they could suggest no better means of settling the question than by the rough expedient of cutting the disputed duchy in two and dividing it equally between the rival claimants. To this arrangement both Brandenburg and Neuburg eventually agreed. But before they could take peaceable possession of their dominions there was another matter to be adjusted. The imperial lawyers undertook to prove from the ancient records of the duchy that Cleves was, and always had been, a male fief; that therefore all the stipulations made in favour of female heirs were null and void; and that as the male line had failed the territory reverted to the emperor as suzerain of Germany. In pursuance of this claim the town and citadel of Juliers were suddenly occupied by a body of imperial troops, to be held, as was alleged, until the question of the succession should be finally adjusted.

This decisive step of the imperial court brought other actors on the scene. Henry the Fourth of France

[1] Jealousy of the house of Brandenburg seems to have been one cause of the delay in settling the question. James the First, it appears, was in favour of the claim of Brandenburg, but the English ambassador at the Hague repeated the following remarkable prophecy of his master:—"Il craint la puissance de "Brandenburg s'il parvient à cette succession d'autant plus qu'à la longueur il "pourroit venir à l'empire."—Letter to Barneveld, 13th June, 1609; Motley's Life of Barneveld, vol. i., p. 61.

regarded as fatal to the interests of his kingdom the extension of the Austrian dominions in that quarter, and, in concert with the Duke of Sully, resolved to oppose it to the utmost of his power. That wise and faithful minister saw clearly that a fresh struggle with Austria and Spain was inevitable, and, thanks to his prudent administration, France had never been better prepared for war than during the latter years of Henry's life. We may smile at the dream of perpetual peace which Henry hoped to realise after he had humbled the house of Austria and chastised the insolence of Spain. But there can be no doubt that the murder of this great king changed the history of Europe. The army which he was about to lead against the imperialists was the finest and the best appointed that France had ever seen,[1] and had his plan of operations proved successful, of which there was every prospect, Germany might possibly have been spared the terrible calamity of the thirty years' war. The dagger of Ravaillac not only destroyed the most valuable life in Europe, but for a time it wholly paralysed France. She became forthwith the prey of furious factions and of a court in which a second princess of the house of Medici seemed, by her scandalous administration, to emulate the infamy of the first. It was not until Richelieu had crushed rebellion and disorder with an iron hand that France regained her influence in Europe.

The murder of Henry had the effect of postponing for eight years the great religious conflict, but they were years of feverish anxiety and silent preparation for the death struggle which was clearly seen to be inevitable. Unhappily there was at this time no central or controlling power in Germany to which the opposing parties could appeal for a settlement of their disputes, and which, if necessary, could enforce obedience to its decrees. Although nothing could be more imposing in

---

[1] See the conversation between the Duke de Sully and Henry on the subject of the proposed expedition.—*Memoirs*, book xxvii.

theory than the Germanic Diet, it had become at this time practically powerless. Composed as it was of princes both spiritual and temporal, of every grade of influence and power, from the electors and great feudatories of the empire to the lords of some petty domain on the Rhine or the Danube, containing, moreover, representatives of the ancient free cities of Germany, and boasting of the first potentate of Christendom as its acknowledged head, the Germanic Diet seemed to exhibit within itself every element of strength, and to be well adapted alike for legislation and for action. But circumstances had entirely changed since Charles the Fifth issued his edicts from Frankfort or from Ratisbon. The Emperor Rudolf the Second and his brother Matthias, who had robbed him of half his dominions, were both alike unfitted to rule in perilous times, and their cousin, Ferdinand of Styria, who eventually succeeded to the imperial crown, was the obedient disciple of the Jesuits and the declared enemy of heresy in every shape. The prospect of his succession was regarded with dread by every Protestant in Germany, and when in the year 1617 he was elected to the crown of Bohemia it was universally believed that the maintenance of peace was no longer possible.

These fears were speedily realised. Nine years before Rudolf had accorded freedom of conscience to his Bohemian subjects. But the royal letter which proclaimed liberty of religious opinion was silent as to freedom of worship. Advantage was speedily taken of this omission. In the course of a few months several Protestant places of worship were closed by the ecclesiastical authorities, and at Klostergrab a church which had been built on the lands of the Archbishop of Prague was levelled with the ground. In consequence of these violent proceedings a remonstrance was presented to the emperor complaining that the promise of toleration contained in the royal letter had been violated, and praying for redress. To this remonstrance a reply was promptly returned in which it was denied that there had been any violation of the royal letter, that whatever had been done had been done in accordance with the law, and that in spite of all opposition the law would continue to be enforced.

This reply could admit of only one interpretation. The leading Protestants regarded it in the light both of a challenge and a threat, and they proceeded to take their measures accordingly. Count Thurn, a nobleman of great influence and of a restless and aspiring temper, had taken a prominent part in preparing the remonstrance to the emperor, and he had gathered around him a band of his brother nobles, who, like himself, were prepared to resort to arms for the maintenance of their religion. They now came to the conclusion that the emperor's reply left them no choice between complete submission and rebellion. They resolved upon the latter.

The emperor at this time resided at Vienna, but he was represented at Prague by ten stadtholders who administered the affairs of the kingdom. Two of these ministers—namely, Martinitz and Slawata—had rendered themselves extremely unpopular by their notorious hostility to the Protestants, and they were generally believed to be the authors of the offensive imperial reply. After much deliberation it was resolved by Thurn and his confederates to murder the two obnoxious ministers in the most public manner. By this act of violence they would at once express the popular feeling of hatred and indignation, and they would render the breach with the emperor irreparable.

On the 23rd of May, 1618, accordingly—a day that will ever remain memorable in German history as the commencement of the thirty years' war—Thurn repaired to the castle of Prague accompanied by a band of his fellow-conspirators, and attended by a body of armed retainers. Making their way into the council-chamber, where they found the two obnoxious stadtholders, they accused them of instigating the emperor to oppress his Protestant subjects, and charged them, moreover, with being the authors of the offensive reply to their late remonstrance. Unaware at first of the real object of the conspirators, the two ministers declared in the most solemn manner that they were not the authors of the imperial reply, for that that had come, not from Prague but from Vienna, and in this they spoke the truth.[1] As there was no actual proof that the stadtholders were the authors of the imperial missive, Count Thurn, in order to justify his conduct, was prepared to make another charge against them, and one that was no less than nine years old. The Emperor Rudolf had proclaimed religious toleration in Bohemia in the year 1609, and his royal letter had been countersigned by all the Catholic nobles of the kingdom with the exception of Martinitz and Slawata, who persistently refused their signatures. In the same year a resolution had been passed in the Diet declaring that whoever refused to subscribe the royal letter was an enemy to the commonwealth. Paul von Rican, one of the conspirators, now produced a copy of this resolution, and, after reading it aloud, asked his confederates if the two stadtholders had not been declared enemies of their country, and if as such they did not deserve death. He was answered by a shout of approval. One or two of the conspirators, moved by pity for the unhappy men, proposed that, instead of being put instantly to death, they should be kept for the present in close confinement, but they were in a hopeless minority. There was a general cry that the stadtholders should be forthwith thrown from the window of the castle. One of the conspirators, approaching Martinitz from behind, seized both his arms; he was instantly surrounded by four others, and dragged to the window of the chamber struggling desperately for his life. He begged hard for a confessor. "Commend your soul "to God," some one exclaimed. "Shall we bring your "Jesuit scoundrels here?" cried another, and the stadt-

---

[1] The author of the imperial reply to the Protestant remonstrance was the Cardinal Khlesol.—Gindley, Geschichte des Dreisigjariger Krieg, vol. i., p. 258.

holder was hurled from the window into the fosse below, a depth of eighty feet, ejaculating "Jesus Maria!" as he fell. "Let us see if his Maria will save him," cried Kinsky, one of the most active of the conspirators. "By "God! his Maria has saved him," he continued in amazement as he watched the stadtholder crawl away from underneath the window apparently unhurt. Slawata and his secretary Fabricius were flung from the window immediately afterwards, and with the same results. All three escaped, not only with their lives, but without serious injury. The adherents of the emperor did not hesitate to assert that their preservation was simply miraculous; their enemies, on the other hand, accounted for it by the fact that they had fallen on a dungheap at the bottom of the fosse.

Thurn and his confederates had failed in their intent to perpetrate a political murder, but their object was nevertheless attained. After the commission of so unpardonable an outrage on the imperial ministers they could only hope to protect themselves against the consequences of their crime by a successful rebellion. They accordingly proclaimed forthwith a provisional government, consisting of thirty directors; they expelled the Jesuits from Bohemia, levied troops, and engaged as their commander a soldier of fortune, Ernest Count Mansfeld, who acted a very conspicuous part in the early part of the thirty years' war. In concert with this adventurer Thurn and his confederates were not only able to set the emperor at defiance, but, relying on the sympathies of the Protestants of Austria proper, marched upon Vienna in the spring of 1619. By this time the Emperor Matthias had died, but Ferdinand was still the titular King of Bohemia, and prepared at all hazards to maintain his rights. Although he had but a handful of troops to oppose to the insurgents, he made resolute preparations to defend his capital, and the latter, being unprovided with artillery for a siege, were compelled to retreat.

The leaders of the Bohemian revolution had now to determine on the permanent form of government to be established in the kingdom, and as a preliminary step they summoned a general Diet of the States, which met on the 17th of August, 1619. By an unanimous vote Ferdinand was declared to be an enemy of the liberties and the religion of Bohemia; that he had employed foreign mercenaries for the oppression of the people; that, in defiance of the national rights, he had by a secret compact bequeathed the kingdom to Spain, and that for these reasons he had forfeited his title to the crown. A few days after this decisive proceeding of the Bohemian Diet—namely, on the 28th of August—Ferdinand was at Frankfort duly elected Emperor of Germany by the name of Ferdinand the Second.

The Bohemians had now to elect a successor to the sovereign they had deposed, and their choice very naturally fell upon the Elector Palatine, Frederick the Fifth. He was the head of the Calvinists in Germany, a kinsman of Prince Maurice of Nassau, and a son-in-law of the King of England. The chief of the Lutherans, John George, the Elector of Saxony, had stood aloof from the leaders of the Bohemian revolt, partly from religious antipathy and partly influenced by the artifices of the imperial court, and he was the only Protestant prince who, in point of territorial importance, could compare with the Elector Palatine. It is said that it was chiefly at the instigation of his wife Elizabeth, the high-spirited daughter of James the First, that Frederick was induced to accept the fatal gift of the Bohemian crown. But James was decidedly opposed to a proceeding so hazardous in itself, and, in his estimation, so subversive of the rights of kings. Frederick himself had grave misgivings as to the prudence of the step, but his scruples were overcome by the glitter of a crown, and on the 4th of November, 1619, his coronation was celebrated at Prague with much pomp and every symptom of popular enthusiasm.

An able and energetic prince in the position in which Frederick was now placed, with the kingdom of Bohemia added to his hereditary dominions, would have rendered himself the most powerful sovereign in Germany. But he was wholly unfitted for the perilous enterprise in which he had embarked. He was an amiable, unambitious, uxorious youth, devoted to his amusements though bigoted in his religion, but without talents of any kind. He offended both Catholics and Lutherans by his strong Calvinistic prejudices, which induced him to strip the churches of Prague of their pictures and ornaments, and all sects of Christians regarded with dismay his alliance with Bethlem Gabor, the semi-barbarous usurper of Transylvania, who, with the aid of the Turks, had made himself master of that province as well as of a considerable portion of Hungary. The emperor meanwhile, resolved on the recovery of his dominions, found powerful and willing allies in the King of Spain and in Maximilian of Bavaria, the most intelligent of the Catholic princes of Germany. An army was soon equipped for the conquest of Bohemia, composed of imperial and Bavarian troops. The latter were led by the veteran Count Tilly, the most successful commander of the day, and by his advice the Bohemian army was attacked and totally defeated in front of Prague on the 8th of November, 1620. Frederick, instead of taking part in the battle which deprived him of his kingdom, was seated at dinner in his palace when the news of the disaster reached him. Without attempting to defend the city he took to flight forthwith, accompanied by his wife and children. The youngest of these was Prince Rupert, then a few months old, but destined in another field to retrieve the pusillanimous conduct of his father. So hurried was his flight that Frederick even left his crown behind him, that crown for which he had risked his all, and which he had worn only for the space of one year and four days.

The Protestants of Bohemia vainly hoped that with

the recovery of his kingdom the emperor would be disposed to forget the past and restore peace to Germany. But they were quickly undeceived. Many of the chief nobility perished on the scaffold, and their estates, as well as those of the leading insurgents, who fled for their lives, were bestowed upon strangers. Of the common people numbers were put to death without trial of any kind, and a decree of the emperor, issued on his sole authority, without the sanction of the Diet, declared Frederick a rebel and deprived him of all his dominions. In further contravention of the laws of the empire, the execution of this sentence was delegated to the King of Spain, who had furnished a body of troops for the Bohemian war, and which forthwith took possession of the Palatinate. With regard to religion, the resolution of Ferdinand was fixed. Filled with implacable hatred of heresy in every shape, he would listen to no kind of compromise with his Bohemian subjects. He tore up with his own hand the Royal letter which his cousin Rudolf had granted eleven years before, and entirely prohibited the exercise of their religion throughout the kingdom.

Frederick meanwhile had taken refuge with his family in Holland, and his position was, to all appearance, utterly desperate, when a single man by his invincible spirit changed the current of events, and, in the name of Frederick and the Protestant religion, defied the whole power of Austria and Spain. This was Count Mansfeld, who, at the head of a few thousand followers, for the most part men of desperate fortunes, drawn from every country in Europe, had maintained himself in Bohemia in spite of all the efforts of the imperialists. He now made his way to the Rhine, gathering recruits as he advanced, and plundering indifferently both friend and foe in the name of the exiled King of Bohemia. It was Mansfeld and his followers who first introduced this lawless mode of warfare, which desolated Germany for thirty years. He soon found an apt imitator and ally in

Prince Christian of Brunswick, a younger brother of the reigning duke. He had been created Bishop of Halberstadt when a child, but nothing could be more unclerical than the character and conduct of Christian. Mansfeld had shown that an army of 20,000 men might be maintained by plunder alone, and he hastened to follow the example of that daring leader by proclaiming himself the "friend of God, the enemy of priests." One half of this boast he fulfilled to the letter by indiscriminately plundering the churches and religious houses of Catholics and Protestants alike. The dwellings of the peasants fared no better at the hands of Christian than did the palaces of the bishops, and what his followers could not consume it was too frequently their custom to burn and destroy. But this army of marauders was no match for the veterans of Tilly, and Christian having rashly attacked the imperial general on the Maine, was totally defeated. With the remnant of his troops he contrived to join Mansfeld, but both were compelled to retreat before the imperialists. They took refuge in Alsace and Lorraine, to the general dismay of the inhabitants, whom they plundered without mercy. Thence they fought their way to the Netherlands, where they entered the service of the Dutch Republic. The adventurers at first received a hearty welcome, as the twelve years' truce with Spain had now expired, and Spinola was besieging Bergen-op-Zoom. Mansfeld and Christian advanced to its relief, and after a desperate fight, in which the latter lost an arm, the Spaniards were compelled to raise the siege. But the Dutch soon wearied of their gallant but unruly allies. They were dismissed after a few months' service, and they marched into North Germany without any definite plan, but content to subsist by wholesale plunder until their services should be again required. It was unfortunate for the credit of Protestantism that its self-appointed champions, Mansfeld and Prince Christian, and we may add their Transylvanian ally, Bethlem Gabor, whose periodical irruptions into the

Austrian dominions were marked by every species of outrage, should have introduced a mode of warfare unequalled for barbarity even in the sixteenth century. The imperial armies, being better paid and under better discipline, contrasted favourably in this respect with their opponents. The private character of Tilly was, moreover, irreproachable, and he did his best to restrain his troops from acts of wanton violence. In the territory of an ally he generally succeeded, but in an enemy's country Catholics and Protestants were alike regardless of the laws of humanity.

Ferdinand, by a very questionable exercise of his prerogative, had already declared Frederick a rebel and placed him under the ban of the empire, and being now in undisputed possession of his dominions, he proceeded to take a step more questionable still. He summoned a Diet at Ratisbon which he opened in person, and after complaining bitterly of the conduct of Frederick as the author of all the recent troubles, he, as suzerain of Germany, in the exercise of his imperial authority now bestowed upon Maximilian of Bavaria, as a recompense for his great services to the empire, the greater portion of the Palatinate, with all the titles and dignities appertaining thereto. The Protestant princes protested against this arbitrary act as a breach of the fundamental laws of the empire; but the Elector of Saxony, the most powerful amongst them, had already been gained over by the gift of Lusatia, which had been bestowed upon him by Ferdinand; and the Catholic Elector of Bavaria was formally invested with the dominions of the unfortunate Frederick.

Hitherto the war had not extended beyond the limits of the empire, but the decisive step, not only of stripping Frederick of his dominions, but of bestowing them upon the Catholic Elector of Bavaria, was a direct challenge to all the Protestant states of Europe, and it was one which, in the interest of their common religion, they felt bound to accept.

In England the popular feeling in favour of the Elector Palatine would have hurried the nation into war on the outbreak of hostilities in Bohemia but for the opposition of the king. James was by no means indifferent to the misfortunes of his son-in-law, but a wholesome dread of entangling himself in the labyrinth of German politics induced him to stand aloof. So long, moreover, as the negotiations for the projected marriage of the Prince of Wales with the Infanta were in progress, he trusted, through the influence of Spain, to obtain the restoration of the Palatinate without resorting to arms. But the breaking off of the Spanish match, which happened contemporaneously with the arbitrary proceedings of the emperor at Ratisbon, entirely changed the aspect of affairs. It had now become apparent that the Palatinate was only to be recovered by force. But for England to engage in a great continental war without effective allies appeared to James to be the height of folly; and as negotiations had commenced for a marriage of the Prince of Wales with Henrietta Maria of France, he naturally, in the first instance, looked to that country for aid. James, moreover, who, notwithstanding his constitutional indolence and irresolution, was much better acquainted with the affairs of Europe than his countrymen in general, was profoundly convinced—and his opinion was fully justified by the result—that should the contest for the Palatinate lead to a general war[1] France would be compelled to take a leading part in the struggle. But Richelieu, who was now minister of Louis the Thirteenth, although fully alive to the dangers of the situation, was not yet prepared to join in the Protestant crusade. He was, in fact, in the anomalous predicament of being compelled to crush Protestant disaffection at

---

[1] "The king is resolved not to break with Spain, nor to give them any occasion to break with him, until he be secure that France will join very close with him and other Catholic princes and states which have the same interest against the greatness of Spain, as being of opinion that *all the Protestants of Europe would be too weak to oppose it.*"—Despatch of Sir Francis Nethersole to Sir W. Carleton, S. P. Dom., clxvii., 28.

home before he espoused the cause of Protestant freedom abroad. He did, indeed, promise, although not in writing, to assist Mansfeld both with men and money on condition that he was also supported by James, and in the spring of 1624 that indefatigable adventurer visited England. He received every attention both from the Prince of Wales and the king; he was lodged in Saint James's Palace, and was followed by admiring crowds whenever he appeared in public. A little army of thirteen thousand men was hastily collected for his service, and James engaged to pay him £20,000 a month for its support. But the men were so badly supplied with necessaries for a campaign that they died in thousands of disease and want after their arrival in the Netherlands. James at the same time applied to the Kings of Sweden and Denmark to aid in the recovery of his son-in-law's dominions. But Gustavus Adolphus was at this time at war with the King of Poland, and the terms he demanded appeared excessive. Christian of Denmark, the uncle of the Electress Palatine, was more moderate in his demands, but James died before the negotiations with that prince had been concluded. Charles, adopting the policy of his father, agreed that the remnant of Mansfeld's troops should join the Danes, and that he should pay the latter a subsidy of £30,000 a month. The threatened Danish invasion, the intervention of England, and the suspicious attitude of France now brought a new and very prominent actor on the scene. This was Count Wallenstein, a nobleman who had greatly distinguished himself in Turkish and Hungarian wars, and who had acquired immense riches, partly by marriage, partly by the wholesale confiscations in Bohemia. He appears to have been a stern, cold, unfathomable man, not without a strain of genuine magnanimity in his saturnine nature, but arrogant, overbearing, and insatiably ambitious. At this crisis of the war, when the empire was threatened with new and formidable enemies, he volunteered to raise from his own resources an army for the service of Ferdinand. The emperor was not in a position to refuse so tempting a proposal, and in the course of a few months Wallenstein was at the head of thirty thousand men. They were composed of many nationalities, but all devoted to their chief. This was the first imperial army, properly so called, that had appeared in Germany since the commencement of the war, and under its renowned commander the prospects of Ferdinand began rapidly to brighten. The year 1626 proved disastrous in the extreme to the cause of Protestantism. On the 25th April Mansfeld rashly attacked Wallenstein at Dessau on the Elbe, but was totally defeated, and a few months later Tilly encountered the King of Denmark at Lutter and won a complete victory. In this year also the two indomitable champions of Protestantism, Mansfeld and Prince Christian of Brunswick, both died, and Bethlem Gabor being thus deprived of his German allies, was rendered comparatively powerless. But the King of Denmark, in spite of his defeat, was still able to maintain himself in Germany through the winter. In the spring of the following year we find Wallenstein in possession of the Northern duchies of Mecklenburg and Pomerania, and seeking to make himself master of the entire Baltic coast. One town only set him at defiance, and in spite of all his efforts and all his boasts he was compelled to raise the siege of Stralsund, which, being open to the sea, received continual supplies of men and provisions from Sweden as well as Denmark. Gustavus Adolphus had by this time made up his mind that sooner or later he would be compelled to take part in the German war, and, in fact, his interference in the defence of Stralsund was practically a challenge to the emperor. On the 3rd of August, 1628, Wallenstein raised the siege.

The successful defence of Stralsund and the prospect of fresh complications seem to have convinced Wallenstein that peace with Denmark would be desirable, and it was probably through his influence that the treaty of

Lubeck was signed in May, 1629.¹ Charles meanwhile, instead of having aided his uncle, the King of Denmark, to the utmost of his power, had allowed his imperious favourite, the Duke of Buckingham, to involve him in two wars, both unnecessary and both alike inglorious, with Spain and France.² The great constitutional struggle in which he soon afterwards became involved obliged him to devote his whole attention to domestic politics during the remainder of his reign.

On the conclusion of the Danish war Ferdinand had a fresh opportunity of giving peace to Germany. But success only confirmed him in his bigotry, and of this he gave a signal proof even before the treaty of Lubeck was signed. Instead of seeking to heal the fatal divisions of his country he took a step which aggravated them tenfold, and rendered certain not only a continuation of the war but the continued intervention of foreign Powers. On the 29th of March, 1629, he signed the famous edict of restitution. It was neither more nor less than a declaration of war to the knife against the Protestant religion. It restored to the Catholic clergy two archbishoprics, twelve bishoprics,³ and about one hundred and twenty smaller ecclesiastical foundations.

But in spite of this most arbitrary and impolitic act the position of the emperor was by no means secure. The Electors regarded with extreme jealousy the elevation of Wallenstein and the extraordinary powers with which he was invested. He had been created Duke of Friedland and Duke of Mecklenburg. He was the absolute master of an army of 100,000 men, and he levied at his pleasure contributions for its support upon Protestants and Catholics alike. No enterprise appeared too vast

---

¹ Dumont.
² The fruitless expedition to Cadiz took place in the autumn of 1625; the disastrous descent of Buckingham on the isle of Rhé in 1627.
³ These were the Archbishoprics of Magdeburg and Bremen, and the Bishoprics of Minden, Halberstadt, Verden, Lubeck, Ratzeburgh, Meissen, Merseburgh, Naumburgh, Brandenburgh, Havelberg, Lebus, and Camin.—See Coxe, Hist. of House of Austria, cap. li.

for his soaring genius, and it is said that at this time he was meditating an expedition against the Sultan. The Turks had often invaded Germany, but the Germans had never invaded the Ottoman dominions, and he would once more plant the imperial eagle on the dome of Saint Sophia. But he was roused from these wild dreams by the proceedings of the Diet which assembled at Ratisbon in July, 1630. Maximilian of Bavaria and the rest of the Catholic Electors, who were strenuously though secretly supported by Richelieu, insisted that Wallenstein should be deprived of his command. The emperor was reluctantly compelled to consent, and, to the surprise of every one, Wallenstein at once, without remonstrance or complaint, laid down his command and retired into private life.[1] A circumstance had taken place before his deposition which probably induced him to conclude that his services would soon be again required.

This was the landing of the King of Sweden in Pomerania, an event which took place on the 24th of June, 1630. With an army of only 15,000 men, and without a single ally, Gustavus had ventured to invade the dominions of the most powerful monarch of the age. In the eyes of the emperor and his flatterers it seemed an act little short of insanity, for throughout Germany and the Netherlands the imperial and Spanish troops must at this time have outnumbered the Swedes by at least ten to one. In Pomerania alone the imperial general, Torquato Conti, had under his command a larger force than Gustavus. But by the rapidity of their movements the Swedes obtained possession of Stettin, the capital of the province. The duke, an aged prince, either through timidity or policy, signed a treaty of alliance with Gustavus, and the imperialists, forced to act on the defensive, were in the course of a few months compelled to evacuate the duchy.[2] In an enterprise of so daring a

---

[1] See proceedings of the Diet with reference to Wallenstein.—Appendix ii.
[2] Harte's Gustavus Adolphus, vol. i., p. 259.

character as that in which Gustavus had embarked it was of supreme importance that a successful beginning should be made, and thus far he had proved to the world that he had miscalculated neither his own resources nor those of his adversaries. Before crossing the Baltic he had, in fact, long and anxiously considered the position of affairs and the chances of success or failure. He saw that the victories of the imperialists had induced Ferdinand, in his zeal for his religion, to trample on the fundamental laws of the empire, and he saw that without foreign aid the Protestant princes were helpless. He knew that both England and France cordially approved of his expedition, the one from religious sympathy, the other from her ever-growing jealousy of Austria. Above all, he was absolute master of the sea, so that in any event his communications with Sweden were in no danger of interruption. But although his expedition had been thus far attended with complete success, his brother-in-law, the Elector of Brandenburg, and the Elector of Saxony both stood obstinately aloof. These princes were the acknowledged leaders of the Protestants of Germany, but much although they dreaded the hostility of the emperor, they dreaded still more the alternative of placing themselves under the protection of a foreign Power. But while the princes stood aloof, volunteers from all quarters flocked to the camp of the Swedish king, and the promising aspect of the expedition enabled him to conclude, on the 13th January, 1631, a treaty with France of a highly-advantageous character, and which materially affected the future progress of the war.

The object of this treaty was declared to be for the defence of the common friends of the two monarchs, for establishing the freedom of the sea, for protecting the states of the empire which had suffered through the war, and for procuring the demolition of the forts erected on the shores of the Baltic. To effect these purposes the King of Sweden was to receive an annual subsidy of

1,200,000 livres[1] from France, in consideration of which he was to maintain an army of 30,000 infantry and 6,000 cavalry. If the war proved successful the Catholics were to be secured in all their religious privileges, and the treaty was to continue in force for six years.[2]

The question here arises whether under the circumstances Gustavus was justified in his invasion of the German empire. Grotius, a favourite authority with the Swedish king, lays down the proposition "that to pre-
"tend to have a right to injure another merely out of a
"possibility that he may injure us is repugnant to all
"the justice in the world."[3] It is possible that Gustavus may have had this passage in his recollection when in the course of his farewell address to the states at Stockholm he expressed himself as follows:—"The object of
"this enterprise is to set bounds to the ever-increasing
"power of a great empire before all resistance becomes
"impossible. Your children will not bless your memory
"if, instead of civil and religious freedom, you bequeath
"to them the superstition of the monks and the double
"tyranny of popes and emperors. We must prevent
"the subjugation of the continent unless we are pre-
"pared *to depend upon a narrow sea as the only safeguard
"of our liberty*, for it is a mere delusion to suppose that
"a mighty empire will be unable to raise fleets where-
"with to attack us if it is once firmly established
"along the shores of the ocean."[4]

The possibility of an imperial fleet appearing in the Baltic was not an imaginary danger. During the siege of Stralsund Wallenstein not only expected a Spanish squadron to aid him in the attack, but he arrogated to himself the lofty title of Admiral of the Ocean.[5]

There can be no doubt that the doctrine laid down

---

[1] Equal to £50,000.
[2] Dumont.
[3] De Jure Belli et Pacis, l. ii., 17. It is said that Gustavus carried with him this famous treatise in all his campaigns.
[4] Life of Wallenstein, by Mitchel, p. 151.
[5] Life of Wallenstein, cap. iii.

by Grotius as to the right of intervention is the true one, although it has on many occasions been departed from in modern times. It appears to be now generally admitted that no state is justified in resorting to an armed intervention unless the danger to be apprehended is immediate and imminent. But who is to judge of the nature of the danger in such a case? Some men are by temperament nervous and apprehensive, some are apathetic, some, again, are over-confident, and each according to his individual character will form his opinion upon the subject. The circumstances of each case, moreover, must differ so essentially that it is obviously impossible to lay down any positive rule as to the right of intervention. All such proceedings are essentially exceptional in their nature; and it has been justly said " that exceptions of this description never can, without " the utmost danger, be so far reduced to rule[1] as to be " incorporated into the ordinary diplomacy of states, or " into the law of nations." In other words, intervention must ever remain a question of public policy and not of public law.

Hostilities, in fact, may be said to have commenced between the emperor and Gustavus before the latter landed in Pomerania. During the war between Sweden and Poland, which had been brought to a conclusion in 1629 though the influence of Richelieu, Wallenstein had sent a body of troops to the aid of the Poles, and during his attack on Stralsund Gustavus had materially assisted the besieged with supplies both of men and provisions. A declaration of war was therefore deemed superfluous, but, in reply to a letter of remonstrance which the emperor addressed to him on his invasion of Pomerania, Gustavus stated at length the motives that had induced him to take up arms, and he expressed his readiness to come to terms provided the

---

[1] See the circular despatch of Lord Castlereagh respecting the intervention of Austria, Russia, and Prussia in the affairs of Naples in the year 1820.—Annual Register, vol. lxii., part ii., p. 737.

princes and free cities of Germany were restored to their just rights and privileges; provided also that his maritime rights in the Baltic should be duly acknowledged, and provided the expenses of the expedition, which he had been compelled, for the protection of himself and his allies to undertake, should be repaid.[1]

The Protestant princes meanwhile, emboldened by the presence of Gustavus in the empire, had recourse to a proceeding of a very extraordinary kind. The Elector of Saxony, on his own authority, summoned a Protestant Diet to meet at Leipsic to consider the position of affairs. It assembled in the beginning of February, and, notwithstanding the remonstrances and menaces of the emperor, who declared the meeting to be wholly illegal, it continued its sittings for upwards of two months. The design of John George and his adherents was to form a third party independent alike of the emperor and the King of Sweden, and to hold the balance between the two. In the meantime they resolved to demand of the emperor the immediate revocation of the edict of restitution, and they declared their intention of employing force, if necessary, to prevent the illegal quartering of troops and the wholesale levying of men and contributions in defiance of the fundamental laws of the empire. In pursuance of this resolution they pledged themselves to raise an army of 40,000 men, and to appoint a permanent council for the direction of their affairs.[2]

While the Protestant princes were debating at Leipsic an imperial army was moving northwards to attack the Swedes. Why this operation had been so long delayed, considering the immense resources at the command of the emperor, it is easy to explain. Shortly after the landing of Gustavus Wallenstein had been dismissed from his command. It then became a question whether Prince Ferdinand, the heir and namesake of the emperor, or Maximilian of Bavaria, should succeed the Duke of

---

[1] See Append. No. iii.
[2] See Append. No. iv.

Friedland. The partisans of both candidates were about equally numerous and powerful; and the emperor, although anxious to promote his son, was unwilling to offend so faithful an adherent as Maximilian, and he finally determined to bestow the chief command on the veteran Count Tilly. The uninterrupted success which had attended that general in all his campaigns amply justified the decision of Ferdinand, and he thus avoided the imputation of favouritism on the one hand, or of ingratitude on the other.

The persistent neutrality of Brandenburg and Saxony obliged Gustavus to confine his operations to Pomerania and Mecklenburg, where the inhabitants, accustomed as they had long been to the unbridled licence of the imperial troops, beheld with surprise and with thankfulness the perfect discipline and orderly conduct of the Swedes. Simple and unostentatious in his habits and sincere in his religion, although wholly devoid of bigotry, the king himself was the model of a Christian soldier. In the unaffected simplicity of his tastes—for his tent and his table were ever furnished in the plainest manner—he presented a singular contrast to his future rival, Wallenstein, who, whether from policy or pride, outvied the emperor himself in the profuse extravagance of his household and the splendour of his equipages. There was another contrast between the two, and one of more importance. Wallenstein, in the course of his campaigns, was by no means indifferent to the sufferings of the unhappy peasantry;[1] but he appears to have taken no effective measures to restrain the rapacity of his followers. Gustavus not only protected the people from violence, but he gave orders that the full market price should be paid for all provisions that were brought into

[1] He seems to have obeyed with reluctance the orders he had received from the court. "'Give the peasantry plenty of time,' 'do not press the peasantry too " 'hard about religion,' 'do not meddle with the peasantry in the mountains,' are " expressions frequently used in his letters. And on one occasion he directs that " a poor widow, who was about to be deprived of her estate because she refused " to change her religion, should be allowed to retain her property."—Mitchell's Wallenstein, p. 205.

his camp. In consequence of these wise and humane measures it is said that any Swedish stragglers who happened to fall into the hands of the peasantry were not put to death[1] or ill-treated, as was almost invariably the case when any of the imperialist troops fell into their hands.

During the occupation of Stettin a Scottish volunteer in the army of Gustavus was hanged by orders of the governor for having beaten a citizen in whose house he was quartered,[2] and this was at a time when the Scots were flocking in numbers to the Swedish camp, where the king was anxious to avail himself of their services.

In consequence of the temporising policy of the Electors Gustavus was forced to remain inactive in the North, while Tilly, before the Protestant Diet had broken up at Leipsic, laid siege to Magdeburg. The capture of this important city was regarded as essential to the honour of the imperial arms, and for the reasons following:—A prince of the house of Brandenburg named Christian William, uncle of the Elector, was archbishop and administrator of Magdeburg at the commencement of the war, but having made an alliance with the King of Denmark during the Danish invasion, he was deprived of his archbishopric by the emperor. The chapter elected in his place Prince Augustus of Saxony, a son of the Elector John George, but the Pope refused to confirm the appointment, and nominated in his stead Prince Leopold, a younger son of the emperor. The Saxon Prince Augustus notwithstanding maintained himself in the citadel until after the arrival of the King of Sweden in Germany; but within a few weeks of that event Christian William, who had been deposed during the Danish invasion, ventured to return to the city, and was once more acknowledged by the magistrates and the people as their archbishop and sovereign. Gustavus,

---

[1] Harte's Gustavus Adolphus, vol. i., p. 249.
[2] Life of Sir John Hepburn, by Grant, p. 86.

although, in consequence of the professed neutrality of the Electors, unable to advance to his support, sent an experienced officer named Falkenberg to take the command of his troops; and in spite of all the efforts of Tilly, seconded by the celebrated Count Pappenheim, Magdeburg held out for several months in the confident expectation that the King of Sweden would be able to raise the siege. In vain did Gustavus, chafing at the delay, which he had too good reason to fear might prove fatal to the beleaguered city, seek a passage for his troops through the territory of Brandenburg. It was persistently refused until a threatened bombardment of Berlin at length overcame the hesitation of the Elector. But the permission came too late. Three days before it was granted Magdeburg had fallen; and of all the terrible scenes enacted in the long tragedy of the Thirty Years' War, the sack of that unhappy city was the most terrible. Early in the morning of the 10th of May, although no breach had been effected in the walls, Magdeburg was taken by storm. The assault was made at four different points, Count Pappenheim being the first to mount the ramparts, and the garrison being completely taken by surprise made but a feeble resistance. The gates were speedily thrown open, and as the imperialist troops rushed in they set fire to the town in several places. A high wind blowing at the time rendered vain every attempt to extinguish the flames, which spread with such rapidity that in the space of a few hours nearly the whole city, with the exception of the cathedral, became a mass of ruins. Falkenberg, the commander of the garrison, was killed shortly after the commencement of the assault, the archbishop was taken prisoner, and for three days and nights the imperialist troops were allowed to wreak their vengeance on the defenceless inhabitants. The Croats of Tilly's army slaughtered indiscriminately men, women, and children, and every kind of outrage was perpetrated by their Walloon and German comrades in search of plunder. Not an attempt was made by the imperial commander to stop this frightful scene until thirty thousand lives had been sacrificed. The few inhabitants who escaped were concealed in cellars or had taken refuge in the cathedral.

It has been suggested that Pappenheim, a furious zealot although a very gallant soldier, was responsible for the massacre of Magdeburg. But this attempt to shield Tilly at the expense of his subordinate seems to be wholly inadmissible. Tilly was the commander-in-chief of the imperial army, and with him and him alone was vested the power of putting a stop to the frightful carnage committed by his troops. It is asserted that he was appealed to on the subject[1] but that he refused to interfere, alleging that the soldiers must have some recompense for the toil and dangers they had undergone. It was not until the fourth day after the assault that he rode in triumph through the smoking ruins of the city, and in solemn mockery of the surrounding scenes caused *Te Deum* to be performed in the cathedral. The terrible punishment inflicted upon Magdeburg was, no doubt, intended to frighten the confederates of Leipsic into submission. But its effect was directly the reverse. The Protestant princes, seeing they had nothing to hope from the clemency of the emperor, were at length convinced that an alliance with Gustavus promised them their only chance of safety, and the eloquent historian of the Thirty Years' War does not hesitate to assert that we must look to the ashes of Magdeburg for the rise of religious liberty in Germany.[2]

The Landgrave of Hesse was the first of the German princes who voluntarily joined Gustavus, and he was followed into the Swedish camp by Bernhard of Saxe-Weimar, then but little known to fame. But the great Electors still stood aloof, and their suspicious neutrality condemned Gustavus to inaction until aid came from an unexpected quarter. The emperor, elated by the capture

---

[1] Harte, p. 330. Schiller, b. iii.
[2] Schiller, b. iii.

of Magdeburg, ordered Tilly to invade Saxony unless John George consented forthwith to disband his army and renounce the Leipsic confederation. The Elector could hesitate no longer. Tilly advanced upon Leipsic and threatened it with the fate of Magdeburg unless it immediately surrendered. The threat sufficed and he took possession of the town, but meanwhile the Elector had made an offer of his alliance and his army to Gustavus. The opportunity for action had come at last, and he availed himself of it on the instant. He had placed garrisons in Spandau and Custrin to insure the fidelity of Brandenburg, and as soon as the Saxon army joined him he marched in search of Tilly, who, with reinforcements recently arrived from Italy, was encamped on the plains of Leipsic. On the 7th of September, 1631, Gustavus at length encountered the imperial army and their veteran commander,[1] who had never in all his campaigns suffered a defeat. The numbers on each side were nearly equal, but the Saxon contingent consisted mostly of raw troops, whereas the imperialist army was composed of seasoned soldiers. Against them the Saxons, who formed the left wing of the Swedish army, made but a feeble resistance. They fled in disorder from the field, accompanied by the Elector; and Tilly, on witnessing their flight, sent off couriers to Munich and Vienna announcing another imperial victory. But Gustavus, who commanded the right wing of the Swedes, repulsed all the attacks of the imperialists. Seven times did Pappenheim, the most famous cavalry leader of the Thirty Years' War, charge the Swedish lines; he was driven back on each occasion with heavy loss. The imperialists were thus thrown into some disorder, and before they recovered themselves, Gustavus, by a rapid and unexpected advance, had turned their flank. A scene of utter confusion followed. Tilly in vain strove to rally his troops, but was at length compelled to fly,

---

[1] Gustavus was exactly half the age of his veteran antagonist—namely, thirty-six. Tilly was seventy-two.

leaving dead on the field some six or seven thousand of his best troops and the whole of his artillery.

The victory of Gustavus was complete. Compared with modern battles the number of combatants engaged was small, not more, apparently, than forty thousand on each side, but the consequences were incalculably great. Twice in modern times it may be said that the fate of Europe has been decided on the plains of Leipsic. The victory of Gustavus in 1631 overthrew the ecclesiastical tyranny of Austria; the victory of the allies over Bonaparte in 1813 rescued Europe from the military tyranny of France.

Some historians have blamed Gustavus for not taking advantage of the consternation produced by his victory, and forthwith carrying the war into the Hereditary States of Austria. But he was probably better able to judge of his position and his prospects than any of his critics, and after an interview with the Elector of Saxony at Halle it was agreed that the Saxons should invade Bohemia, while Gustavus should march against the imperial and Spanish forces on the Rhine. But as he advanced he found no enemy to oppose him. Fortress after fortress and town after town surrendered without striking a blow. As he approached the Palatinate the imperial and Spanish troops retired; and at Frankfort he was joined by the unfortunate Frederick, who hoped that his dominions were at length about to be restored to him. But although Gustavus acknowledged his title to the crown of Bohemia, he declined to reinstate him in his hereditary dominions. The conduct of the Swedish king on this occasion has given rise to various surmises as to his ulterior designs in Germany. But it is to be observed that he broke no promise in thus declining, at this stage of the war, to restore the Palatinate. He was under no obligation to do so, and Frederick, by continuing to remain in the Swedish camp, seems to have tacitly acknowledged that he had no good ground of complaint against Gustavus.

The succession of disasters which had befallen the imperial arms, and the presence of a victorious enemy in the very heart of the empire, although regarded with dismay throughout Catholic Germany, failed to shake the constancy of Ferdinand. Tenacity of purpose was the predominant feature in his character; he ever appeared to the greatest advantage in adversity, and in the apparently desperate condition of his affairs he was still full of energy and hope. He knew that the extraordinary success of Gustavus was regarded with uneasiness by Louis the Thirteenth. He had aided the Swedish king, it is true, in his attack upon the empire, but he had no desire to see a Protestant emperor in the place of Ferdinand. There was another consideration which weighed still more with the timid and superstitious Louis. The Swedish army was now close to the French frontier, and it was artfully insinuated by imperial emissaries that Gustavus was in correspondence with the Huguenot leaders, and that in alliance with them he might suddenly march upon Paris instead of Vienna. It required all the vigilance and decision of Richelieu to counteract these insidious counsels, and to keep his master to his engagements with Gustavus, who never appears to have entertained any such wild schemes as were now attributed to him by the emissaries of Ferdinand.

Gustavus had fixed his winter quarters at Mentz, and meanwhile the Elector of Saxony had invaded Bohemia and entered Prague without opposition.[1] Wallenstein resided in the Bohemian capital at this time, and it is said that it was by his advice that the city surrendered to the Saxons. At Prague he had built a palace, and his immense wealth enabled him to live in more than regal splendour, and to attract to his service a host of dependants of all ranks and all nations. To him they looked, notwithstanding his dismissal and disgrace, for present support and future promotion, con-

[1] On the 11th of November, 1631.—Schiller, b. iii.

vinced that his day of triumph would come; and they were not disappointed.

Failing to break off the alliance between France and Sweden, the emperor was thrown entirely on his own resources. Tilly was in Bavaria still at the head of a considerable force, and this was the only army which could be relied upon for the defence of the hereditary imperial dominions. That the King of Sweden would move in this direction in the spring was all but certain, and could Tilly, after his crushing defeat at Leipsic, be relied upon to stop him? And if not, what was to be done? There was but one man living who could be deemed a match for the King of Sweden, and that was Wallenstein. It was an act of bitter humiliation for the emperor to be compelled once more to seek the services of the general who had been so unceremoniously set aside. But necessity obliged him to approach his subject almost in the attitude of a suppliant. Wallenstein was not the man to forget an injury, and in his retirement at Prague we do not know what schemes of vengeance may have flitted through his brain, for although he was surrounded by innumerable dependants he had no friends. To the first overtures of Ferdinand he replied with cold indifference; but this was only to enhance his price. With his energetic and imperious nature he was doubtless eager to return once more to active life. But he would have his revenge. He, and he alone, should dictate the terms upon which he would serve the emperor; and never before were such conditions proposed by a subject and accepted by a sovereign.

The King of Spain and Maximilian of Bavaria both protested against the reappointment of Wallenstein, but Ferdinand was prepared to sacrifice his pride for the safety of his empire, and he finally agreed to all the conditions demanded by his imperious subject. These declared the Duke of Friedland to be commander-in-chief of all the imperial and Spanish forces in Germany; he was to have the nomination of all the officers, and the distribution of all rewards and punishments. He was to be allowed to levy contributions without restriction of any kind, and to dispose of all confiscated property without the intervention of the Imperial Chamber or of any other tribunal, and no peace or truce was to be made without his sanction. Finally, the Duchy of Mecklenburg was to be restored to him on the conclusion of peace.[1]

While these negotiations were proceeding Gustavus entered Bavaria and took Donauwerth by storm. He then advanced against Tilly, who had taken up a strong position on the banks of the Leck. The river, swollen by the melting snow, was deep and rapid, but on the 5th of April Gustavus succeeded in constructing a bridge for the passage of his troops. Tilly defended his post with his accustomed intrepidity, but in the midst of the action he was carried off the field mortally wounded, and on the loss of their general the Bavarians retreated upon Ingolstadt, where he died a few days afterwards. Fortune had finally deserted him since the slaughter of Magdeburg.

On the retreat of the Bavarian army Augsburg fell into the hands of the Swedes, the Protestant religion was re-established, and the magistrates took an oath of allegiance to Gustavus. He then advanced upon Munich, which had been left defenceless, and entered the city in triumph, accompanied by the Elector Palatine, who had the satisfaction of witnessing the capital city of his bitterest enemy laid under contribution by a foreign invader. But Gustavus had soon to encounter an antagonist more formidable than Tilly. Wallenstein had engaged to raise an army of 40,000 men in the space of three months for the service of the emperor, and he kept his word. Adventurers from all parts of Europe as well as from the Catholic States of Germany came flocking to his standard, attracted no less by his fame as a commander than by his reputation for libe-

[1] Append. No. v.

rality to those who served him. Maximilian of Bavaria, who had taken the most active part against him at Ratisbon, felt now the humiliation of being compelled to serve under the orders of the man whom he both feared and hated. But Wallenstein was too much master of himself to exhibit either triumph or resentment towards his former enemy, and on the junction of the imperial and Bavarian armies the two commanders, to all appearance at least, had become cordial friends. Threatened by such formidable odds—for the imperial and Bavarian forces numbered upwards of 60,000 men—Gustavus took prompt measures for the safety of his army. He was in the heart of Germany with not more than 20,000 men under his immediate command, while the remainder of his forces were scattered in garrisons over an immense extent of country. Under these circumstances he fixed upon Nuremberg as the headquarters of his army. From this point his communications were open with the Maine and the Rhine, whence he could draw whatever reinforcements he required, and in a strongly-intrenched camp which he had formed outside the town he waited the approach of Wallenstein. On arriving in front of the Swedish lines, which were defended by 300 pieces of cannon, the imperial general declined to attack so formidable a position. He trusted that want of provisions would soon oblige Gustavus to abandon it. But in this he was mistaken. The Chancellor Oxenstiern arrived in the Swedish camp on the 16th of August with a reinforcement of 36,000 men drawn from the fortresses in Northern Germany and on the Rhine; he also brought with him a large supply of provisions.

Wallenstein meanwhile had taken up a very strong position on a rising ground to the north of Nuremberg, and he had fortified it with the utmost care, resolved apparently to act entirely on the defensive. The two greatest armies which had appeared since the commencement of the war were now opposed to each other, and

the country far and near was pillaged in the most merciless manner by marauders from both camps. Gustavus did his utmost to preserve discipline, but finding all his efforts vain, he summoned a meeting of his officers of all grades, and addressed them in language which those who heard it were not likely to forget. It appears that the chief offenders were not the Swedes or the foreign troops who served with them, but the Germans themselves, and it was to them especially that he addressed himself as follows:—" You princes, lords, and gentle-
" men, and you my generals, lieutenant-generals, and all
" you my inferior officers, I have ever esteemed you for
" brave cavaliers, and I bear you witness that upon all
" occasions of service offered you have in battle given
" me sufficient demonstration of your valour. But when,
" having you all here before me, I am put in remem-
" brance of your ravages, robberies, and plunderings, and
" that you yourselves are guilty of these atrocities, my
" hair stands up on end with horror. Let yourselves be
" judges. Is it not a doleful and a lamentable case, yea,
" most odious in the sight of Almighty God, that one
" Christian should pillage another? one friend—nay,
" one brother—should ransack, spoil, and undo one
" another? The very devils in hell are more loving
" and trusting, one to another, than you Christians are
" among those of your own country.

" My heart almost fails me, yea, my bowels yearn
" within me, as often as I hear complaint made that the
" Swedish soldiers are more merciless than the enemy.
" But they are not the Swedes, they are the Germans,
" that commit these outrages. Had I known that you
" Germans had been a people of this temper, that you
" had no natural affection for your country, I would
" never have saddled horse for your sakes, much less
" have hazarded my own kingdom and my life in your
" behalf. No, I would rather have suffered you to
" remain in the miserable condition in which you were
" of a hopeless slavery.

"You will say, perchance, that you want money. But when I have the means to satisfy you, and you by pillaging, robbing, and plundering deprive me of those means, whose, I ask you, is the fault that you are not satisfied? What share have I at any time received out of all your plunder? I do protest before God that I have not by all this war enriched myself to the value of a pair of boots, and I declare withal that I would rather ride without boots than make myself the richer by the plunder and the ruin of these poor people. Since leaving my own kingdom I have had full forty tons of gold sent over to me, all which I have spent for your good, and for the re-establishment of such princes as are united with me in the same truths of religion. I might, perhaps, on this matter have been silent; but I must remind you, in addition, of the loss I have sustained by the deaths of so many brave and worthy cavaliers, whom I valued beyond all the riches in the world. And you for your parts, what have you contributed towards all these wars? This is all that henceforth I shall desire at your hands, that you spoil not others of their goods, but leave to every man his own possessions. The choler and the manhood that you have, score it, in God's name, upon the fronts of your enemies, but stain not the honour of a soldier by outraging unarmed innocence. Live upon your means like soldiers, and not by pilfering and spoiling like highway robbers. This if you do not you shall ever be infamous, and I with such help shall never be victorious."

It is said that these simple yet eloquent words drew tears from many that heard them, but Gustavus was not satisfied with these passing tokens of compunction or repentance. He issued a proclamation declaring that henceforth he would pardon no man, whatever might be his rank or condition, of whom just complaint was made. And he added that if to avoid punishment any number of them should conspire together in a general meeting, he with his Swedes and Finlanders would speedily reduce them to obedience. In token of his sincerity he caused a lieutenant to be hanged for some act of violence, and on the complaint of a peasant[1] that a soldier had stolen his cow he replied to the delinquent, who pleaded for pardon, "My son, it is better that I should punish thee "than that the wrath of God for thy misdeeds should "fall on me."[2]

We do not find on the part of Wallenstein any such vigorous denunciations of robbery and violence, but it is pleasing to find that at this time, when the opposing armies were in daily expectation of a decisive struggle, he was by no means unobservant of the courtesies of warfare. A colonel in the Swedish army having been taken prisoner by the Croats, Wallenstein not only sent him back without ransom to the camp of Gustavus, but he also sent a message to the Swedish king with the assurance that he entertained for him the highest regard and looked upon him as the greatest soldier in the world. He also sent back without ransom a Swedish captain, saying that nothing would give him greater satisfaction than to be the means of bringing about a peace between Gustavus and the emperor.[3] There were, indeed, at this time some faint attempts at negotiation, but to no purpose. As provisions were rapidly failing in the Swedish camp, and Gustavus saw that Wallenstein was resolved to remain immovable behind his intrenchments, he determined, notwithstanding the immense strength of his position, to attack him. On two successive days the Swedes assailed the imperialist lines; but in spite of all their efforts, directed by the king in person, they were driven back on both occasions with heavy loss, and Wallenstein could boast that he had shown at last that Gustavus was not invincible.

Gustavus now broke up his camp, and after leaving

[1] Swedish Intelligencer, part iii., pp. 24 and 25.
[2] Ibid. p. 27, supposed to be reported by Colonel Munro, a Scottish officer in the service of Gustavus.
[3] Mitchell's Wallenstein, p. 235.

a garrison in Nuremberg directed his march towards the Danube; but instead of following him Wallenstein invaded Saxony, where he has been unjustly accused[1] of allowing his troops unbounded licence to pillage and destroy in revenge for the defection of the Elector. On the contrary, he gave the strictest orders to his officers that the peasants should not be plundered, and for a very sufficient reason. "Let nothing," he said, "be "destroyed or taken from the peasantry, for we must live "during the winter on the supplies we can find here,"[2] and he added in a postscript to the letter containing these injunctions, "The Croats must not, under pain "of death, be allowed to take a single thing from the "people." It was his intention to select some strong position in Saxony in which, as at Nuremberg, he might bid defiance to the Swedes. But Gustavus penetrating his design speedily followed, and on this the last march of the Swedish king he was everywhere received with more than royal honours. At Naumburg, as he passed through the city, the people fell down on their knees and hailed him as their deliverer; some pressed round his horse and kissed the sheath of his sword, while he gently upbraided them for making him the object of such idolatry.

Although he knew that Gustavus was on his track, Wallenstein had rashly ventured to divide his forces. While he himself took post at Lutzen, he despatched Pappenheim to the Rhenish bishoprics, desiring him to seize Halle by the way. Gustavus did not fail to take prompt advantage of his adversary's blunder, and early on the morning of the 6th of November he was again in front of the imperial army. Wallenstein, constant to his defensive tactics, had intrenched himself as strongly as the nature of the ground allowed, and after despatching orders for the immediate return of Pappenheim, awaited the onset of the Swedes. Gustavus, as at

---

[1] By Schiller, b. iii.
[2] Mitchell, p. 210.

Leipsic, commanded the right wing of his army, and charging at the head of his cavalry, as was his custom, the imperialists in front after a stubborn resistance were driven from the field. But Bernhard of Saxe-Weimar, who commanded the left wing of the Swedes, was reported to be hard pressed by the enemy, and Gustavus galloped off to his assistance with only a few attendants, when he fell mortally wounded. The loss of their beloved monarch roused the Swedes to fury, and although Pappenheim arrived on the field with 8,000 horse in time to take part in the battle, the imperialists were beaten at all points, that gallant leader being himself among the slain.

It has been said that the death of Gustavus at Lutzen was a fortunate event for Europe and for himself. He had accomplished the great work he had undertaken; he had rescued the Protestant princes and people of Germany from the thraldom of Austria and Spain, and he died in the very zenith of his fame and glory. Had he lived longer, had he utterly defeated the imperial armies and become the conqueror of Germany, who can say what would have been the result? It is asserted[1] that the imperial crown was the ultimate object of his ambition. But this is pure conjecture. It is most probable that at the time of his death he had no fixed designs except a resolution to prosecute the war to a conclusion. However that may be, and whatever dreams of future grandeur he may have entertained, we cannot but allow that Gustavus, dying, as he did, at the early age of thirty-seven, was the most immaculate of conquerors. His only defect, if it was a defect, was a certain warmth and irritability of temper which was not at all times under control,[2] but which never, even during the most exciting scenes of his busy and eventful life, hurried him into any act of unseemly violence. It was this impetuous spirit

[1] By Schiller, b. iii.
[2] See the interview between Gustavus and the Marquis of Hamilton.—Burnet's Dukes of Hamilton, p. 18.

which in the day of battle too often led him to forget that he was a king and a commander, and to court danger apparently for its own sake. It is well known that at Lutzen he wore no armour, and it is said that before he fell he had slain six men with his own hand.

Bernhard of Weimar took the command of the army on the death of the king, and Wallenstein retreated during the night, leaving the whole of his artillery on the field. But notwithstanding his retreat Lutzen was claimed as a victory at Vienna and Madrid, and the death of the Swedish king was regarded as a visible interposition of Providence on behalf of the imperial arms. It was hoped that the Swedes, deprived of their great king, would be desirous of peace on almost any terms. Christina,[1] the only child and heiress of Gustavus, was but seven years old, and her kinsman the King of Poland had not renounced his claim to the Swedish crown. But the Chancellor Oxenstiern, in spite of the unpromising aspect of affairs, resolved on the prosecution of the war as the only means of obtaining for Sweden an honourable peace. He knew that France had regarded with ill-concealed jealousy the victorious career of Gustavus, but now that he was gone she would be disposed to co-operate more cordially with the Swedes and the Protestant princes against the house of Austria. On the 23rd April, 1633, he summoned a meeting of the German allies of Sweden at Heilbron. The Elector of Saxony, ever vacillating in his policy, alone declined to attend, and did his utmost to thwart the schemes of Oxenstiern. But the latter succeeded not only in obtaining the consent of the princes to a league for the prosecution of the war, but that he as plenipotentiary of Sweden should be entrusted with the chief direction of all military operations. To strengthen his position and to conciliate England and the Netherlands, Oxenstiern determined to restore the Palatinate to the rightful heir. The unfortunate Frederick had died a few months after

[1] See Append. No. vi.

Gustavus; but his eldest son, Charles Louis, was formally invested at Frankfort with the inheritance of his ancestors. There are few diplomatic triumphs more remarkable than that by which Oxenstiern, in spite of innumerable obstacles, acquired an ascendency in Germany hardly inferior to that which had been exercised by Gustavus.

After his defeat at Lutzen Wallenstein fell back upon Bohemia. He established his winter quarters at Prague, where, with his accustomed munificence and his accustomed severity, he distributed his rewards and punishments among his followers. To those who had distinguished themselves he gave out of his own resources large sums of money and valuable presents; while those who had misbehaved in presence of the enemy were punished without mercy. On the 4th of February, 1633, twelve officers were publicly beheaded. Others were cashiered and had their swords broken by the public executioner, and the names of forty who had absconded were affixed on the gibbet. All these punishments were inflicted on the sole authority of Wallenstein, not in the heat of the moment while smarting under his defeat, but three months after that event; and as many of the victims belonged to families of distinction and no appeal was allowed to the emperor, Wallenstein was not only accused of undue severity on this occasion, but it was alleged that he had sought by the sacrifice of innocent blood to efface the stain of his defeat. Others asserted that he had resorted to these extreme measures chiefly or solely to proclaim his independent authority. But it is a singular fact that while he was thus asserting his military supremacy he seems to have been sincerely desirous of peace. With this object in view he earnestly recommended the emperor to proclaim a general amnesty and to offer fair terms to the Protestant princes. Whatever may have been his faults Wallenstein had no bigotry in his nature; but he appealed in vain to a prince who, with many amiable qualities, regarded toleration as a deadly sin, and although the war had now raged for fifteen years, he still hoped, in spite of his reverses, to re-establish his ecclesiastical supremacy.

It is creditable alike to the judgment and the humanity of Wallenstein that at a time when the death of Gustavus had spread consternation throughout Protestant Germany he should, instead of urging the emperor to take advantage of that event, which an ambitious soldier might naturally have done, have recommended a policy of conciliation. That he was perfectly sincere in his desire for peace there is not the smallest reason to doubt. In fact, it was his obvious reluctance to engage in active hostilities during his last campaign which furnished his enemies with the alleged proofs of his treasonable conduct. He had entered Saxony, where he had commenced a correspondence with the Elector, and he had remained inactive while Bernhard of Weimar overran Bavaria and captured Ratisbon. Wallenstein refused to stir for the protection of the dominions of his enemy Maximilian, and while the emperor was urging his imperious general to move to the South for the defence of Austria Proper, the latter was seeking the alliance of the two Northern Electors with the intention apparently of once more advancing to the Baltic. He also made overtures to Oxenstiern, but that wary minister declined to commit himself to any scheme proposed by the imperial general. It would appear from the military inactivity of Wallenstein at this time, and his correspondence with the Saxons and the Swedes, that it was his object to force the emperor to a peace. But Maximilian of Bavaria, the Jesuit advisers of Ferdinand, and the court of Spain were all resolved on the prosecution of the war, and all animated with jealousy and hatred of Wallenstein, whom they never ceased to accuse of the most treasonable schemes, and whom they finally persuaded the emperor to deprive of his command. But this step was too hazardous to be attempted simply by an imperial mandate. The resolution of the court was communicated to Wallenstein in another way. He was commanded to occupy Passau, to send a portion of his forces to the Netherlands, and with the remainder to march forthwith to Ratisbon and retake that important fortress. He was then to take up his winter quarters in the territory of the enemy.

Wallenstein might complain that this interference on the part of Ferdinand was a breach of the terms upon which he had agreed to re-enter the imperial service. But he wasted no time in useless remonstrances. It was plain that his enemies were all-powerful in Vienna, and were resolved on his ruin and disgrace. He summoned before him the colonels of his different regiments and informed them that his enemies at court were persuading the emperor to remove him from his command, that he had determined to resign rather than await his dismissal, that he was quite content to retire into private life, and that his only regret was that he should be unable to reward as they deserved so many brave and faithful comrades.

This artful address had the effect for which it was no doubt intended. Wallenstein was earnestly entreated not to resign the command, and a memorial was signed, it is said, by all the officers present, pledging themselves to support the general at the risk of their lives and fortunes. Whether Octavio Piccolomini signed this paper is a question, but it is known that he hastened to Vienna and acquainted the emperor with its contents. This Italian adventurer had received many favours at the hands of Wallenstein. But he not only deserted his benefactor in the hour of danger, but he obtained an imperial order to return forthwith to Bohemia, and to take him dead or alive. Wallenstein had by this time quitted Pilsen and retired to Egra. Gordon, the commandant of this fortress, had owed his promotion to the imperial general, and on his fidelity Wallenstein implicity relied. But Piccolomini found that this man was ready like himself to desert his benefactor, and as it would have been hazardous to attempt to make a prisoner of the general, they resolved that he should be murdered. It is to be observed that no countryman of Wallenstein was implicated in this foul plot. The principal conspirators, besides Piccolomini, were Gordon and a Colonel Leslie, who were both Scots, and Colonel Butler and Captain Devereux, who were both Irish. On the night of the 24th February, 1634, Gordon invited the chief partisans of Wallenstein to supper, and after the wine had circulated freely, a band of soldiers at a given signal rushed into the apartment and the unsuspecting guests were massacred on the spot. Devereux then called on a party of the assassins to follow him, and bursting open the door of Wallenstein's chamber they found him standing on the threshold in his nightdress. He had been roused from his bed by the noise outside, but silent and inscrutable to the last, he received his death-wound from the hand of Devereux, and fell to the ground without uttering a word.

The death of Wallenstein proved welcome news at Vienna, and the murderers were handsomely rewarded. The King of Hungary, the son and heir of Ferdinand, was appointed to the chief command of the imperial armies, and the emperor had soon occasion to congratulate himself on his choice of a successor to Wallenstein. In the course of the summer, Ratisbon, which had been captured by Bernhard of Weimar, surrendered to the King of Hungary, and on being joined by the cardinal infante and a body of troops from Italy he laid siege to Nordlingen. In front of this place, on the 6th of September, 1634, they encountered the main army of the Swedes, commanded by Bernhard and Gustavus Horn. The Swedes were totally defeated, with the loss of 10,000 men and 6,000 prisoners. It was by far the greatest overthrow they had sustained since the commencement of the war.

The imperial victory of Nordlingen threatened at first to undo the great work of Gustavus. The league of Heilbron was paralysed by this terrible blow, and Oxenstiern with infinite reluctance turned to France, the only quarter whence in so desperate an emergency he could look for aid. He well knew the price he should have to pay for French support.[1] He knew that Richelieu would not only claim the chief direction of the war, but a chief share in its spoils. But as he saw no prospect of aid from any other quarter he was compelled to accept the terms upon which alone the French Ministry would agree to support, or it may be said to save, the Swedes. In addition to the subsidy already granted, France paid down a sum of half a million of livres to enable Oxenstiern to put his army again in motion; she likewise agreed to declare war against Spain; to provide a corps of 12,000 men to be employed in Germany; and to supply an additional number to act on the Rhine as occasion might require. In return France was to retain possession of the greater portion of Alsace, with the towns of Philipsburg and Spire, till the conclusion of a peace. The confederates were to respect the neutrality of any Catholic prince of Germany who should claim the protection of France; they were also to assist in the conquest of Brisac and the fortresses on the Upper Rhine as far as Constance, and in the recovery of Philipsburg, which during the negotiations had been captured by the imperialists. This treaty, by which the keys of Germany were delivered into Richelieu's hands, was signed at Heilbron in March, 1636. The prediction of James the First was then fulfilled, that if the religious troubles in Germany should lead to a general war, France would be forced to take a principal part in the contest.

Another important treaty had in the meantime been concluded between the emperor and John George of Saxony. The Elector, who had been saved from ruin by Gustavus, hastened to desert his Swedish allies in their hour of need, and once more made his peace with Ferdinand. As a preliminary to the negotiations which

[1] Coxe, cap. lvi. Schoell, t. i., p. 100.

commenced soon after the battle of Nordlingen, the emperor, in order to gain the most important of the Protestant princes, consented, with unwonted liberality, to abandon, in favour of the Saxon Lutherans, the edict of restitution, and on this basis a treaty was finally concluded at Prague on the 30th of May, 1635.

Germany had now for sixteen years been the theatre of a war unsurpassed in history for its calamities and horrors, and it was intended that the treaty of Prague should form the basis for a general pacification. But these anticipations proved wholly groundless. The treaty of Prague repeated the fatal blunder of the treaty of Passau by recognising no form of Protestantism except the Lutheran, and further, the worship of the Confession of Augsburg was to be tolerated only among the free nobility or in those imperial cities which were not bound by a previous arrangement with the emperor, but from this concession Bohemia and the other possessions of the house of Austria in the empire were formally excluded. A general amnesty was granted to all who acceded to the treaty, with the restitution of all conquests made since the landing of Gustavus Adolphus. From this clause, however, were excepted the Duke of Wurtemberg, the Prince of Baden, and the Landgrave of Hesse, as well as the subjects of the house of Austria who had taken up arms against the emperor. The Elector of Saxony was to retain Lusatia, and the archbishopric of Magdeburg was assigned to his second son. The proscription against the Elector Palatine was proclaimed afresh; but his widow, the Princess Elizabeth of England, was to receive her jointure from the Elector of Bavaria. Finally, the two contracting parties, with all who should accede to the treaty, were to unite their forces for the purpose of expelling all foreigners from the empire.[1]

There cannot be a doubt but that for the active intervention of France at this crisis of the war the Swedes

[1] Dumont, tom. vi., p. 99.

must have been driven out of Germany, and at the first the French were almost everywhere unsuccessful. They were less experienced in regular warfare than their imperial and Spanish adversaries, and no commander of note had as yet appeared to lead them. In the year 1636 the cardinal infante invaded France and threatened an attack on Paris. But the resolute attitude of Richelieu, who appealed to the patriotism of his countrymen of all creeds and of all degrees, caused the invaders to pause and finally to retreat beyond the frontier. In the North, too, the Swedes had been attacked by the Elector of Saxony, who hoped to drive them across the Baltic, but he was totally defeated in Pomerania by Baner, one of the ablest of the pupils of Gustavus, who, with only 12,000 men, advanced into Saxony and once more threatened the imperial territories. His numbers rapidly increased until he found himself at the head of an army large enough to defy the imperial commanders, and he was concerting a plan of advancing simultaneously upon Vienna with Bernhard of Weimar when the career of that enterprising leader was cut short by a fever of which he died in Alsace at the early age of thirty-five. As Bernhard had made a conquest of this province it was his intention to retain it, and he bequeathed to his brothers all the rights over it which he possessed. The emperor, the Swedes, the Prince Palatine, and Richelieu on the part of France, all competed with the heirs of Bernhard for the possession of so valuable a prize. But the superior address of Richelieu prevailed, and Alsace became a portion of the French dominions.

The emperor was now dead. At an earlier period of the war his death might have led to important consequences, for his unconquerable bigotry was the great obstacle to peace. But all the great Continental powers had now become involved in the struggle, and as the contest proceeded it became more and more evident that it could only be terminated by the exhaustion of one or of both the combatants. The King of Hungary, who succeeded to the imperial crown by the title of Ferdinand the Third, although less inclined to ambitious counsels than his father, was no less resolute in his determination to maintain the ascendency of his house, and with the aid of his gallant kinsman, the cardinal infante, he had every prospect of success. But although the admirable discipline of the Spanish armies was still maintained, the vast empire of Charles the Fifth and Philip the Second was giving at this time unmistakable symptoms of dissolution.

In the year 1639 a great Spanish fleet—the last that was sent to the North Sea—was attacked and destroyed by the Dutch in the English Channel. The circumstances under which this feat was accomplished were peculiar and unprecedented. The Spanish fleet, consisting, with transports, of seventy sail, had taken refuge in the Downs. It was followed by the Dutch admiral, Van Tromp, whose force was superior to that of the Spaniards, the two hostile fleets being both within the territorial waters of England. The two fleets were watched by an English squadron in the Downs to prevent any breach of the peace in the neutral waters. It so happened that at this time Charles the First was in urgent need of money. The Scottish covenanters had risen in arms against the ecclesiastical innovations which he had sought to introduce, and he was in want of means to equip an army to reduce them to obedience. For a sum of one hundred and fifty thousand pounds he undertook that the Spanish fleet should be protected until it reached its destination in Flanders. The cardinal infante, then governor of the Spanish Netherlands, agreed to these terms, but the Dutch admiral, Van Tromp,[1] was not to be balked of his prey. On the morning of the 11th of October he addressed a letter to the English admiral, Sir John Pennington,[2] but as it was written in

---

[1] The excuse given by Van Tromp was that the Spaniards had first fired upon him.—See his letter, Record Office, October 11th, 1639.

[2] The Earl of Suffolk, Warden of the Cinque Ports, writes from Deal Castle, October 11th, 10 a.m.:—" At this instant the Spaniards and the Hollanders are in " a bloody fight in the Downs. The admiral of Holland began the fight. There

Dutch he did not understand it, and it was obviously the intention of Van Tromp that it should not be understood. But an explanation swiftly followed; he opened fire on the Spanish fleet, and in the course of a few hours the greater part of the ships were either captured, or burnt, or driven ashore. Some thirty escaped to sea, but of these only ten reached the Netherlands in safety. The cardinal infante complained loudly of this gross breach of neutrality, and Charles was at once indignant at that and disappointed of the sum he had expected to obtain as the price of his protection. But in the difficult position in which he stood, with growing disaffection in England and Scotland actually in rebellion, he was content to accept a formal apology from the Dutch, which eventually was tendered by an ambassador expressly sent to London for that purpose.

The destruction of her fleet was not the only misfortune which happened to Spain at this time, for the Catalans had risen in revolt, and in the following year Portugal, which had been annexed by Philip the Second, reasserted her independence under the Duke of Braganza. The premature death, in 1642, of the cardinal infante, who had given abundant proofs of his military skill in

"are six Lubeckers already run ashore, and it is probable that more will follow.
"A few hours more will decide the particulars, and then you shall hear further
"from me.
"To Secretary Windebank."

(From the same to the same.)
"3 p.m.
"Since writing the Spaniards and Hollanders being under sail made their way
"from the Downs westward, fighting as they passed. I saw two of the Spanish
"fleet fired close under Walmer Castle. There are many Spaniards already come
"ashore, for whose accommodation I have given orders."

On October 12th the Lord Warden writes:—"Two of the Spaniards being two "leagues from Dover, towards Folkestone westward, were taken, and another "Spanish ship within a league of the same place fired and blown up. It is further "reported that five more of the Spaniards have blown up themselves." And he adds, "This is certain, that the greater part of the Spanish fleet is ruined." The following incident may show that the people on the shore were exposed to some danger during the action :—"A minister, whose calling might have restrained "his curiosity, riding upon the seashore to see the fight, had his horse killed "under him by a rolling shot, though his life was preserved."

After his victory Van Tromp anchored in the Downs, and, lowering his flag in token of the king's supremacy, fired a salute of nineteen guns.—Ibid.

two successful campaigns against the French, was a serious loss to Spain at this critical period of her history, and she sustained a still more serious blow in the following year at Rocroi, where a youthful Bourbon prince, subsequently known as the "great Condé," annihilated the flower of the Spanish infantry, which had long been deemed invincible. Richelieu did not live to hear of this great French victory, but his policy was faithfully followed by Mazarin and Condé, and Turenne found a powerful ally in the Swedish general Torstenson, the ablest and the most successful of all the disciples of Gustavus. But the princes of the house of Austria have generally appeared to the greatest advantage in adversity, and Ferdinand the Third, although deprived of the support of Spain and eventually deserted by Bavaria, showed no disposition to abandon the struggle. That he was superior to the prejudices of his race we may learn from the significant fact that towards the close of the war he appointed Melander, a Calvinist, his commander-in-chief. But this new leader was totally defeated by Turenne, who in May, 1647, had penetrated to the banks of the Danube with the purpose of invading the Austrian dominions. He was prevented from following out his plan by the inundations of the river Inn, and the war dragged on for another twelvemonth. Peace was at length concluded in the autumn of 1648. The formidable task of humbling the house of Austria, which Germany and Denmark had attempted in vain, had been triumphantly begun by Gustavus Adolphus, and was finally accomplished by Condé and Turenne.

The condition to which Germany had been reduced by this frightful war had long rendered all parties desirous of peace, and for some years negotiations had been proceeding with a view to this essential object. But the difficulties in the way of a final settlement were enormous. Some years elapsed even before a place of meeting for the plenipotentiaries of the different states could be agreed upon; but it was finally determined, in

1642, that the representatives of Austria, Spain, France, and the Catholic states should meet at Munster under the mediation of the Pope and the republic of Venice; and that the representatives of Sweden and the Protestant states should meet at Osnaburg under the mediation of the King of Denmark; but no meeting actually took place until the spring of 1644.

But much had to be done before the business of the congress was commenced; for while battles were being fought with varying success on the Rhine and the Danube, diplomatists at Munster were wrangling over disputed points of precedence and ceremonial. And it is somewhat curious to find that upon these points the representatives of republics appear to have been more sensitive and more exacting than the representatives of monarchies. On his arrival at Munster, Contarini, who had been appointed by Venice to act as mediator along with the Papal Nuncio, made a formal complaint against the Count d'Avaux, the first plenipotentiary of France. The Venetian alleged that he had not been treated with becoming courtesy, and for the following reasons:—He said that when he waited by appointment on the French minister, the latter advanced five steps down the stairs of his hotel to receive him, and further that when he took his leave his host accompanied him to the foot of the stairs. But Contarini insisted that this was not enough. The French minister, he said, ought to have accompanied him to the door of his residence and to have witnessed his departure, for this attention had been paid to him in England and in other countries. The point was warmly discussed for some time, and eventually it was referred to Mazarin for his decision. The cardinal finally gave instructions that the demand of the Venetian should be complied with.[1]

The Dutch, although their independence had not yet been recognised by Spain, were not less tenacious of their dignity than the Venetians. The former made it

[1] Bougeant, Histoire de Traité de Westphalie, t. ii., l. i.

a condition of their entering the congress that they should be received at Munster with the same honours as the representatives of a monarch—that is to say, they were to receive the title of excellency, and the French minister was to offer them his hand. The Count d'Avaux was willing to concede the title, but he demurred to taking by the hand a bevy of Dutch burghers. He offered to compromise the matter by offering his hand to any one of the number they chose to name. This proposal did not satisfy the Hollanders, and eventually they were received with the same honours as were accorded to the Venetians.[1]

The Spaniards, it appears, notwithstanding their proverbial pride, stood less upon their dignity than their revolted subjects. When the Bavarian deputies arrived at Munster they visited first the plenipotentiaries of France before waiting on those of Spain. The slight was keenly felt, but it was felt in silence. To complain would have been undignified when they must have complained in vain.[2]

Between the representatives of the Hanse Towns and the French ministers a dispute arose which might have led to serious consequences. The Hanse deputies were received by both the French ministers, the Count d'Avaux and M. Servien, and after taking their leave they were expected to pay a visit to M. Servien alone. But instead of so doing they repaired straight from the plenipotentiaries of France to those of Spain. This was regarded as a serious affront by M. Servien, and he took prompt means to avenge it. He appointed a day for the visit of the Hanse deputies at his residence, and when they arrived they were detained for some time, and they were then informed[3] that he was occupied and could not receive them. Their surprise and indignation at this preconcerted insult may be easily imagined. They

[1] Bougeant, t. ii., l. i.
[2] Ibid.
[3] Ibid.

prepared a memorial complaining bitterly of the conduct of the French minister; but the dispute was finally arranged, although with difficulty, through the mediation of the deputies of Hesse, some time afterwards. Innumerable questions of this nature absorbed for months the entire attention of the plenipotentiaries at Munster. The son of the Chancellor Oxenstiern represented Sweden at this famous congress. Was it in the midst of these diplomatic squabbles that his illustrious father reminded him of the amount of wisdom displayed in the government of the world?

Never before had there assembled in Europe so great a concourse of diplomatists and statesmen; never before did so many great and perplexing questions await discussion. With the exception of Great Britain, all the principal states of Christendom were represented. And of the minor Powers, in addition to the Electors and princes of the empire, the King of Portugal, the Dukes of Savoy, Tuscany, Lorraine, Mantua, and the Swiss cantons all sent deputies to Osnaburg or Munster. For upwards of a twelvemonth no real progress was made. After the many questions of precedence and ceremonial had been settled, the exorbitant pretensions and demands on the one side and on the other rendered all agreement impossible. And such demands rose or fell with the success or failure of the military operations, which were in no way relaxed during the negotiations. It was not until the summer of 1645 that specific propositions were lodged with the mediators, and for two years these continued to be discussed without any prospect of a satisfactory result. Each party, in fact, looked more to the progress of the war than to the interminable discussions of the diplomatists. How long this state of things might have continued it is impossible to say, had not the condition of Spain induced her to seek for a cessation of hostilities. In addition to her other misfortunes, a revolution in Naples in 1647 threatened to deprive her of her Italian dominions, and thus pressed on all sides she consented at length, after a struggle of eighty years, to recognise the independence of the Dutch republic. This important treaty was signed on the 30th of June, 1648, and the progress of France and the Swedes at this time, and the utter exhaustion of the imperial territories, rendered Ferdinand willing to accept peace on any reasonable terms. Sweden was no less thoroughly exhausted, for her armies were now composed for the most part of mercenary troops, and France was desirous of peace with Austria that she might employ the whole of her resources against Spain. The principal Powers being thus at length of one accord, the Treaty of Munster, after three years of active negotiation, was finally signed on 9th September, 1648.

As the war had been virtually brought to a close by the combined action of France and Sweden, they naturally claimed the chief share in its spoils. The three bishoprics of Metz, Toul, and Verdun, which had been seized by France in 1552, were now formally annexed to that kingdom. The emperor also surrendered Upper and Lower Alsace with the city of Strasburg to France, and a provision was inserted in the treaty that no fortress should be erected on the right bank of the Rhine from Basle to Philipsburg. France also obtained from the Duke of Savoy the town of Pignerol in Piedmont. By these important concessions both Germany and Italy became open to invasion—a circumstance which they soon found ample reason to deplore. Sweden, too, acquired a considerable extension of territory—namely, Upper Pomerania and the Isle of Rugen, with various towns on the Baltic, and Bremen and Verdun converted into a principality. The Swedes were also to receive a sum of five millions of crowns for the expense of maintaining an army in the empire until the treaty was carried into execution.

The Lower Palatinate was restored to Charles Louis, the son of the unfortunate Frederick; but the Upper Palatinate was confirmed to Maximilian of Bavaria,

and an eighth electorate was established in his favour.
The treaty, moreover, contained a variety of provisions
as to the territories of the minor princes, and the Swiss
cantons, which in theory formed a portion of the empire,
were now declared to be independent.

But so far as Germany and the Germans were concerned the most important provisions of the Treaty of
Munster related to religion. It was the struggle
between the old creed of Christendom and the new
which led to the rebellion in Bohemia, and finally
involved, directly or indirectly, all the European Powers.
After so fierce and so prolonged a contest it might have
been anticipated that the total overthrow of one sect and
the complete triumph of the other would have been the
result. Such had been the result in Britain, such had
been the result in France, and such, in all probability,
would have been the result in Germany had Germany been composed of one great monarchy. But
the number of different states of which the empire
was made up—some Catholic, some Lutheran, and
some Calvinist—was essentially favourable to the cause
of religious equality, and the establishment of this
equality was the most memorable work of the Treaty of
Westphalia.

The Treaty of Passau of 1555 was recognised as the
groundwork of the new religious peace; and the Calvinists were at length admitted to equal privileges with
the Lutherans. A perfect equality was to be maintained among the princes and states of the empire,
whether Catholic, Lutheran, or Calvinist. All ecclesiastical benefices were to be restored to the same condition in which they were on the 1st of January, 1624,
which was termed the definitive year, but in regard to
the dominions of the Elector Palatine, the Margrave of
Baden, and the Duke of Wurtemberg, the year 1618
was fixed as the definitive period on account of the
changes, both in civil and ecclesiastical affairs, introduced by the imperialists and Spaniards during their

invasion of the Palatinate on the outbreak of the war.

The Germanic empire, as finally constituted by the Treaty of Westphalia, was composed of no less than three hundred and fifty-five states, each claiming the right of sovereignty, but of very unequal extent and power. Among these, in addition to the emperor, there were one hundred and fifty secular states governed by hereditary Electors, dukes, landgraves, marquises, counts, and burgraves, one hundred and twenty-three ecclesiastical states governed by archbishops, bishops, abbots, and other dignitaries chosen for life; and of sixty-two imperial cities privileged to choose their own magistrates, and which, in fact, were governed as republics. That the theory of equality among so many states differing so widely in extent and resources should have been thus publicly acknowledged was an important step in the progress of society. The constitution of the empire as settled by this treaty was framed with the wise purpose of protecting the weaker states against their more powerful neighbours, and so far as the Germans themselves were concerned the result was in many respects beneficial. But as regarded their foreign relations the diminution of the central or imperial power was attended with very serious consequences. It enabled the kings of France to form alliances with the different princes, and under the pretext of supporting the weaker states to exercise an undue influence over the policy of the empire. The great work of humbling the house of Austria, projected by Henry the Fourth, had, in short, been accomplished by Richelieu and Mazarin. The house of Austria still continued to play a prominent part in the politics of Europe, but it never afterwards recovered the exorbitant power of which it was deprived by the Treaty of Westphalia.

CHAPTER VIII.

FROM THE TREATY OF WESTPHALIA TO THE TREATY OF THE PYRENEES.

The plenipotentiaries of France and Spain had failed to come to terms at Munster, and the war between the two monarchies still continued. During the childhood of Louis the Fourteenth Mazarin administered the affairs of the kingdom, not without ability, but he proved unequal to the task of preventing the outbreak of a destructive civil war which, under the name of La Fronde, rendered France for several years comparatively powerless abroad. During this interval Spain recovered Catalonia and various places in Flanders, including the important seaport of Dunkirk. In this war Condé, imitating the evil example of his famous ancestor the Constable Bourbon, fought under the flag of Spain against his country. But Condé found a formidable opponent in Turenne, who espoused the cause of his youthful sovereign; and in 1655 Mazarin was fortunate enough to form an alliance which proved of decisive influence on the progress of the war.

Charles the First had perished on the scaffold in 1649, and under Cromwell England had once more become a formidable military power. In his transactions with foreign states the Protector displayed the same remarkable energy and the same unscrupulous spirit which were conspicuous in his domestic policy. His attack upon the Spanish colonies in 1655, which resulted in the conquest of Jamaica, was alike unjustifiable and impolitic. He had not only no cause of quarrel with Spain, but Philip the Fourth to secure his friendship and alliance had offered him the most favourable terms.[1] But he listened to Mazarin instead, and lent his powerful aid to augment the rapidly-growing strength of France. While Blake and Montague swept the Spaniards from the seas, six thousand Ironsides fought under Turenne at Dunes,[2] and contributed essentially to that important victory. When Cromwell made up his mind to break with Spain she had ceased to be an object of alarm. In every quarter of her dominions she had exhibited decided symptoms of weakness and decay, and Austria, her faithful ally, had been bridled by the Treaty of Westphalia. It was now the turn of France to threaten the general peace, and the foreign policy of Cromwell contributed directly to strengthen that formidable power.

It has been said in defence of the Protector that his grand scheme of Continental policy was defeated by his death, and that his intention was, after having humbled Spain, to turn upon France. But this defence, so discreditable to the sagacity of the Protector, seems to refute itself. If he had designed by turns to attack both France and Spain it is to the last degree improbable that he would have commenced with the weaker power. However that may be, the fact is undeniable that at this critical period of her history France was deeply indebted to Cromwell for the consolidation of her strength.

As the price of his alliance Cromwell obtained Dunkirk, an acquisition which entailed a considerable annual outlay. One of the few wise acts of Charles the Second, for which he was mercilessly abused by all parties, was the sale of this place to France for the large sum of £400,000. Of the statesmen of the day Clarendon alone approved of the transaction, and apparently for very sufficient reasons. It is plain that the possession of a seaport in Flanders could have been of no real advantage

---

[1] See Thurloe i., 761; ii., 54, 154, 570.—Dumont.

[2] This battle, in which the Spaniards under the Prince of Condé were totally defeated, was fought on the 14th of June, 1658.

to England unless she had intended to revive the aggressive policy of the Edwards and the Henries. There can be no doubt that when Cromwell took possession of Dunkirk he entertained the project of making further acquisitions on the Continent. As a means of averting attention from his despotic policy at home he had an obvious motive in seeking employment for his army abroad. His troops were famed throughout Europe for their discipline and valour, and the civil war had produced a host of able officers, many of them discontented with the state of affairs at home, but all eager to embark on active service. All schemes of foreign conquest, however, died with the Protector,

During the Protectorate of Cromwell a brother of the Portuguese ambassador was charged with being concerned in an outrage which raised an important question of public law. Dr. Zouch, the most eminent English civilian of the day, who was appointed along with other legal authorities to inquire into the matter, has stated the facts of the case as follows:—

" On the 22nd November, 1653, there happened an
" unlucky accident in a mad but premeditated riot which
" was raised by the retinue of the Portuguese ambas-
" sador, chiefly upon account of his brother. For an
" English gentleman walking in the New Exchange at
" London, and thinking no harm, was basely killed by a
" pistol-shot. The Lord Protector showing a just
" concern both for the blood of an English subject and
" the pretended privilege of an ambassador, consulted
" the most eminent professors, both of the common and
" civil law, how such a barbarous murder might be
" punished. But these disagreeing amongst themselves,
" his highness thought fit to leave the decision of the
" affair to a court of delegates, consisting of the Chief
" Justice and two other judges, the same number of gen-
" tlemen, and three doctors of the civil law. When the
" ambassador's brother and the other offenders were
" brought before this court, he who was supposed by

"some to be a colleague in the embassy vaunted there
"he was his king's ambassador and subject to the juris-
"diction of no one else; but producing the King of
"Portugal's letters, all that appeared from them was
"that the king intended in a little time to recall his
"brother and to give him commission to manage his
"affairs in England. But this being judged insufficient
"to prove him an ambassador, he was, without any fur-
"ther regard to the privileges of that character, ordered
"himself as well as the rest to plead to the indict-
"ment. And accordingly he pleaded not guilty. But
"witnesses appearing and relating the whole matter of
"fact upon oath, they were all convicted and condemned
"to die. The ambassador's brother having been dis-
"covered in an attempt to make his escape was after-
"wards executed, together with an English servant
"of his."

It appears that on the night before the murder in question was committed a quarrel had ensued between four Portuguese gentlemen and a Colonel Gerard on the New Exchange. On the following evening Don Pantaleon Sa, the brother of the Portuguese ambassador, accompanied by two knights of Malta and a number of armed attendants, returned to the Exchange. A serious riot ensued, in the course of which various persons were wounded, and a gentleman of Lincoln's Inn, named Greenway, who had taken no part in the fray, but only happened to be passing at the time, was killed by a pistol-shot. By whom the shot was fired did not appear; but that serious mischief was premeditated by the Portuguese, and that the brother of the ambassador was their leader on the occasion, there seems to be no doubt.

The rioters were eventually dispersed by a troop of horse, who followed them to the house of the Portuguese ambassador, and demanded that the ringleaders should be given up. The ambassador at first refused on the ground of privilege, but he was finally induced to surrender his brother and several of his companions. On the following day they were taken before the Lord Chief Justice Rolles, who committed them to Newgate in order that they might be brought to trial for the murder of Mr. Greenway.

On the 13th of December Don Pantaleon made his escape from prison, but he was retaken and a day appointed for his trial. But it was postponed from time to time, and in the interval the question of his liability to be tried like any ordinary criminal was much discussed both in England and in foreign countries. In the latter it was generally considered that, as he formed a part of the household of the ambassador, he was privileged from arrest and punishment. But for very obvious reasons the Spanish ambassador took the opposite view. He declared that "Don John of Portugal was a usurper and no "lawful king, and that Don Pantaleon might be executed "without violating the rights and privileges of ambas- "sadors." The brother of the unfortunate youth, who was only nineteen years old, had various interviews with the Protector on the subject, and also with reference to a treaty of commerce with Portugal. But eventually the law was allowed to take its course. Don Pantaleon was brought to trial before a mixed jury on the 5th of July, 1654. There were arraigned along with him an English servant and the two knights of Malta. As a foreigner unacquainted with the laws of England he requested to be allowed the aid of counsel, but he was informed that on a charge of felony counsel could not be allowed. All the prisoners were convicted, and on the 10th of July Don Pantaleon was conveyed in a mourning-coach and six to Tower Hill and was there beheaded. His English servant was hanged at Tyburn; the others were reprieved.

It so happened that early on the morning of this day the treaty of commerce, after much negotiation and delay, was signed by the ambassador of Portugal, and it has been insinuated that he was induced to sign it in the belief that his brother's life would be spared.[1] The coincidence, to say the least of it, is suspicious; but without some positive proof so serious a charge of perfidy against the Protector cannot be entertained.[2]

The opinion of Zouch was that if the ambassador himself had committed murder he would not have been amenable to the law of England, but that this immunity did not extend to his suite, and that therefore Don Pantaleon was justly executed.[3] But he admits that Grotius was of a different opinion, and that he maintained the immunity from the jurisdiction of foreign law the suite of an embassy as well as the ambassador himself. We may add that two very eminent authorities on the criminal law of England—namely, Lord Hale[4] and Justice Foster[5]—have both maintained that an ambassador was punishable by the law of England. But they rest their opinion on moral grounds alone. There can be no doubt that the immunity of ambassadors from the criminal law of the country to which they are accredited is a principle now universally recognised among civilised states; and this immunity, in accordance with the opinion of Grotius, is generally held to extend to their suite.

After the disastrous defeat of Dunes Philip the Fourth was anxious to come to terms with France. But for some time the position of the Prince of Condé proved an insuperable obstacle to peace. The King of Spain, to whom he had rendered such important service, insisted that the distinguished rebel should be restored to all his dignities and all his vast possessions. It was precisely a repetition of the demands of Charles the Fifth on

---

[1] Carte, History of England.

[2] In a letter from La Bastide de la Croix to De Baas, dated 10th July, 1654, it is said :—"This morning at eight of the clock the Portugal ambassador signed his "treaty and departed for Gravesend at ten. His brother was beheaded this "afternoon and his man hanged at Tyburn."—Thurloe, p. 439.

[3] Solutio questionis de Legati delinquentis, competente judicio.

[4] "If the ambassador or his associates commit any capital offence they may be "proceeded against by indictment as other aliens committing like offences."—Pleas of the Crown, vol. i., p. 99.

[5] Foster's Crown Law, p. 188.

behalf of the Constable Bourbon after the battle of Pavia. But the circumstances were very different. France had then suffered a terrible defeat, and her monarch was a prisoner. She was now victorious, and hoped to be able to obtain peace on her own terms. Mazarin refused, therefore, to restore Condé to his honours and estates, but proposed that without any express stipulations he should simply trust to the generosity of the king. To these terms Philip declined to accede, but being anxious to bring about a marriage between his daughter and Louis a suspension of hostilities took place on the 8th of May, 1659, and it was agreed that the plenipotentiaries of the two kingdoms should meet on the frontiers of Spain for the purpose of concluding peace.

The island of pheasants in the river Bidassoa was the spot selected for the meeting, and Mazarin far outvied the representative of Spain in the splendour of his appointments. On the 13th of August he appeared on the banks of the Bidassoa with twenty-seven carriages, each drawn by six horses,[1] and containing representatives of the first families in France, who again were accompanied by innumerable pages and attendants in gorgeous liveries. The plenipotentiary of Spain was Don Louis de Haro, prime minister of Philip, and, as was usual in this age, many days were spent in discussing questions of ceremonial and precedence. But as both parties were by this time anxious for peace, the question of the Prince of Condé was no longer allowed to delay the negotiations, and it was finally agreed that he should be restored to his dignities and his estates.

The territorial acquisitions which were secured to France by this treaty were numerous and important. She retained the county of Artois and various towns in the duchy of Luxembourg, and on the southern frontier she obtained the county of Roussillon, which was finally ceded by Spain, and the Pyrenees henceforth became the

[1] Schoell, Hist. de Traités.

boundary of the two kingdoms. A still more important acquisition was a large portion of Lorraine—namely, the duchy of Bar and the county of Clermont. The duke complained loudly of the partition of his territories, but he was not only compelled to submit to the terms imposed upon him by Mazarin, but rather than suffer further acts of spoliation he agreed to allow at all times a free passage through his territories to the armies of France.

By the thirty-third article of the treaty it was agreed that a marriage should be solemnised between the young King of France and the Infanta of Spain, Maria Theresa, the daughter of Philip the Fourth, with whom Louis was to receive a dowry of 500,000 crowns. Both by the treaty and the contract of marriage it was expressly stipulated that the infanta for herself and her descendants renounced all claim to the crown of Spain, and this renunciation was confirmed conjointly by herself and her husband after their marriage. The worthlessness of these precautions was questioned at the time and with reason, for this Spanish alliance was eventually the cause of many wars.

By the Treaty of the Pyrenees, which was signed on the 7th of November, 1659, France acquired a dangerous ascendency in the politics of Europe. Cromwell was now dead;[1] but there can be little doubt that her alliance with the Protector contributed essentially to this result. Without his powerful aid by land and sea it is highly improbable that Spain would have been reduced to the necessity of acceding to the terms now imposed upon her. Mazarin did not long survive his diplomatic triumph. He has been accused of insatiable avarice as well as of inordinate ambition, but it cannot be denied that to this foreign adventurer belongs the credit of having concluded the two most important treaties of the seventeenth century, and that both of these contributed materially to the aggrandisement of his adopted country.

[1] On the 3rd of September, 1658. Mazarin died in 1661.

Emancipated from the tutelage of Mazarin, Louis the Fourteenth became the absolute master of France at twenty years of age. The aggressive spirit of Spain and Austria had each in their turn brought innumerable calamities on Europe, but both had been effectually humbled. It was now the turn of France to follow in their footsteps, and eventually to share their fate.

CHAPTER IX.

FROM THE TREATY OF THE PYRENEES TO THE TREATY OF RYSWICK.

ALTHOUGH Louis the Fourteenth had, by the treaty of the Pyrenees, solemnly renounced for himself and his descendants all territorial claims which might arise by virtue of his marriage with the infanta, events soon proved that he had no intention of keeping his engagements. So long as Mazarin lived the young monarch left to him the entire management of public affairs, but from the moment of his death Louis assumed to himself the sole responsibilities of government. His celebrated reply when he was asked the name of Mazarin's successor was not only true to the letter, but it remained true until the day of his death.

Mazarin died in the year 1661, and in the following year Louis concluded a treaty, offensive and defensive, with the United Provinces for twenty-five years. The true object of this treaty was to prevent the republic making common cause with Spain, whose possessions in the Low Countries it was his intention, sooner or later, to add to his dominions. A dispute which occurred in London on a point of precedence between the ambassadors of France and Spain would have led to war between the two crowns had not an ample apology been made by Philip the Fourth to his son-in-law. For an affront which had been offered to the French ambassador at Rome by the Papal guard, reparation of a more extraordinary kind was demanded and exacted. Louis not only insisted that a special envoy should be sent to

[1] On the 27th of April, 1662.—Dumont.

Paris to ask his forgiveness, but that a pyramid should be erected at Rome on which was inscribed a brief narrative of the affair.[1] This excessive jealousy of the honour and dignity of his crown was a conspicuous feature in the character of Louis throughout his long and memorable reign.

In the year 1665 war broke out between England and Holland. Charles the Second has been accused, apparently without reason, of having for his own ends brought about the rupture. The commercial rivalry between the two rising maritime Powers was no doubt the true cause of the war, and there are no sea-fights on record of so desperate, and, we may add, of so indecisive a character, as those which now took place between the English and the Dutch. On the 1st of June, 1666, a battle was fought off the North Foreland, which lasted for four successive days. The Dutch were commanded by De Ruyter, the most famous seaman of the age, and by Van Tromp, the son of the admiral of that name; the English by Monk, Duke of Albemarle, and Prince Rupert, the son of Frederick, the unfortunate Prince Palatine; and, after a combat unprecedented in naval warfare, both sides seem to have claimed the victory, although probably the Dutch were best entitled to that honour.[2] The degree of perfection to which the arts of destruction have now been carried would render any such protracted struggle impossible. For so rare an exhibition of unflinching courage modern warfare offers no opportunity. Four hours, instead of four days, would be more than sufficient in the present age to decide the fate of any naval battle.

John De Witt, one of the most eminent men that the Dutch Republic had produced, and conspicuous alike for his capacity as a ruler and his private virtues, was at this time at the head of affairs in Holland. He had

[1] This pyramid stood for three years, but was, by permission of the French king, removed in the year 1667, during the pontificate of Clement the Ninth.—Daniel, Hist de France, t. x., p. 97.
[2] Such is the opinion of Lingard, vol. ix., p. 62.

claimed from Louis the Fourteenth, on the outbreak of the war, the aid which, under the treaty of 1662, France was bound to supply. Louis was ambitious at this time of creating a fleet, and, with the aid of his able and energetic minister Colbert, he had succeeded. But he was unwilling to expose it to the risk of a naval war with England, and although he did not actually repudiate his engagements with the Dutch, he took no active part in the war, being well content to see the two great maritime Powers engaged in a struggle which was weakening the resources of both. Louis considered he had sufficiently fulfilled his engagements by sending six thousand troops to oppose the Bishop of Munster, who had declared war against the States.

During this war London was the scene of two unprecedented calamities. In 1665 the plague, it is said, carried off upwards of a hundred thousand of its inhabitants, and in the following year a large portion of the city, extending from the Tower to the Temple, was destroyed by the great fire. These misfortunes disposed Charles and his ministers to listen to proposals for peace, which were offered through the mediation of Sweden. Plenipotentiaries were appointed by both countries, and a mediator by the King of Sweden, and, after some discussion, Breda was agreed upon as the place of meeting. Meanwhile, owing to the heavy losses sustained by the trade of London in consequence of the late calamities, it was found impossible to raise money sufficient for the maintenance of the fleet. It had been customary for the government to borrow from the merchants and bankers on the security of the revenue for this and other purposes of state, and this expedient was no longer practicable. It was therefore proposed to lay up the larger ships, and to keep afloat only a certain number of frigates. The proposal was strenuously opposed by the Duke of York, who had greatly distinguished himself in the war, but the difficulty of obtaining money and the prospect of a speedy peace induced Charles to consent to a measure which he soon found occasion deeply to regret.

On the meeting of the plenipotentiaries at Breda, Charles, for very obvious reasons, proposed an armistice—a proposal which, for reasons equally obvious, was rejected by the Dutch. They had, upon the whole, suffered more severely from the war than the English, and a tempting prospect of retaliation was now offered them through the parsimony or the necessities of their rivals. With a fleet of seventy ships De Ruyter anchored off the Nore, and, finding nothing to oppose him, sailed with a portion of his squadron and several fireships up the Thames and the Medway as far as Chatham. The damage done by this daring expedition was comparatively small, but the disgrace was long and keenly felt; and, although the king was much less to blame than his ministers, he was accused of having planned the attack on Chatham in concert with his enemies. It was insinuated that to humiliate the nation was the surest means of preparing the way for the establishment of a despotic government. These rumours seem to have been utterly without foundation. Charles always took a lively interest in naval affairs; and, in fact, the only business to which he ever seriously applied himself was that of the Admiralty.[1]

It might have been anticipated that the affair at Chatham would have interrupted the negotiations at Breda; but, as both parties were desirous of peace, and the questions at issue were not difficult of adjustment, the treaty was signed on the 31st of July, 1667. Each Power retained whatever had been acquired during the war. Thus England acquired New Amsterdam, which was henceforth named New York, the Dutch acquired Surinam, and the vessels taken during the war remained the property of the captors.[2]

Louis had meanwhile matured his plans for the invasion of the Spanish Netherlands. His father-in-law,

---

[1] Pepys' Diary.
[2] Schoell, Traités de Paix, cap. iii.

Philip the Fourth, had died in the year 1665, and Louis forthwith laid claim to the duchy of Brabant, the lordship of Malines, Antwerp, Upper Guelders, and Namur, together with various places in the duchy of Luxembourg, and the whole of Franche-Comté. He rested his claim upon two grounds—first, on the so-called law of *devolution* which prevailed in those provinces; and, secondly, that the dowry of the infanta had not been paid.

By the law of *devolution* the children of a first marriage were entitled to succeed to the immovable property of their parents, to the exclusion of the children of a second marriage. By his first marriage Philip the Fourth had two children, Don Baltazar and the infanta, the queen of Louis the Fourteenth. Charles the Second, who succeeded his father as King of Spain, was born of a second marriage, and Don Baltazar being dead, Louis maintained that the whole of the territories in question had vested in his wife in virtue of the law of *devolution* as sole heiress of Philip the Fourth by his first marriage. Louis further maintained that the renunciations made by the infanta, in accordance with the Treaty of the Pyrenees, having been made during minority, were not binding upon her nor her descendants.

To this the Spanish ministers replied that the law of *devolution* applied only to the property of private persons; that, by the fundamental laws of Spain, the territorial possessions of the monarchy, wherever situated, were indivisible and belonged of right to the king, and that no precedent could be shown for any such claim as that now made by France.

John De Witt attempted, but in vain, to mediate between the rival monarchs. He saw that, in the event of war between France and Spain, it would be difficult for the States to remain neutral. But Louis had now commenced that course of aggressive policy which, after inflicting incalculable mischief upon all his neighbours, proved eventually most disastrous to France. Unfortunately for Europe and for himself, he was at first eminently successful in all his undertakings. In the campaign of 1667 he captured a number of important towns in the Spanish Netherlands, including Charleroi, Tournai, Douai, Courtrai, Oudenarde, and Lille, and early in the following spring the Prince of Condé made himself master of Franche-Comté.

The rapid progress of the French arms alarmed the neighbouring Powers, and a treaty, well known under the name of the Triple Alliance, was concluded at the Hague, chiefly through the influence of the English ambassador, Sir William Temple, between Great Britain, Holland, and Sweden.[1] This treaty is chiefly remarkable for the expedition with which it was concluded. In an age of diplomatic trifling, the negotiations were begun and ended in three days. An explanation of so singular a phenomenon is to be found in the simple fact that both the negotiators, De Witt and Temple, were able and honest men who had no interests to serve except the interests of their respective countries.

The Treaty of Aix-la-Chapelle, concluded on the 2nd of May, 1668, under the mediation of the Pope, put an end to the war between France and Spain. France retained the conquests she had made in the Spanish Netherlands, but she restored Franche-Comté. No reference was made in the treaty to the pretensions of the Queen of France to any of the territories in question, which, in fact, had been the sole pretext for the war. Having succeeded in establishing a footing in the Netherlands, Louis was discreetly silent as to the means he had employed in accomplishing his purpose.

As the Triple Alliance had obliged Louis to stop short in his career of conquest, he spared no expense to bring about the dissolution of a league which formed so formidable a barrier in his path, and he eventually succeeded. He knew that between Charles and his

[1] Dumont.

Dutch allies there was no real sympathy; he knew that the English king preferred the friendship of France to that of any other country; above all, he knew the easy and pliant temper of Charles, which rendered him incapable of pursuing any consistent course of policy. It was not without reason, therefore, that Louis calculated on the speedy breaking up of the Triple Alliance, and the means by which it was effected showed that he had formed a true estimate of the character of the English king.

While at Dover in the summer of 1670 Charles received a visit from his favourite sister the Duchess of Orleans.[1] The real object of her visit, which had been planned by Louis, was not suspected at the time, but its result was the famous secret treaty, the text of which has only come to light in the present age. The principal articles were:—First, that the King of England should publicly profess himself a Catholic at such time as should appear to him most expedient, and thereafter should join with Louis in a war against the Dutch Republic at such time as the French king should think proper. Second, that to enable the King of England to suppress any insurrection which might be caused by his conversion the King of France should grant him an aid of two millions of livres by two payments, one at the expiration of three months, the other of six months after the ratification of the treaty, and should, moreover, assist him with an armed force of six thousand men if the employment of such a force should be deemed necessary. Third, that Louis should faithfully observe the Treaty of Aix-la-Chapelle, and Charles be allowed to maintain that treaty in conformity with the conditions of the Triple Alliance. Fourth, that if eventually any new rights in the Spanish monarchy should accrue to the King of France the King of England should aid him with all his power in the

---

[1] She was accompanied by Mademoiselle Querouaille, who afterwards became Duchess of Portsmouth.

acquisition of those rights. Fifth, that both princes should make war on the Dutch Republic, and that neither should conclude peace without the consent of his ally. Sixth, that the King of France should take on himself the whole charge of the war by land, receiving from England an auxiliary force of six thousand men. Seventh, that by sea Charles should furnish fifty and Louis thirty ships of war; that the combined fleet should be placed under the command of the Duke of York; and that to enable the King of England to support the charge of the naval armament he should receive every year the sum of three millions of livres from the King of France. Eighth, that out of the conquests that might be made his Britannic majesty would be satisfied with Walcheren, Sluys, and the island of Cadzand; and that in separate articles provision should be made for the interests of the Prince of Orange. Ninth, that to unite more closely the interests of the two countries the treaty of commerce which was being negotiated should be concluded as speedily as possible.[1]

The ministry of Charles at this time consisted of the famous *cabal*, so named from the initial letters of their respective names; and that men like Buckingham, and Shaftesbury, and Lauderdale were ready to embark in any enterprise which promised them a fresh lease of power, and fresh opportunities of plunder, we can well believe. But that a prince of so easy and careless a temper as Charles should be willing to risk his crown in the pursuit of schemes so dark and dangerous was to all appearance highly improbable. Of the nature and purpose of the treaty there can be no question. It was simply a conspiracy between the two kings for the overthrow of the religion and liberties of England. But whether Charles was sincere in acceding to the dangerous projects of Louis seems to be more than doubtful. He was ready and willing to aid the French king in an attack upon Holland, as the event proved. But to the pressing

[1] See the treaty in Lingard, vol. x, Append.

invitations of Louis, again and again repeated, that he would publicly renounce the Protestant religion and declare himself a Catholic, Charles invariably returned evasive answers. The truth appears to be that Charles, being always in want of money, could not resist the temptation of the bribes held out to him. In his hostility to the Dutch he was at least sincere, and he repeated the blunder of Cromwell by aiding to the utmost of his power, instead of opposing, the aggrandisement of France.

Charles had not only no cause of quarrel with Holland, but he was bound by every consideration of honour and sound policy to support her against her ambitious and aggressive neighbour. Louis himself seems hardly to have expected that he would have been so blind to the interests of his country as to have violated the Triple Alliance, and supported him in his attack on the republic. But to his great satisfaction, Charles, in accordance with the secret treaty, issued on the 17th March, 1672, a declaration of war against the Dutch, and it has been truly said that reasons more false and frivolous to justify a recourse to arms have never been set forth.[1] Charles having renounced the Triple Alliance, Sweden was induced to follow his example, and in the course of the following month she concluded a separate treaty with France.[2]

De Witt was well aware that he had incurred the mortal enmity of Louis by his alliance with England and Sweden, and now that that alliance was at an end he saw his country exposed to the dangers of a simultaneous attack by the first military and the first naval Power in Europe. Unfortunately since the termination of their great struggle with Spain the Dutch had neglected their land defences. Many of their fortresses were dismantled and their forces were few in number, comparatively speaking, undisciplined and without experience in war. They

---

[1] Hume, chap. lxv.
[2] On 11th April, 1672.—Dumont.

still possessed a formidable fleet, and that was commanded by De Ruyter; but against the overwhelming forces which Louis was able to bring against them on land resistance appeared to be hopeless. But an incident which happened in 1670 had the effect of procuring them two important allies. In that year Louis, in violation of the Treaty of the Pyrenees, had taken possession of the entire duchy of Lorraine, thus cutting off all direct communication between Franche-Comté and the Spanish Netherlands. This proceeding brought about an alliance between Spain and her revolted subjects; and Frederick William, the Elector of Brandenburg, with a view to the security of his territories on the Rhine, concluded a treaty with De Witt by which he engaged to provide in case of need an army of twenty thousand men, the expense of which was to be equally divided between the Elector and the republic.[1]

In the spring of 1672 Louis invaded the United Provinces with a great army. His most experienced commanders took part in the expedition—namely, Condé, Turenne, Luxembourg, and Créqui—and the Hollanders were utterly unable to make head against the overwhelming forces opposed to them. Town after town fell into the hands of the invaders, and they were threatening an attack upon Amsterdam when terms of peace were proposed by De Witt. The French king was holding his court at Utrecht with all the pomp and splendour in which he took delight when the Dutch deputies laid their proposals before him. They offered to cede various important frontier towns, and to pay a sum of ten millions of francs towards the expenses of the war. The more prudent of his ministers advised Louis to accept these terms, but fortunately for the interests of Holland and of Europe he was induced to reject them. He demanded instead a war indemnity of twenty millions of francs, that the provinces of Utrecht and Gueldres with various other places should be ceded

[1] Dumont.

to France, that the Catholic religion should be established throughout the republic; and lastly followed the most degrading condition of all—namely, that every year a golden medal be presented to the king as *the preserver of the liberties of the republic*, and that it should bear an inscription to that effect. This astounding piece of insolence is without a parallel even in the history of Louis the Fourteenth.

On the part of the King of England the demands were that the English flag on board a ship of war should at all times be saluted by the Dutch; that a million sterling should be paid towards the expenses of the war; that ten thousand pounds a year should be paid on account of the herring-fishery; and that the Prince of Orange should be restored to his rank as captain-general and admiral of Holland. Until these conditions were complied with the island of Walcheren and several seaports were to be held in pledge.

The Prince of Orange, although a very young man, had displayed the utmost energy in opposing the invaders, and while the negotiations were proceeding at Utrecht it was rumoured that De Witt was about to betray his country to the French. In the apparently hopeless condition to which the republic was reduced these utterly groundless slanders were eagerly caught up. A victim was required on whom the popular rage might vent itself, and John De Witt and his brother Cornelius, who had been his faithful colleague in the government of the States for twenty years, were brutally murdered by an infuriated mob. The Prince of Orange had been already proclaimed stadtholder, and by his advice the further progress of the French was checked by opening the dykes and inundating the country, as had been the practice in the Spanish wars. He indignantly rejected the degrading terms proposed by Louis and Charles. The Duke of Buckingham, who was at this time ambassador at the Court of France, was subsequently authorised to offer him the sovereignty of Holland, with the guarantee of England and France; but this, too, he peremptorily refused. Buckingham, to gain his end, employed every argument that was likely to influence a generous mind, and at length asked if he did not see that the commonwealth was already ruined? The reply of the prince was worthy of his great ancestor and namesake. "There "is one certain means," he said, "by which I can be "sure never to see the ruin of my country. I will die "in the last ditch."

While the French armies overran the greater part of the United Provinces the combined fleets of England and France fought a series of battles with the Dutch navy, commanded by De Ruyter. None of these actions were decisive, but the Dutch admiral had the glory of protecting his coast against an enemy whose forces were far superior to his. It was suspected, however, that the French commanders purposely abstained from taking an active part in these encounters, as the object of Louis was to allow the two maritime Powers to waste their strength while he encouraged by every means the development of his naval resources.

This most unjust and most impolitic war had never been regarded with favour in England. Although the Dutch were regarded as commercial rivals, it was clearly seen that the overthrow of the republic by France, which seemed to be the aim of Louis, would give an immense preponderance to a Power whose ambitious and aggressive spirit was already a source of constant danger and alarm to all her neighbours. Of the wild and wicked schemes of the *cabal* the nation was profoundly ignorant; but the character of the men who composed it rendered them open to general suspicion, and the proceedings of the government were watched with extreme jealousy. On the opening of Parliament,[1] Shaftesbury, then Lord Chancellor, made a violent speech in favour of the war with Holland. He maintained that the Dutch were not only the commercial enemies of England, but the enemies

[1] In 1673.

of all monarchies; that nothing would satisfy their ambition but the subversion of all existing governments; that even in the state of distress to which they had been reduced they scornfully rejected all overtures of peace, and that the only maxim applicable to such a state was *delenda est Carthago*, for it was only by its destruction that the general welfare could be secured.

It is probable that this violent language was used in the belief that Charles was now about to fulfil his engagements under the secret treaty. In addition to the Guards, a considerable force had been assembled at Blackheath under a foreign officer, Marshal Schomberg, and there is little doubt that Shaftesbury and his colleagues were quite prepared to resort to force in the pursuit of their nefarious schemes. But Charles, if he ever was sincere in the business, which seems very doubtful, displayed more discretion than his ministers, and refused to plunge the country into a second civil war. With characteristic inconstancy Shaftesbury soon joined the opposition, and became no less conspicuous for his hostility to the Crown than he had been to the liberties of the people.

The reluctance of Parliament to vote supplies for the Dutch war, and the intervention of Spain on behalf of the States, finally induced Charles to violate his secret engagements with Louis and to conclude a separate peace. Through the mediation of the Spanish ambassador in London a treaty was concluded at Westminster on the 19th of February, 1674, by which Charles obtained in substance the terms he had demanded two years previous. The States consented that their ships and fleets should lower their flags and topsails to every British man-of-war on any part of the sea from Cape Finisterre to Van Staaten in Norway as a matter of right; that the English settlers in Surinam should be freely permitted to leave that colony in English ships; that all subjects of dispute between the East India Companies of the two nations should be referred to the decision of arbitrators, to sit in London; that the States should pay to the King of Great Britain the sum of eight hundred thousand crowns. Charles had formerly demanded for the Prince of Orange the title of stadtholder, but the States had already conferred that dignity upon him and his heirs shortly before the commencement of the negotiations.[1]

In the meantime the tide of fortune had turned in favour of the Hollanders. Nothing apparently could be more hopeless than their condition when they rejected the humiliating terms proposed by Louis. But while they possessed champions like the Prince of Orange on the land, and De Ruyter on the sea, they could not despair of the republic, and the heroic spirit displayed by the States in their misfortunes awakened both the sympathies and the fears of their neighbours. The Elector of Brandenburg, whose Rhenish territories were threatened by the aggressive policy of Louis, had wisely taken part with the republic, and through his influence the Emperor Leopold was induced, after some hesitation, to follow his example. A few months after the treaty of peace was concluded between England and the States the emperor declared war against France;[2] an imperial army joined the Prince of Orange at Bonn, which surrendered after a short siege. The Duke of Brunswick and various other princes of the empire joined the allies, and the French were compelled to abandon nearly all their conquests in Flanders. On the Upper Rhine Turenne was now opposed to the imperialists, who had invaded Alsace with a powerful army, but he compelled them to recross the river. He followed them to Sasbach, in the territory of Baden, but was killed by a random shot while preparing to give them battle.[3] On the death of their great commander the French recrossed the

[1] Dumont.
[2] When Charles concluded the Treaty of Westminster he stipulated that he was still to be allowed to provide a body of troops for the service of Louis. But he bound himself not to increase their number—a condition which he did not observe.
[3] In July, 1675.

Rhine. During the retreat a contingent of English troops, which, in terms of the engagements between Louis and Charles, served in the French army, greatly distinguished themselves. Among them was a young captain named John Churchill, who received his first lessons in the art of war in this campaign. Little did the French commander think that his pupil was one day to become the most formidable enemy that France had ever seen.

After the treaty had been concluded between Charles and the States, Sir William Temple, the English ambassador in Holland, had sought to bring about a general peace. But he found the Prince of Orange so resolutely bent on the prosecution of the war that his task was hopeless. It was chiefly through the energy, the prudence, and the invincible spirit of the prince that the States had been able to make head against the overwhelming power of France, and patriotism or ambition induced him to refuse all terms of accommodation so long as Louis was in a position to pursue his arbitrary and aggressive schemes. The prince lived in an age when military glory was the ruling passion among the great, and he was eager for distinction in a field in which he naturally deemed himself qualified to excel. But it was his misfortune to be opposed by the most renowned commanders of France, and in his most important military operations he was generally unsuccessful. At Senef, one of the bloodiest battles of the war, and which is said to have cost the lives of more than twenty thousand men, he was compelled by the great Condé to retreat after a struggle of fourteen hours. At St. Omer, when preparing to invade France, he was subsequently defeated by Luxembourg. But although unaccustomed to victory he never despaired in defeat, and the deliberation with which he matured his plans, and the unswerving constancy of purpose with which he pursued them, led him to be universally regarded as a firm friend or a most dangerous enemy.

Freed from all risk of an attack from England, De Ruyter sailed for the Mediterranean in search of the French fleet. An insurrection had broken out at Messina, and the French had taken part with the insurgents, and, for the first time since the Sicilian Vespers, attempted to gain a footing in Sicily. De Ruyter fought two battles with the French, the one off the Lipari Islands, the other in the Straits of Messina. In the last of these the great admiral fell,[1] leaving behind him a reputation for valour and for patriotism unsurpassed in the annals of his country.

For some time negotiations had been going on between France and Holland. Louis was willing to make peace with the Dutch provided he was allowed to retain his conquests in the Spanish provinces, and the Hollanders were weary of a war which had not only loaded them with debt, but which had thrown a large portion of their trade into the hands of the English. The Prince of Orange, in no wise daunted by his want of success, and confident that if his allies remained true to their engagements they must eventually prevail, would listen to no terms which promised an increase of territory to France. His betrothal to the Princess Mary, the eldest daughter of the Duke of York, brought to his side, at least for a time, a new and very important ally. It is difficult to imagine two characters in all respects more unlike than those of the Prince of Orange and Charles the Second. The former was a model of prudence and propriety, the latter exactly the reverse; but Charles could admire in others those qualities in which he himself was notoriously deficient. From the first he seems to have formed a highly-favourable opinion of his nephew, and through his influence a treaty offensive and defensive was concluded between Great Britain and Holland on the 3rd of March, 1678.[2]

Charles was now in a position, in concert with Hol-

---

[1] On the 22nd of April, 1676.
[2] Schoell, Histoire des Traités, t. i., p. 364.

land, the emperor, and the King of Spain, to have put a stop to the aggressive schemes of France and restore the balance of power, which she threatened to overturn. Upon him alone it seemed to depend whether the peace about to be concluded should be of a permanent nature, or whether, by yielding to the demands of Louis, it should merely prove the prelude to future wars. That was the opinion generally entertained by the allies, and apparently by Louis himself. The French king was well aware that so long as the confederates continued to act in concert it would be in vain for him to realise his schemes, and he spared no pains to come to separate terms with each. From his knowledge of the character of Charles he confidently hoped to be able to detach him from the cause of the allies. But he was disappointed. Charles on this occasion displayed an amount of energy and resolution which, if he had been supported by his Parliament, must have had a most important influence on the affairs of Europe. He was now apparently quite alive to the designs of France, and, in spite of his engagements with Louis, was prepared to declare war rather than allow him to dictate terms of peace. He was strenuously supported in this resolution both by the Prince of Orange and the Duke of York, and he resisted all the attempts of Louis to turn him from his purpose. But in the midst of his preparations he was thwarted by the leaders of the Opposition in the House of Commons, who at first were clamorous for war with France, and then refused the necessary supplies. That the French king was responsible for a result in which he was so deeply interested is certain. That the Parliamentary leaders were, even at the time, not above suspicion we have abundant proof.[1]

[1] June 18th, 1678. A test was proposed for the discovery of such members in that House as had received bribes or any other consideration for their votes, either from the English Government or foreign Powers. The popular leaders spoke warmly in its favour, but before the last division took place about one hundred members slipped out of the House, and the motion was lost by a majority of fourteen.—C. Journals Parl. Hist. iv., p. 1,000.

It was not, therefore, as has been asserted by many historians, the fickle temper of the king, but the factious proceedings of the House of Commons, which enabled Louis at this critical time to conclude peace on his own terms. Disappointed in their hopes of aid from England, the confederates were no longer in a position to prolong the contest. The emperor was threatened with a Turkish war; the condition of Spain was truly represented by the royal invalid, Charles the Second, who then occupied the throne; and the Dutch were overwhelmed with debt. The refusal of the English Parliament to grant supplies for the war under these circumstances rendered peace inevitable, and it was concluded at Nimeguen in the autumn of 1678.[1]

By this treaty the King of Spain ceded to France the whole of Franche-Comté, together with various important towns in Flanders—namely, Valenciennes, Bouchain, Condé, Cambray and Cambresia, Airé, Saint-Omer, Ypres, Warwick, Warneton, Bailleul, Cassel, and several others.

These acquisitions were the principal results of the war, and they gave to the King of France a preponderance among the Powers of Europe of which they were soon made painfully aware. In addition to the territories ceded to him by the Treaty of Nimeguen he claimed various places which he alleged belonged to him as sovereign of the districts in question, and among others the important frontier towns of Luxembourg and Strasbourg. After much negotiation his title to these places and to various others was acknowledged by the King of Spain and the emperor by a treaty known as the Truce of Ratisbon in the autumn of 1684.

Important events had meanwhile taken place in the

---

[1] It was not the fault of Charles and Prince William that the peace of Nimeguen was concluded upon terms which founded the preponderance of Louis the Fourteenth in Europe. That result was owing far rather to the fact that France had gained over the domestic adversaries of Charles and William, the members of the opposition in the States General and in the English Parliament.—Ranke, Hist. of England, vol. iv., p. 486.

empire. A series of insurrections in Hungary, fomented by French intrigue on the one hand and by the active intervention of the Sultan on the other, had for some time occupied the chief attention of Leopold; and in March, 1683, he concluded an alliance with John Sobieski, King of Poland, in anticipation of an invasion of his dominions by the Turks. This treaty was a most fortunate incident in the history of the house of Hapsburg. In the autumn of this year an immense Turkish army, commanded by the Grand Vizier, advanced unopposed to the gates of Vienna. The emperor and his ministers fled from the capital, followed by thousands of the citizens. But the Duke of Lorraine, who was in command of the garrison, although sorely pressed by the besiegers, was able to hold out until the appearance of Sobieski, who on the 12th September, 1683, totally defeated the Turks under the walls of Vienna, and was justly hailed by the inhabitants as the saviour of the city. To the Polish monarch belongs the glory of repelling the last great Mohammedan invasion of Christendom.

Louis the Fourteenth had now reached the zenith of his power and fame. For more than twenty years he had been invariably successful in all his wars and in all his negotiations. He was absolute master of the richest kingdom in Europe. He possessed an immense standing army, and although Turenne was now dead and Condé had retired into private life, he could still command the services of Luxembourg and Vauban, of Catinat and Boufflers, and of many other experienced officers. He had, moreover, created, with the aid of Colbert, a very formidable fleet, so that he plainly aimed at supremacy on the sea as well as on the land. It is estimated that at this time his land and sea forces consisted of more than half a million of men. Even the most warlike of the Roman emperors could never boast of so great a military force as that which was now possessed by a king of France.[1]

[1] Gibbon, cap. i.

There was not, indeed, at this time a Power in Europe that was capable of offering effectual resistance to his ambitious schemes. England was vitally interested in preventing France from becoming supreme at sea, as she was already on the land; but Charles the Second was her pensioner. Charles the Second of Spain was in a hopeless decline, weak alike in body and in mind. The Emperor Leopold was harassed by the chronic disaffection of his Hungarian subjects and by a Turkish war. The princes of the empire were still more jealous of each other than of the King of France, and the Scandinavian kingdoms were comparatively little interested in the politics of Western Europe. There was only one enemy who at this time Louis had cause to dread, and that was the Prince of Orange. He alone was ever ready to oppose the ambitious projects of the French king, and it was his persistent hostility which led eventually to their defeat.

During the days of his greatness Louis acquired and deserved the reputation of being a munificent patron of literature and art. But unfortunately for his reputation as a man, when his power was at its height he showed the greatest disposition to abuse it. His invasion of the duchy of Luxembourg in the year 1683 was not only wholly unjustifiable, but the operations were conducted with extraordinary barbarity. Unfortified towns were bombarded with red-hot shot; and in retaliation for one village that had been burnt by the Spaniards Louis ordered fifty to be burnt by his troops.[1]

His attack upon Genoa in the following year was more unjustifiable still. Ever since the days of Charles the Fifth that republic had been on terms of amity with Spain; and Louis, who was at this time apparently resolved to force a quarrel on the Genoese, complained, among other matters, that they were building four galleys for the service of the Spanish king. A powerful fleet was despatched to Genoa to seek redress, and the

[1] H. Martin, tom. xiv., p. 17, note.

terms demanded were of the most humiliating kind. The French admiral, a son of the famous Colbert, not only insisted that the galleys should be given up to him, but that the Doge, with four senators, should come to Versailles, which had recently been built at enormous expense, to ask pardon of the French king. To this outrageous message no reply was returned, and on the 18th of May, 1684, the French fleet opened fire. The bombardment continued for four successive days, during which upwards of 13,000 bombs were thrown into the city. The palace of the Doge was burned to the ground; many other palaces and public buildings and whole streets in the lower part of the city were destroyed. It was in vain that the Genoese appealed for assistance to Spain and to the Pope. The Spaniards were themselves helpless, and the Pope at this time was not on friendly terms with the King of France. But Louis was not satisfied with the havoc that had been wrought, although he abated some of his demands; in addition to the bombardment of their capital, he still insisted on inflicting on the Genoese a humiliation unprecedented in the history of a free people. He required the chief of the republic, along with four senators, to appear at Versailles and there to ask pardon for their alleged offences. On the 5th of May, 1685, accordingly, Lescaro, the Doge of Genoa, accompanied by the senators Lomellino, Garibaldi, Durazzo, and Salvago, arrived at Versailles. It is said that they were treated with studied insolence by Louvois, the minister of war. But they were mollified by the courteous reception accorded to them by the king, who seemed to regard them, not as rebellious and repentant vassals, but as friends and allies. The unrivalled urbanity of his demeanour even led them to forget, while in his presence, as they themselves confessed, the wrongs he had inflicted on their country.[1] Of such inestimable value are pleasing manners in the conduct of public affairs.

[1] Martin, tom. xiv., p. 16.

Whether a neutral State is justified in supplying ships of war to a belligerent is a question which has been much debated in modern times, and it is with the avowed purpose of preventing international disputes that the two principal maritime States of the world have now by express legislation prohibited their subjects from furnishing such vessels. The restriction thus imposed by Great Britain and the United States[1] is unquestionably founded on sound policy. It may affect the profits of a few individuals, but it would be unreasonable to maintain that upon that account the public peace should be seriously endangered. In the dispute between Louis and the Genoese the question did not arise, as France was not at war with Spain when the attack upon their capital took place.

But an event more startling than the bombardment of Genoa soon occupied the attention of Europe. On the 17th October, 1685, the Edict of Nantes, that most wise and just measure of Henry the Fourth, was revoked, and the demon of religious discord was once more let loose in France. To escape persecution it is estimated that not less than half a million of her citizens abandoned their country, and carried with them to foreign lands, not only their intelligence and industry, but an undying

[1] In 1793 the United States prohibited the furnishing of ships of war to a belligerent Power under the following circumstances:—In that year, during the second Presidency of General Washington, war had been declared by the French Republic against Great Britain, and a number of privateers had been fitted out with the sanction of the French Government to prey upon British commerce. The French maintained that in virtue of their commercial treaties with the United States they had a right to fit out such vessels; but this was disputed by the American Government. Washington and his ministers clearly saw that this privilege could not be conceded to France without the imminent risk of a renewal of the war with Great Britain; and being anxious to maintain peaceful relations with all European States, an Act of Congress was passed prohibiting any person within any "of the ports, harbours, bays, rivers, or other "waters of the United States, to fit out and arm, or procure to be fitted out and "armed, or knowingly to be concerned in the furnishing, fitting out, or arming, "of any ship or vessel with intent that such ship or vessel should be employed in "the service of any foreign prince or State, to cruise or commit hostilities upon "the subjects, citizens, or property of another foreign prince or state with whom "the United States were at peace," &c. On the model of this Act of Congress the two British Foreign Enlistment Acts of 1818 and 1870 have been framed. See "The Foreign Enlistment Act," by Frederick Waymouth Gibbs, C.B., p. 30.

S

hatred of the great king who had driven them into exile. It is stated by Vauban[1] that in the course of four years after the revocation of the edict nine thousand sailors, the best in France, twelve thousand soldiers, and six hundred officers had entered the service of the enemies of Louis. His flatterers had persuaded him that the "conversion" of the heretics was a sacred duty, that the principle of toleration proclaimed by his great ancestor was a fatal error, and that the lawful supremacy of the Church which a royal mandate had overthrown another royal mandate could restore. Louis had by this time married Madame Scarron. Bigotry, or the affectation of it, had become fashionable at court, and when the people were amused by the splendid ceremonials of Versailles and the edifying devotion of the courtiers, the heretics of Languedoc and Poitou were being hunted from their homes, and fortunate if they escaped torture or murder at the hands of the royal dragoons who were sent, in the language of the day, to "convert" them to the true religion. The barbarous treatment of these poor people produced a profound impression, not only in all Protestant countries, but throughout Europe; and it is certain that no act of Louis the Fourteenth more powerfully contributed to consolidate the strength of his enemies than the revocation of the Edict of Nantes.

During the persecution of the Huguenots the affairs of the Palatinate once more attracted the attention of the neighbouring States. In 1685 Charles Louis, the last male heir of his house, died, and the Duke of Neuburg succeeded without dispute as the nearest collateral relation of the deceased prince to all his feudal rights and dignities. But the King of France laid claim, in right of the Duchess of Orleans, the sister of the deceased prince, to all the *allodial* lands in the principality, which were of great extent, as well as to all the movable property belonging to the prince, including the artillery and all the munitions of war in the different

[1] H. Martin, t. xiv., liv. lxxxvi.

fortresses. These pretensions following so closely on the persecution of the Huguenots revived the fears of Catholic as well as Protestant States as to the designs of Louis. Not content with tyrannising over his own subjects, he seemed to be ever inventing new pretexts for meddling with the affairs of his neighbours, and the Emperor Leopold, who disputed his claims on the Palatinate, was induced to conclude at Augsburg a defensive league with the Prince of Orange, the object of which was to protect their respective dominions against the aggressions of the French king.

The Prince of Orange, who never ceased to regard Louis as the mortal enemy of his country and of Europe, was the real author of this league, and he fully expected and prepared for an attack upon Holland as soon as its existence became known at Versailles. But, fortunately for the prince, Louis was persuaded by Louvois, his minister of war, instead of attacking Holland to undertake the invasion of the Palatinate.

In the autumn of 1688 the Dauphin crossed the Rhine at the head of an army of 80,000 men, and speedily overran the whole electorate. This decisive step induced the King of Spain, the Duke of Savoy, and the Kings of Sweden and Denmark to join the League of Augsburg.[1] Meanwhile the ever-memorable revolution which placed the Prince of Orange on the English throne had taken place. The prince has been severely censured by many historians, more especially by those of France, for deposing his father-in-law, James the Second. But it may perhaps be said with greater truth that James deposed himself. As Duke of York he had given many proofs both of his courage and his aptitude for business; but from the time that he inherited the crown, in 1685, his infatuation was so extraordinary, his violations of the law were so flagrant, that nothing short of a miracle could have enabled him to retain it. A prince more scrupulous or less ambitious than William would have declined to

[1] Schoell, t. i., p. 394.

take advantage of the fatal errors of his father-in-law. But the position of the Prince of Orange was peculiar. From his youth upwards he had been engaged in a most unequal struggle with the colossal power of France, and to his energetic and enterprising spirit the prospect of being able to continue the contest on more equal terms as King of England was a temptation too strong to be resisted. It is impossible, therefore, to absolve him of the charge of ambition; but it cannot be denied that the bloodless revolution which placed him on the throne was eminently conducive to the peace and happiness of this island, as well as to the general interests of Europe.

The attack on the Palatinate happened most opportunely for William and his English adherents, for had the French invaded Holland instead, as had been originally intended, it would have been impossible for him to undertake an expedition to England at this time. As it was, he was speedily enabled, as King of Great Britain, to place himself at the head of the coalition against Louis, and threatened at once by so many enemies the French were forced to retire from the Palatinate.

And now commenced a scene to which even the dismal records of the Thirty Years' War afford no parallel. Previous to the evacuation of the Palatinate, Louvois, the minister of war, a man of a most insolent and arbitrary temper, obtained from the French king an order that the country should be laid waste. The savage edict was obeyed to the letter, and Heidelberg with its famous castle—magnificent still in its ruins—was first given to the flames. Spires, Mannheim, Worms, Oppenheim, Frankenthal, with innumerable villages, shared the same fate. It was in the midst of winter that these atrocious scenes were enacted, and thousands of the wretched inhabitants thus ruthlessly driven from their homes perished of cold and hunger. Even the dead were not spared, for at Heidelberg the tombs were rifled by marauding parties in search of buried treasures, and the remains of the electors scattered about the streets.

When Louis issued this infernal mandate, which made a desert of one of the fairest regions of Europe, he, no doubt, persuaded himself that he was acting in strict accordance with the laws of war, although he would have found some difficulty in showing a precedent, at least among Christian States, for his conduct. But what advantage he could expect from stirring up against him and his country the deadly hatred of the whole German race it is impossible to see. It has been said in extenuation of his conduct that he did not witness the frightful havoc that had been made, and further that when Louvois proposed to add Treves to the list of the proscribed cities he gave a prompt and peremptory refusal. It is further stated that he so far forgot his habitual self-possession as to aim a blow at that imperious minister when he said that he had already, without the knowledge of his master, sent orders for the burning of Treves. Louvois had told a falsehood simply to obtain the king's consent, and Treves did not share the fate of Heidelberg and Mannheim.[1] It is very possible, therefore, that upon reflection Louis may have regretted that his orders for the devastation of the Palatinate had been so cruelly obeyed. But the broad fact remains that without his sanction the work of destruction could not have been performed.

The intense exasperation created throughout Germany by these terrible scenes was speedily expressed in a resolution of the Diet expelling from the empire all French subjects of whatever grade or profession, and prohibiting, under pain of treason, all commercial intercourse with France.[2]

Only one ally now remained to Louis, and that was the exiled King of England, who, notwithstanding his misfortunes and his follies, had been received at the

---

[1] It is said that the king would have struck his minister but for the presence of Madame de Maintenon. Madame Scarron had now assumed this name, and she interposed in time to prevent so scandalous a scene.—Saint Simon, t. xiii., p. 32.

[2] H. Martin, t. xiv., p. 107.

French court with every mark of courtesy and consideration. It was of paramount importance to France, surrounded as she was by exasperated enemies, to replace James on his throne, and no efforts were spared to effect this object. William had been with all legal and constitutional formalities acknowledged as king both in England and in Scotland; but the people of Ireland, or at least a great majority of them, adhered to the ancient faith, and were prepared, as soon as an opportunity offered, to espouse the cause of a monarch who had lost his throne mainly through his zeal for his religion. Ireland, therefore, was the most vulnerable point in William's new dominions, and to Ireland accordingly James repaired in the spring of 1689. He landed at Kinsale on the 22nd of March, and on the 20th of May he summoned a Parliament at Dublin, which acknowledged him as lawful king of Great Britain and Ireland.

Louis had by this time, with infinite pains, created a great navy. It was his undoubted object to make France the dominant Power at sea as she already was on land; and he was enabled, without interruption from the English cruisers, to send a small army to Ireland for the support of James. It was expected at the time, from the interest that he took in this expedition, that Louis, among his many other projects, entertained the design of eventually annexing Ireland to his dominions. But there seems to have been not the slightest foundation for this suggestion.[1] Louis had quite enough on his hands without attempting a conquest which, if successful, must have weakened instead of strengthening his dominions. His motives for supporting James were sufficiently strong and obvious to account for all he did on his behalf.

The presence of James in Ireland, the growing strength of the French navy, and the incessant rumours of Jacobite plots both in England and Scotland, ren-

---

[1] Ranke, Hist. of England, vol. iv., p. 535, note.

dered the position of William extremely critical at this time. But on the 12th of July, 1690, he encountered his rival and his French auxiliaries on the banks of the Boyne, and he there won his first and last decisive victory. James made no attempt to rally his adherents after his defeat, but retired once more to France, to the great disappointment and displeasure of Louis. Two days before the battle of the Boyne the French fleet, under the command of Admiral Tourville, had defeated the combined English and Dutch fleets off Beachy Head. The French navy had now proved to be a match, and more than a match, for the two maritime Powers, and Louis even hoped, with the superiority thus acquired, to prevent the return of William to England until a rising had taken place in favour of the banished king. But all these projects were defeated by the flight of James.

The victory of Beachy Head was not the only French success of this year. On the 1st of July the Prince of Waldeck, who commanded the allies in Flanders, was totally defeated at Fleurus by Luxembourg. On the 18th of August the Duke of Savoy was defeated by Marshal Catinat at Marsaglia in Piedmont, and in Catalonia the Duc de Noailles was still master of the greater portion of the province. Except in Ireland the French were everywhere victorious. Another battle, far more disastrous to the Irish Catholics and their French allies than that of the Boyne, was fought at Aughrim on the anniversary of William's victory.[1] The Irish on this fatal day sustained a crushing defeat, and both Galway and Limerick soon afterwards surrendered to the conquerors.

In this year Louis had taken the field in person; but beyond the capture of Mons,[2] which the royal invalid of Spain imagined to be in England, no action of importance took place. The French king had not yet abandoned his

---

[1] The battle of the Boyne was fought on the 12th of July, 1690; that of Aughrim on the 12th of July, 1691.
[2] Mons was taken on the 9th of April, 1691.

purpose of restoring James to his throne, and two powerful fleets were fitted out, the one at Brest, the other at Toulon, with the design that when united they should make a descent upon the English coast. But Tourville, who commanded the Brest squadron, emboldened by his success at Beachy Head, ventured to attack the English fleet without waiting for the Toulon contingent, and was defeated and driven back to La Hogue with heavy loss. To William this victory was of immense importance. It not only avenged the disaster of Beachy Head, but it proved fatal for the time to the hopes of James and his adherents.

William, meanwhile, had taken the field in Flanders, but the most remarkable feature of the successive campaigns in which he now engaged was their singularly indecisive character. Town after town was taken and retaken, great battles were fought entailing an immense loss of life, but at the end of each year the issue seemed as doubtful as at the commencement. On the 3rd of August, 1692, William surprised Luxembourg at Steinkirk. The battle was long and doubtful; but the French commander, by the most heroic efforts, eventually succeeded in defeating his assailants. On this occasion the princes of the blood, among whom was the Duke de Chartres, a boy of sixteen, especially distinguished themselves. At the most critical period of the day they leaped from their horses and charged on foot, at the head of the household troops and Swiss guards, bearing down all opposition and committing terrible havoc among the English regiments, which consisted chiefly of raw levies.[1] The loss on both sides seems to have been nearly equal, but William was finally driven back at all points.

In the following year[2] was fought the great battle of Landen. William was on this occasion attacked by

---

[1] Macaulay says that five regiments were entirely cut to pieces. William also lost on this occasion many officers of distinction.—Vol. iv., p. 282.
[2] On the 18th of July, 1693.

Luxembourg, and once more defeated, with the loss, it is said, of not less than 20,000 men. At the close of this terrible day there occurred one of those pleasing incidents which occasionally relieve the stern realities of war. Ruvigny, a distinguished Huguenot, who, to escape persecution, had abandoned his country and entered the service of William, was taken while retreating from the field. His captors knew well what fate awaited him if he were made a prisoner; but in the spirit of true chivalry they pretended not to recognise him, and in the hurry and confusion allowed him to escape.[1]

So great was the number of standards and other trophies taken in this battle that Luxembourg was nicknamed "the upholsterer of Notre Dame." But he turned this great victory to no account. Instead of marching upon Brussels, which he might have captured at this time without striking a blow, he remained inactive in his camp while William was receiving reinforcements from every side and steadily preparing for a fresh encounter. The indecisive character of these campaigns is, therefore, best explained by the character of the two commanders. Luxembourg never lost a battle, and William never gained one; but it might be said that the one was never more inactive than after a victory, and the other rarely more formidable than after a defeat.

Notwithstanding the defeat at La Hogue, France still remained powerful enough at sea to cause serious interruption to the commerce of the maritime States. Having little commerce of her own to protect, she was enabled to employ her whole naval power in destroying that of her rivals. In this year a great fleet of English and Dutch merchantmen, proceeding to the Mediterranean under convoy, was intercepted and dispersed by Tourville, and the loss sustained on this occasion by London and Amsterdam was immense.[2] At this time, too, Jean Bart, a noted sea-rover—the Paul Jones of the

---

[1] Martin, vol. xiv., p. 177.
[2] Macaulay, vol. iv., p. 413.

seventeenth century—being provided with letters of marque by the French king, became the terror of the North Sea from the wholesale depredations committed by his cruisers.

The campaign of 1694 was productive of no incident of importance, but in the following year William laid siege to Namur. He no longer had Luxembourg for an opponent, but Namur was gallantly defended by Marshal Boufflers, who only surrendered after all hope of relief had failed. The capture of this important fortress was the most signal triumph achieved by William in this war. Hitherto Louis had been invariably successful, but his enemies were now persuaded that the tide had turned. Meanwhile he had been negotiating in secret to bring the war to a close, not that he desired a permanent peace, but to enable him to prepare for another conflict which he saw impending, and in which he had resolved to take a leading part. The King of Spain was in a hopeless decline, and on his death the question of the succession to his still vast dominions was one which must occupy the immediate attention of Europe. To break up the Grand Alliance Louis first made overtures to the Duke of Savoy, and concluded with that prince a separate treaty of peace. He next opened negotiations with the Dutch, and eventually it was agreed that plenipotentiaries of all the Powers should meet at Ryswick in the spring of 1697 with the view of concluding a general peace. But, as was invariably the case in this age, months were spent in diplomatic bickering without any prospect of a result until the two commanders—Boufflers and the Earl of Portland—met one day by appointment in an orchard near Brussels, and after an hour's friendly converse settled between them the preliminaries of a treaty between their respective sovereigns. It was this incident which caused it to be said at the time that while the ambassadors were making war, the generals were making peace.

The most important article of the treaty as it regarded William and Louis was the recognition of William's title to the crown of Great Britain. Louis had steadfastly up to this time maintained the doctrine of hereditary right as paramount and indefeasible, and he must have been sincerely desirous of peace to consent to acknowledge as a lawful king a prince who owed his crown to his own subjects. Louis also pledged his royal word that he would not directly or indirectly lend assistance to any of the enemies of William. This provision referred to James the Second and his family, who still continued to reside in France; and William, on his part, engaged that the jointure which had been settled by Act of Parliament on Mary of Este, the queen of James, should continue to be paid.

Between the States of Holland and France the only important article of the treaty referred to Pondicherry, which was ceded to the French king.

To Spain Louis undertook to restore Barcelona and various places in Catalonia; and in Flanders the duchy of Luxembourg and various towns, but by no means all, that he had captured since the treaty of Nimeguen.

After this treaty had been signed by the representatives of Savoy, Great Britain, Spain, and Holland, the ambassadors of the emperor loudly complained that they had been deceived. They insisted that their allies ought not to have concluded peace without their consent. To this the allies replied that it was in consequence of the unwarrantable procrastination and indecision of the imperial court that they were compelled to come to terms without its concurrence. After some months of further negotiation the emperor finally acceded to the treaty, and for a few years at least peace was restored to Europe.

With respect to the claims of the Duchess of Orleans on the Palatinate, which had originally furnished a pretext for the war, it was agreed that the matters in dispute should be settled amicably by the emperor and the King of France, and in case of their disagreement that the decision of the Pope should be final. Various towns and fortresses which had been captured during the war were restored to the emperor, but the important city of Strasburg was formally ceded to France, and the navigation of the Rhine was declared to be free, not only to the subjects of the contracting parties, but to all nations. It was further provided that no additional imposts should under any pretext be levied on the vessels navigating the river.[1] We are agreeably surprised to find in a treaty of the seventeenth century provisions for the encouragement of commerce so liberal and just.

The Duke of Lorraine was restored to his dominions, but it was stipulated that the fortifications of Nancy should be razed, and the same provision was made as to the fortifications of Bitsche and Hombourg. The towns of Sarrelouis and Longwi were ceded to France, and she retained the right of a free passage through the duchy at all times for her armies.[2] The Duke of Lorraine, who was now restored to his dominions, was the son of him who had shared with John Sobieski in 1684 the glory of defeating the Turks under the walls of Vienna. Unlike his father, he did not seek distinction in war, but throughout his reign devoted all his energies to promote the welfare of his people, and the lord of this petty principality has been justly eulogised as the most virtuous and enlightened prince of the age in which he lived.[3]

A short time before acceding to the treaty of Ryswick the Emperor Leopold had obtained a signal success over the Turks. On the 11th September, 1697, the imperial commander, Prince Eugene, encountered the Sultan in person at Zanta, on the banks of the Theiss, and gained a decisive victory.[4] The loss of the

---

[1] Schoell, tom. i., p. 441.
[2] Ibid., p. 443.
[3] See the character of this prince in Voltaire, Siècle de Louis XIV., cap. xvii.
[4] Hammer Purgstall, vol. iii., p. 899.

Turks in this battle was enormous, and the treaty of Carlowitz was the result, by which they surrendered many of their most important conquests in Europe. To the emperor they abandoned, after a struggle of two hundred years, their acquisitions in Hungary and the whole of Transylvania; to the Venetians they surrendered the Morea and a considerable portion of Dalmatia; to the Czar of Muscovy Azoff; and to the King of Poland Kaminieck and the fertile province of Podolia. But the Sultan refused to deliver up to the Austrians a distinguished Hungarian refugee, Tekeli, who had sought an asylum in his dominions.[1] We have seen in the present age a similar demand made on the Sultan by the Austrian Government with a similar result.[2]

[1] Martin, Hist. de France, vol. xiv., p. 350.
[2] As to the demand of the Austrian Government for the Hungarian refugees after the war of 1849, see the Annual Register of that year.

CHAPTER X.

FROM THE TREATY OF RYSWICK TO THE TREATY OF UTRECHT.

The general peace restored by the treaties of Ryswick and Carlowitz was but of short duration. The great question of the Spanish succession still remained unsettled, and threatened at any moment to lead to endless complications. Unless the leading Powers could come to some definite arrangement before the death of the king a renewal of the war on a more extended scale than ever might be regarded as inevitable. With the professed object of guarding against these obvious dangers Louis made secret overtures to William, as King of England and Stadtholder of Holland, and a treaty[1] was eventually concluded between them, the purpose of which was to effect an amicable partition of the Spanish dominions on the death of Charles the Second.

By the law of Castile which regulated the succession of the monarchy, the dauphin, being the eldest son of the eldest daughter of Philip the Fourth, was the undoubted heir of Charles. But Maria Theresa, the mother of the dauphin, had on her marriage not only renounced for herself and her descendants all claim to the crown of Spain, but this renunciation was confirmed by the treaty of the Pyrenees, and subsequently by the Cortes.

The second daughter of Philip the Fourth, Margaret Theresa, had married the Emperor Leopold, and dying soon afterwards had left an only daughter, who was married to the Elector of Bavaria. She, too, soon died after her marriage, leaving an only son. It was contended that this prince had a preferable claim to that of the dauphin because, although his grandmother Margaret

[1] In October, 1698.

Theresa had on her marriage with the emperor renounced all claim to the crown of Spain, that renunciation had not been confirmed by the emperor.

Lastly, the Emperor Leopold claimed as being the only lineal male descendant of Philip and Joanna, the parents of the Emperor Charles the Fifth.

Between these three claimants Louis, wholly disregarding the treaty of the Pyrenees, now proposed that the Spanish dominions should be partitioned on the death of Charles the Second.

By the first of the so-called partition treaties it was agreed between England, Holland, and France that the dauphin should have the kingdom of the Two Sicilies, together with various ports in Tuscany, and the province of Guipuzcoa; that the Archduke Charles, the second son of the emperor, should have the duchy of Milan; and that the electoral prince of Bavaria, a boy of six years old, should succeed to the whole of the remaining dominions of Spain, as well in Europe as in America. But this the first of the partition treaties was of very short duration, for the electoral prince of Bavaria, upon whom it had been designed to settle the crown of Spain, died[1] of the small-pox a few months after its conclusion. This unexpected event led to a second treaty of partition between Louis and the maritime Powers, by which, in addition to the territories allotted to him by the first, the dauphin was to obtain Lorraine, and in exchange for his paternal dominions the Duke of Lorraine was to be invested with the duchy of Milan. The remainder of the Spanish dominions were to be settled on the Archduke Charles, provided he agreed to accept the terms proposed within three months after the execution of the treaty.

It may be asked why William, who had all along so steadily opposed the aggressive designs of Louis, was induced to consent to terms which promised so materially to strengthen the naval power of France, if not to

[1] On 8th February, 1699.

render her mistress of the Mediterranean. To explain his conduct we must look to the circumstances in which he was placed at the time by the action of the political parties in England. No sooner was the treaty of Ryswick signed than an earnest desire was manifested throughout the country for the immediate disbanding of the naval and military forces. By the people at large the maintenance of the balance of power among the Continental States was regarded with comparative indifference, but as the ruler of Holland William considered it essential to the security of the United Provinces, and he regarded the interests of the two maritime Powers as identical. As both the rival factions in England agreed in opposing his views, and even insisted on the dismissal of his Dutch guards, he was so deeply mortified at the attitude of the House of Commons that he seriously thought at this time of resigning his crown and retiring to Holland.[1] It was while thus wholly deprived of the support of Parliament that he was induced to consent to the partition treaties. One great object he, no doubt, sought to effect by means of these treaties—namely, the exclusion of the house of Bourbon from the throne of Spain.

The partition treaties were never carried into effect, but they unhappily furnished precedents which throughout the last century, and even in this, have led to an incalculable amount of mischief. And, indeed, the notion of parcelling out whole provinces, and even kingdoms, without regard to the interests or the inclinations of the inhabitants, is so opposed to every principle of sound policy and justice that we cannot be surprised at the result. It is to be observed, however, that the attempt in the present instance to arrange the affairs of Europe in anticipation of the death of the Spanish king was far more justifiable than various transactions of a similar kind that have taken place since. The circumstances were peculiar and unprecedented; the danger to be apprehended was great and imminent; and it cannot be

[1] Ranke, vol. v., p. 190, and the letters to Heinsius there cited.

doubted that, whatever may have been the secret views of Louis, William at all events was sincere in his desire to avert it. It is further to be observed that if the Prince of Bavaria had lived there was a strong probability that peace might be preserved. But the death of that child placed the rival houses of Bourbon and Hapsburg in immediate and direct antagonism, and the prospect of an amicable adjustment of their claims became all but hopeless.

When the existence of the partition treaties became known at Madrid the indignation of the king was extreme. That two foreign potentates, one of whom was the descendant of "that arch rebel," William the Silent, should have arrogated to themselves the right of disposing of his dominions he not unjustly regarded as an unpardonable affront, and he felt the insult the more inasmuch as he was wholly powerless to resent it. Nothing, indeed, could be more pitiable than the condition of Charles during the last year of his life. The rival partisans of France and Austria by turns gained the ascendency over the unhappy king; and, unable to decide between them, he turned at length in despair to his spiritual advisers, and by them the great question of the Spanish succession was eventually decided.

Portocarrero, the Archbishop of Toledo, a most able but unscrupulous prelate, had been gained over by the emissaries of France, and at his instigation Charles applied to Pope Innocent the Twelfth, by whose decision he declared that he was willing to abide. "Having no " children," he said, " and being obliged to appoint an " heir to the Spanish crown from a foreign family, we " find such great obscurity in the law of succession and " in the circumstances of the case that we are unable to " form a settled determination. Strict justice is our " aim, and to be able to decide with that justice we " have offered up constant prayers to the Supreme Being. " We are anxious to act rightly, and we have recourse " to your holiness as to an infallible guide, entreating

T

"you to consult with the cardinals and divines whom you judge to be most able and sincere, and after having attentively examined the testaments of our ancestors, from Ferdinand the Catholic to Philip the Fourth, the decrees of the Cortes, the renunciations of the Infantas Anna and Maria Theresa, the marriage articles, compacts, and all the Acts of the Austrian princes from Philip the Handsome to the present time, to decide by the rules of right and equity."[1] Thus was the question of the Spanish succession, which for twenty years had perplexed the statesmen of Europe, eventually referred to the decision of the Pope. Never, even when the Papal power was in its zenith, had a cause of more vast international importance been discussed at the Vatican than that which was submitted to Innocent the Twelfth.

But the day had long gone by when the Pope could have acted as an independent umpire between the rival monarchs of France and Austria. Portocarrero had not ventured to propose a reference to Innocent the Twelfth without the certain knowledge that the Pontiff was at this time, from jealousy of the designs of Austria, devoted to the interests of France. But the question notwithstanding was discussed at the Vatican with all due formality and deliberation. The competing claims of France and Austria were submitted by the Pope to the cardinals Albani,[2] Spinola, and Spada, who, after an interval of forty days, reported in favour of the dauphin. In announcing the decision to the Spanish king the Pope expressed himself as follows :—"Your majesty ought not to put the interests of the house of Austria in competition with those of eternity, and of that account of your actions which you are soon to give before the great Judge of Kings, who is no respecter

---

[1] Coxe, House of Austria, vol. ii., p. 472.
[2] Innocent the Twelfth died a few weeks before the King of Spain—namely, on 27th September, 1700. He was succeeded by the Cardinal Albani, who was elected on the 23rd November following, and who assumed the title of Clement the Eleventh.—Martin, Hist., tom. xiv., p. 373.

" of persons. Neither should you be ignorant that the
" children of the dauphin are the rightful heirs of the
" crown, and that in opposition to them neither the
" archduke nor any member of the Austrian family has
" the smallest legitimate pretension. In proportion to the
" importance of the succession the more flagrant will be
" the injustice of excluding the rightful heirs, and the
" more surely will you draw on yourself the vengeance
" of Heaven. It is therefore your duty to omit no
" precaution which your wisdom can suggest to render
" justice where justice is due, and to secure by every
" means in your power the undivided succession of the
" Spanish monarchy to a son of the dauphin."[1]

At first the letter of the Pope instead of relieving only added to the perplexity of the unhappy king. Although incapable himself of coming to any decision, the ties of blood induced him to lean to the side of Austria; but, on the other hand, he justly dreaded the immense power of France, and he dreaded still more the spiritual censures of the Church and the terrible consequences they might entail both in this world and in the next. His superstitious fears eventually prevailed, and on the 2nd of October, 1700, he was induced to sign a will, which had no doubt been previously prepared, and which declared the Duke of Anjou, the second son of the dauphin, to be his heir. On the 1st of November following the last Spanish king of the Austrian branch ended his miserable life.

On the day of his death the will was read in the presence of the Council of State, and with reference to the succession it contained the following passage:—
" From various consultations of the ministers of state
" and justice, it appears that the reason on which the
" renunciations of the Infantas Anna and Maria Theresa,
" the Queens of France, our aunts, were founded, was
" the danger of uniting the succession of France and
" Spain in the same person. That fundamental objec-

[1] Coxe, vol. ii., p. 472.

"tion being removed, the right of succession subsists in the nearest relation, conformably to the laws of Spain; and this relation is the second son of the Dauphin of France. For this reason he is declared successor to the Spanish dominions."[1] It was further provided that should the Duke of Anjou die without issue, or become heir to the French crown, the Duke of Berri, the third son of the dauphin, was to succeed on the same conditions. Failing him, the Spanish monarchy was entailed on the Archduke Charles, but on condition that the crowns of Spain and of the empire should not be united; and failing all these heirs, the succession was to devolve on the house of Savoy.

Louis had displayed consummate skill in obtaining for his grandson the crown of Spain. The hesitation he publicly expressed before accepting that splendid inheritance has even induced some historians to believe that he took no part in the intrigues at Rome and at Madrid, and that, in fact, the transfer of the Spanish monarchy to the house of Bourbon "was the work of "Providence, and conducted without the artifices of "man." It is only necessary to observe that before arriving at this conclusion we must close our eyes to all the previous and all the subsequent policy of Louis the Fourteenth.

On the 24th of November the Duke of Anjou was proclaimed King of Spain, at Madrid, by the title of Philip the Fifth, and on the 18th of February following he made his entry into the capital, and was received by his new subjects with every mark of enthusiasm. The most important provision in the treaty of the Pyrenees was thus deliberately set aside; but Louis contended that although the letter of the treaty was violated its spirit was preserved, as ample provision had been made by the testament of Charles to prevent the union of the two crowns. With the exception of the emperor, the other Powers either expressly or tacitly acknowledged

[1] See copy of the will in Dumont, vol. ii., part 2, p. 485.

the new king. But Leopold regarded as a mortal affront to his house the elevation of a French prince to the Spanish throne, and resolved forthwith to dispute his title. But he sought in vain for allies to aid him in the struggle. England had no desire at this time to recommence the war; the princes and states of Italy were for the most part in the interest of France, and the princes of Germany were at this time watching with alarm the triumphant progress of the youthful King of Sweden, Charles the Twelfth. No sooner had that monarch succeeded to the crown than the neighbouring princes of Denmark, Russia, and Poland, presuming on his youth and inexperience, formed the design of robbing him of a large portion of his dominions. But to the amazement of Europe, the King of Sweden, who was only eighteen years old, replied to this base attempt of his neighbours by suddenly invading Denmark, marching upon Copenhagen, and compelling the king to sue for peace. He next advanced against the Russians and defeated them at Narva with heavy loss. He next invaded Poland, and defeated a combined army of Poles and Saxons with a force which did not number by one half that of his enemies. Whichever way he turned the youthful conqueror seemed irresistible, and the German princes intently watched his movements, uncertain whether he might not, like his great predecessor Gustavus, lead his victorious battalions to the Rhine or to the Danube. To France he would no doubt be a welcome ally, but fortunately for Austria Charles was not disposed to meddle with the politics of Western Europe. He had not yet sufficiently humbled his two most potent enemies, the King of Poland and the Czar. The emperor meanwhile sought to gain to his side two of the German princes by raising to the dignity of an elector the Duke of Hanover, and acknowledging the Elector of Brandenburg as King of Prussia. The latter prince was proclaimed at Kœnigsberg on the 15th of January, 1701, under the title of Frederick the First. It is worthy of note that the Pope protested against the royal title being bestowed on the Elector of Brandenburg,[1] on the ground that the Pontiff alone had the privilege of creating kings. The favour thus shown to Prussia and Hanover excited much irritation among the princes of the empire, and a secret treaty was concluded between Bavaria and France,[2] the professed object of which was the maintenance of the treaties of Westphalia, Nimeguen, and Ryswick.

Louis was well aware when he accepted the crown of Spain for his grandson that war with Austria was inevitable; but it was entirely his own fault that the contest, which at first promised to be a duel between the rival houses of Bourbon and Hapsburgh, involved eventually the whole of the Western Powers. No sooner was his grandson proclaimed at Madrid than Louis claimed in his name to garrison with French troops the line of Spanish fortresses in the Netherlands. To prevent these fortresses from being annexed to France an infinite amount of blood had been shed, and this outrageous claim of the French king created the utmost alarm both in Holland and in England. But as Louis well knew, England, in obedience to the popular clamour, had disbanded her army and was practically powerless, and in the name of the King of Spain he proceeded forthwith to place French garrisons in Luxembourg, Namur, Maure, Charleroi, and even the seaports of Nieuport and Ostend.

The emperor meanwhile had commenced the war without a single ally, but it soon appeared that with Prince Eugene to lead his armies he required none. That enterprising chief, who, in defiance of the orders of the Aulic Council, had fought and annihilated the army of the Sultan at Zanta, crossed the Tyrolese Alps by forced marches in the summer of 1701, and defeated Catinat, the most renowned of the French commanders,

---

[1] Martin, vol. xiv., p. 367.
[2] On 9th March, 1701. Schoell, t. ii., p. 22.

at Carpi. Marshal Villeroi, who was sent to supersede Catinat in consequence of his misfortune, subsequently attacked Eugene in the neighbourhood of Brescia, but was repulsed with heavy loss, and in spite of all the efforts of the French and Spaniards, powerfully aided by the Duke of Savoy, Eugene maintained himself in Lombardy throughout the winter.

But although the emperor had drawn the sword, and Louis was in possession of the Spanish fortresses, it was still the opinion of William that a general war might be avoided. With this object he commissioned the Earl of Marlborough to negotiate a treaty with Holland and the emperor. The antecedents of Marlborough had not been such as to inspire confidence in any party. He had been enriched and ennobled by James the Second, but had deserted that prince at the most critical period of his career, and since his desertion was suspected of having carried on a secret correspondence with the exiled family. But political honesty is rare in times of revolution, and William, although doubtful hitherto of the character and objects of Marlborough, was well aware of his great abilities when he was sent on this important mission. On the 7th of September, 1701,[1] a treaty was concluded between the emperor, the States, and England, which, so far as the latter Power was concerned, might probably have remained a dead letter but for the subsequent conduct of the French king. He not only did not reject the terms proposed by the allies, but professed in general terms his earnest desire for the restoration of peace. Within a very few days, however, after the treaty was signed an event occurred which rendered the maintenance of peace impossible.

On the 16th of September, 1701, James the Second died at St. Germains, and Louis, in direct violation of the fourth article of the treaty of Ryswick, forthwith acknowledged the son of James and of Mary of Modena

[1] Schoell, t. ii., p. 29.

as the King of Great Britain and Ireland. It is said that Louis was induced to take this dangerous step by the solicitations of Mary and of Madame de Maintenon,[1] and that he yielded partly from his inability to resist their entreaties, and partly from a chivalrous sentiment of compassion for the exiled family, whom it is admitted upon all hands he invariably treated with princely hospitality. If Louis had never broken any other treaty the explanation would be a plausible, perhaps even a creditable one. But he so frequently and so flagrantly violated his engagements that we are driven to the conclusion that he took this extraordinary step in the belief that the English were at this time so averse to a renewal of the war that he could take it with impunity.

But in this he was egregiously mistaken. William was in Holland at the time when the tidings reached him, and he forthwith desired his ambassador to quit Versailles without taking leave. In England the indignation was all but universal. That Louis should, in open contempt of his engagements, seek to set up, as a rival to the throne, a son, and, as many said, a supposititious son, of the exiled king, was regarded as a national affront of the most unpardonable kind; and when William reached London in the autumn of this year he was received with an amount of genuine enthusiasm which he had never before witnessed. With the eye of the experienced statesman he saw and seized his opportunity. Although the House of Commons was not a twelvemonth old, he resolved on a fresh appeal to the nation; and the result was a Parliament which readily voted all the men and money that he desired. He was once more in a position to take the field against the indefatigable enemy of European liberty and peace; but

[1] The ministers of Louis did their utmost to dissuade him from a course so dangerous in itself and so fatal to his reputation. Fénélon, who had been preceptor to the Duke of Burgundy, the elder son of the dauphin, and was now Archbishop of Cambrai, joined in the remonstrance of the council; but nothing could shake the resolution of Louis.—Voltaire, Louis XIV., cap. xvii.; Macaulay, vol. v., cap. xxv.

his great career was fast drawing to a close, and he never left England again. A constitution never strong was worn out by incessant toil of mind and body. He died on the 8th of March, 1702, an old man at fifty-one.

Voltaire has drawn a comparison between William and Louis very much to the advantage of the latter; and it must be admitted that the English king was wholly deficient in those attractive qualities which were conspicuous in his great rival. But beyond his liberal patronage of literature and art it may well be asked what benefits Louis conferred upon the world in the fifty years during which he was absolute master of France? It cannot be denied that he cruelly persecuted his subjects on account of their religion, and that in pursuit of the phantom of universal monarchy he involved his neighbours in perpetual strife. And what was the result of all his deeply-laid intrigues, his broken treaties, and his successful and unsuccessful wars? To bring upon his country an amount of misery and disaster only to be surpassed in the history of him who in the early part of the present century followed in his footsteps, who reaped a still richer harvest of glory, and whose downfall was still more signal and decisive. At times, too, William has been compared to Cromwell; but between the great Protector and the hero of the Revolution the resemblance is faint indeed. Cromwell, in the present age, has been the object of more unbounded eulogy than he ever was before; but what real service he rendered to his country, or to the world at large, it would be hard to say. That a private individual should have rendered himself the absolute master of three kingdoms was a circumstance unprecedented in modern times, and the homage paid by foreign States to the successful leader of the great rebellion was flattering to the national vanity. To the serious errors of his foreign policy allusion has been already made—errors which it required all the heroic energy of William and all the genius of Marlborough to repair; and of his barbarous policy in Ireland we are still reaping, and are likely to continue to reap, the bitter fruits. Nor was he more successful in his domestic policy, for all his attempts at legislation culminated at last in the establishment of a despotism far more intolerable than that which he had overthrown. To William belongs the distinction of having solved, perhaps, the most difficult of all political problems. He proved to the world, during his reign of thirteen years, that a constitutional monarchy was a practicable form of government. It must have been a hard task, for a prince of his strong will, and with his habits of command, when thwarted by opposing factions, to walk within the limits of the constitution which he had sworn to observe. We can perceive, from his confidential letters, that the effort was a painful one;[1] but it was fortunate alike for his reputation and for his adopted country that he was restrained by a sense of duty, or of interest, from following the evil example of his predecessors. Yet, with all his great qualities, William was never a popular king. Although constant in his attachments, like most men of grave and earnest natures, his manner, except to intimate friends, was cold and reserved, even at times ungracious; and those who remembered the unaffected affability and ready wit of Charles were apt to draw comparisons by no means flattering to his nephew. But the defects of William were essentially of a superficial kind. The great and permanent importance of the work he accomplished must ever render him one of the most prominent characters of modern history.

To oppose the dangerous ascendency of France had been the ruling passion of William's life, and he may be said to have bequeathed to Marlborough the task of completing the work that he had left unfinished. There have been many great commanders in the world, but if we are to believe the concurring testimony of friends and enemies, none greater than that renowned

[1] See his letters to Heinsius.—Ranke, vol. v., p. 190.

general. Of him it has been truly said that he never laid siege to a town or a fortress that he did not take, and that he never fought a battle that he did not win. His enemies were wont to add that he never served a prince or a cause that for an adequate consideration he was not ready to betray. But in times of revolution consistency is rare among public men; and whatever may have been the political delinquencies of Marlborough, it is universally allowed that he possessed in a pre-eminent degree every quality requisite for success in war. And this was not all; for a temper that was absolutely imperturbable, an unerring knowledge of men, and a clear and solid judgment, rendered him no less formidable in negotiation than in the field.

Queen Anne, on her accession, lost no time in expressing her intention of following in the footsteps of her predecessor, "who," she declared in her first speech in Parliament, "was the great support, not only of these " kingdoms, but of all Europe,"[1] and she recommended two measures to their special attention : the first that every effort should be made in concert with her allies " to reduce the exorbitant power of France;" the second to consider the best means of effecting a union with Scotland—a matter which William had always considered of the first importance, and which he had recommended to the attention of Parliament only a week before his death.

War was formally declared against France and Spain by the Allied Powers on the 15th of May, 1702; and Marlborough, not without much opposition on the part of the Dutch, was appointed commander-in-chief in the Netherlands. His army, consisting of English, Dutch, Prussians, and Hanoverians, numbered about 60,000 men; and as the enemy persistently declined to risk a battle, he resolved to attack the line of fortresses on the Meuse; and he besieged and captured in succession, in

[1] History of Queen Anne by Lord Stanhope, p. 39.

the course of two months, Venlo, Ruremond, and the important city of Liège, thus cutting off the communications of the French with the Lower Rhine.

Although Boufflers, who commanded the army of Louis in the Netherlands, declined at this time to meet the allies in the field, he is said to have given his sanction to a design which could not be justified by the rules of warfare recognised and practised by Christian States. The scheme in question is explained in a despatch from the English envoy at the Hague as follows:[1]—" Here is
" discovered a most villainous design to pierce a *digue* in
" North Holland to drain the whole country. It was
" first proposed by a Papist gentleman of this country of
" a good estate, bred by the Jesuits at Emmerich: his
" name Van Eysel. He proposed it to Monsieur d'Avaux
" when last bred, who recommended him to Boufflers,
" then in Flanders, *who relished it so well* as to send him
" with it to Monsieur Torcy at Paris, and after it had
" all their approbations, and the man came back hither
" to execute it, he and two of his accomplices were seized,
" and finding their own letters produced against them,
" besides two witnesses *vivâ voce*, they have confessed
" the fact." The three persons in question were afterwards put to death.

Questions of ceremonial were frequently debated in the course of this war, and seem at times to have exercised an important influence over the policy of princes. In this year the young King of Spain visited his Italian dominions, and it had been arranged that an interview should take place between him and the Grand Duke of Tuscany at Leghorn, but Philip insisted that when they met the duke should take his place on his left side. The duke on his part was equally resolved that his proper place was the right, and as neither would give way the projected interview did not take place.

A meeting did take place between Philip and the Duke of Savoy at Acqui; but not only did the King

[1] History of Queen Anne by Lord Stanhope, p. 55.

of Spain refuse his right hand to his own father-in-law,[1] but he refused to allow him the use of an armchair. It has been suspected, and it seems highly probable, that this stupid adherence to the rigid ceremonial of Versailles in which Philip had been trained induced the Duke of Savoy shortly afterwards to renounce his engagements with France and Spain and join the Grand Alliance. That Marlborough was superior to the puerile prejudices of the day we learn from the fact that he so far forgot his dignity as commander of the allied armies as on a certain occasion to hand a napkin while at supper to the newly-created King of Prussia. It is said that his Prussian majesty was so flattered by this piece of unlooked-for courtesy that he cheerfully continued to supply his contingent to the allied army throughout the war.[2]

In the following year the Duke of Savoy abandoned the French and joined the Grand Alliance; and his example was followed by the King of Portugal, who, on the promise of certain frontier towns in Estremadura, consented to acknowledge the Archduke Charles as King of Spain, and to furnish, at his own cost, a contingent of 15,000 men. The treaty was signed on the 16th of May, 1703, by Mr. Paul Methuen, ambassador of Queen Anne at Lisbon, on the part of England, and as it guaranteed to England several important commercial advantages, it is generally known by his name.[3]

The desertion of the Duke of Savoy and the accession of the King of Portugal to the ranks of his enemies were not the only misfortunes which befell Louis at this time. A serious insurrection in Languedoc, the result of the cruel measures adopted for the suppression of the Protestants, led to innumerable atrocities on both sides, and gave employment to a considerable body of troops

---

[1] There was a double connection between the houses of Bourbon and Savoy, two grandsons of Louis—namely, the Duke of Burgundy and the Duke of Anjou—having married two daughters of Victor Amadeus of Savoy.
[2] Voltaire, cap. xviii.
[3] Schoell, t. ii., p. 30.

whose presence was required elsewhere. Marlborough meanwhile had been entirely thwarted in his plans by the obstinacy or the jealousy of the States. He had resolved on the capture of Antwerp and Ostend, but he was opposed at every step by his allies; and a defeat of a considerable Dutch force at Eckeren, upon whose co-operation he had relied, obliged him to abandon his design. He was so dispirited at this time by the obstacles that were thrown in his way that he had serious thoughts of resigning his command. Fortunately for his country and for Europe he was dissuaded by Godolphin, who was now Lord Treasurer, and by Heinsius, the friend and counsellor of William, from taking this decisive step.

In the spring of the following year the preparations of France for carrying on the war were on a more extensive scale than ever. One army was required to chastise the Duke of Savoy for his apostasy, another to attack the King of Portugal, another to watch the insurgents in Languedoc. Boufflers and Villeroi were in Flanders with orders to remain on the defensive, while an attack in overwhelming force was directed against the heart of the empire, with the object, by one great effort, of finishing the war. A rebellion in Hungary, fomented by French intrigue, happened at this time most seriously to augment the dangers to which the empire was exposed, for it was a part of the grand design of Louis that while his armies descended the valley of the Danube, Ragotzky, the Hungarian chief, should advance upon Vienna, and by a joint attack upon his capital compel Leopold to submit to their terms, with the alternative of losing his crown.

Marlborough saw that if the empire was to be saved speedy and effective means required to be taken to arrest the progress of the French, and with this view he formed the daring and, apparently, impracticable scheme of transporting his army from the Rhine to the Danube. Observing the profoundest secrecy as to his real design he moved upon Coblentz and made a feint of occupying the line of the Moselle. Having by this means deceived the enemy as to his intentions, he steadily pursued his march, and at Heilbron he met Prince Eugene, and there concerted with the imperial general the plan of operations that each was to pursue. It was the first occasion on which these eminent commanders had met, and they mutually conceived for each other a degree of confidence and regard which never diminished during their respective lives. It may be doubted whether the annals of war furnish any such example of genuine friendship between two such rivals in military fame.

Having received some reinforcements from the Margrave of Baden, Marlborough advanced upon Donauwerth, which was occupied by a Bavarian force, and on the second of July he stormed the lines of Schellenberg by which the town was defended. After the surrender of Donauwerth the Elector retired to Augsburg, and an attempt was there made to induce him to abandon the French alliance. But he made the most extravagant demands as a condition of his joining the allies against the common enemy. He insisted that not only the Tyrol but the Duchy of Milan should be added to his dominions. Counter-proposals were made by the allies, but on learning that Tallard with a fresh army of 30,000 men was advancing to his assistance he abruptly broke off the negotiations. The emperor and the German princes were, under the circumstances, not unnaturally disposed to regard the Elector as a traitor to the Fatherland. It was only in accordance with the usages of war, as they were then recognised, that his dominions were laid waste by the invaders. Marlborough had many enemies, but no one has accused him of inhumanity in the conduct of his campaigns, and in announcing the final resolution of the Elector to adhere to the French alliance, he spoke with regret of the retaliatory measures which the obstinacy of the Elector had provoked. "However," he said, "we are in his country and he

"will find it difficult to persuade us to quit it. We
"sent this morning 3,000 horse to his chief city of
"Munich with orders to burn and destroy all the
"country about it. This is so contrary to my nature,
"that nothing but absolute necessity could have obliged
"me to consent to it, for these poor people suffer for their
"master's ambition. There having been no war in this
"country for above sixty years these towns and villages
"are so clean that you would be pleased with them."
And again, "You will, I hope, believe me that my nature
"suffers when I see so many fine places burnt."[1]

On the 13th of August, Marlborough and Eugene having united their forces, at length found themselves in front of the Franco-Bavarian army. It occupied a strong position on a rising ground, with the village of Blenheim on their right, a thick wood protecting their left flank, and an extensive morass lay in front. Like Gustavus Adolphus, Marlborough was the assailant in all his great battles, and he directed his first attack against the right wing of the French, while Prince Eugene advanced against the left. Neither attack was successful, but it was in another quarter that the English general had determined to make his main effort. Tallard knew that the marshy ground in his front had been impassable some months before, and he rashly concluded that it was impassable still. But Marlborough had ascertained that it had been sufficiently hardened by the summer heats to be practicable even for cavalry, and the French general saw to his astonishment a large body of horse advancing against his centre, which, believing to be safe from attack, he had seriously weakened to strengthen his wings. The attacking force was led by Marlborough in person, and after several vigorous charges the French centre was broken through. The battle was now won, for although the French posted at Blenheim continued to defend themselves with unflinching courage their condition was hopeless, and they were

[1] Coxe, vol. i., p. 376.

finally compelled to surrender. The victory was decisive and complete. The Franco-Bavarian army had consisted of about 60,000 men, and of these at least two-thirds were either killed, wounded, or taken prisoners. Among the latter was Tallard, their commander-in-chief. No such disaster had befallen France since her king was defeated and taken prisoner at Pavia in the days of Charles the Fifth.

Blenheim was not the only English victory achieved in this eventful year. A few days before that battle was fought Gibraltar was captured[1] by a small force landed by Sir George Rooke, and has ever since remained an important dependency of the British Crown.

The campaign of 1704 had saved the Empire. It was the design of Marlborough and Eugene in the following spring to carry the war into the heart of France. But this plan was frustrated by the recall of Eugene to Piedmont, and by the refusal of the Margrave of Baden to co-operate with the English general. Marlborough, notwithstanding, ascended the valley of the Moselle, prepared to give battle to Villars, the most successful of all the French commanders who was now opposed to him. But Villars had strict orders to avoid a general engagement, and Marlborough was condemned to inactivity during the greater part of this year.

In the following spring he was more fortunate. He was opposed in Flanders by Villeroi, who, confident in his veteran troops and in himself, was eager to give battle to the allies; but he was totally defeated at Ramillies, where Marlborough won a complete victory by unexpectedly turning his adversary's flank. This celebrated battle was fought on the 23rd of May, 1706, and its results were most important. In consequence of their defeat the French abandoned the whole of the Spanish Netherlands; and Brussels, Bruges, Ghent, Louvain, Malines, and Oudenarde fell into the hands of the allies. Vendome was hastily recalled from Italy to

[1] Gibraltar was captured on the 3rd of August.

oppose their progress, and that able commander saved to France Douay, Tournay, and Valenciennes.

The disastrous defeats of Blenheim and Ramillies proved fatal to the military ascendency of France. Her great natural resources still enabled her to prolong the war, but from this time there can be no doubt that she became sincerely desirous of terminating a contest which, in addition to her losses in the field, threatened to involve her in financial ruin. We find, accordingly, that shortly after the battle of Ramillies Louis made secret overtures of peace to the emperor. Leopold, who had commenced the war, was now dead, but his son and successor Joseph refused to entertain the proposals of Louis, although they were highly favourable to the house of Hapsburg. Louis offered to acknowledge the title of the archduke to the crown of Spain on condition that Philip was invested with the kingdom of the Two Sicilies. He further undertook to cede to the Dutch certain of the barrier towns in the Spanish Netherlands. But these important concessions did not satisfy either the emperor or his Dutch allies. They believed, or affected to believe, that the overtures of the French king were made solely with the view of breaking up the Grand Alliance, and an opportunity of bringing the war to a conclusion on equitable terms was thus thrown away.[1]

The French sustained this year in another quarter a defeat not less serious than Ramillies. On the 7th of September Prince Eugene gained a decisive victory over Marshal Marsin in front of Turin, and some months afterwards a secret treaty was concluded with the

---

[1] Schoell, t. ii., p. 61. It was the decided opinion of Lord Bolingbroke that peace should have been made at this time on the basis proposed by the French. He says:—"To have humbled and reduced, in five campaigns, a Power that had "disturbed and insulted Europe almost forty years; to have restored in so short "a time the balance of power in Europe to a sufficient point of equality, after it "had been more than fifty years—that is, from the treaty of Westphalia—in a "gradual deviation from this point—in short, to have retrieved in 1706 a game "that was become desperate at the beginning of the century—to have done all "this before the war had exhausted our strength—was the utmost sure that any "man could desire who intended the public good alone; and no honest reason ever "was, or ever will be, given why the war was protracted any longer."—Letters on History, p. 318.

emperor, by which the French agreed to evacuate Piedmont. The Duke of Savoy was now restored to his dominions, and, accompanied by Prince Eugene and a powerful force, he soon afterwards undertook the capture of Toulon. But that important place was so vigorously defended, both by land and sea, that the besiegers, in consequence of the heavy losses they sustained, were compelled to abandon the enterprise.

In consequence of the determination of the French to act strictly on the defensive no action of importance took place in the Netherlands in the year 1707. But in the spring of that year a diplomatic success of a very important kind was achieved by Marlborough in another quarter. Charles the Twelfth had by this time completed the conquest of Poland, and he had encamped with his victorious Swedes in the vicinity of Leipsic, undecided, apparently, as to his future projects. In the contest that was raging throughout Western Europe his sympathies were supposed to be on the side of France, and there was a general dread on the part of the Grand Alliance that he might be induced by the blandishments of Louis to take an active part in the war. Charles, moreover, had made certain grave complaints against the emperor. He demanded reparation for an insult which, he alleged, his chamberlain had received from an officer of the imperial court; he complained that the Protestants of Silesia were prohibited from building churches, and he insisted on the surrender of 1,500 Russians who had taken refuge in the Austrian dominions. We learn with surprise and regret that Marlborough recommended the emperor to satisfy the King of Sweden on all these points, and even to accede to his most unwarrantable demand[1] for the surrender of the fugitives. But Joseph gave a prompt and peremptory refusal to a proposal which the law of nations and the honour of his crown alike forbade him to entertain. He did, however, promise

---

[1] Letter from Count Wratislaw, May 14, 1707.—Coxe's House of Austria, cap. lxxii.

that reparation should be made for the affront to his chamberlain of which Charles complained, and that religious toleration should be established in Silesia. But the attitude of the Swedish king, who had taken up his quarters in the heart of Germany, apparently for the purpose of enforcing his demands, was of so menacing a character that Marlborough undertook the delicate task of paying him a visit with the view of ascertaining his real intentions. A substantial bribe to Count Piper,[1] the confidential minister of Charles, obtained for the English general a courteous reception in the Swedish camp and a speedy interview with the king. That indefatigable warrior, it is well known, utterly despised all the luxuries and elegances of life; but he was by no means impervious to flattery, and on their first meeting Marlborough administered to him a dose which might have turned a more sensitive stomach, but was not too strong for him:—"I present to your majesty," he said, " a letter, not from the chancery, but from the heart of " the queen my mistress, and written with her own " hand. Had not her sex prevented it she would have " crossed the sea to see a prince admired by the whole " universe. I am in this particular more happy than the " queen, and I wish I could serve some campaigns under " so great a general as your majesty, that I might learn " what I yet want to know in the art of war."[2]

It is said that Charles was visibly delighted with the fulsome compliments thus paid to him by the conqueror of Blenheim and Ramillies; and to the queen's message he replied in the following terms:—" The Queen of Great " Britain's letter and your person are both very acceptable " to me, and I shall always have the utmost regard for " the interposition of Her Majesty of Great Britain and " the interests of the Grand Alliance. It is likewise " much against my will if I have been obliged to give " the least umbrage to any of the parties engaged in it;

---

[1] Lediard, Life of Marlborough, vol. i., p. 456.
[2] Ibid., p. 460.

"but your excellency cannot but be convinced that I
had just cause to come into this country with my troops.
On the other hand, you may assure the queen, my
sister, that my design is to depart from hence as soon
as I have obtained the satisfaction I demand. *But not
sooner.* However, I shall do nothing that can tend to
the prejudice of the common cause in general, or to
the Protestant religion in particular, of which I shall
always glory to be a zealous protector.[1]"

It is generally admitted that in consequence of Marlborough's visit to the Swedish camp the matters in dispute between Charles and the emperor were amicably arranged, and the Swedish king shortly afterwards set out for that fatal campaign in Muscovy which closed his victorious career.[2]

Important events had meanwhile taken place in Spain. In the summer of 1705 the Earl of Peterborough sailed from England with 5,000 troops, and if that eccentric nobleman had possessed a tithe of Marlborough's prudence it is probable that a Bourbon dynasty would never have been established in the Peninsula. By a series of daring achievements he in a very short time rendered himself master of the important provinces of Catalonia and Valencia, and he was ready and eager to follow up his successes by a march upon Madrid, but his reckless conduct, and his still more reckless tongue, alarmed and offended his best friends, and being opposed in all his views by the "Vienna crew," as he was wont to call the advisers of the archduke, he left

[1] Lediard, vol. i., p. 461.
[2] According to Voltaire, Marlborough discovered the real intentions of Charles on their first interview. He says, "The duke had learned by long experience the art of penetrating into the minds of men. When he spoke to him of war in general, he imagined that he saw in his majesty a natural aversion towards France, and that he took a secret pleasure in speaking of the conquests of the allies. He mentioned the Czar to him, and took notice that his eyes kindled whenever he was named. He moreover remarked that the king had a map of Muscovy lying before him on the table. This was sufficient to convince him that the King of Sweden's real design was to dethrone the Czar as he had already done the King of Poland," &c. But this account of the interview is disputed by Lediard, and apparently upon good grounds. See Lediard, vol. i., p. 462, et seq.

the country in disgust.¹ During his absence a combined army of English and Portuguese advanced into Castile from the side of Portugal. They were opposed by the Duke of Berwick, who commanded the French. It was a circumstance most singular, and, indeed, unprecedented in the history of the two nations, that on this occasion the English should have been commanded by a natural-born Frenchman, Ruvigny, the Huguenot refugee, who had been created Earl of Galway by King William, while the French were commanded by a natural-born Englishman, the Duke of Berwick, who was a son of James the Second by Arabella Churchill, and consequently a nephew of Marlborough. Galway, although a brave soldier, was but an indifferent commander, and he and his Portuguese colleague, Das Minas, were generally at variance respecting the conduct of the campaign. Although inferior in number to the French they ventured to attack them on the 25th of April at Almanza, but were totally defeated, with the loss, it is said, of 12,000 men. This was the most important battle fought in Spain during the war of succession, and although the allies continued the struggle, it was a blow from which they never appear to have recovered.

In spite of all her losses and defeats France was still able in the following year to open the campaign in the Netherlands with an army of 100,000 men. They were nominally under the command of the Duke of Burgundy, the favourite grandson of Louis, but he was supposed, erroneously as it proved, to be subordinate to Vendome, who accompanied him. In the beginning of July they captured Ghent and Bruges, and they had invested Oudenarde when the allied army under Marlborough and Eugene rapidly advanced to the relief of that important place. On the morning of the 7th they were fifteen miles distant from the main body of the

---

¹ "What fools we are to fight for such a couple of louts!" he was wont to say, referring to both the claimants of the Spanish crown.—Stanhope's Reign of Queen Anne.

French, and the Scheld ran between the opposing armies; but the allied commanders, notwithstanding the difficulties of the march, attacked the French on the afternoon of the same day. There were about 80,000 men on each side, but while the allied commanders acted in perfect harmony—for on this occasion Eugene led the British, while Marlborough led the Dutch and Germans—Vendome and Burgundy were disputing as to the disposal of their troops. Even in the middle of the action a charge ordered by the marshal was countermanded by the duke. The result was a victory for the allies, by no means so decisive as those of Blenheim or Ramillies, but Oudenarde was saved, and Lille was shortly afterwards invested. After a siege of two months, chiefly famous for the number of distinguished persons who took part in it,[1] this city surrendered on the 22nd of October, and the campaign closed with the recovery of Ghent and Bruges, which were once more wrested from the French.

While England was engaged in a war which seemed interminable, a work of immense importance to the national welfare had been accomplished at home. Scotland had been united to England for upwards of a century, but so long as the legislatures of the two countries were separate and independent the union was incomplete, and from the days of King James and Lord Bacon to those of King William and Lord Somers the subject had engaged the attention of the ablest British statesmen. We have seen that King William in the last speech that he addressed to Parliament spoke of the projected union as one of extreme importance. So long, in fact, as there was war with France there was danger from the side of Scotland, for the Jacobite faction in that country placed all their hopes on France, and if Louis had been more fortunate in his wars they would not have looked to that quarter in vain. The utter

---

[1] See a full description of the siege in Alison's History of the Duke of Marlborough.

failure of the Darien expedition, which the Scots attributed, not without reason, to the jealousy of the English colonists in the West Indies, had created a dangerous amount of irritation on both sides of the Tweed, and immensely increased the difficulties attendant on the projected union. But if there was danger in the excited state of public feeling in forcing on the treaty, there was still more danger in delay, and to Lord Somers belongs the chief credit of accomplishing this great national work. The patience, the firmness, and the liberal spirit displayed by that eminent statesman finally overcame obstacles that up to that time had proved insurmountable. On the one hand, the Scots were loath to surrender their national independence, and on the other, the English were unwilling to share with their Northern neighbours, whom from time immemorial they had regarded with no friendly eyes, their great and rapidly-expanding colonial trade. Eventually, but not without an infinite amount of negotiation, both points were surrendered, and on the 6th of March, 1707, a treaty was signed which has proved eminently conducive to the welfare of this island.

In a transaction of this kind it was of paramount importance that the weaker of the two kingdoms should retain her own laws and her own religion; and both of these were guaranteed to Scotland. But although the union may be said to have become a necessity for both countries, it was popular in neither. We can respect the prejudices and admire the spirit of Lord Belhaven and Fletcher of Saltoun, who persistently denounced the treaty as fatal to the best interests of their country. It was a bitter pang for Scotland to sacrifice that national independence which in times past she had made such heroic efforts to maintain. But notwithstanding the patriotic opposition of the Scots, it must be admitted that the terms of the treaty were upon the whole equitable and just; and that is the true reason why it has proved more successful in its results than its most ardent advocates could have anticipated. The progress of Scotland, both material and moral, during the eighteenth century, notwithstanding two Jacobite rebellions, has been more remarkable than that of any other country in Europe.[1]

A question, which might have led to serious consequences, arose about this time between the British Government and the Czar of Muscovy—better known by the title of Peter the Great—respecting the rights and privileges of ambassadors. In the summer of 1708 the Russian ambassador accredited to the court of Queen Anne was arrested for a debt of £300 due by him to certain London tradesmen. It so happened that the arrest was made in a very public and offensive manner. His carriage was stopped in the open street, he was deprived of his sword, and he was conducted to a common "spunging-house" and was there detained for several hours among debtors of the least reputable kind. As soon as the affair was known he was liberated on bail, and he complained in very indignant terms of the treatment to which he had been subjected, and demanded the immediate punishment of every one who had taken part in the outrage. It was explained to the envoy of the Czar that there was no power to punish any one in England without trial; but that the queen was grieved beyond measure at the occurrence, and that proceedings should be taken against the persons implicated as soon as the forms of law allowed. These explanations did not accord with Muscovite notions of justice, and the ambassador demanded his passports and set out for the Hague. There was every disposition on the part of Queen Anne and her ministers to give satisfaction to the Czar by punishing the perpetrators of an outrage which threatened to lead to a breach of the friendly relations that, from the days of Elizabeth, had existed between the two countries.

---

[1] In two recent works—namely, in Burton's History of Queen Anne, and in Lecky's History of the Eighteenth Century, the subject of the Union with Scotland has been very fully and ably discussed.

But the law was found ineffectual for the purpose. Proceedings were taken by information in the Court of Queen's Bench against the parties implicated, and a verdict of guilty was pronounced against them by a special jury; but the law had provided no specific punishment for the offence, and no punishment appears to have been inflicted. The Russian Government insisted that the question was not one of municipal law, but that the law of nations had been violated in the person of its ambassador, and that it was the right and the duty of every government to punish such offences in a summary and signal manner. They reminded the Secretary of State that an English ambassador, the Earl of Manchester, had recently received an affront at Venice, and that the offenders were forthwith sent to the galleys on the complaint of that nobleman without any recourse being had to the ordinary tribunals of the republic. And the Secretary of State was further reminded that the affront in question had not been offered to the English ambassador in person, but to one of his suite. The matter was meanwhile discussed by the diplomatic body in London at a meeting summoned by Baron Spanheim, ambassador of the King of Prussia, and an Act of Parliament was eventually passed for the protection of ambassadors and their retinue in future.[1] But this concession did not satisfy the Russian Government, for Pultowa[2] was fought and won and the King of Sweden had become a fugitive in Turkey while the diplomatic correspondence was proceeding; and Peter, after crushing his great adversary, had acquired a prominent position among European sovereigns. It was therefore finally arranged that a formal apology should be made to the conqueror of Charles the Twelfth. Lord Whitworth, ambassador extraordinary of Queen Anne at the court of the Czar, in accordance with his instructions, in presence of Peter and his court expressed the sincere regret of his mistress at the occurrence. The apology

---

[1] See Appendix No. vi.
[2] The battle of Pultowa was fought on the 8th of July, 1709.

was graciously accepted, and after the lapse of some eighteen months the affair was amicably settled.

After the defeat of Oudenarde and the capture of Lille, Louis renewed his overtures to the allies. In addition to her continued disasters, France was at this time threatened with a famine, and the king was prepared to make extraordinary sacrifices to restore peace to his suffering country. It was at this time that he sought to bribe the Duke of Marlborough to induce the allies to come to terms. The offer was made through Torcy,[1] the minister who had been specially sent to the Hague to negotiate a peace. Louis was now prepared, as he had been after Ramillies, to abandon the claim of his grandson to the crown of Spain; but he desired to retain for him Naples and Sicily, and for himself Strasburg, and Landau, and Dunkirk, with their forts and arsenals. If the English commander could bring about a peace on these terms he engaged to pay him no less than four millions of livres. We have the account of this attempt to corrupt the great duke from Torcy himself, and it is satisfactory to know that Marlborough did not even deign a reply. There is one sure inference to be drawn from the offer of this enormous bribe, and that is, that Louis was at this time sincerely desirous of peace. Yet the allies affected to believe all along that he only desired to gain time and to break up the confederacy arrayed against him. But moderation in success is the rarest of virtues, and the terms on which they now offered to conclude peace were hard in the extreme. They consisted of forty articles, among which it was provided that within two months the Duke of Anjou should finally quit Spain and retire to France, and if he failed to comply Louis was to join the allies against his grandson, and compel his abdication of the Spanish crown. These humiliating terms were at once rejected by Louis with the cordial approval of his ministers. "If I must wage "war," he said, "I would rather wage it against my "enemies than against my children."

[1] See Schoell, t. ii., p. 64, note.

Among the numerous charges made against Marlborough, his enemies were wont to allege that he used all his influence to prolong the war for the sake of the great emoluments which he derived as commander-in-chief. But, like many other imputations that have been made against him, this charge seems to be wholly groundless. That he loved money is not to be denied, and that is a passion which is found in many men who have risen from obscurity to wealth and fame. But, instead of desiring to protract the war, we learn from his private and confidential letters that he was all along anxious for peace. To his kinsmen Godolphin and Sunderland, and to the Duchess of Marlborough, his language on this point is uniform. When he began his victorious career he was no longer a young man, and in his letters to his wife he invariably expressed his desire for the restoration of peace ; he frequently alludes to his declining years, and even at times to his failing memory. It may be said that these were not his real sentiments ; but we must bear in mind that this great man had more dread of his wife's tongue than of all the armies of France ; and it is incredible that he should have ventured to deceive her on a point so interesting to both.

In anticipation of a speedy peace Marlborough seems to have carried on his negotiations with Torcy in the most friendly spirit. He expressed his sincere respect for the French monarch, and said he should never forget that he had learned his first lessons in the art of war from Turenne. But the anti-Gallican prejudices of the English ministers,[1] the greed of the Dutch, and the ambition of the Hapsburg princes, rendered a continuation of the war inevitable ; and after five years more of

---

[1] We find that even so enlightened a politician as Lord Somers was not above the prejudices of the day. "The late Lord Oxford told me that my Lord Somers "being pressed, I know not on what occasion, on the unnecessary and ruinous "continuation of the war—instead of giving reasons to show the necessity of it, "contented himself to reply, that he had been bred up in a hatred of France. "This was a strange reply for a wise man; and yet I know not whether he could "have given a better then, or whether any of his pupils could give a better "now."—Bolingbroke's Letters on History, p. 339.

needless slaughter, they all finally consented to a peace on terms less favourable than those that now were offered, for it left a Bourbon prince in possession of the Spanish crown.

During the negotiations in 1709 the allies appear to have concluded that France was wholly incapable of resisting their demands. But although her armies had been again and again defeated, although her finances were ruined, and there was famine in the land, her resources were not yet exhausted. In his distress Louis appealed to the people, and he did not appeal in vain. He roused their dormant patriotism by publishing the humiliating conditions which the allies had sought to impose upon France; and recruits for the army came swarming from every quarter of the kingdom. The very sufferings of the rural population tended to swell their numbers, for to the young and active the life of a camp was infinitely preferable to starvation at home. The nobles displayed no less enthusiasm in the cause of their country; and Villars, the only one of the French commanders who had never suffered a defeat, marched to the northern frontier to oppose the allied armies. They on their part were not less active, and Eugene declared that as the French king had refused their terms, 150,000 armed plenipotentiaries should dictate peace at the gates of Paris.[1] We do not find that Marlborough indulged in any such confident anticipations of speedy and decisive success. He knew the character of his opponent, for it was Villars who, by his skilful tactics on the Moselle, had four years before saved France from invasion, and the result proved that the new French general was the most formidable antagonist the allies had yet encountered.

The allies commenced the campaign with the capture of Tournay, and they next determined to invest Mons. The misery of the rural population of France at this time is frequently referred to by Marlborough. In

[1] Coxe, vol. iii., p. 55.

writing to his wife after the capture of Tournay he says, "That which gives the greatest prospect for the happiness of being back to you is that certainly the misery of France increases, which must bring us to a peace. The misery of all the poor people we see is such that one must be a brute not to pity them."[1] In the meantime Villars had taken up a strong position at Malplaquet, and on the 11th of September, 1709, the allied generals determined to attack him. The ground chosen by the French commander was admirably adapted for defence. Each of his wings was covered by a dense forest, and in front his line was protected by deep intrenchments and trunks of trees obtained from the neighbouring woods. His army consisted of about 100,000 men, but of these, according to the opinion of Eugene, four-fifths were raw recruits;[2] and in spite of the opposition of the Dutch he was strongly in favour of an immediate attack. Marlborough, it is said, on examining the formidable position of the French, expressed some hesitation, but finally assented to the opinion of Eugene, and the battle that ensued bore much resemblance to that of Blenheim. Eugene, as at Blenheim, assaulted the left wing of the French. He was again and again repulsed, and returned again and again to the attack. The Prince of Orange assailed the right wing of the enemy with heavy loss upon both sides. Villars had not repeated the fatal error of Tallard at Blenheim of leaving his centre unprotected, but after several hours' fighting he was compelled to weaken it to fill up the gaps in either flank. Marlborough now saw his opportunity, and after a desperate struggle he succeeded in breaking through the French line. The battle was now won, but at a terrible cost. The number of men actually killed on the side of the allies at Malplaquet more than doubled the loss of Wellington at Waterloo.[3]

[1] Burton's Reign of Queen Anne, vol. iii., p. 45.
[2] Histoire de Jean Churchill, à Paris, 1808, t. iii., p. 99.
[3] The number of men actually killed on the side of the allies at Malplaquet was 5,544.—See Lediard, vol. ii., p. 195. At Waterloo the number of killed was 2,090.—See Alison's History of Europe.

Villars had been severely wounded during the battle, but Boufflers, who was next in command, retreated in good order, the French, owing to the strength of their position, having suffered much less than their assailants. "A deluge of blood was spilt to dislodge them, for we "did no more at Malplaquet." Such were the words of Bolingbroke upon this bloody but barren victory, which, beyond the surrender of Mons, had no perceptible influence on the progress of the war.

This was the last great battle in which Marlborough was engaged, and we may observe that in the course of his victorious career he was invariably the assailant; that he invariably deceived his enemy as to the real point of attack; and that he never failed without loss of time to follow up a victory. That with these great qualities his disposition was essentially humane we have a striking proof after Malplaquet. As he rode over the field on the morning after the battle he was so much affected by the ghastly scene that he became seriously unwell for several days;[1] but this did not prevent him from giving orders that every attention should be paid to the French wounded, numbers of whom still lay on the ground.

Meanwhile the war in Spain dragged on. In the summer of 1710 an English force under General Stanhope, and a German contingent under Marshal Staremberg, encountered and defeated the army of Philip at Saragossa, and after their victory they carried the archduke in triumph to Madrid. But the coldness of his reception convinced the allies that the people of Castile were devoted to the cause of Philip, and want of provisions soon compelled them to quit the capital. Unfortunately, moreover, the two commanders, Staremberg and Stanhope, agreed no better than their predecessors Galway and Das Minas, and having unwisely separated their forces, they were, while retreating through Aragon, de-

[1] He says in a letter to Godolphin that he could not sleep on the two succeeding nights, and he adds, "the lamentable sight and thoughts of it has given me "so much uneasiness that I believe it is the chief cause of my illness."—Stanhope, p. 397.

feated in detail by Vendome, who had assumed the command of Philip's forces.

It was the opinion of Stanhope, after the campaign of 1710, that from the attachment the people had displayed to Philip the prospects of the archduke had become hopeless. He said, "that armies of twenty or "thirty thousand men might walk about that country till "Doomsday without effect; that wherever they came the "people would submit to Charles the Third out of terror, "and as soon as they were gone proclaim Philip the "Fifth again out of affection. That to conquer Spain "required a great army, and to keep it a greater."[1]

In this year Louis made another attempt to restore peace to his unhappy country, and the allies lost another opportunity of bringing the war to a conclusion on terms alike favourable to them and humiliating to France. A Conference met at Gertruydenberg, in the neighbourhood of Breda, for the purpose of arranging the conditions of peace, but four months of negotiation were spent without result. Louis now agreed to abandon the claim of his grandson to the Spanish monarchy, provided only that the island of Sicily and certain places in Tuscany were secured to him. He also offered to pay to the allies one million of livres a month for the expenses of the Spanish war. But they insisted in addition that Louis should engage that Philip the Fifth should finally quit Spain and retire to France within two months. In other words, they required the French monarch to undertake that which was wholly beyond his power to accomplish; for Philip, supported as he was by the great majority of his subjects, had expressed his determination at this time to maintain to the last his title to the Spanish crown. We may infer from the fact of the allies insisting upon a condition which they knew to be impracticable, that while professing a sincere desire for peace they were resolved on a renewal of the war.

The capture of several towns by the allies followed

[1] Bolingbroke on the Study of History, Letter 8.

the breaking up of the Conference. But these successes were more than counterbalanced by the fall of the Godolphin ministry and the accession to power of Harley and St. John, who were known to be in favour of peace. A few months after the change of ministry in England, another event occurred which entirely altered the aspect of affairs. This was the unexpected death of the Emperor Joseph.[1] By this event his brother Charles, the claimant of the Spanish throne, succeeded to all the dominions of the house of Austria, and he was soon afterwards elected emperor under the title of Charles the Sixth. But he had no intention, notwithstanding, of abandoning his claim to the Spanish crown, and to this resolution he adhered with all the pride and obstinacy of his race.

Portugal and Savoy had contributed but little to the success of the allies, but after the death of the emperor they declared they would no longer aid in placing the crown of Spain on the head of his successor, for that would be, in effect, to revive the gigantic empire of Charles the Fifth. They had consented to join the Grand Alliance when the independence of Europe was threatened by the aggressive policy of France, and were they now to aid in creating a power far more formidable than that which had been wielded by Louis the Fourteenth in the zenith of his greatness? These questions were, in fact, unanswerable, and yet the war went on, with no other object, apparently, than that of undoing the work of the treaty of Westphalia and aggrandising the house of Austria. But it was not in the nature of things that to gratify the ambition of the emperor the war should be continued much longer, for the maritime Powers were quite as much interested in opposing the undue ascendency of Austria as that of France. "The scales of the balance of "power," it has been truly said,[2] "will never be

[1] He died of small-pox on the 17th of April, 1711, at the early age of 33.
[2] Bolingbroke, Letters on History, No. 8.

"exactly poised. It is sufficient in this as in other
"human affairs that the deviation be not too great.
"Some there will always be." These are the words of
the minister who was mainly responsible for the peace of
Utrecht, and who believed that in the disasters and the
humiliation of France the object of the Grand Alliance
had been attained. But it is right to observe that Marlborough was of a contrary opinion. He rarely spoke in
public; only, indeed, on occasions when it would have been
unbecoming in him to remain silent. But in the House
of Lords, after the accession of the Tory Ministry of
Harley and St. John, he declared that, while always
anxious for an honourable and lasting peace, he was of
opinion "that the safety and liberty of Europe would be
"in imminent danger if Spain and the West Indies were
"left to the house of Bourbon." Shortly before making
this speech he had achieved his last victory. Marshal
Villars had constructed a line of defences from Montreuil-sur-mer to the Scheld, which, believing them to be
impregnable, he had described as the *ne plus ultrâ* of the
allies. But, by a series of masterly manœuvres, the
duke not only slipped through without losing a man,
but he crossed the Scheld and besieged and captured
Bouchain in spite of all the efforts of Villars to relieve
that important fortress.[2] While engaged in this siege
we learn that Marlborough gave strict orders for the
protection of the estates of Fénélon, who was now Archbishop of Cambray, and stationed a sufficient force at
Cateau Cambresis for that purpose.

It was the design of Marlborough, after the capture
of Bouchain, to carry the war, in concert with Eugene,
into the heart of France; but on the last day of this
year he was not only deprived of all his employments,
but he was exposed to every species of abuse and mis-

---

[1] Stanhope, p. 501.
[2] Writing to Godolphin, the duke says:—"If we can succeed in this siege we shall have the honour of having done it in the face of an army many thousand men stronger than we are."—Stanhope, p. 486.

representation which ignorance and party malice could supply.[1]

Meanwhile there had been secret negotiations between the new English ministry and the French Government, and certain preliminaries had been agreed upon, of which the following were the most important:—That the King of France should recognise the title of Queen Anne and of the provisions made in favour of the house of Hanover; that Gibraltar and Minorca should

---

[1] The following is Thomas Carlyle's highly-characteristic account of the dismissal of Marlborough:—

"Kaiser Karl the Sixth, head of the Holy Roman Empire at this time, was a "handsome man to look upon, whose life, full of expense, vicissitude, futile labour, "and adventure, did not prove of much use to the world. Describable as a "laborious futility rather. He was second son of that little Leopold, the solemn "little Herr in red stockings, who had such troubles, frights, and runnings to and "fro with the sieging Turks, liberative Sobieski's acquisitive Louis the Four- "teenth, and who at length ended in a sea of futile labour, which they call the "Spanish succession war.

"This Karl, second son, had been appointed 'King of Spain' in that futile "business; and with much sublimity, though internally in an impoverished "condition, he proceeded towards Spain, landing in England to get cash for the "outfit. Arrived in Spain and round about there as titular king, for some years "with the fighting Peterboroughs, Galways, Starembergs, but did no good there, "neither he nor his Peterboroughs. At length his brother Joseph, father "Leopold's successor, having died, Karl came home from Spain to be kaiser. "At which point Karl would have been wise to give up his titular kingship in "Spain; for he never got nor will get anything but futile labour from hanging "to it. He did hang to it nevertheless with notable obstinacy. To the woe of "men and nations: punishment, doubtless, of his sins and theirs!

"Kaiser Karl mere amazement and indignation when the English "tired of fighting for him and it. When the English said to their great Marl- "borough:—'Enough, you sorry Marlborough! You have beaten Louis the "'Fourteenth to the suppleness of washleather, at our bidding; that is true, and "'that may have had its difficulties, but after all we prefer to have the thing "'precisely as it would have been without any fighting. You therefore, what is the "'good of you? You are a —— person whom we can fling out like sweepings, "'now that our eyesight returns, and accuse of common stealing. Go and "'be ——!'

"Nothing had ever so disgusted and astonished Kaiser Karl as this treat- "ment—not of Marlborough, whom he regarded only as he would have done a "pair of military boots or a holster pistol of superior excellence, for the uses that "were in him—but of the Kaiser Karl, his own sublime self, the heart and focus "of political nature, left in this manner, now when the sordid English and Dutch "declined spending money for him further. 'Ungrateful, sordid, inconceivable souls,' "answered Karl, 'was there ever since the early Christian times such a martyr as "'you have made of me?' So answered Karl in diplomatic groans and shrieks to "all ends of Europe. But the sulky English and allies, thoroughly tired of paying "and bleeding, did not heed him; made their peace of Utrecht with Louis the "Fourteenth, who was now beaten supple; and Karl, after a year of indignant "protests and futile attempts to fight Louis on his own score, was obliged to do "the like," &c.—Carlyle's Frederick the Great, vol. i., p. 546.

remain under the dominion of Great Britain; that the contract of *assiento*,[1] or the privilege of supplying the Spanish colonies with negro slaves, should be transferred from France to Britain; and that Newfoundland and the territory of Hudson's Bay should be ceded to Britain.

The King of France further agreed that effective measures should be taken to prevent the union of the crowns of France and Spain under the same prince; and he further agreed that certain fortresses should be ceded to the Dutch to protect them from invasion on the side of France.

Such were the preliminaries which formed the basis of the treaty of Utrecht. The English ministers have been severely censured as well for the conditions which they now offered to France as for the circumstances under which they were made—namely, without the knowledge of their allies. But the conditions were in themselves reasonable, and it was clearly for the interest of England to terminate a war in which her object had been fully attained. That object had been, in fact, accomplished years before, for in 1706 the armies of France had been utterly defeated in Germany, in Italy, and in the Netherlands. England had nothing more to fear from that great Power which in the days of William the Third had threatened the independence of Europe. But the English were induced to continue the struggle partly on account of their allies, partly because they had the greatest soldier in the world to command their armies, and the opponents of the war were silenced by his success. Had the Emperor Joseph lived it is impossible to say how long the contest might have continued, but the death of that prince may be said to have restored peace to Europe. The impracticable character

---

[1] The Emperor Charles the Fifth had made a concession of this lucrative but degrading traffic to the Flemings; but in 1532 the Spaniards resumed the privilege of supplying their own colonies with slaves. In 1580 Philip the Second confirmed the right on the Genoese, who are said to have realised immense sums by the traffic. On the accession of Philip the Fifth he transferred it to France for a period of twelve years.—See Schoell, t. ii., p. 80.

of his successor, and his obstinate adherence to his Spanish claims, rendered a new arrangement of the affairs of Europe imperative. And, considering the attachment the Castilians had displayed to their Bourbon king, there appeared to be no better mode of settling the vexed question of the succession than by acknowledging his right to the Spanish crown, but with this essential condition, that under no circumstances should the crowns of Spain and France ever be united. Between this scheme and the revival of the empire of Charles the Fifth there was, in fact, no choice; and that the latter was infinitely the more dangerous of the two will not be disputed.

But admitting that the preliminary terms of peace proposed by England and accepted by France were reasonable in themselves, it is said, and truly said, that they ought not to have been made without the consent of the allies. Harley and St. John were, no doubt, open to censure upon this point. The negotiations, in fact, were conducted with the utmost secrecy, the agents employed being a French priest named Gaultier, who was a resident in London; Matthew Prior, the poet; and a merchant of Rouen, named Ménager, who was well versed in commercial affairs. The work upon which these men were engaged was not unattended with personal risk, for they knew that the partisans of the late ministry, who were strenuously opposed to peace, were ready to proceed to any extremity to accomplish their purpose.

When the preliminaries were finally agreed upon it became necessary to communicate the result to the allies, and both the Dutch and the imperialists expressed the utmost surprise and indignation at the terms of the proposed peace. Count Gallas, the imperial ambassador in London, took an especially active part in denouncing, both in public and in private, the conduct of the English Government in proposing terms to the French king without the knowledge of the allies. There can be no doubt that upon this point he had a good ground of complaint; but, on the other hand, it is morally certain that Harley and St. John would never have obtained the assent of the emperor to abandon his claim to the Spanish crown, and were they to prolong the war indefinitely and squander the resources of the nation in the pursuit of a policy which, if successful, must once more have endangered the liberties of Europe? These, we may presume, were the motives which induced the English ministers to propose terms to the French king, and, under all the circumstances, they seem to have been justified in adopting the steps they did to put an end to this most unnecessary war. It was, no doubt, a grievous disappointment to the emperor to find that the English were no longer disposed to spend their blood and their subsidies on his behalf. His ambassador, Count Gallas, who seems to have been a meddlesome and insolent person, not only took every opportunity of denouncing the conduct of the queen's ministers, but he set up a printing-press in his house in Leicester-square, whence anonymous lampoons were issued, ridiculing the conditions of peace which had been communicated to him in confidence, but which he ventured to publish without authority. This breach of diplomatic usage enabled the ministers to get rid of an adversary so mischievous and unscrupulous. The master of ceremonies waited on the Austrian count and informed him that his behaviour of late had been such that he could no longer be received at court. Any communication, however, which the emperor might desire to make through any other minister would receive due attention. Gallas required to be furnished with the reasons of the queen's displeasure, but he was informed that these should be furnished to the emperor. The ambassador wrote to the Secretary of State to inquire when he was expected to leave the kingdom. St. John replied that he might go whenever he thought fit.[1]

[1] Wyon, vol. ii., pp. 319, 320.

But it was not among the queen's allies alone that an outcry was raised against the proposed terms of peace. Pamphlets innumerable issued daily from the press, denouncing the ministers as the tools of France and the allies of the Pope and the Pretender. The truth is that, in spite of all that philosophers and poets have said and sung in praise of peace, war has at all times been popular with the English. Whether this pugnacious spirit is inherited from their Scandinavian and Saxon and Norman ancestors, or whether it is to be accounted for from the circumstance that many generations have passed away since an invading army has set foot on their shores, or from both causes combined, there can be no doubt of the fact. The Duke of Ormond had been appointed successor to Marlborough in the Netherlands, and during the negotiations with France he had been ordered to act strictly on the defensive. The attitude of the new English commander, so different from that of his predecessor, had given deep dissatisfaction to the allies, as well as to the war party in England, and on the 7th of December, although the ministers had recruited their ranks by the creation of twelve new peers, a motion was carried in the House of Lords, by a majority of 62 votes to 54, "That no " peace could be safe or honourable to Great Britain or " Europe if Spain and the West Indies were allotted to " any branch of the house of Bourbon."

The ministers were more fortunate in the House of Commons, where, on the same question, they obtained a decisive majority of 232 to 106. But the resources of the war party were not yet exhausted. A few weeks after the debates in Parliament Prince Eugene arrived in England, but he soon discovered that he had come too late to prevent the meeting of the Congress, which it had been arranged should forthwith assemble at Utrecht to settle the terms of peace on the basis already agreed upon between England and France. He was received with cold politeness by the queen, whose health was now rapidly failing, and he was grieved to find his old and honoured comrade, by whose side he had so often marched to victory, not only in disgrace but accused of embezzling the public money.[1] The Tory pamphleteers had now discovered that he possessed neither the qualities of a commander nor the courage of a soldier; and Swift, who had become an ardent partisan of the new ministry, did not hesitate even in private to speak in disparagement of the man who had rendered such eminent services to his country and to Europe.[2] But it is satisfactory to know that he was punished for

[1] Eugene received a hint on his arrival in England that the less attention he showed to Marlborough the better pleased the queen would be. But the prince was too little of a courtier to desert a friend in trouble, and the first visit he paid in London was to his old companion in arms.—Wyon, vol. ii., p. 360.

[2] "The Duke of Marlborough was at court to-day, and nobody hardly took "notice of him." In the same letter he adds, "I confess my belief that he has "not one good quality beside that of a general, and even that I have heard denied "by several great soldiers."—To Stella, December 29, 1711.

Of Prince Eugene he says some weeks afterwards:—"I saw Prince Eugene at court to-day. He is plaguy yellow, and literally ugly besides."

The following is an extract from the *Examiner*, No. 16, one of Swift's most celebrated attacks on Marlborough:—

"There is an active and a passive ingratitude: applying both to this occasion, "we may say, the first is, when a prince or people returns good services with "cruelty or ill usage; the other is, when good services are not at all, or very "meanly rewarded. We have already spoken of the former; let us therefore in "the second place examine, how the services of our general have been rewarded; "and whether upon that article either prince or people have been guilty of "ingratitude?

"Those are the most valuable rewards, which are given to us from the certain "knowledge of the donor, that they *fit our temper best:* I shall therefore say "nothing of the title of *duke*, or the *garter*, which the queen bestowed upon the "general in the beginning of her reign; but I shall come to *more substantial* "*instances*, and mention nothing, which hath not been given in the face of the "world. The lands of *Woodstock* may, I believe, be reckoned worth £40,000; "on the building of *Blenheim* castle £200,000 have been already expended, "although it be not yet near finished; the grant of £5,000 *per annum* on the "post office is richly worth £100,000; his principality in *Germany* may be com- "puted at £30,000; pictures, jewels, and other gifts from foreign princes, "£60,000; the grant at the *Pall-mall*, the rangership, etc., for want of more "certain knowledge, may be called £10,000; his own and his duchess's employ- "ments at five years value, reckoning only the known and avowed salaries, are "very low rated at £100,000. Here is a good deal above half a million of money; "and, I dare say, those who are loudest with the clamour of ingratitude, will "readily own, that all this is but a trifle, in comparison of what is *untold*.

"The reason of my stating this account is only to convince the world, that we "are not quite so ungrateful either as the *Greeks* or the *Romans*; and in order "to adjust this matter with all fairness, I shall confine myself to the latter, who "were much the more generous of the two. A victorious general of *Rome*, in the "heighth of that empire, having *entirely|subdued his enemies*, was rewarded with "the larger triumph, and perhaps a statue in the *Forum*, a bull for a sacrifice, an "embroidered garment to appear in, a crown of laurel, a monumental trophy

the scandalous libels he published against Marlborough by a fit, not of compunction, but of abject terror for his life. So precarious did he consider the position of the ministry, notwithstanding their victory in the Commons, that he besought St. John to appoint him to some embassy abroad where he should be protected against personal violence. But St. John was by no means disposed at this time to dispense with the services of the most famous writer of the day, and both he and Harley did their best to assure him that his fears were imaginary, and that notwithstanding all the efforts of their enemies and the visit of Eugene, the treaty was secure.[1]

Eugene, in fact, soon discovered that he had visited England to no purpose. All his movements were narrowly watched, and not only did his popularity rapidly decline, but the most ridiculous accusations were made against him by a Jesuit spy named Plunket, as well as by anonymous libels. It was alleged that he was conspiring with the Duke of Marlborough and the late ministers to excite an insurrection, and even to set fire to the city and seize the person of the queen. That the ministers were in any degree responsible for the currency of these outrageous rumours is not alleged,

"with inscriptions, sometimes five hundred or a thousand copper coins were struck
"on occasion of the victory, which, doing honour to the general, we will place to
"his account; and lastly, sometimes, although not very frequently, a triumphal
"arch. These are all the rewards, that I can call to mind, which a victorious
"general received after his return from the most glorious expedition; having
"conquered some great kingdom, brought the king himself, his family, and nobles,
"to adorn the triumph in chains; and made the kingdom either a *Roman* province,
"or at best a poor depending state in humble alliance to that empire. Now, of
"all these rewards I find but two, which were of real profit to the general; the
"*laurel crown,* made and sent him at the charge of the publick, and the *em-*
"*broidered garment;* but I cannot find, whether this last was paid by the senate
"or the general."

No one knew better than the Dean that this elaborate piece of rhetoric was sheer nonsense. He intended his readers to believe that the only rewards a successful Roman general received were a sprig of laurel and an embroidered robe, for which he probably paid out of his own pocket. No one knew better than the Dean that a successful Roman general looked for his pecuniary recompense not to his fellow-citizens but to the plunder of the province or the people he had subdued.

[1] Journal to Stella.

but they are accused of having taken insufficient means to detect and punish their authors.[1]

On the 29th of January, 1712, the Conferences were at length opened at Utrecht. But before the work had seriously begun Europe was shocked by a series of domestic calamities at Versailles, and the question of the Spanish succession once more threatened to present an insuperable obstacle to peace. The dauphin had died during the previous year, leaving as his heir the Duke of Burgundy, and in the course of one week both this prince and his duchess, Marie of Savoy, who was universally beloved on account of her amiable disposition and attractive manners, died of a distemper which appears to have been measles of a peculiarly malignant type.[2] They left two boys, the Duke of Brittany and the Duke of Anjou, the one five and the other two years old. Both of these children were soon afterwards seized with the same disease which had proved fatal to their parents, and on the 8th of March the Duke of Brittany died, being the third dauphin of France who had died in the space of twelve months. The Duke of Anjou, a weakly child, contrary to general expectation, survived the attack, and failing him and his great-grandfather, now in his seventy-fourth year, the next heir to the French crown was Philip of Spain. This unexpected state of things led to an adjournment of the Conferences at Utrecht until the question of the Spanish succession was definitely settled. The French minister proposed that in the event of the crown of France devolving upon Philip he should at once elect whether he would accept it, and if so he should at once renounce for himself and his descendants all claim on the crown of Spain. But to this proposal the English minister gave an emphatic refusal. In a remarkably able paper St. John pointed out the dangers attendant on any prospective arrangement. And he concluded with these words:—" No

---

[1] Stanhope, p. 511.
[2] The duchess died on the 12th February; the duke a few days after.

"expedient will give any real security unless the prince who is now in possession of Spain will make his option *at this very hour*, and unless his option so made be an article in the treaty of peace."[1]

It is clear that this counter-proposal of St. John was intended as an ultimatum, and that upon its acceptance or rejection the question of peace or war depended. The momentous issue rested solely with the King of Spain, and after full deliberation he consented to the terms proposed by the English minister, and declared his readiness to make a full renunciation of his contingent claim to the crown of France. This serious obstacle to the treaty having been removed, the plenipotentiaries at Utrecht resumed their work. There was much difficulty in arranging a barrier for the Dutch, and the emperor would upon no account abandon his claim to the Spanish crown. In order to expedite the negotiations, St. John, created in this year Viscount Bolingbroke, repaired to France, and in concert with Torcy finally arranged the terms of peace between Britain and France. Now that the question of the Spanish succession was settled it was plainly the intention of the English ministers to bring the war to a close, if possible with the sanction of the allies, but without their sanction if they were found to be impracticable.

An armistice meanwhile had been proclaimed by the British and French commanders in the Netherlands; but the good fortune of Eugene, who commanded the imperialists, deserted him in this campaign. Villars, who was opposed to him, surprised and routed a body of 8,000 men who had been posted at Denain. He subsequently compelled Eugene to raise the seige of Landrecies, and he invested and captured Douay in spite of the efforts of the imperial general to relieve it. Villars crowned his successes in this campaign by the recovery of Bouchain, the last of Marlborough's conquests.

The disastrous results of this campaign and the

[1] Bolingbroke Correspondence, vol. i., p. 448.

desertion of England finally induced the Dutch to come to terms, and separate treaties of peace were finally concluded between the different Powers and France. The emperor alone stood aloof, as he still claimed to be the lawful King of Spain. England acquired by the treaty all that she had demanded—namely, Gibraltar, Minorca, Hudson's Bay, Nova Scotia, and Newfoundland, and the demolition of the forts of Dunkirk. She also obtained from France a recognition of the Act of Settlement and a pledge that the Pretender should be expelled from the French dominions. England also obtained through the Assiento treaty the right of supplying the Spanish colonies with negro slaves for thirty years. No provision in the treaty of Utrecht appears to have given such general satisfaction as this. The profits from this new source of wealth were expected to be enormous, and not a voice was raised against a traffic which a century later was prohibited under the severest penalties. We turn from this dark spot[1] in the treaty to a provision of a more legitimate character, and one of vast importance to commerce in time of war.

We have stated elsewhere[2] that France by an ordonnance of the year 1543 laid down a new rule of maritime law by which she declared that not only the property of an enemy found at sea but also the vessel in which it was embarked was liable to capture and confiscation. This was an unprecedented innovation in the maritime law of Europe, but during the Spanish war of succession it was rigorously enforced by France. She now consented to abandon in favour of Great Britain this iniquitous practice, for which not a shadow of right could be shown, but she made no such stipulation with regard to other Powers.

The Dutch had to restore to France some of the towns which were in their possession—namely, Lille, Aire, Bethune, and St. Venant—but they retained in

---

[1] See Append. No. vii.
[2] Ante, cap. vi., p. 170.

their hands the fortresses in the Spanish Netherlands, which it was agreed should eventually be ceded to the emperor. By this means it was intended that Holland should be protected against France. The Spanish dominions in Italy, with the exception of the island of Sicily, were also ceded to the emperor. The Duke of Savoy obtained some addition to his territories in Piedmont as well as Sicily, and the recognition of his title to the Spanish crown in the event of a failure of the line of Philip the Fifth. France ceded to the King of Portugal an extensive tract of territory in South America, and she also at length recognised the title of the King of Prussia, which up to this time she had persistently refused to do. The treaty of Utrecht was concluded between Great Britain and France on the 13th April, 1713, and with the other Powers in the course of the following summer.

The emperor having done his utmost to prevent the restoration of peace, would upon no account abandon his claim to Spain. His father, Leopold, had commenced the war without an ally, and he was resolved to continue it on the same conditions. He relied on the prowess of Eugene and on the exhausted state of France, but he received but cold support from the princes of the empire, who regarded with some uneasiness the extension of his dominions in Italy and in the Netherlands, and who were, moreover, weary of the war. Eugene once more found himself opposed to his old adversary Villars, who laid siege to Landau in June of this year. Eugene found himself unable to relieve the place, which surrendered after a stubborn defence. The French commander next crossed the Rhine and invested Fribourg, which in a few weeks shared the fate of Landau. These losses following the desertion of his allies at length induced the emperor to come to terms, and Prince Eugene and Marshal Villars met at Rastadt in March, 1714, to discuss the conditions of peace. In the course of these the imperial general insisted that the ancient privileges of the Catalans, who had made so many sacrifices for the house of Austria, should be restored. Villars replied that he had no instructions upon this point, and the matter seems to have dropped. The emperor still refused to recognise the title of Philip to the Spanish crown, but notwithstanding this difficulty peace was eventually concluded between the emperor and the King of France on the 6th March, 1714, and the war of the Spanish succession was at an end.

The question of the Catalans still remained unsettled, and it was one in which England, as well as the emperor, was directly interested. The Catalans had fought valiantly under Peterborough and Stanhope for the archduke, and were now threatened with the vengeance of his successful rival. Although their position was desperate, they still continued in arms in defence of their *fueros*, and although abandoned both by England and Austria, they defended Barcelona against the combined forces of France and Spain for upwards of a twelvemonth. That city was taken by storm on the 11th September, 1714, and the ancient privileges of the Catalans were finally abolished. The desertion of the Catalans was wholly inexcusable. The allies in their diplomatic correspondence had clearly admitted their obligation to protect them. Yet when the crisis came they deliberately abandoned them to the vengeance of their enemies.

Queen Anne had died in the previous month universally lamented on account of her many amiable qualities,[1] and thirteen months later Louis the Fourteenth ended his long and eventful reign.[2] If we are to believe his biographers the retrospect gave but little satisfaction to the aged king. "Beware, my child," he said to the sickly boy who inherited his crown—"beware of indulging

[1] She seems to have been at all times anxious for the restoration of peace. To Ménager, who was sent with Gaultier and Prior to arrange the terms in 1711, she said:—"It is a good work; pray God prosper you in it. I am sure I long for peace. I hate this dreadful work of blood."—Stanhope, p. 493.

[2] Anne died on 1st August, 1714; Louis on 1st September, 1715.

" a taste for extravagance and war, for they bring ruin
" on the people." Unfortunately for his country and
for mankind, he learned these simple truths too late.

The treaty of Utrecht terminated an important period
of modern history. After the decline of the feudal
system and the rise of the great Continental monarchies
we find that at three different epochs three powerful
princes threatened the peace and the independence of
Europe. But Charles the Fifth found a Maurice of
Saxony, Ferdinand the Second a Gustavus Adolphus,
and Louis the Fourteenth a Marlborough to oppose and
overthrow their deep-laid schemes of aggrandisement.
We may, perhaps, conclude from these and from subsequent examples that since the establishment of standing
armies it is the tendency of some particular State to
become too powerful for the peace and tranquillity of its
neighbours. For this state of things there is, as all
history proves, but one remedy. The notion of preserving
the balance of power in the European system has been
derided by many writers in the present age, and it is true
that to maintain a perfect balance is impracticable. But
the instinct of self-preservation is paramount among
nations as among men, and we may rest assured that the
rise of any European Power to an exorbitant degree of
power would lead to results similar to those that have
been again and again witnessed in the past.

APPENDIX No. I.

THE LEAGUE OF CAMBRAY.

EXTRACT of a Despatch from the Council of Ten to the Venetian Consul in London, with instructions to him to seek an interview with Henry the Seventh, and to point out to the King of England the dangers of allowing France to accomplish her ambitious designs in Italy, dated 12th of February, 1509:—

"His Majesty of his great wisdom should consider that if the King of France is allowed to occupy Italy the immediate result will be the violent usurpation of the Popedom, to which Rouen (Cardinal d'Amboise) ardently aspires. Thus would France become monarch of the world, for the overthrow of the empire would certainly follow, which with the spiritual authority she would then unite in herself. Such unbecoming and immoderate projects should be opposed by every Christian sovereign, especially by such as have the greatest grace and power from the Almighty, like his Majesty the King of England."

The Venetians were at this time endeavouring to detach the Emperor Maximilian from the League, and with reference to this point the despatch contains the following instructions:—"Labour with all thine ability to induce His Majesty of England to reconcile and unite us to the Emperor. Thou shalt also dispose him against France in order to deter her from the invasion of Italy; and the greater and more speedy his demonstration to this effect the more will it prove to the purpose, and should he forthwith write a strong letter to the King of France in such grave terms as his Majesty of his wisdom will well know how to employ, it would be a very profitable and salutary commencement; and it would also produce great effect were his Majesty to write to the Pope acquainting him with his mind, and pointing out the perils of Christendom, which would be augmented by the introduction of such troubles into Italy, and most especially by the disorder of our state, and we consider it indubitable that his Holiness, who is well aware of the snares laid for him, would conform himself throughout to the will of his Majesty.

"There is no occasion for us to say more, save that the negotiation which we place in thy hand is of extreme importance, and therefore the more strenuously thou performest this commission the more wilt thou deserve praise, commendation, and reward from our Liguory," &c.

On the 16th of February, 1509, the following instructions were forwarded by the Council of Ten to the imperial ambassador, Luca de Renaldi.

After expressing their entire confidence in his prudence and loyalty, as well as in his regard for the Emperor Maximilian, the despatch proceeds as follows:—"Expatiate on the long-tried devotion of the Republic to the Emperor and his ancestors, and on the identity of interests between the state of Venice and the entire German nation. If last year their deeds seemed at variance with this inclination, and if they were unable to obey the Emperor, this did not proceed from any lack of desire to do even much greater things for his Majesty, but from an inability to act, they being then bound by another engagement. From that tie they are now released, as they told him, and are therefore ready and anxious to return to their natural course, the Emperor likewise being bound by no law, either divine or human, to keep faith with those who break it so easily with others, and who so often and so unworthily have infringed and violated their oath to his imperial Majesty.

"Their reverence for the Emperor and the Holy Roman empire, coupled with their zeal for the Christian commonwealth, whereof his Majesty is the head, protector, and governor, induce them therefore to explain to him the snares now prepared under the veil and pretext of advantage, in order to usurp the imperial dignity and transfer the same from Germany to France. This result is to be effected by the invasion of Italy and the occupation of the apostolic see in order to secure for France the spiritual and temporal monarchy of that country. The Emperor should interpose in time, not only for his own safety, but also for that of the Christian religion, which will otherwise incur great peril from the infidels. The Republic desires to form a perpetual alliance with the Emperor, offer and promise him all the resources at its disposal, including money for the recovery of the Milanese territory, now in the hands of the

French, agree to advance 200,000 Rhenish guilders for the above purpose, 50,000 to be paid on the ratification of a formal treaty; 50,000 on the Emperor invading the Milanese territory; 50,000 at the end of a month from that period, and the residue at the end of the second month. Declare the firm intention of the Republic of adhering perpetually to the Emperor, and of considering him the father and protector of the state. They are persuaded the Emperor will accept their offers, together with so excellent an opportunity of avenging the many bitter injuries done him by his ancient and natural enemies, and that all Italy, which abhors the French, will side with the Emperor.

"Motion made that should Dom Luca de Renaldi bring the said negotiation to a good end, he is to receive benefices in the Venetian territory of the annual value of 2,000 ducats; that until put in possession he is to be guaranteed 1,000 ducats a year from the funds of the Council of Ten; and that there be forthwith given as a gift to Dom Luca 500 Rhenish guilders." [*]

APPENDIX No. II.

THE complaints of the Electors against Wallenstein at the Diet of Ratisbon, 1630.

" The Electors, in a great and solemn answer, insisted upon the miseries of the present times, the outrages committed in the wars, and the excessive impositions, laying all the fault upon the author of all these, the new Duke of Mecklenburg, General of the Emperor's great army; seeing that unto him he had given so large commission (and that without the consent of the Princes of the empire) as never before him any had. That there had an infinite army been gathered, to no use unless to the destruction of their country; that war had commenced against various princes without a declaration; that the impositions which by the law of the empire it had been fit to have assessed by the joint consent of the princes, had, at the pleasure of the said Duke, been imposed and most rigorously exacted. They at the same time also affirmed

[*] Calendar of State Papers (Venice), edited by Rawdon Brown vol. 1, pp. 338, 339.

how that the Elector of Brandenburg alone in the few years past (besides the incalculable damages which usually accompany the wars) had to contribute (and that under the name of tribute) to the value of twenty millions of florins.

"At which time these several complaints were also given in. The Duke of Pomerania complained himself for ten millions drawn out of his principality of Stettin alone; and that only in one year there had been one-and-thirty thousand foot and seven thousand five hundred and forty horse billeted upon Pomerania. William, Landgrave of Hesse, for his tribute of some certain years, seven millions; the Duke of Wirtemberg contributed monthly an hundred and twenty thousand florins. The city and state of Nuremberg twenty thousand a month; others likewise complained of some more, some less, that had been raked from them. They highly complained of the prodigal luxury of the said Duke, his colonels and captains for their flaunting in such rich clothes and household stuff of gold and silver, and the incredible high keeping and trappings of their horses.

"At the same time there was a little book showed up and down, wherein the ordinary provisions of his house, the officers of his camp, and the names of those that had principal charge about him were contained; and all these with larger allowances (as it was said) than those of the Emperor's own palace. Then was his so much envied house, built at Prague, out of the spoils of the empire, and upon ruins of an hundred houses (purposely plucked down for him) everywhere spoken of. Nor could any of these things be denied. * * * *

"Unto Wallenstein, therefore, there were sent John Baptista Verdenberg and Gerard Questenberg, Barons, both of them, and both ot them enriched by him with many a mighty gift; and both of them always believed to be at court the great advancers of his projects. But even therefore were they made choice of before any others as the fittest men to preside with him. The task which they under took seemed to be the difficultest of all the rest, it being believed that Wallenstein being a man of a most haughty spirit, accustomed to military command, one that had been courted by the greatest princes and upheld by infinite riches, would never duly endure such an affront, nor by his free will ever stoop again into a private life. Cause to fear, moreover, he had, lest they who never durst do it when he was a general would yet require their own of him when he should become a private man. And the Duchy of Mecklenburg (they believed) likely thereby to be exposed to most certain danger. All men's minds now full of expectation what would be the event of that message; all were now afraid of new hurly-burlies; behold now what everybody much admired at: Wallenstein immediately obeys the commandment of the Emperor," &c.

From the *Swedish Intelligencer*, London, 1630.

The contents of the conditions whereupon the Duke of Friedland hath re-accepted of the generalship, which, in the name of his imperial Majesty, hath by divers privy councillors (both of war and peace) been offered unto him.

1.

"The Duke of Friedland shall be Generalissimo, not only for the Emperor but also for the King of Spain and the whole House of Austria, and for ever so continue.

2.

"The Generalship shall be wholly and plenarily conferred upon the Duke of Friedland, in the most absolute form that may be.

3.

"His royal Majesty Ferdinand the Second shall not be personally present in the army; much less have any command over it. But when the kingdom of Bohemia shall be again recovered, his Majesty shall personally keep court at Prague and Don Balthasar di Marradas for his better security shall wait upon him with 12,000 men in Bohemia until there be an universal peace established in Germany. For the Duke of Friedland well perceiveth that the Bohemians both must and will have their King to be personally resident among them. By this means also shall both the Emperor and his General rest the better assured that no rebellion shall be there attempted.

4.

"His imperial Majesty shall give him security in the best manner that he shall have some Lordship given him in inheritance in Austria for his ordinary recompense.

5.

"He shall for his extraordinary recompense have the highest rank in any of the recovered countries of Germany.

6.

"He shall have the disposal of all the confiscations in the empire, after the most absolute manner, so that neither the Imperial Council, nor Exchequer, nor the Chamber at Spires shall pretend any interest in them, either in part or in whole, nor have anything to do with the decision of them.

7.

"The Duke of Friedland shall have absolute power to dispose, not only in matters of confiscation but of pardon also, and notwithstanding there should from the Emperor's court be granted any letters of safe-conduct or of pardon, yet that without the Duke of Friedland's confirmation they shall be of no value, and extend no further than unto life and honour, and not unto goods or estate; the real and absolute pardoning whereof shall be granted by him alone. For his imperial Majesty is too gracious and too good, and pardoneth every one who sues to his court for it, which if it should be so still, then should the higher and lower colonels and officers of the army have their rewards taken away; and the soldiery, that which should give them content.

8.

"And if there should ere long happen to be a peace treated upon in the empire, that then the Duke of Friedland's own interest to the Dukedom of Mecklenburg should be contained in the capitulation.

9.

"All the charges and expenses for the continuation of the war shall be given unto him.

10.

"All the hereditary dominions of his imperial Majesty shall at any time be open unto him and his army."*

---

* The *Swedish Intelligencer*, second part, published in London, 1632, p. 225.

APPENDIX No. III.

LETTRE de l'EMPEREUR au ROY de SUEDE.*

NOUS Ferdinand par la grace de Dieu, empereur des Romains, &c. Au serenissime prince Gustave, Adolphe, roy de Suede, des Goths & Vandalles, &c. nostre amitié, dilection, & salut. Serenissime prince & tres cher amy, il nous a esté rapporté de divers lieux, dignes de foy, que vostre dilection a dressé n'agueres une puissant armée de cavalerie & infanterie, dont elle a inopinément fait entrer une partie, aprés avoir passé la mer, dans les isles de l'empire Romain, & en terre ferme au duché de Pomeranie, s'y estant emparce, non seulement de quelques places, villes, & chasteaux d'importance : mais a aussi outre cela commencé d'usurper les gabelles & peages (qui en vertu de droict royal, n'appartiennent qu' à nos) & est encores en volunté de nous assaillir par toute sorte d'hostilité, & d'empieter d'avantage sur les pays dudit empire. Nous n'avons point souvenance, que depuis que nous soustenons cette grande charge d'empereur il soit arrivé entre nous aucun contraire ou sinistre accident, ou que nous ou l'empire ayons donne occasion de trouble ou dissension, moins d'une si ouverte hostilité Et pourtant il nous semble fort estrange, que vostre dignité a entrepris de jetter contre nous & l'empire, les fondemens d'une guerre, possible tres facheuse à l'une & à l'autre des parties, & ce pour quelque different particulier, touchant la ville de Stralsond, duquel vostre dignité n'a deu concevoir aucun ombrage de danger ou prejudice. Car tout cela s'est passé dans nostre terriore, & de l'empire, & concerne les droicts, & privileges d'iceluy, esquels vostre dignité n'a non plus de droict de nous faire la loy, qu'avec raison elle se trouveroit offenceé, qu'en semblables debats l'on entreprist, de la maistriser en son royaume de Suede. Et ce d'autant plus, qu' à nostre opinion ledit different pouroit facilement estre composé & assoupy, sous des conditions equitables, sans venir à aucune hostilité ou effusion de sang, par l'entremise du roy de Dannemarc, qui n'a fait aucune difficulté de s'en charger, aussi promptement qu'on le luy avoit

* Mercure François, tom. xvi., p. 334, &c.

proposé & conseillé, si vostre dignité s'y fust portée de mesme zele
& affection que nous, & qu'elle eust au temps prefix & assigné
envoyé ses ministres avec instruction suffisante. Mais comment que
ce soit, il estoit plus que raisonnable par le droict des gens, que
vostre dignité (supposé, qu'elle eust creu d'estre assez bien fondée
de nous attaquer par armes & de rompre toute amitié) nous eust
prealablement denoncé la guerre par un deffi public & legitime,
avant qu'envahir l'empire si injustement, asseurant vostre dignité,
que nos preparatifs de guerre prez la mer Baltique, & ailleurs, n'ont
point esté faits pour l'offencer, ny cy devant, ny à present: ains
qu'au contraire nous avons eu le desir, de continuer entre nous les
effets de bon voisinage & toute amitié mutuelle, comme nous avons
encore cette mesme affection, pourveu que vostre dignité par ses
procedures contraires ne nous donne plus de sujet de nous porter à
d'utres resolutions, & qu'elle fasse cesser cette guerre non neces-
saire. C'est pourquoy nous l'exhortons amiablement, de ne s'ingerer
plus avant és affaires de l'empire & que (ne luy ayans donné nulle
occasion) elle n'offence ny nous, ny les membres dudit empire, ains
qu'elle retire son armée, au plustost des isles & terres d'iceluy par
elle occupées : Qu'elle n'empesche plus par ses navires, la navigation & le commerce maritime, & qu'elle ne nous incommode point,
soit par mer, soit par terre, en la perception des droicts de l'empire. Que si au contraire (ce que nous n'estimons pas) il arrive,
que vostre dignité en mesprisant nostre presente declaration imperiale, & confidente assurance de nostre amitié, persiste en cette
hostilité, & s'opiniastre à retinir les places par elles prises, par ruse
de guerre, ou par force ; nous, avec l'ayde & conseil des electeurs de
l'empire mettrons promptement en estat pour les recouvrer, &
prendrons à cœur la conservation de nostre reputation & de l'empire, ensemble la defence & manutention des estats, qui continueront
la fidelité & obeyssance qu'ils nous doivent, afin d'obvier à une
plus grande calamité. Nous esperons, que vostre dignité ne per-
mettra point, que l'affair vienne à cette extremité ; & selon qu'elle
aura deferé à nos presentes lettres imperiales, nous serons tres
prompts & disposez à luy faire paroistre par bons offices nostre
amitié & bien-veillance en ce qui luy sera agreable. Donné à
Ratisbonne, le dix huictiesme Aoust, mil fix cens trente. D. V. D.
cousin & affectioné,

FERDINAND.

LETTRE du Roy de Suede à l'Empereur.*

AU serenissime & tres puissant prince Ferdinand II. de ce nom, empereur esleu des Romains, d'Allemagne, d'Hongrie, Boheme, Dalmatie, Croatie, & Sclavonie, roy, archiduc d'Austriche, duc de Bourgogne, Stirie, Carniole & Virtemberg, comte de Habsbourg & Tirol, nostre tres cher cousin & amy.

Serenissime & tres puissant empereur, cousin & tres cher amy. Nous avons (non sans admiration) entendu par la lettre de vostre serenité, datée du 18 d'Aoust, & a nous renduë seulement le 6 de ce mois, en nostre camp de Ribnitz, qu'elle s'emerveille beaucoup, que cet esté passé nous soyons entrez avec nostre armée en Allemagne, & que vous taschez de nous rendre coulpables, tant de cette entreprise mesme, que de ce qu'elle soit faite sans aucune denonciation ou defi public. Certainement nous ne pensions jamais que vostre serenité eust peu tomber en une si profonde oubliance des choses passées, ny se mesprendre contre la personne de celuy qui a commencé d'offenser l'autre par ses armes, puis que nous nous sommes tousjours promis de son equité, qu'elle n'imputeriot jamais à la partie innocente ce que la coulpable avoit commise, & ne chargeroit l'une de la faute de l'autre; attendu que c'est le maistre de camp de vostre serenité, qui sans aucune prealable denonciation (nous ne rapporterons icy par le menu une infinité de cruantez & de hostilitez contre nous exercées) nous a jetté sur les bras és années passées une grande & puissant armée, tant de cheval que de pied, sous les estendarts ou aigles de l'empire Romain. Ce qui est notoire, & autant manifeste comme il est tres veritable que nous n'avons que trop experimenté les mauvaises intentions & violences de ladite armée, losquelles, ny neus-mesmes, par nostre innocence, ny le conseil de nostre royaume, par ses remonstrances bien fondées & tres equitables, n'avons peu faire arrester ny revoquer. C'est pourquoy, bien que nous le pezions en gros, ou en detail, nous ne pouvons comprendre sous quel pretexte ou titre on nous pourroit charger de le cause de cette guerre, & par quelle raison on pourroit precisément demander de nous la denonciation, laquelle vostre serenité a mesme negligée, estant certain que nous n'avons travaillé qu'à tenir pour nostre seureté la guerre esloignée de nous, sans la faire à autruy. Nous ne voyons aussi aucune

* Mercure François, tom. xvi, p. 347, &c.

raison, qu'on nous charge du crime commis contre le droict des gents, puis que ce droict contient en son vray sens, qu'és guerres deffensives les defits ne se sont tousjours par des herauts ou rois d'armes, mais par la nature & qualité mesme de telles guerres, quand on se sent contre le droict tout-a-fait offensé, & ouvertement assailly : voire qui plus est, pour ne manquer à une denonciation, quoyque superfluë, & pour ne donner sujet de se plaindre de nous avec fondement, comme si nous eussions trompé le monde par les projets d'une paix, au envahi l'empire à l'improviste, nous nous sommes servis de cette precaution d'escrire à deux diverses fois aux electeurs de l'empire Romain, comme aussi nous avons admonesté vostre serenité par un deputé de nostre dit conseil vers le general de vostre serenité, que si l'on n'avoit esgard à nos justes plaintes, en nous donnant satisfaction des fautes contre nous commises, nous serions constraints de pourvoir par autre voye à la seureté & conservation de nostre estat & dignité.

Vostre serenité dit bien, que depuis son advenement à la dignité imperiale elle n'a commis ou permis aucune chose tendante au prejudice ou danger de nostre estat ; que vos appareils & preparatifs par terre & par mer, n'ont jamais eu le but d'apporter aucun dommage à nous ou à nos estats, & que par des moyens paisibles on eust peu composer nos differents, n'estans pas d'une telle importance, qu' avec raison on se pouvoit formaliser pour troubler l'empire. Mais sur cela nous disons que nous n'avons pas l'intention de debatre icy, si ces protestations ne sont directement contraires aux actes & effects si evidens, remettans tout au jugement libre de tout le monde. Et que nous ne scavons pas aussi exactement, si vostre serenité (dont les pensées nous sont incogneues) ait eu quelque intention de nous faire du mal, ou de nous offencer : mais que sons l'ombre & l'authorité du nom, & de la haute dignité imperiale, soit par vostre commandement, ou par une grande connivence nous nous trouvons offencez, & outragez de beaucoup de dommages & affronts. Nous le scavons & sentons, veu qu'il est aussi manifeste, que si quelqu'un se vouloit amuser à en faire des demonstrations ou deductions plus amples, ce seroit esclairer le soliel en plein midy. Dont nous appellons sans difficulté à la conscience de vostre serenité, laquelle nous prendrons pour tesmoin ou juge. Et quant à l'appareil de guerre, & de ce que nous en avons deu juger, nous rapportons à la cognoissance que tout le monde en a, & aux discours tant passez que presents de vos ministres et officiers ; mais principalement à leurs actes, traictez, entreprises, excez, desseins & conseils, lesquels comme trop suspects & apparents, descouvrent assez ce que nous en avons deu attendre. Et si tout cela n'estoit assez notoire, le duché de Pomeranie & les provinces voisines pourroient tesmoigner, que sous le faux pretexte de la crainte de nos armes, mais en effect à dessein de nous desplaire & faire du mal, les gens de vostre serenité les ont tourmentez, pillez et entierment ruinez.

Nous advoiions bien clairement & simplement, que les differents survenus entre nous pouvoient estre utilement terminez par autres moyens que par armes, d'autant qu'il seroit à souhaiter que vous n'eussiez enterpreté sinistrement, ains acunement souffert nostre secours justement donné à la miserable & trop injustement oppressée ville de Stralsond, sans prejudicier en aucune façon à l'empire Romain, ains plustost pour garentir les decrets de vostre serenité, comme nous avons de bon cœur, et d'un courage endurcy à la patience & constance, postposé à la commune tranquilitié, et au repos public de la Chrestienté, toutes les indignitez et offences que nostre cousin le duc de Holstein, par vostre commandement, et sous les enseignes de l'empire nous a faites. Par ainsi nous ne doutons point que nous n'eussions peu venir à quelque accommodement, au lieu qu'an rebours on nous a contrains d'assembler avec grande despence une puissante armée, et la passer et loger en Allemagne, pour obvier en temps aux perils et dangers qui s'advancoient et nous menacoient trop evidemment. Mais puis qu'il a pleu a vostre serenité de choisir une voye contraire, et vos subdeleguez, lors presens en la ville de Lubec, pour assister au traicté qui s'y faisoit avec le roy de Dannemarc, s'estans enhardis, contre le droict des gens, de refuser et defendre l'accez à nos embassadeurs y envoyez à cette fin, pour travailler à la composition de l'affaire de Stralsond ; joinct aussi que les armées de vostre serenité se sont ouvertement declarées de nous en vouloir, & l'ont confirmé par toutes sortes d'hostilitez ; nous avons cette grande confiance, qu'il n'y aura ame vivante, aimant le droicht & l'equité, laquelle estant authorisée pour juge ou arbitre, ne declare que la faute ou couple n'est pas en nous, mais bein en vousmesmes, qui avez mieux aimé de preferer la guerre à la paix par une certaine malveillance & inimitié conceue contre nous sans aucun sujet. Or combien que nous sentons si iniquement

& sans aucune juste cause provoquez nous voyans hors de toute esperance de venir à quelque accommodement, estans bien certains qu'on ne nous imputera jamais aucun dessein ou attentat inique, ny destraisonnable, pour lequel nous, pour estre plus exempts de tout sinistre soupçon, ne serions plus obligez d'entendre à la paix, quon nous a voulu vendre trop chere : toutefois pour manifester à la Chrestienté nostre zele & ardeur au bien & tranquilitié publique, nous n'avons point voulu desister de nos conseils & intentions dirigées à icelle, ains par nos serieuses & assidues recherches, avons esmeu le roy de Dannemarc, à ce que par son interposition, durant l'hyver passé, il nous preparast le chemin d'une amiable conference, qu'on feignoit devoir estre entamée entre nos commissaires de part & d'autre en la ville de Dantsick, ou nous avions envoyé, nostre chancelier avec les adjoincts, bien munis de suffisant pouvoir & instruction. Et afin que les factions de guerre ne troublassent ou empeschassent les propositions & deliberations de paix, nous avons arresté & dilayé de faire advancer nostre armée, non sans grande perte de temps, desadvantage notable, & frais extraordinaries. Pour lequel soin particulier, qui ne visoit qu'au repos universal de la Christienté, nous avons pour recompense, que non seulement nos bonnes & salutaires pensees ont esté aneanties par plusieurs illusions & subterfuges : mais que vostre serenité ose encores nous imputer la malheureuse issue dubit traicté, au lieu qu'avec raison elle devoit plustost examiner les actions & procedures de son commissaire, par lesquelles vostre serenité auroit cogneu, qu'il a empesché que les mediateurs de cette affaire estans à Dantsick ne peussent mesmes venir à quelque entreveuë avec nos ambassadeurs, pour donner fondement a un traicté selon que la coustume & la raison requierent en tel cas.—Vostre serenité eust aussi outre cela mieux fait, de considerer que ledit traicté se pouvoit autant commodément & bien faire en quelque autre lieu, qu'en la ville de Dantsick, puis que cette place, pour quelques differents survenus entre nos officiers & ladite ville, s'estoit renduë suspecte. Et vostre serenité eust deu quitter toute opiniastreté plustost que de causer au repos publique des prejudices & dangers si grands, ou de rompre totalement & à dessein tout traicté;—principalement à l'esgard que nos commissaires esprouverent assez clairement par des raisons manifestes & urgentes, qu'il ne leur estoit plus loisible de condescendre a aucun traicité au susdit lieu de

Dantsick, bien que vostre commissaire sist des instances toutes contraires.

Quand donc tout cecy, tant en general qu'en particulier, sera bien consideré, nous pouvons fort librement laisser le jugement à toute personne sincere & exempte de passion, lequel de nous deux a plus juste cause de se plaindre ; & sans aller plus loin, nous remettons tout a l'interieur de vostre conscience, afin qu'elle en soit juge, veu que la nostre nous asseure fermement, que vous mesmes nous tenez pour inculpables.

Vostre serenité dit bien, qu'elle veut conserver avec nous & nostre royaume de Suede une amitié indissoluble, à condition que nous quittions & rappellions nos armées. Mais les choses sont venuës trop avant, & ne sont plus en leur entir, puis que les dangers qui ont menacé & menacent tousjours nous & nos sujets, ne sont point imaginatifs, mais reels & effectifs : outre ce qu'on nous a, non par paroles, ains par armes, rudement attaqué, en exercant contre nouse toute sorte d'hostilité, tant par mer que par terre. Et pourtant nous esperons que vostre serenité nous excusera, si pour nostre seureté nous ne pouvons accepter telles offres & promesses, que vous appellez des sincerations, veu qu'icelles ne nous pourront jamais donner aucune satisfaction, parce que nous sommes plus griesument blessez & offencez en effect, que de simples paroles : & croyons que vostre serenité ne prendra en mauvaise par nostre resolution, de tenir fermes nos armes, que la necessité inevitable, & vos outrages nous ont fait prendre ; & de ne ceder, ny ployer en aucune maniere, jusques à ce que nous soyons exempts par vrayes & parfaictes cautions, du peril trop evident qui penche sur nous, & que les grandes offenses, & violents affronts à nous faits, soient reparez par une solide & reelle satisfaction sans aucune tache de nostre reputation. En cette constante & tres-juste intention, nous attendrons constamment tout ce qui nous arrivera de la main de Dieu, à la bonté duquel, comme à la justice de nostre cause, nous avons tout remis, & recommandé.

Mais si d'aventure vostre serenité est cependant touchée d'un sentiment, qu'il soit desormais que le vaisseau de la Chrestienté, agité & tourmenté par des orages de guerre, soit en fin conduit au port de la paix, autant salutaire & profitable, comme souhaitée de tant d'oppressez soubs le joug des miseres, sans l'abandonner plus aux tempestes furieuses des ravages & desolations, & que pour cet effect le renouëment d'un traicté de paix aggréera à vostre serenité: nous donnons parole d'y vouloir promptement entendre, & d'y apporter tout ce qui sera en nostre pouvoir pour l'advancement & le progres d'un œuvre si sainct & glorieux.

Ce qui aura lieu, si vostre serenité promet & demonstre, effectivement ; que les princes & villes d'Allemagne, comme respectivement nos tres chers cousins, beaux freres, parents, amis, alliez & voisins, seront restituez en l'estat au quel ils estoient devant ces derniers troubles, en sorte que nous puissions esperer cy-apres de joüir d'une entiere seureté, pour nostre estat, de ce costú là : que l'amitié & bonne correspondence entre nostre royaume & ledites provincis soit restablie, & que nous scachions estre cassez, aneantis, & revoquez, tous appareils & equipages de guerre par mer, comme nous estans trop suspects & contraires à la prerogative que nous avons de protecteur de la mer Baltique ; & que finalement les despenses par nous faites pour nostre defense, à laquelle nous avons esté obligez & constraints par vos injures & offenses, viendront en juste deuë consideration. Alors vostre serenité n'aura pas si tost de son costé accomply ces choses, que par effect elle trouvera que nous ferons voir à tout le monde combien nous sommes poussez d'ambition à maintenir, tant avec vous qu'autres nos voisins, une amitié inviolable, sincere & constante, & que nous desirons sur toute chose vous vaincre & surpasser par toute sorte d'amitié & de bons offices, apres que la bonne intelligence entre nous sera restablie, & tous malentenduës ostes. Les choses doncques estans remises en tel estat, nous ne voudrions veritablement donner aucun subjet à personne de soupçonner, ou de se plaindre justement que nous melassions impertinemment ou presomptueusement des affaires qui ne nous touchent point, ou peu. Car comme nous ne sommes accoustumez de nous ingerer aux affaires d'autruy, quand elles ne sont tellement joinctes à nos interests, que celles là trainent ceux-cy avec elles : tesmoin nos deportements, durant le temps de la guerre par tout allumée en Allemagne, où nous n'avons songé qu'à ce qui concerne nostre royaume, & non à la Germanie jusques au temps que par outre evidence & iniquité de vos ministres, les affaires esloignées nous sont venuës sur les bras, & par leur union, consequence, & reflexion, nous ont poussé & engagé à prendre soin de celles d'autruy, comme des nostres propres. Par ainsi l'on nous trouvera maintenant & à l'advenir en si bonne intention, que nous ne tenons, ny ne voudrions tenir, en aucune façon que ce soit, les affaires d'Allemagne, pour les nostres, & vous asseurons de ne vouloir vous y donner la moindre fascherie.

 Nous concluons donc avec cette sincere & saincte protestation, que tout cecy soit entendu, ou droictement, ou sinistrement, & que cette affaire se tourne, ou en paix, ou en guerre : que nous ne couvons aucune inimitié ou hostilité contre l'empire Romain, jaçoit que vous taschiez de vous servir de telles expositions pour vostre descharge & excuse, & pour nous charger de hayne & de blasme. Mais tant s'en faut, que nous voulussions jamais songer à aucune chose, tendante à son prejudice ou dommage ; qu'au contraire nous declarons, de vouloir continuer & conserver une pure & vraye amitié & correspondence aussi longuement, que de sa part on s'abstiendra de toute hostilité contre nous, & qu'on ne favorisera par assistance nos ennemis, pour ne nous forcer de venir à des oppositions & revenges legitimes. Et tout ce que dit est vous suffra pour le present d'une declaration bien nette de nostre affection & volonté sur ce sujet. Vous recommandant à la saincte grace de Dieu. Escrit à Stralsond ce dernier jour d'Octobre mil six cents trente. De vostre serenité tres-affectionné cousin,

GUSTAVE ADOLPHE.

APPENDIX No. IV.

A short NARRATION of the PROTESTANT DIET held at LEIPSIC: beginning February the 8th, 1630-1, and ending April the 3d, 1631. Printed at London, 1632. See Harte's Gustavus Adolphus, vol. ii., Append.

THE imperial diet at Ratisbon thus ending November $\frac{3}{13}$, left matters in a far worse state than it found them: for that men perceived now their very hopes to be taken away, as their liberties and goods had been before: and the protestant princes finding themselves startled by four things especially, perceived it high time now for them to take the alarm. The first of the four was this: that whereas the duke of Saxony had, in the time of the diet, written advice unto the emperor, of the king of Sweden's approaching; the emperor tells him again, how he hoped that himself (the elector of Saxony) and Brandenburg would well aid him with money, ammunition, and other necessaries. By which answer, the elector of Saxony perceived a new bill of charges coming upon the protestants next those parts where the king of Sweden was landed. The second was this: the compendious course taken by the emperor for the recovering of the church lands; which neither the elector of Saxony was able to stop by his letters unto the emperor, nor the elector of Brandenburg, and other princes, with their presence at the diet:* but that even before their own faces, daily commissions were sent out against them. A third was this: the rigid course (taken by advice of the jesuits) for reformation of the protestant churches and schools, and the forbidding of the liberty of the Augustan confession. The fourth was, that decree of the emperor (published four days before the breaking up of the diet, though projected long before) for the continuance of the wars against the king of Sweden: whereas the way had been propounded and advised upon before,

---

* Harte says—"We have proved the contrary of this assertion, in the part of "our history that relates to it: the two electors alleging, by way of excuse for their "personal absence, that the imperial troops had rendered them unable to defray the "expences of such a journey." *See also Memoirs of the House of Brandenburg.*

how to compound the matter, rather than how to continue the troubles. And what aggravated the decree for the wars being, not only that the princes were to be at the charges of it, but that the levies were to be laid and collected, not by the consent of those who should pay them, but at the pleasure of the imperial commissaries: for the moderating of whose power, and repressing the numbers and insolencies of the soldiers, notwithstanding some slight promises were now made, yet how far they would be kept, was in their own pleasures. The protestants by these arguments being not only made suspicious, but sensible too, that there were not over many good intentions in the emperor towards them, their estates or religions, began to enter into a consultation for their own safety. The plot for it was laid thus. That whereas there had been a conference between them and the catholics at the former diet, concerning the church lands, the further treaty thereupon was referred unto a diet (procured by the catholics) to be held at Francfort upon Mayn, in August following; the duke of Saxony should write his letters unto the emperor (which was seconded by the mediation of the electors of Mentz and Bavaria), intreating liberty for the protestants to hold a diet by themselves, in some convenient place; that so by their united councils they might be provided, for an answer at the future diet of Francfort.

The imperial assent being thus obtained, the protestant princes, by their letters and ambassadors, agree upon the diet; the place to be Leipsic, and the time the 8th of February. That the several princes and states therefore might know beforehand, what instructions to give unto the ambassadors they were to send, the duke of Saxony, in his invitatory letters to each of them, lays open the purpose of the intended diet; fairly communicating the main propositions, both unto them and to the emperor. The contents whereof were, first, to consult how the church might with a good conscience be maintained in her ancient liberties and happy state. Secondly, how to keep their due obedience to the emperor, and yet preserve the ancient constitutions and peace of the empire. Thirdly, how to maintain correspondency with the catholic princes. And, fourthly, what to answer for themselves both in general and particular, as well concerning the maintenance of the reformed religion, as to the emperor's edict concerning the church lands, when they should come to meet at the diet of Francfort.

z

The princes thus invited, and the time now come, upon the 4th of February, 1631, the elector of Saxony enters Leipsic in great state, and the elector of Brandenburg a little after him. Thither in person came these protestant princes also; Christian, another marquis of Brandenburg, John, William, and Bernard, dukes of Saxe Weymar. William landgrave of Hesse-Cassel, Frederick marquis of Baden, Augustus prince of Anhault, Frederick count of Solmes, John, George, and Ernest Lodowicke, counts of Mansfeilt, and the deposed dukes of Mecklenburg. The following princes sent their deputies, the duke of Deuxponts, John Ernest, another duke of Saxony, Frederick Ulrick, duke of Brunswick, the duke of Lunenburg. The several princes of the Circles of Suabia and Franconia,* the lady of the abbey of Quidlinburg, the bishop administrator of Mecklenburg, the counts of Stolberg, the barons of Reussen and Schonberg. These towns and states sent their agents also: Norimberg, Strasburg, Francfort, Lubec, Bremen, Brunswick, Hildesheim, Mulhausen, and Northausen.† Duke Lodowic Frederick, administrator of the dukedom of Wirtemberg, was newly dead, and duke Julius not yet settled; and therefore being not able to come himself, he sent the vice-chancellor of the dukedom, called Dr. Loefler, and some other counsellors, as deputies for that duchy. And these are the protestant party in the empire; some whereof being Lutherans and some Calvinists, they first of all agree to have that distinction of names (which had caused so much schism and hatred heretofore) to be utterly taken away, making a general decree, that both professions should from thenceforth be called by one name of Evangelical.

No man was suffered to stay within the town, whose business was not known: the streets ends were chained up and barricadoed; guards set at the several ports; and the keys of the gates every night brought into the duke's chamber; and all this was to prevent spies and surprises. The duke, elector of Saxony (on whose greatness and countenance the party and action very much depended) makes a speech first of all, which had reference unto his former letters of invitation unto them; protesting withal, his own firmness and forwardness for the peace of the empire, and the maintenance

---

* Duke of Saxe-Altenberg; add likewise John Casimir duke of Saxe-Coburg, Augustus count Palatine, and Augustus prince of Anhault.
† Add the deputies of the archbishoprick of Bremen.

of the Religion; and that he would be ready to venture both life and goods in the cause; so desiring every man freely to give his counsel in such manner as they might be able to render a fair account of it unto the emperor. Unto this meeting, the king of Sweden also sends his ambassador, Dr. Chemnitius, who in his master's name delivers them this assurance: that his majesty's intentions were no other, than to restore the empire to her ancient peace, the princes to their liberties, and to defend the church in her religion; telling them moreover, that the French king was newly entered into a league with him for five years to come. The ambassador had both speedy audience and honourable entertainment. The diet, to be brief, broke up on Palm Sunday, the 3d of April following. The conclusions agreed upon, themselves express in their letters, in humble and complaining manner, enlarged in many sheets of paper, sent by an express courier unto the emperor, in which their joint desires were thus signified.

Their complaint and remonstrance I reduce into these propositions:—

That the golden bull and constitutions of the empire had of late been all abused; that the emperor's late edict for restitution of the church lands, and his endavours to root out the protestant religion, were the main causes of these late troubles. The first of these, breeding jealousies and discontents betwixt the protestants and the papists, and the second tending to the utter ruin of the two electors of Saxony and Brandenburg. Then they complain of injustice done unto particular princes and cities, some of which were injured by the violent taking away of their church lands: as the dukes of Wirtemberg and Brunswick, the prince of Anhalt, the counts of Hohenloe, Stolberg, Lippe, Waldec, Werthimb, Erpach, &c. the town of Augsburg, and others; some hindered in the exercise of their religion, as Augustus and Frederick, princes Palatine, and younger brothers unto Wolfgang William, Palatine of Newburg, now turned papist. Others had their estates confiscated, as the lady electress Palatine,* and her son Lewis, prince Palatine, the dukes of Mecklenburg, &c. for whom the whole college of electors had interceded in the late diet, but not prevailed. Others complain of the violent altering of the feods and tenures of their lands and

* The mother and brother of the king of Bohemia, Lewis being duke of Simmern.

lordships, as the last beforenamed princes and John Casimir elector of Saxony, into whose lands the imperial commissaries have with force and arms intruded, changing the tenures of the tenants, and altering the religion. Ernestus, marquis and elector of Brandenburg, complains of the same wrongs offered unto his pupils, the young marquises of Onspach*. Ulme duke of Brunswick complains, first, of the ravages of his lands done by Tilly, upon pretence of monies owing to the king of Denmark, and made over by the said king unto the emperor, who employed Tilly thus to strain for them. Secondly, of the seizure of his bishoprick of Hildesheim. And, thirdly, that the chief town of his own residence, Wolfenbuttle, had been forced to take an imperial garrison.

Others complain, how they might not have the benefit of the law, but were driven away by threatenings and discourtesies. The electors and princes complain of contempts and indignities offered unto their persons, some of them having been threatened the bastinado by some of the emperor's soldiers. The cities and circles of the empire complain, that undue and excessive impositions and taxes had been laid upon them, not by the consent of themselves (as the imperial laws command) but at the pleasure of any of the emperor's commissaries. That, under colour of protecting them, they have been forced to afford quarter and maintenance unto the imperial armies, who, when they should indeed have defended them, most cowardly ran away. That when they would not endure the soldiers insolencies, they have been declared enemies of the empire, and forbidden to defend themselves; that their lands have been given to soldiers, as if they had been conquered. That they have been forced to contribute to imaginary companies of soldiers (perchance to four or five), as if they had been a complete band. That the commissaries have assigned quarters and passages unto the soldiers, without ever asking leave of the princes or countries: that people have been tortured for their money, had their cattle driven away, their houses fired, and all commerce driven out of their country. That the soldiers neither observed martial discipline nor moral honesty, neitheir keeping the laws, nor fearing God; that virgins and women have been ravished upon the high altars; that if the weekly contributions were not paid at the commissaries absolute pleasure, the soldiers then spoiled the country.

* Which are of the house of Brandenburg: their lands lying by Nuremberg.

The marquis of Brandenburg complains, that notwithstanding the king of Sweden had two parts of his country (the old and the new Mark) yet was he forced to pay a full contribution for the whole marquisate to the Imperialists. That himself, by the soldiers being so long in his country, was left so poor, that he was not able to entertain a garrison for the defence of his own palace, and was fain to abridge even the necessary provisions of his own table and family; that the soldiers, entertained by the protestants for their own defence, have been turned against them, to take away the church lands; that trebly more contributions have been raised against no enemy, than ever were when the Turks were in Germany. That when the princes of the house of Saxony, as, namely, Altenburg, Weymar, and Coburg, had excused themselves of disability to pay each of them 1454 dollars a month, which the commissary Ossa had required of them; then Tilly threatened to draw 10,000 more dollars a month out of them. That considering all this, they could perceive nothing else, but that the emperor had intended their utter ruin; whereas he had dealt more gently with those of his own hereditary dominions. That all this is most contrary unto the oath of the emperor, and unto the laws of the empire, inasmuch as such hath been complained of by the several electors and princes, and by them protested against in the late diet of Ratisbon; wherefore they now humbly petition to be relieved, protesting otherwise that they are no longer able to endure, but shall be enforced to defend their persons, consciences, estates, and subjects; resolving notwithstanding to continue their due loyalty and obedience unto the emperor, humbly now desiring a fair and gracious answer from him. Leipsic, March 18, 1631.

Their conclusions were answerable unto their propositions.

1. That considering it was their sins which deserved these punishments, they command public prayers to be made unto Almighty God for the diverting of these miseries.

2. That means might be thought upon, and a friendly treaty appointed with the catholic princes, for removing all jealousies, and restoring good terms and concord betwixt them, as for seventy years before it had been.

3. That when the time and place for this treaty were once appointed, the protestants should there appear a little before, to prepare themselves what to say in it.

4. And the more fairly to dispose both Cæsar and the Catholics unto their intentions, that their grievances should in humble manner be beforehand, by letter, presented both unto the emperor and the three catholic electors.

5. That these grievances should in those letters be pressed to be contrary unto the emperor's oath, the imperial laws, the privileges of the princes, the honour and safety of the empire. That the wars would undo all; the insolencies of commissaries and soldiers were so insufferable, as that it stood neither with their consciences, their safeties, nor their honours, to suffer themselves and subjects to be any longer thus abused; and that they would hereupon desire the benefit of the emperor's so often promised protection.

6. That seeing these greater and fuller assemblies were both chargeable and tedious, they agreed, that certain deputies should, as necessity required, be, in the names of all the rest, appointed, both to treat and determine of what should seem convenient for the common cause.

7. The decree of levies of soldiers (both of horse and foot) to be made in their several dominions and divisions, without crossing the constitutions of the empire, or offence of any, and only in their own defence.

8. That whereas in a diet of the empire held in 1555, it had been decreed, how that neighbouring princes should live neighbourly, and if any oppressed others, the rest should relieve them; this relief they now promise one another, desiring, that if in these troublesome times, the levies and other carriages could not possibly be every way agreeable to the constitutions of the empire, that it might not be interpreted to be done on purpose.

9. They decree the continuance of their loyalty and obedience unto his imperial majesty.

10. They agree also upon the proportion of the levies.

Thus the elector of Saxony engages himself to raise six regiments, Brandenburg three. The several Circles of Suabia, the Rhine, and Franconia, three regiments apiece; and the Circle of Lower Saxony agreed to furnish monies for the raising and paying of one regiment. Each regiment of foot was to be 3,000 strong, and of horse 1,000. And thus the diet being ended upon Palm Sunday with a sermon, Saxony displays his defensive banner, beats up his drums, begins his levies, and so at their coming home do the rest of the princes.

These conclusions and resolutions of the protestants were not a little boggled at at court, did not slightly displease the emperor, and startle the catholic leaguers, with their adherents. The protestants hear of it in both ears; for this are they, both by words and writings, threatened and reviled; yea, their new league and strength were by some confidents not a little scoffed and scorned at. But they that had been used to hard deeds before, were sufficiently hardened against foul words now; they were not to be discouraged this way, they did their business, and let the others talk their talks. Things going thus on, it was by the middle of May every where perceived, how that these leaguers of Leipsic were now in very good earnest. For now upon the taking of Magdeburg, the protestants strongly suspecting by the inhuman cruelty there used by the imperialists, that it was not a heat of war alone, but that there was a core of malice discovered in it, not an imperial, but a popish spite, unto that city above others, for having been one of the first that harboured Luther and his religion; they begin to make it their own case, and that, for their religion's sake, they were all not likely to be much better used. Some therefore of the neighbour princes (those, namely, of Saxony and Suabia) demand of the cities of Ulm and Memmingen, &c. situate in Suabia by the river Danube (which were of the protestant league with them) to entertain for garrisons some of these new levied forces. Memmingen consents; but Ulm, being a greater city, relies upon her own strength. These things being done, command is given by the emperor unto Eggon count of Furstenburg (appointed general of the Circle of Suabia) to employ those 8,000 (lately come out of Italy, after that the wars of Mantua were ended) together with 8 or 10,000 more, against those towns aforesaid. Furstenburg presses so hard upon Memmingen, that about the beginning of June, he enforceth it to renounce the new league, and to purchase the emperor's pardon at the rate of 50,000 florins ready pay, and 25,000 monthly contribution. The protestant league being now noised abroad, and another meeting at the latter end of May at the same Leipsic intended, thither come the ambassadors of England, Sweden, Saxony, and Brandenburg; there is the uniting of their forces with the king of Sweden propounded, but not concluded; only the passage of

Wirtemberg, heretofore denied him by Saxony, is now yielded to, to be open for his army. M. Tilly about the same time dispeeds a message unto Saxony with overtures of peace, promising shortly to come himself with sufficient commission to confirm it. This being suspected to be a plot, either to divert or stagger the resolution of the duke, or a trick to gain time, and that Tilly's commission might perchance be in his scabbard, the message was not accepted, notwithstanding that Tilly did, in the mid June following, come in person indeed, and at Oldsleben had treaty with the duke's ambassadors.

When this would not do, and the emperor, by the duke's second letter (dated the day after the end of the late diet), understanding the resolution of the leaguers, which by their general levies he perceived them ready to maintain; and hearing withal, the king of Sweden to be victoriously already advanced quite through Pomerania and Mecklenburg, into some places of Brandenburg, out thunders he his imperial ban against the Leipsic leaguers, dated at Vienna, May 14, peremptorily forbidding any place of the empire to grant either relief, passage, or place of quarter, muster, or rendezvous, unto any of their forces; commanding every man to destroy, kill, and persecute them as enemies: and the easier to dehort the leaguers, his majesty offers to release them of their oaths taken in prejudice of him at Leipsic, and to grant pardon to as many as should come in: upon pain of death forbidding all their subjects either to contribnte to their levies, or to serve under their ensigns, but to turn both their monies and persons towards the advancement of his imperial service, promising the freedom of conscience and estates to all that should thus obey him.

Divers people are naturally afraid of thunder; some of the leaguers, therefore, (and especially the grave-headed burghers in the richer cities) began now to quake at the noise of this so hideous a proclamation: which fear of theirs much cooled their blood, made them the less zealous and warm in the resolution; but he that hath not courage enough to fight, hath wit enough commonly to excuse his cowardice. So fell it out here; divers of the backwardest palliating their own remissness with the news they pretended to have heard, of the mammering of the chief man in the action, the duke of Saxony. And this had like to have arrested the whole design. Saxony hearing of all this, notwithstanding he was at this instant hard laid at, by Hagenmüller, the emperor's ambassador, to come over to his master; yet (to prevent a jealousy) would he not so much as once speak with him, then at Torgau, but referred him for audience over unto his privy council.

Hagenmüller's propositions were these four:—

1. To consult how the business about the church lands might best be compounded.

2. How the inconveniencies occasioned by the wars might be eased.

3. That the agreement of Leipsic, for standing upon their own defence, might be cancelled.

4. That he would advise how a peace might honourably be concluded with the Swede, and that the duke would mediate it.

The answer of the duke's council is too long to insert; and, to be brief, the ambassador returns not well satisfied. Immediately hereupon, the duke dispatches his letters unto the several leaguers, assuring them of his own constancy, and inviting them with all speed to hasten their preparations.

These letters of Saxony brought about the matter again; and he, to shew that he meant to do more than write letters, lays sure guards upon his own frontiers some eight or ten thousand men; proceeding warily hitherto, and all upon the defensive. The protestant princes of Suabia (which lie along the Danube, between the dukes of Wirtemberg and Bavaria) do hereupon assemble at Essingen, resolving to stick close to the articles of Leipsic, reinforcing their levies thereupon. And now the fair city of Norimberg in the Upper Palatinate returns to her former resolution, notwithstanding the particular threatenings of the emperor, to give the spoil of it unto their great neighbour the duke of Bavaria. The city of Strasbourg arms also; and the city of Ulm, encouraged by the new administrator of Wirtemberg, duke Julius, refuses to give passage to the late troops coming that way out of Italy, and sends 300 musqueteers to aid their neighbours of Memmingen against them.

The landgrave of Hesse-Cassel (against whose country it was generally reported that Tilly would forthwith come, and that he was already for that purpose upon his march as far as Duringen) bestirs himself all this while, levies men, and fortifies his frontiers. Tilly sends before he comes to him, with these four demands:—

1. To pay the arrear of the contribution due unto the emperor.

2. To give sufficient hostages or security for the future; directly professing him either a friend or a foe to the emperor.

3. Immediately to cashier his army.

4. To lay open his passages for the emperor's forces, to receive imperial garrisons into Cassel and Sichenheim, and to give quarter to five other regiments.

Hard terms all. Unto which the landgrave returns though a negative yet a modest answer. This way not speeding, it seems the way of practice and of treachery was attempted, for the landgrave presently upon this discovers some correspondency entertained by two or three of his own chief lords with Tilly, for the delivering up his two chief towns of Cassel and Sichenheim, for which they are executed. Tilly after this in a rage sends three several troops into his country, his own intended expedition against him being diverted by news of the king of Sweden.

All this while (namely, until the latter end of June) was there no assurance of the protestant princes purpose to unite with the king of Sweden; but they all stood upon terms of neutrality, kept their obedience unto the emperor, standing only upon the defensive, without once offering any act of hostility, where they were not first provoked. Saxony had now 17,000 foot and 3000 horse all in a readiness. Upon the same terms stands the marquis elector of Brandenburgh, who, notwithstanding the near alliance betwixt the king of Sweden and himself (the king having married the sister of the said marquis) yet that he seemed far enough from uniting with him, appears by an action of his, which had like to have cost him dearly. The elector denies a request of the king's, for two passages for his army (now in the Brandenburger's country), and especially for that the marquis now desired his town of Spandau again, which upon some terms had at the first been lent unto the king; which the king taking very unkindly, (divers circumstances perchance occurring) all of a sudden besieges the elector's town of Berlin, bending his cannon upon the very palace, threatening to pillage it. The difference is at length appeased by the electress, together with the promise of 30,000 rix-dollars a month, and to have the town of Spandau (Custrin he also desired) again consigned over unto him as before.

APPENDIX No. V.

CHRISTINA, the only child of Gustavus Adolphus, succeeded her father as Queen of Sweden, and an incident in the life of this princess raised a question of international law which led to much discussion among Continental jurists at the time, although at the present day there would probably be no difference of opinion on the subject.

Christina was only seven years old when she inherited her father's crown. As she grew up she displayed uncommon powers of intellect, but was at times eccentric and wayward in her conduct, and to the astonishment of Europe when only twenty-eight years old she abdicated her crown in favour of her cousin Charles Gustavus and retired to France. At Versailles she received every attention, but her manners and conversation were not such as to inspire general esteem. She was in the habit of speaking slightingly and coarsely of the Lutheran religion, in which she had been brought up. She affected to despise women, and the only one of her own sex to whom she showed partiality was the notorious Ninon de l'Enclos. After residing some time in France she repaired to Rome, where she renounced the religion of her fathers, and professed herself a Catholic. In 1656 she returned to France, where apartments were assigned to her in the palace of Fontainebleau, and where the tragedy of which we are about to speak took place.

There was in her service at this time an Italian nobleman, the Marquis Monaldeschi, who, from some reason, had given her mortal cause of offence. On the 10th of November, 1657, she summoned this man before her and accused him of having defamed her in certain letters, some of which it appears were produced. What was the nature of the defamatory matter of which she complained we do not know, but the result was that she ordered him to be put to death forthwith. This cruel sentence was most cruelly executed, for the unfortunate man, apparently suspecting danger, wore armour underneath his clothes; and the two guards who carried out the orders of their mistress stabbed him in many places before they inflicted a mortal wound.

It seems to be impossible at the present day to ascertain the nature of the charge upon which Monaldeschi was put to death; we only know that when confronted with Christina she denounced him as a traitor. But whether innocent or guilty it is clear that her conduct was wholly indefensible. Even if she had been Queen of Sweden at the time she could have had no jurisdiction in a foreign country to commit such an act. As a private individual, which she had become, of her own free will, she could not have a shadow of right for taking the life of this man. Some authorities, however, have undertaken to defend, and others to extenuate, her conduct; but at the present day the execution of Monaldeschi can only be regarded as a deliberate murder.

The affair, as might have been supposed, created a profound sensation at the French Court, but no judicial investigation was made, so that the mystery was never cleared up. Christina not long afterwards took up her residence in Rome, where she spent the remainder of her days. She died unmarried on the 19th of April, 1689.[1]

APPENDIX No. VI.

L'INSUFFISANCE des lois anglaises rendirent toutefois inutiles les poursuites faites contre les individus; ils furent déclarés coupables par les jurés sans que l'on pût leur infliger aucune peine. La reine se vit donc obligée de viser à d'autres moyens pour donner au czar une satisfaction telle qu'il la demandait, et ce fut à cet effet que S. M. revêtit Lord Withworth, son Envoyé extraordinaire à la cour de Russie, du caractère d'ambassadeur extraordinaire, et l'autorisa à faire en son nom, dans une audience publique, ses excuses à Pierre I.

Ce fut lors des fêtes qui, au retour du czar de la campagne victorieuse contre Charles XII., eurent lieu à Moscou et qui durèrent six semaines, que Lord Withworth s'acquitta de sa commission.

[1] Martin's Causes Célèbres, t. i.; see also Biographie Universelle.

APPENDIX. 349

Le 5 Février, jour fixé pour cette solennité, M. Basile de Soltikof, écuyer-tranchant de S. M. Impériale, accompagné de M. Athanase de Dmitreef Mamonof, échanson, faisant fonction de maître de cérémonie, se rendit à l'hôtel de l'ambassadeur dans un carrosse de S. M. pour le prendre; ils furent suivis par vingt autres carrosses occupés par les principaux seigneurs de la cour ou destinés en partie à recevoir les secrétaires et les gentilshommes de l'ambassade.

A l'arrivée de l'ambassadeur au château, les régiments des gardes Preobrazenski et Semanofski qui occupaient l'intérieur de la cour, battirent aux champs et restèrent en parade pendant tout le temps de l'audience. M. de Narischkin, gentilhomme de la chambre de l'empereur, vint au-devant de l'ambassadeur au bas de l'escalier; le prince George de Scherbatof, conseiller d'État, lui rendit le même honneur au haut de l'escalier; et M. de Mussin Pouchekine, conseiller privé, le complimenta dans l'antichambre d'où il le conduisit, selon le cérémonial usité, jusqu'à la salle d'audience, où l'empereur se trouva debout et découvert sous un dais, appuyé sur une table, ayant un fauteuil derrière lui, et entouré des grands, des ministres et des généraux de l'armée.

Après les trois révérences d'usage l'ambassadeur ayant monté la première marche de l'estrade, restant debout et découvert, prononça son discours en anglais, dont le secrétaire d'ambassade lut la traduction allemande, signée de la main de l'ambassadeur, afin que les ministres étrangers qui avaient été invités dans les formes pour assister à cette solennité, en entendissent le contenu; après quoi un des secrétaires de l'empereur en fit autant en langue russe pour les grands et les seigneurs de la cour.

Discours prononcé par Lord Withworth.
(Traduction française.)
"Très-Haut et Très-Puissant Empereur! [1]

"C'est avec une douleur bien vive que je me vois obligé aujourd'hui de rappeler à V. M. Impériale l'attentat qui fut commis sur la personne de son ambassadeur à la cour de la Grande-Bretagne. Mais je me félicite d'avoir reçu des ordres exprès de S. M. la reine pour déclarer combien elle a mis de soins pour donner

[1] Ce fut en cette occasion que pour la première fois la Grande-Bretagne donna au Czar le titre d'*Empereur*.

à V. M. une satisfaction éclatante qui puisse servir de témoignage de l'amitié constante qu'elle a eue de tous temps pour V. M. Impériale, et qu'elle a à cœur de conserver inviolablement envers sa personne sacrée.

"A peine la reine eut-elle connaissance de cet évènement fâcheux, que les coupables ressentirent son indignation royale; ils furent arrêtés, examinés devant S. M. dans son conseil, emprisonnés et poursuivis en justice selon la rigueur des lois; et bien que celles-ci fussent insuffisantes, on ne déclara pas moins les coupables infâmes, du consentement unanime de toute la nation, dans le parlement assemblé, qui par un acte public a fait connaître au monde, combien il a en horreur un pareil acte et combien il a été empressé à prendre les précautions nécessaires, pour en prévenir de semblables pour l'avenir. L'on ne s'en tint pas là; les coupables ont été déclarés indignes de toute grâce et exclus du pardon général que S. M. a fait accorder à tous ses sujets, même à ceux qui avaient attenté contre sa personne sacrée.

"Enfin pour manifester publiquement les sentiments d'équité comme ceux de l'amitié sincère qu'elle a pour V. M., S. M. la reine a daigné me revêtir du caractère éminent de son ambassadeur extraordinaire, commissaire et plénipotentiaire, afin de représenter sa personne royale, comme si elle-même était présente, pour témoigner le chagrin et la juste et haute indignation qu'elle ressent de cet acte de violence commis sur un ministre public, et notamment sur celui pour lequel S. M. la reine a une estime toute particulière, et pour faire agréer à V. M. ses excuses de ce par le défaut des lois de son royaume (le cas d'une violation si extraordinaire du droit des gens n'étant point prévu par la loi), il n'avait point été possible de punir les coupables avec toute la rigueur qu'ils méritaient, et selon le désir de V. M. Impériale, et d'exprimer enfin, combien S. M. la reine est portée à entretenir l'ancienne amitié et la bonne intelligence subsistant depuis si longtemps entre les deux couronnes, et dont V. M. Impériale trouvera les sentiments exprimés dans la lettre que je dois avoir l'honneur de lui remettre de sa part.

"C'est avec instance que je prie V. M. Impériale au nom de S. M. la reine de daigner recevoir ses excuses avec une affection fraternelle, et de ne point imputer à S. M. la reine, ni à la nation anglaise, un événement dont quelques perturbateurs se sont rendus coupables, mais qu'elle veuille les oublier et conserver pour S. M. la reine et pour ses peuples les sentiments d'amitié et d'intérêt qu'elle leur a portés jusqu'à présent.

"Quant à moi, je m'estimerai très-heureux, si je puis contribuer en quelque manière à ce grand œuvre si avantageux aux deux couronnes et si nécessaire à l'état de l'Europe.

"Les bienfaits et les marques de bonté dont V. M. a daigné m'honorer pendant l'exercice de mes fonctions comme envoyé extraordinaire de S. M. la reine, et dont le souvenir ne s'effacera qu'avec ma vie, me font espérer qu'elle voudra bien m'accueillir avec cette même bonté toutes les fois que par ordre de ma souveraine j'aurai l'honneur de lui faire quelques propositions.

"Que V. M. me permette de recommander à la haute protection de V. M. Impériale les sujets de S. M. Britannique habitat ce pays, pour le libre exercice du commerce que leurs ancêtres ont commencé les premiers à établir à Archangel à grands frais."

Ce discours fini, et la lecture des deux traductions en langue allemande et russe ayant été faite à haute voix, l'ambassadeur remit encore dans les mains de l'empereur une lettre autographe de la reine, dont la traduction en russe était jointe. L'empereur l'ayant donnée au comte Golofkin, grand-chancelier de l'empire, fit en personne la réponse suivante au discours de Lord Withworth.

Réponse de S. M. l'empereur au discours ci-dessus.

"Il convenait que S. M. la reine nous eût donné la satisfaction demandée en punissant les criminels selon toute la rigueur, et ainsi qu'il est d'usage dans tous les pays du monde; mais comme S. M. vous a ordonné de nous en faire des excuses en qualité de son ambassadeur extraordinaire revêtu tout exprès pour cette occasion, et de nous exposer les motifs qui ne lui ont point permis d'infliger aux coupables un tel châtiment, vu l'insuffisance des lois existantes dans son royaume, et qu'elle a fait passer un acte du consentement unanime du parlement pour assurer à l'avenir les priviléges des ministres publics, nous agréons toutes ces choses comme une marque de l'affection qu'elle a pour nous et comme la satisfaction même qui nous est due ; nous donnerons les ordres à nos ministres, pour que cette affaire soit terminée définitivement avec vous, dans une conférence."

L'audience finie, l'ambassadeur fut reconduit à son hôtel avec les mêmes cérémonies, et par ordre de l'empereur traité pendant trois jours par M. de Soltikof avec la plus grande magnificence.

Ce fut dans une conférence qui eut lieu le 9 Février chez le comte Golofkin, grand-chancelier de l'empire, à laquelle assistèrent les autres ministres de l'empereur, que cette affaire fut définitivement terminée à la satisfaction mutuelle. Il y fut arrêté :

Que l'empereur ordonnerait à M. de Mathweof, son ambassadeur à La Haye, d'instruire d'abord la reine d'Angleterre de ce que Lord Withworth revêtu tout exprès du caractère d'ambassadeur pour faire ses excuses à S. M. Impériale s'était acquitté de sa commission ; que S. M. déférant aux instances de la reine avait bien voulu recevoir ses excuses faites en son nom comme satisfaction pour l'outrage fait à son ambassadeur, afin de lui prouver qu'il appréciait l'amitié de S. M. la reine ; que l'empereur oublierait la conduite criminelle des auteurs de cet attentat et demandait leur grâce à S. M. britannique ; que par égard aux services signalés que son ambassadeur lui avait rendus et en souvenir des services importants qu'avait rendus feu son père, Artemon Serge de Mathweof, premier ministre et Boyare du règne du père et du grand-père de S. M., S. M. la reine, à titre d'une satisfaction particulière due à M. de Mathweof écrirait à cet ambassadeur une lettre analogue aux circonstances, et le dédommagerait des frais qu'il avait eus ; que l'empereur enfin ordonnerait à M. de Mathweof de demander sa lettre de récréance, ainsi que le présent d'usage ; et que lorsque tout ceci aurait eu lieu, l'empereur en témoignerait sa satisfaction à S. M. la reine d'Angleterre par une lettre autographe qui serait remise à Lord Withworth.

Anno Septimo Annæ Reginæ, A.D. 1708, Cap. XII.

An Act for preserving the previleges of Ambassadors, and other public Ministers of Foreign Princes and States.

(For the *History* and *particular occasion* of this Act being made ; and the Privileges secured by it, see 3 Bur. 1478. 1 Blac. Com. 255. 4 Id. 70.)

"Whereas several turbulent and disorderly Persons having in
" a most outrageous manner insulted the person of his Excellency
" *Andrew Artemonowitz Mattueof*, Ambassador Extraordinary of his
" Czarish Majesty, Emperor of *Great Russia*, her Majesty's good

"friend and Ally, by arresting him, and taking him by Violence out of his Coach in the publick Street, and detaining him in Custody for several Hours, in Contempt of the Protection granted by her Majesty, contrary to the Law of Nations, and in Prejudice of the Rights and Privileges which Ambassadors and other publick Ministers, authorized and received as such, have at all Times been thereby possessed of, and ought to be kept sacred and inviolable;"

Be it therefore declared by the Queen's most Excellent Majesty, by and with the Advice and Consent of the Lords Spiritual and Temporal, and Commons, in Parliament assembled, and by the Authority of the same, That all Actions and Suits, Writs and Processes commenced, sued or prosecuted against the said Ambassador, by any Person or Persons whatsoever, and all Bail Bonds given by the said Ambassador, or any other Person or Persons on his Behalf, and all Recognizances of Bail given or acknowledged in any such Action or Suit, and all Proceedings upon or by Pretext or Colour of any such Action or Suit, Writ or Process, and all Judgments had thereupon, are utterly null and void, and shall be deemed and adjudged to be utterly null and void, to all Intents, Constructions, and Purposes whatsoever.

II. And be it enacted by the Authority aforesaid, That all Entries, Proceedings, and Records against the said Ambassador or his Bail, shall be vacated and cancelled.

III. And to prevent the like Insolences for the future, Be it further declared by the Authority aforesaid, That all Writs and Processes that shall at any Time hereafter be sued forth or prosecuted, whereby the Person of any Ambassador, or other Publick Minister of any Foreign Prince or State, authorized and received as such by her Majesty, her Heirs or Successors, or the Domestick, or Domestic Servant of any such Ambassador, or other publick Minister, may be arrested or imprisoned, or his or their Goods or Chattels may be distrained, seized, or attached, shall be deemed and adjudged to be utterly null and void, to all Intents, Constructions, and Purposes whatsoever.

IV. And be it further enacted by the Authority aforesaid, That in case any Person or Persons shall presume to sue forth or prosecute any such Writ or Process, such Person and Persons, and all Attorneys and Solicitors prosecuting and soliciting in such Case, and all Officers executing any such Writ or Process, being thereof convicted, by the Confession of the Party, or by the Oath of one or more Credible Witness or Witnesses, before the Lord Chancellor, or Lord Keeper of the Great Seal of *Great Britain*, the Chief Justice of the Court of *Queen's Bench*, the Chief Justice of the Court of *Common Pleas* for the Time being, or any two of them, shall be deemed Violaters of the Laws of Nations, and Disturbers of the publick Repose, and shall suffer such Pains, Penalties, and Corporal Punishment, as the said Lord Chancellor, Lord Keeper, and the said Chief Justices, or any two of them shall be judged to be imposed and inflicted.

V. Provided, and be it declared, That no Merchant or other Trader whatsoever, within the Description of any of the Statutes against Bankrupts, who hath or shall put himself into the Service of any such Ambassador or Publick Minister, shall have or take any Manner of Benefit by this Act; and that no Person shall be proceeded against as having arrested the Servant of an Ambassador or Publick Minister, by virtue of this Act, unless the Name of such Servant be first registered in the Office of one of the Principal Secretaries of State, and by such Secretary transmitted to the Sheriffs of *London* and *Middlesex* for the Time being, or their Under-Sheriffs or Deputies, who shall, upon the Receipt thereof, hang up the same in some publick place in their Offices, whereto all Persons may resort, and take Copies thereof, without Fee or Reward.

VI. And be it further enacted by the Authority aforesaid, That this Act shall be taken and allowed in all Courts within this Kingdom as a Publick Act; and that all Judges and Justices shall take notice of it without Special Pleading; and all Sheriffs, Bailiffs, and other Officers and Ministers of Justice, concerned in the Execution of Process, are hereby required to have regard to this Act, as they will answer the Contrary at their Peril.

APPENDIX No. VII.

"Traité de l'Assiento. Conclu entre leurs Majestez Britannique et Catholique, par lequel la Compagnie Angloise s'oblige à fournir aux Espagnols, aux Indes Occidentales, des esclaves négres, pendant le terme de trente ans, à compter du premier jour de Mai de la présente année 1713, jusques au même jour de l'an 1743."—Actes, Mémoires, &c., concernant la Paix d'Utrecht, v. 72.

The following are the leading clauses:—

"I. En premier lieu, pour procurer par ce moyen, mutuellement et reciproquement l'avantage des souverains et des sujets des deux couronnes, sa Majesté de la Grande Bretagne offre et s'oblige, pour les personnes qu'elle nommera et autorisera pour cet effet, de faire transporter aux Indes Occidentales de l'Amerique, appartenant à sa Majesté Catholique à commencer du premier jour de Mai 1713, jusques au même jour de l'année 1743, le nombre de cent quarante quatre mille négres, piezas de India, des deux sexes et de tous les âges, sur le pied de quatre mille huit cent négres piezas de India par an, pendant le cours des dites trente années, à condition, que les personnes, qui se transporteront aux Indes Occidentales pour travailler aux affaires de l'assiento, se garderont de rien faire qui puisse offencer ; car en ce cas, ils seroient poursuivis en justice, et punis de la même manière, qu'ils l'auroient été en Espagne, supposé qu'une faute de la même nature y eut été commise.

"II. Que les assientistes, ou la Compagnie de l'Assiento, payera de châque négre, pieza de India, suivant le modèle régulier de sept quatiers n'étant ni vieux ni de défectueux, selon ce qui a été pratiqué et établi jusques à present aux Indes, la somme de trentetrois pièces de huit, Escudos, et la troisième partie d'une pièce de huit, en y comprenant tous les droits d'Alcavala, de siza, d'union de armas, de Boqueron, ou aucun autre droit, de telle nature qu'il puisse être, d'entrée ou de régale, qui sont ou qui pourroient être imposez à l'avenir, appartenant à sa Majesté Catholique, en sorte qu'on ne pourra rien exiger au de la. Et au cas, que les gouverneurs, officiers royaux ou autres ministres en prissent d'avantage, on en tiendra compte aux assientistes et cela sera rabattu sur les droits des 33 pièces de huit et un tiers susmentionnez, qu'ils doivent payer à sa Majesté Catholique, la chose étant prouvée par un certificat authentique, qui ne pourra être refusé par un notaire public, à la requisition des assientistes. Et pour cet effet on sera publier un ordre ou une cédule générale, dont la teneur sera la plus ample qu'il se pourra.

"III. Que les dits assientistes avanceront à sa Majesté Catholique, pour suppléer, aux besoins pressans de la couronne, la somme de deux cent mille pièces de huit ou Escudos, en deux payemens égaux, de cent mille pièces de huit chacun, dont le premier se sera deux mois après, que sa Majesté aura approuvé et signé cet assiento; et le second au bout de deux autres mois, après le premier payement; et cette somme ainsi avancée ne sera remboursée qu'après le terme échu des vingt premières années de cet assiento, et alors on pourra la déduire par portions égales, pendant les dix années restantes, sur le pied de vingt mille pièces de huit par an, qu'on rabattra sur les droits imposez sur les négres, payables pendant le cours de ces années là."—Actes, Mémoires, &c., v. 74-77.

"XLI. Que tout le contenu du présent contract, et des conditions qui y sont inférées, comme aussi de tout ce qui y sera joint ou en dépendra, sera accompli et exécuté avec sincérité et exactitude, en sorte qu'il ne s'y trouve aucun obstacle, sous quelque pretexte, cause ou motif que ce soit. Et pour cet effet sa Majesté doit suspendre, comme elle suspend par cet article, toutes les loix, ordonnances, proclamations, privilèges, établissemens, usages et coutumes, qui y sont contraires, dans tous les ports, lieux et provinces de l'Amerique appartenant à sa Majesté, ou elles pourroient subsister, pendant le terme de trente ans, que cet assiento doit avoir lieu, outre les trois années accordées aux assientistes pour retirer leurs effets, et ajuster leurs comptes, comme il a déjà été dit. Cependant ces loix là etc., doivent demeurer en pleine force et vigueur, dans tous les cas qui n'auront point de rapport à ce contract, et dans tous les tems à venir, après l'expiration de ses trente-trois années."—Actes, Mémoires, &c., v. 130, 131.

Among the obligations for working the contract harmoniously are the following:—

"XVIII. Qu'à compter du premier jour de Mai de la presente année 1713, jusques à ce qu'ils aient pris possession de l'assiento ni après qu'ils l'auront prise il ne sera plus permis à la Compagnie Françoise de Guinée, ou à qui que ce soit de transporter des esclaves négres aux Indes : Et au cas qu'ils le fîssent, sa Majesté Catholique les déclarera, comme elle les déclare par cet article, confisquez en faveur et à l'avantage des assientistes, qui en prendront possession en payant les droits des négres introduits ainsi contre cet article, et le réglement établi par ce contract. Et pour cet effet, aussi tôt qu'il sera signé on dépêchera, de la manière la plus ample, des ordres circulaires en Amerique, pour empêcher qu'on n'y admette aucuns négres dans les ports, sur le compte de la Compagnie Françoise, et la même chose sera notifiée à leur agent. Et afin que ceci soit plus effectuel et plus avantageux au revenu royal, on est convenu, que lors que les assientistes seront informés qu'aucun vaisseau chargé de négres, ne leur appartenant pas, sera arrivé sur les côtes, ou entré dans aucun port, il leur sera permis d'équiper, d'armer et de mettre en mer immédiatement les vaisseaux qu'ils auront en propre, ou aucuns de ceux de sa Majesté Catholique ou de ses sujets, avec lesquels ils conviendront de prendre, de saisir, et confisquer de pareils vaisseaux et leurs négres, de telle nation qu'ils puissant être, et à quelques personnes qu'ils puissant appartenir. Pour cet effet les dits assientistes et leurs facteurs auront la liberté de prendre connoissance, et de visiter tous les vaisseaux qui arriveront sur les côtes des Indes, ou dans ses ports, et dans lesquels ils auront lieu de croire ou de soupçonner qu'il y aura des négres de contrebande ; bien entendu, que pour faire de pareilles recherches, et autres procédures comme dessus, il faudra qu'ils en aient premièrement la permission des gouverneurs, aux quels ils communiqueront ce qui se passera, et les prieront d'y interposer leur autorité ; mais il faudra, que la paix soit proclamée avant que ceci puisse se faire, ou que cet assiento ait lieu.

"XIX. Que les dits assientistes, leurs facteurs et agents auront la liberté de naviger et de transporter leurs esclaves négres, selon leur contract dans les ports septentrionaux des Indes Occidentales de sa Majesté Catholique, sans en excepter la Rivière de Plata ; avec défense à tous autres, soit sujets de la couronne ou étrangers, d'y transporter ou introduire aucuns négres, sous les peines établies par les loix faites pour ce contract de commerce : De plus, sa Majesté Catholique, s'oblige en soi et parole de roi de maintenir les dits assientistes dans la pleine et entière possession de tous ces articles, et de les faire exécuter, pendant le terme dont on est convenu, sans permettre ou conniver à quoi que ce puisse être, qui soit contraire à leur ponctuelle et exacte exécution, sa Majesté en faisant sa propre affaire ; bien entendu qu'ils ne transporteront pas, ni dans la dite Rivière de Plata ni à Buenos Ayres, au dessus de douze cent piezas de négres accordez, par le 8 article de ce traité.

"XX. Qu'au cas, que les dits assientistes fûssent troublez dans l'exécution de cet assiento, ou que l'on s'opposât à leur trafic ou à leurs privilèges par des procès, ou de quelqu'autre manière, sa Majesté Catholique déclare qu'elle s'en réservera la connoissance uniquement, et de tous les procès, qu'on pourroit leur susciter à cet égard, avec défense à tous les juges, quels qu'ils puissant être, d'examiner et de prendre connoissance des causes, procès, omissions ou fautes, qui pourroient se commettre dans l'exécution de cet assiento.

"XXI. Que lors que les vaisseaux des dits assientistes arriveront dans les ports des Indes avec leurs cargaisons de négres, les capitaines des dits vaisseaux seront obligez de certifier, qu'il n'y a aucun mal contagieux sur leur bord, afin d'obtenir des gouverneurs et officiers royaux la permission d'éntrer dans les dits ports n'y pouvant être admis sans de pareils certificats."—Actes, Mémoires, &c., v. 98-103.

INDEX.

Aborigines, slave trade and, 170.
Achæan League, wars of the, 13.
Acre, siege of, 69.   [165.
Admiralty Courts, maritime law of the,
Adrianople:
  Turks capture, 73.
  Turks reign at, 75.
Adriatic, sovereignty in the, 56.
Adriatic provinces, Maximilian and, 134.
Adultery, Frederick II. accused of, 46.
Africa:
  Ferdinand V. in, 136.
  slave trade and, 170—2.
  see also Slave Trade.
Age of Chivalry, 79—130.
Agincourt, battle of, 122.
Aix-la-Chapelle, treaty of, 241.   [127.
Alain Blanchard, wanton execution of,
Alaric, King of the Goths, humanity of, 24.
Albert of Austria, Boniface VIII. and, 59.
Albigenses, Innocent III. and the, 42
Alessandria, siege of, 37.   [—3, 61.
Alexander III.:
  Lateran Council and, 36
  papal power and, 35.
  slavery and, 26, 36.
  Thomas à Becket and, 35.
Alexander VI.:
  Borgias rendered odious by, 133.
  perfidy of, 133.
  territorial ambition of, 133.
Alexius Comnenus, 65.
Alfred the Great:
  amelioration by, 28.
  Christianity promoted by, 28.
  Danes and, 28.
  execution of pirates by, 28.
  Guthrum and, 28.
  piracy put down by, 28.
  severity of, 28.
  warfare and, 28.
  Winchester executions by, 28.
Allia, battle ou the, 4.
Alliances:
  ancient, 12.
  Greek, 13.
Allied Powers:
  balance of power and, 305—6.
  Charles XII. and the, 291.
  Duke of Savoy joins the, 285.
  England makes treaty with, 285.
  France made war upon by, 283.
  King of Portugal joins the, 285.

Allied Powers:
  Louis XIV. makes peace with, 301.
  Madrid entered by, 303.
  Mons invested by, 301.
  Peace of Utrecht and, 309.
  Portugal and the, 305.
  Savoy and the, 305.
  Spain made war upon by, 283.
  Tournay captured by, 301.
  Vendome defeats army of, 304.
Alps:
  Francis I. crosses the, 139.
  Prince Eugene crosses the, 278.
Alsace:
  Bernhard of, Weimar and, 217.
  Count Mansfeld takes refuge in, 184.
  France acquires, 215, 224.
  Richelieu and, 217.
Amasis, Temple of Delphi and, 2.
Ambassadors: [236.
  dispute between French and Spanish,
  English law of, 229—32.
  Feciales as, 17.
  immunities and liabilities of, 156—9.
  insult at Rome to one of the French, 236—7.
  outrages upon, 2—3.
  privileges of, 6.
  rights and duties of, 3.
  Roman law as to, 157.
  sacred regard for, 4.
  war made by, 267.
Amboise, Huguenot conspiracy of, 152.
America:
  maritime law of, 165.
  slave trade and, 170—1.
Amiens, Edward III. reaches, 109.
Amphictyonic Council, 10, 61.
Amphictyons, arbitrations by, 12.
Amsterdam:
  Louis XIV. threatens, 245.
  maritime law of, 166.
  marine losses of, 265.
Ancient law of nations, 1—22.
Ancient manners, simplicity of, 5.   [14.
Ancient rivalries, endeavour to lay aside,
Ancient slavery, 22.
Ancona, Venetians and, 56.
Anglesea, Llewellyn and, 80.   [by, 26.
Anglo-Saxon kings, slavery prohibited
Anglo-Saxon slaves, 25.
Angora, battle of, 75.
Anjou, houses of Aragon and, 56.
Anna of Cleves, 175.

Arabia, permission by Prince of, 6.
Aragon:
　houses of Anjou and, 56.
　see also King of Aragon.
Arbitration:
　ancient, 12.
　appeals to, 83.
　England and Holland resort to, 238—9.
Archbishop of Cambray, Marlborough and, 306.
Archbishop of Milan, rebuke by Ambrose, the, 23.
Archduke Charles:
　Austrian crown passes to, 305.
　Madrid rejects, 303.
　Philip V. and, 285.
　Spain rejects, 303—4.
　Spanish succession and, 276.
Aristotle:
　Greeks criticised by, 13.
　Machiavelli compared to, 161—2.
　slavery and, 25.
Armada:
　driven from the Channel, 155.
　sailing of the, 154.
Armed intervention:
　justification of, 193.
　law of nations and, 193.
Armenian king, creation of, 42.
Artois retained by France, 233.
Asia Minor, Turks overrun, 66.
Assassination:
　chivalry and, 119.
　preaching of, 121.
Asylum, respect for law of, 7, 8.
Athenian captives, cruelty to, 15.
Athenians, outrage by, 3.
Athens:
　aggressive spirit of, 13.
　blockade of, 9.
Augsburg:
　Diet of, 149.
　Gustavus Adolphus takes, 203.
　religious liberty confirmed at Diet of, 151.
Austria:
　Bethlem Gabor's irruptions into, 185.
　Bohemia added to, 144.
　Cleves and, 174.
　close of struggle between France and, 151.
　Condé and, 220.
　Count Mansfeld defies, 183.
　Duke of Sully opposed to, 175—6.
　France and, 176.
　French co-operation against, 210.
　French rivalry with, 139.
　Gustavus Adolphus and, 191.
　Gustavus Adolphus beats, 209.
　Henry IV. opposed to, 175—6.
　humbled, 226.
　Hungary added to, 144.
　Henry IV. and the humbling of, 226.
　Louis XIV. prepares for war with, 278

Austria:
　Mazarin and the humbling of, 226.
　overthrow of ecclesiastical tyranny of, 200.
　peace imposed upon, 220.
　powerlessness of house of, 131.
　power wrested from, 226.
　prominent part continued to, 226.
　Richelieu and the humbling of, 226.
　Spain and, 176.
　Sultan threatens, 254.
　Turenne and, 220.
Azoff, Turks abandon, 269.

Babylon, Frederick II. and Soldan of, 46.
Bagdad, Constantinople and, 65.
Bajazet, grandson of Othman, 73.
　Bulgarian resistance to, 73.
　Constantinople besieged by, 74.
　death of, 75.
　descendants of, 75.
　first Sultan, 73.
　French resistance to, 73.
　Greeks promise tribute to, 74.
　Hungarians defeated by, 73.
　imprisonment of, 75.
　rapid conquests of, 73.
　Rome threatened by, 73.
　St. Peter's threatened by, 73.
　Sigismund and, 73.
　surnamed the Thunderbolt, 73.
　terrible retaliation of, 73.
　vain boasts of, 73.
Balance of power:
　Allied Powers and the, 305—6.
　ancients and, 12.
　Greeks and, 13.
　origin of, 15.
Baldwin elected Emperor of the Eastern Empire, 71.
Baliol:
　Abdication of, 89.
　Edward I. and, 86—9.
　fealty sworn by, 88.
　obligations upon, 88.
　Philip the Fair and, 88.
　unfitness of, 89.
Baltic:
　Count Wallenstein on the coast of the, 188.
　destruction of forts on the, 191.
　Gustavus Adolphus claims rights on the, 191.
　Gustavus Adolphus crosses the, 191.
　Spanish squadron expected in the, 192.
Baner:
　Elector of Saxony defeated by, 217.
　Saxony invaded by, 217.
Bannockburn, battle of, 100.
Bar acquired by France, 234.
Barbarians, Persians and Gauls as, 4.
Barbarian conquerors, Christianity respected by, 24.
Barbarossa, Frederick I. See Frederick I.

INDEX.

Barcelona, Spain acquires, 267.
Basil I., 65.
Basil II., legions of, 66.
Basil III.:
  death of, 66.
  defeat of Bulgarians by, 66.
Bavaria:
  annexation by, 174.
  Bernhard of Weimar overruns, 212.
  Ferdinand of Styria disposes of, 185.
  Ferdinand III. deserts, 220.
  France makes treaty with, 278.
  Gustavus Adolphus enters, 203.
  Tilly retains a force in, 202. [263.
Beachy Head, French naval victory off,
Belisarius:
  achievements and humanity of, 24—5.
  victories of, 29.
Belligerents:
  maritime law of, 164—5.
  neutrals and, 257.
Benedict XII., Edward III. and, 102.
Benevento:
  battle of, 51.
  prisoners taken by, 26.
Bergen-op-Zoom:
  Count Mansfeld relieves, 184.
  Spinola besieges, 184.
Berlin, threat to bombard, 197.
Bernhard of Weimar:
  Alsace and, 217.
  Bavaria overrun by, 212.
  command of Swedish army entrusted to, 210.
  death of, 217.
  Gustavus Adolphus sacrifices his life in defence of, 209.
  Gustavus Adolphus joined by, 198.
  Ratisbon captured by, 212.
Bertrand du Guesclin:
  Brittany and, 108.
  captivity of, 112.
  Charles V. lends money to, 113.
  ransom of, 112—13.
Berwick-on-Tweed:
  judgment at, 88.
  Parliament at, 90.
  siege of, 89.
Bethlem Gabor: [185.
  Austria suffers from irruptions by,
  Frederick V. allied with, 182.
  Hungary partly acquired by, 182.
  powerlessness of, 188.
  Protestantism and, 184.
  Transylvania usurped by, 182.
  Turks in alliance with, 182.
Beurnanville, beheading of, 115.
Bishop of Beauvais, Richard I. and, 40.
Bishops of Rome, Constantine and the,
Bishop of Ross: [29.
  Elizabeth and, 156.
  Lord Burghley and, 157—9.
Bishop of Toledo, Spanish succession and, 273.

Blackheath, force assembled at, 233.
Black Prince:
  battle of Poitiers and, 110.
  Bertrand du Guesclin and, 112—13.
  Bordeaux started from by, 110.
  burning and destroying by, 110.
  carried into Limoges, 114.
  Chandos and the, 113.
  courtesy of, 110.
  disasters to the, 113.
  expedition of the, 110.
  five hundred towns and villages laid in ashes by, 110.
  Guienne governed by the, 112.
  hearth-tax imposed by the, 113.
  inconsistency of, 114.
  insurrection against, 113.
  John of France and, 110.
  last enterprise of, 114.
  laying waste by, 110.
  Limoges besieged by, 113.
  march upon Poitiers by, 110.
  massacre by, 114.
  Pedro the Cruel and the, 112.
  pillage and destruction by, 110.
  rebels put to death by, 114.
  Spain invaded by the, 112.
  three thousand inhabitants massacred by, 114.
  Toulouse marched upon by, 110.
Blake, Spain and, 228.
Blenheim, battle of, 289.
  French ascendency destroyed at, 290.
Blockading, practice of, 8.
Bohemia:
  Austria absorbs, 144.
  Count Mansfeld draws followers into, 183.
  Count Wallenstein and, 187. [211.
  Count Wallenstein falls back upon,
  Count Wallenstein resides in capital of, 201.
  defeat of army of, 182.
  Elector of Saxony invades, 201.
  Ferdinand of Styria elected to crown of, 177.
  Jesuits expelled from, 180.
  king created for, 42.
Bolingbroke:
  on Malplaquet, 303.
  peace of Utrecht arranged by, 315.
Boniface VIII.:
  Albert of Austria and, 59.
  bull by, 57—8.
  burning of letter of, 57.
  Church and, 60.
  claims to dispose of Scotland, 93—6.
  College of Cardinals and, 58.
  Colonna and, 59.
  Count of Flanders and, 59.
  crimes imputed to, 58.
  damnation declared by, 58.
  death of, 59.
  defeat of, 59.

INDEX.

Boniface VIII.:
  denunciation of, 58.
  disconcerted, 58.
  Edward I. and, 60.
  Edward I. replies to, 95.
  excommunication by, 57.
  famous bull by, 58.
  France and, 58.
  makes concessions to Edward I., 96.
  Philip the Fair and, 56.
  Philip the Fair resists, 57.
  rashness of, 56.
  Scotland and, 60.
  seizure of person of, 59.
  striking of, 59.
  succession of, 59.
  vain claims of, 57.
Bordeaux:
  Black Prince at, 112.
  Black Prince starts from, 110.
  duel proposed at, 55.
Borgias:
  Church and the, 30.
  odious name of the, 133.
Bosphorus, conquerors on the, 63.
Bouchain, Villars recovers, 315.
Bouffers:
  Earl of Portland meets, 266.
  Marlborough evaded by, 284.
  William III. opposed to, 266.
Boulogne, English capture of, 148.
Bourbon (Constable):
  Clement VII. and, 142.
  killed in battle, 142.
  reinstatement of, 141,
Bourbons:
  Hapsburg duel with, 278.
  Hapsburgs and, 272.
  Spain and the, 272.
  Spain spared to the, 301.
Boyne, battle of the, 263.
Brandenburg:
  Cleves and, 175.
  Gustavus Adolphus and the Elector of, 191.
  Gustavus Adolphus seeks passage through, 197.
  persistent neutrality of, 195.
Breda, negotiations at, 239.
Bremen, maritime law and, 166.
Brennus, Gaulish king, 3.
Brescia, siege of, 44.
Bretigni, treaty of, 110—11.
Bristol:
  revival of slavery at, 27.
  slaves exported from, 26.
Brittany:
  Bertrand du Guesclin and, 108.
  Charles of Blois and, 103, 108.
  Count de Montfort and, 103, 108.
  desolation of, 108.
  rival claimants of, 108.
  Sir John Chandos and, 108.
  violence and treachery in, 108.

Brittany:
  wager of battle in, 108.
  war of succession in, 108.
Bruce:
  caging of sister of, 98.
  Edward I. and, 82—4.
  humanity of, 100.
  vengeance upon adherents of, 97.
Brutus, march upon Rome by, 4.
Bulgaria:
  king created for, 42.
  subdued by Bajazet, 73.
Burghley, see Lord Burghley.
Burgundy: [24.
  House of Orleans and House of, 119—
  John of France renounces, 111.
  Philip, first Duke of, 111.
  suzerainty of, 99.
  Vendome thwarted by, 294.
Byzantine Empire:
  commerce passed from, 72.
  Crusaders and the, 70.
  Crusades and the, 63—78.
  culminating point of, 66.
  death-wound of the, 72.
  history of the, 63.
  last Emperor of, 76.
  laws decayed of, 72.
  Leo III. and, 63.
  Mahommedans and the, 70.
  pre-dependence of the, 73.
  prolongation of the, 74.
  Turks overrun the, 66.
Byzantines excelled the West, 65.

Cabal ministry, 243.
Cadmeia, retaking of, 10.
Cæsar unfavourably compared, 24.
Caius Pontius:
  magnanimity of, 18, 19.
  surrender to, 17.
Calais:
  attempt at recovery of, 106.
  disposal of, 151.
  English subjects in, 106.
  French compelled to leave, 106.
  Froissart on siege of, 104.
  Henry V. marches on, 125.
  massacre of inhabitants of, 127.
  possession of, 106.
  siege of, 104.
  surrender of, 105, 127.
Calvinists: [220.
  Catholic command given to one of the,
  Frederick V. head of the, 181—2.
  Lutherans distinguished from, 173.
  Lutherans placed on an equality with,
Cambray: [225.
  League of, 133—7.
  Peace of, 143.
Cambyses:
  conquest of Egypt by, 5.
  invasion by, 4.
  permission obtained by, 6.

Camden, contraband and, 169.
Cannon, battle of Creci and, 104.
Capet, end of male line of, 101.
Cardinal d'Amboise, Louis XII. and, 134.
Cardinals:
    College of, 31.
    imprisoned, 45.
    scarlet hats first worn by, 46.
Carlowitz, treaty of, 269.
Carpi, battle of, 279.
Carthage:
    armament sailed from, 6.
    escape of, 5.
    outbreak and mutiny at, 9.
    rising power of, 5.
    sues for peace, 6.
Carthaginians:
    courtesies of war and, 20.
    destruction of fleet of, 6.
    fine imposed upon, 6.
    frustrated, 7.
    sacrifice of children by, 6.
    treaty with, 5.
    victory over, 6.
Castile:
    Duke of Berwick in, 294.
    England advances into, 294.
    French victory in, 294.
    Innocent the Third and, 41.
    law of succession in, 270.
    Philip V. preferred in, 303.
    Portugal advances into, 294.
    see also Spain.
Catalonia:
    Peace of Utrecht and, 318.
    Peterborough invades, 293.
    revolts against Spain, 219.
    Spain acquires parts of, 267.
    Spain recovers, 227.
Cateau Cambresis, treaty of, 151—2.
Catherine de Medici:
    betrothed to Duke of Orleans, 143.
    Machiavelli and, 161.
    three sons of, 152.
Catholics:
    Count Wallenstein levies upon, 180.
    Count Wallenstein resisted by, 180.
    Ferdinand of Styria favoured by, 201.
    Frederick V. offends, 182.
    humanity disregarded by, 185.
    Louis XIV. excites fears of, 259.
    Oxenstiern in alliance with, 215.
    restorations to the, 189.
    Richelieu makes stipulations in favour of, 215.
Catinat, Prince Eugene defeats, 278.
Caudine Forks, affair of the, 17.
Cecil, Elizabeth and, 155.
Celestine, Richard the First and, 37, 39.
Celtic races, Reformation rejected by, 160.
Chandos, the Black Prince and, 113.
Charlemagne:
    breaking up of empire of, 30.

Charlemagne:
    chivalry and, 79.
    Christianity extended by sword of, 27.
    distinct epoch of reign of, 27.
    laying waste by, 27—8.
    Mahomet compared with, 27.
    Saxons beheaded by, 27.
    usurpation of, 27.
Charles of Anjou:
    atrocious cruelty of, 52.
    Clement IV. and, 51.
    death of, 55.
    duel proposed by, 53.
    execration of, 55.
    insurrection against, 54.
    Parliament summoned by, 52.
    progress to Rome of, 51.
    retribution upon, 54.
    satellites of, 53.
    Sicilian monarchy created by, 51.
    son of, 54.
Charles of Blois:
    defeat and death of, 108—9.
    Duke of Brittany and, 103.
Charles the Bold, Nanci besieged by, 115.
Charles I.:   [189.
    Christian of Denmark neglected by,
    constitutional struggle of, 189.
    Count Mansfeld befriended by, 187.
    Duke of Buckingham influences, 189.
    Dutch apology to, 219.
    France at war with, 189.
    perished on the scaffold, 227.
    Scottish covenanters and, 218.
    Spain bribes, 218.
    Spain at war with, 189.
Charles II.:
    cabal ministry of, 243.
    Catholic leanings of, 242—4.
    Dunkirk sold by, 228.
    fickle temper of, 253,
    Holland and, 237—9.
    Louis XIV. forced to peace by, 252.
    Louis XIV. makes secret treaty with, 242—3.
    Louis XIV. pensioned, 255.
    Prince of Orange admired by, 251.
    Prince of Orange resists, 246—7.
    William III. contrasted with, 282.
Charles II. of Spain:
    anticipated death of, 271.
    Austrian leanings of, 275.
    childless fate of, 273.
    Church domination over, 275.
    death of 275.
    France dreaded by, 275.
    indignation of, 273.
    Innocent XII. appealed to by, 273.
    Louis XIV. opposed by, 259.
    pitiable condition of, 273.
    succession signed away by, 275.
    superstitious fears of, 275.   [275.
    vengeance of Heaven threatened upon,
    will of, 275.

INDEX.

Charles V. of Austria:
  Bertrand du Guesclin and, 113.
  challenge between Francis I. and, 143.
  deception upon Francis I. practised by, 147.
  dissimulation of, 143.
  Duke of Guise resists, 150.
  election of, 140.
  Ferdinand, brother of, 144.
  France invaded by, 146.
  France visited by, 146.
  Francis I. entertains, 147.
  Francis I. makes final peace with, 148.
  Henry VIII. makes treaty with, 148.
  Machiavelli and, 161.
  Maurice of Saxony befriended by, 149.
  Maurice of Saxony defeats, 150.
  Metz advanced upon by, 150.
  Montmorency resists, 146. [145.
  new rivalries between Francis I. and,
  Provence invaded by, 146.
  refuses to fulfil his promise, 147.
  religious liberty conceded by, 151.
  retreat of, 146, 150.
  resignation of, 151.
  war again breaks out between Francis I. and, 147.
Charles VI. of Austria:
  accession of, 305.
  Archduke Charles becomes, 305,
  impracticable character of, 309, 316.
  Spain and, 305.
  Spanish claims of, 305.
Charles VI. of France:
  derangement of, 119.
  Duke of Burgundy cousin of, 119.
  Duke of Orleans brother of, 119.
  merciless execution by, 115.
Charles VII.:
  English exposed in chains by, 116.
  prosperity in time of, 131.
  standing army of, 132.
Charles VIII.:
  Alps crossed by, 132.
  forty thousand soldiers of, 132.
  Italy invaded by, 132.
  Milanese assistance to, 132.
  Naples abandoned by, 133.
  Naples seized by, 132.
  Venetian resistance to, 132.
Charles XII.:
  Allied Powers and, 291.
  Copenhagen marched upon by, 277.
  Denmark invaded by, 277.
  designs against, 277.
  Europe amazed by, 277.
  German princes alarmed by, 277.
  Gustavus Adolphus, predecessor of, Joseph and, 291. [277.
  Leipsic quarters of, 291.
  Louis XIV. and, 291.
  Marlborough sides with, 291.
  Marlborough visits, 292—3.
  Muscovy campaign of, 293.

Charles XII.:
  Poland invaded by, 277.
  Polish conquest of, 291.
  Protestants of Silesia and, 291.
  Russians advanced upon by, 277.
  Russian fugitives and, 291.
  Saxons beaten by, 277.
Charles Louis:
  invested at Frankfort, 211.
  Palatinate and, 224.
  Palatinate restored to, 211.
Chatham:
  De Ruyter attacks, 239.
Children, sacrifice of, 6.
China, Tamerlane and, 75.
Chios, baseness of people of, 8.
Chivalry:
  Age of, 79—130.
  assassination and, 119.
  barbarous treatment of prisoners in days of, 114—15.
  Charlemagne and, 79.
  Edward I. and, 80.
  French cruelty and, 119.
  Germany and, 79.
  Homeric age and, 79.
  institution of, 79.
  Middle Ages and, 79.
  most brilliant records of, 104.
  origin of, 79.
  Richard I. and, 80.
  Rome and, 79.
  women and, 79.
Christian II.:
  deposition of, 160.
  Gustavus Vasa and, 160.
  Protestantism and, 160.
  tyranny of, 160. [161.
  Christian III., Lutheran religion and,
Christian IV.:
  Charles I. neglects, 189.
  moderate demands of, 187.
  refuge in Germany of, 188.
  Tilly defeats, 188.
Christianity:
  Alfred the Great promoted, 23.
  barbarian conquerors and, 24.
  champion of, 30.
  Constantine the Great and, 23.
  extended by sword, 27.
  Germany and, 27.
  Gothic respect for, 24.
  introduction of, 23.
  law of nations affected by, 23.
  little influence of early, 23.
  pillage in times of, 24.
  power of, 23.
  slavery and, 25.
  warfare and, 21, 23.
Christians, surrender of, 69.
Church:
  Borgias and the, 30.
  crimes of the, 30.
  dark annals of the, 30.

Church:
- denunciation of revenues of the, 47.
- empire and, 44.
- Europe and the, 61.
- European princes and the, 60.
- France and the, 57.
- Frederick the Second's struggle with the, 45—50.
- Frederick V. tears down pictures of the, 182.
- generosity and the, 52.
- humanity and the, 61.
- images and the, 64.
- knowledge incompatible with claims of the, 62.
- Leibnitz and the, 62.
- lost dominion of the, 61.
- odious spirit of the, 61.
- persecution of the, 61.
- revolt against the, 61.
- ridicule of the, 45.
- rivalry with the, 60.
- scandals of the, 30.
- schism in the, 59.
- Scotland and the, 61.
- seizure of lands of the, 173.
- stretch of authority by the, 50.
- superstitious veneration for the, 62.
- tenth century of the, 30.

Churches:
- diversity between East and West, 66.
- plunder of, 45.
- Prince Christian plunders, 184.

Civilisation:
- dark spots of, 21.
- French modern, 27.

Clement IV.:
- Charles of Anjou and, 51.

Clement V.:
- Sicily and, 53.

Clement VII.:
- Constable Bourbon and, 142.
- punishment of, 142.   [142.
- repudiation of treaty sanctioned by,

Clement VIII.:
- niece of, 145.
- pretended solicitude of the emperor for, 143.
- ransom demanded for, 143.
- surrender of, 143.

Clergy:
- France and the, 57.
- marriage of, first forbidden, 31.
- taxes and the, 57.

Clermont acquired by France, 234.

Cleves:
- Anna of, 175.
- Austria and, 174.
- Brandenburg and, 175.
- disputed succession to, 174.
- lunatic and childless Duke of, 174.
- male fiefdom of, 175.
- Maria Eleonora of, 174—5.
- Netherlands and, 174.

Cleves:
- Neuburg and, 175.
- partition of, 175.
- rival sisters of, 175.
- vain stipulations about, 175.

Clusium, siege of, 3.
Coalitions, Greek, 13.
Coblentz, Marlborough moves upon, 287.
Colbert, admiral of French fleet, 254.

College of Cardinals:
- election of Popes by, 32.
- Ferdinand and the, 53.

Colonna, Boniface VIII. and, 59.
Colossus, overthrow of the, 2.
Columbus, Ferdinand and, 136.

Commerce:
- French destruction of, 265.
- warfare and, 21.

Commons:
- England and the, 60.
- see also House of Commons.

Concubines, Frederick II. accused of consorting with, 46.

Condé:
- Austria and, 220.
- Mazarin and, 233.
- Philip IV. pleads for, 332.
- Prince of Orange defeated by, 250.
- restored to his dignities and estates, Richelieu and, 220.   [233.
- Spanish infantry annihilated by, 219.
- treachery of, 227.

Confiscation of Protestant estates, 183.
Conqueror, slavery during reign of, 26.

Conradino:
- Constantina and, 53.
- Duke of Austria and, 52.
- Elizabeth of Bavaria and, 52.
- execution of, 53.
- grandson of Frederick II., 52.
- heroic death of, 53.
- infancy of, 50.   [60.
- Queen of Scots compared with, 159—
- Rome entered by, 52.
- total defeat of, 52.

Consolato del mare, 164—5.   [141.
Constable Bourbon, reinstatement of,
Constable d'Eu, beheading of the, 109.
Constance, Diet of, 33.

Constantina of Aragon:
- Conradino and, 53.
- daughter of Manfred, 52.
- magnanimity of, 54.
- wife of King of Aragon, 54.

Constantine the Great:
- Bishops of Rome and, 29.
- Christianity and, 23.
- Rome and, 29.
- Saracens and, 63.
- Slavonians and, 63.
- tribute by successors of, 75.

Constantine IX.
- beheading of body of, 77.
- death of, 77.

Constantine IX.:
    glorious fall of, 77.
    last Byzantine Emperor, 76.
Constantinople:
    Bagdad and, 65.
    besieged and taken, 42.
    French attack, 70.
    Greek emperors of, 71.
    Greek Church and, 65.
    Latin emperors of, 71,
    Mahomet II. captures, 76—7.
    Rome and, 64.
    sacking of, 71.
    siege of, 74.
    Venetians attack, 70.
Constitutional monarchy, William III. initiates, 282.
Contarini, Count d'Avaux and, 221.
Contraband of war:
    ancient, 9, 169.
    Camden on, 169.
    Charles V. and, 169.
    Drake on, 169.
    Edward I. and, 169.
    Elizabeth on, 169.
    Europe and, 169.
    Hanseatic League and, 169.
    treaty concerning, 9.   [277.
Copenhagen, Charles XII. marches upon,
Coriolanus, considerate conduct of, 16.
Cortanuova, battle of, 44.
Costumbres maritimos, 164.
Council of:
    Lyons, 46, 56.
    Trent, 149.
Count d'Artois, Edward III. and, 102.
Count d'Avaux, Contarini and, 221.
Count of Evreux, France and the, 101.
Count of Flanders, Boniface VIII. and the, 59.
Count Gallas, Peace of Utrecht and, 309—10.
Count of Holland claims to succeed Frederick II., 49.
Count Mansfeld:
    Alsace a refuge for, 184.
    Austria defied by, 183.
    Bergen-op-Zoom relieved by, 184.
    Bohemia a base for, 183.
    Charles I. befriends, 187.   [188.
    Count Wallenstein totally defeats, death of, 188.
    Dutch service entered by, 184.
    England befriends, 187.
    James I. supports, 187.
    lawless warfare introduced by, 183.
    Lorraine a refuge for, 184.
    Netherlands reached by, 184.
    North Germany ravaged by, 184.
    plundering by, 183.
    Prince Christian imitates, 184.
    Prince Christian joins, 184.
    Protestantism and, 180, 184.
    reverses in the Netherlands of, 187.

Count Mansfeld:
    Rhine advanced upon by, 183.
    Spain defied by, 183.
Count de Montfort:
    Brittany and, 103.
    does homage to Edward III., 103.
    Salic law interpreted by, 103.
    victory and succession of, 108—9.
Count Pappenheim, storming and sacking of Magdeburg by, 197—8.
Count Thurn:
    aspiring temper of, 178.
    murder attempted by, 178—80.
Count Tilly, see Tilly.
Count Wallenstein:
    amnesty recommended by, 211.
    army of, 188.
    arrogation, of, 192.
    artillery abandoned by, 210.
    attack refrained from by, 204.
    Baltic coast approached by, 188.
    bigotry not in the nature of, 211.
    Bohemian confiscations in favour of,
    Catholics levied upon by, 189. [187.
    Catholics resist, 184.
    character of, 187.
    cold-blooded executions by, 211.
    commandership-in-chief given to, 202.
    confiscated property assigned to, 203.
    Count Mansfeld totally defeated by, 188.   [207.
    courtesies of warfare observed by,
    created Duke of Friedland and Duke of Mecklenburg, 189.
    Croats cautioned by, 208.
    defeat and rout of army of, 209.
    defiance of, 188.
    dependants of, 201.
    deprivation of command of, 190.
    deprivation second time of, 213.
    Devereux murders, 214.
    Diet of Ratisbon and, 190.
    Egra retired to by, 213.   [212.
    Elector of Saxony corresponds with,
    falls back upon Bohemia, 211.
    Ferdinand of Styria hates, 212.
    Ferdinand of Styria rewards the murderers of, 214.
    Ferdinand of Styria sacrifices his pride to, 202.
    Gordon and Piccolomini conspire against and contrive murder of, 213—14.
    Gordon deserts, 213.
    Gustavus Adolphus contrasted with, 195.   [207.
    Gustavus Adolphus driven back by,
    Gustavus Adolphus on track of, 208.
    Gustavus Adolphus resists, 188.
    Gustavus Adolphus resolves to attack, 207.
    Gustavus Adolphus seriously menaced by, 204.

INDEX. 367

Count Wallenstein:
  Gustavus Adolphus threatened with renewed hostilities of, 203.
  humanity of, 212.
  indifference pretended by, 202.
  Irish conspirators against, 214.
  jealousy of, 189.
  King of Hungary succeeds to the command of, 214.
  King of Spain protests against, 202.
  massacre of partisans of, 214.
  Maximilian of Bavaria protests against, 202.
  Maximilian of Bavaria resists, 190.
  Mecklenburg possessed by, 188.
  Mecklenburg promised to, 203.
  military inactivity of, 212.
  murder of, 214.
  offer to restore, 202.
  officers beheaded by, 211.
  officers cashiered by, 211.
  100,000 men at his disposal, 189.
  Oxenstiern refuses overtures of, 212.
  peace desired by, 211—12.
  peace sought by, 207.
  Piccolomini and Gordon conspire against and contrive murder of, 214.
  Piccolomini betrays, 213.
  Pilsen quitted by, 213.
  plundering denounced by, 208.
  Poles aided by, 193.
  Pomerania possessed by, 188.
  Prague palace of, 201.
  Prague winter quarters of, 211.
  prisoners returned by, 207.
  profuse extravagance of, 195.
  Protestants levied upon by, 189.
  Protestants recommended to fair terms by, 211.
  rapacity of followers of, 195.
  resignation of, 213.
  restoration of, 202—3.
  retirement of, 190.
  retreat during the night of, 210.
  reward of murderers of, 214.
  Richelieu opposes, 190.
  Saxony invaded by, 208.
  Scotch conspirators against, 214.
  splendour of, 195.
  Stralsund besieged in vain by, 188.
  strong position of, 204.
  Sultan threatened by, 190.
  treasonable schemes imputed to, 212.
  Treaty of Lubeck and, 189.
  victory falsely claimed by, 210.
  winter quarters of, 211.
Countess of Buchan, cruel degradation of, 98.
Countess Matilda, Hildebrand and, 33.
Court of arbitration, Roman, 16.
Court of international appeal, first, 12.
Creci, battle of, 104.
Crema, siege of, 36—7.

Crespy, Treaty of, 143.
Croats:
  indiscriminate slaughter by, 197.
  marauding by, 208.
Cromwell (Oliver):
  death of, 229.
  despotic policy of, 229.
  Dunkirk acquired by, 228—9.
  energy of, 227.
  European fame of troops of, 229.
  formidable power of, 227.
  France augments strength of, 228.
  France influenced by, 234.
  Jamaica acquired by, 227.
  Mazarin listened to by, 228.
  Philip IV. makes offers to, 227.
  reputation of, 281—2.
  Spanish colonies attacked by, 227.
  unscrupulous spirit of, 227.
  William III. compared with, 281.
Crusaders:
  atrocities of the, 68.
  Byzantine Empire and, 70.
  ferocity of the, 67.
  Innocent III. and the, 71.
  Jerusalem sacked by, 68.
  plunder of churches by, 71.
  Saracens and, 69.
  unparalleled brutality of, 68.
Crusades:
  Byzantine Empire and, 63—78.
  fallacy of the, 69.
  Frederick II. and the, 45.
  inevitable result of the, 72.
  maritime law affected by, 164.
  Mohammedan retaliation for the, 72.
  Popes sanctioned, 69.
  stupendous folly of the, 72.
Cumberland, invasion of, 89, 91.
Cyprus, Duke of Savoy claims, 134.
Cyrus:
  illness of, 2.
  revolt against, 8.

Dalmatia, Turks abandon, 269.
Danes, Alfred and the, 28.
Danube:
  Euphrates to the, 66.   [208.
  Gustavus Adolphus marches to the,
Darius, ambassadors of, 3.
Dark Ages, initiation of the, 30.
Dauphin:
  death of the, 314.
  Rhine crossed by the, 259.
  Spanish succession decided in favour of the, 275.
David, brother of Llewellyn, fate of, 81—2.
David of Israel, Henry VII. compared to, 128.
David II., John of France and, 111.
Days of chivalry:
  travellers in, 117.
  see also Chivalry.

368 INDEX.

Dead:
  outraged, 260.
  respect for the, 20.
Debased coin condemned by Innocent III. 42.
Delphi, burning of Temple of, 1.
Demetrius Poliorcetes, severity of, 9.
Demosthenes on Greek policy, 13.
Denmark:
  Charles XII. invades, 277.
  Christian of, 187, see Christian.
  Innocent III. and, 60.
  James I. and, 187.
  Louis XIV. opposed by, 259.
  Lutheran religion in, 161.
  Sweden and, 160.
De Ruyter, the Dutch admiral, 237.
  Chatham attacked by, 239.
  death of, 251.
  Mediterranean entered by, 251.
  naval battles of, 251.
  Thames entered by, 239.
Dessau, battle of, 188.
Devereux, an Irish captain, Count Wallenstein murdered by, 214.
De Witt:
  capacity of, 237.
  Louis XIV. and, 238.
  Louis XIV. at enmity with, 244.
  peace between France and Spain promoted by, 240—1.   [245—6.
  peace proposals by Louis XIV. to, private virtues of, 237.
  treachery imputed to, 246.
  Triple Alliance and, 241.
Diet of Augsburg, 149.
  religious liberty confirmed at, 151.
Diet of Constance, 33.
Diet of Leipsic, 194.
Diet of Ratisbon, 185, 190.
Diet, Protestant, 181.
Divine wrath, effort to avert, 3.
Donauwerth:
  Gustavus Adolphus storms, 203.
  Marlborough advances upon, 287.
  religious riot at, 173.
Don Louis de Haro, plenipotentiary of Spain, 233.
Drake:
  contraband and, 169.
  heroic conduct of, 155.
Dreux, battle of, 158.   [149.
Duke of Alva, Protestantism and the,
Duke of Anjou:
  heir to France, 314.
  proclaimed as Philip V., 276.   [275.
  Spanish succession settled on the,
Duke of Austria, 38.
  beheading of, 53.
  Conradino and, 52.
  penitence of, 39.
Duke of Bedford, Regent of France:
  Earl of Douglas and, 117.
  French exploits of, 129.

Duke of Berri, Spanish succession and,
Duke of Berwick: [276.
  Castile entered by, 294.
  Marlborough, uncle of, 294.   [127.
Duke of Bourbon, death in captivity of,
Duke of Brittany:
  Charles of Blois and, 103.
  death of, 314.
  granddaughter of, 103.
Duke of Brunswick, France resisted by, 249.
Duke of Buckingham, Charles I. influenced by, 189.
Duke of Burgundy:
  audacity of the, 120.
  Battle of Agincourt and, 122.
  Charles VI. and, 119.
  Charles VII. and, 123.
  crime and flight of, 120.
  driven from France, 122.
  eulogy of the, 121.
  heir to France, 314.
  murder of, 124.
  Philip, son of, 124.   [264.
Duke de Chartres, gallant conduct of,
Duke of Clarence, defeat and death of,
Duke of Cleves: [128.
  lunatic and childless, 174.
  sisters of, 174.
Duke of Guise:
  Charles of Austria resisted by, 150.
  humanity of, 150.
  Metz defended by, 150.
Duke of Hanover:
  Electorate given to, 277.
  King of Denmark and, 160.
Duke of Lorraine:
  restoration of the, 268.
  Vienna defended by, 254.
Duke of Marlborough, see Marlborough.
Duke of Norfolk, Elizabeth and, 156.
Duke of Orleans:
  captivity in England of, 127.   [145.
  Catherine de Medici betrothed to,
  Charles VI. and, 119.   [121.
  John Petit justifies the murder of,
  murder of the, 120.
  praised for murder, 121.
  ransom of, 127.
Duke of Ormond, Marlborough succeeded by, 311.
Duke of Savoy:
  Allied Powers joined by, 285.
  Cyprus claimed by, 134.
  Louis XIV. opposed by, 259.
  Louis XIV. appeals to, 266.
  Philip V. and, 285.
  Prince Eugene joined by, 291.
  restoration of dominions of, 151.
Duke of Sully, Austria opposed by, 175
Dunes: [—6.
  after defeat of, 232.
  battle of, 228.
Dunfermline Abbey, destruction of, 96.

INDEX. 369

Dunkirk:
  Charles II. sells, 228.
  Cromwell acquires, 228—9.
  Spain recovers, 227.
Dutch: [219.
  Charles I. exacts apology from the,
  Count Mansfeld enters service of the, 184. [184.
  Prince Christian enters service of the,
  Prince of Parma resisted by the, 155.
  Spanish fleet destroyed by, 218—19.

Earl of Buchan, Henry V. and, 128.
Earl of Douglas, quarter refused by, 117.
Earl of March:
  Henry V. and, 124.
  restored to liberty, 126.
Earl of Murray:
  Elizabeth and, 155.
  Randolph and the, 158.
  Tamworth and the, 158. [156.
Earl of Northumberland, Elizabeth and,
Earl of Peterborough:
  Catalonia mastered by, 293.
  recklessness of, 293.
  Spain and, 293.
  Valencia mastered by, 293.
  Vienna crew and, 293.
Earl of Suffolk:
  extradition and imprisonment of, 118.
  Shimei compared with, 118.
  treacherous execution of, 118.
Earthquake at Rhodes, 2.
Eastern Empire, see Byzantine Empire.
Ecclesiastical authority only check to licence, 60.
Ecclesiastics exempted from taxes, 51.
Edict of Nantes:
  abandonment of, 216.
  Henry IV. of France and, 257.
  promulgation of the, 153.
  revocation of the, 257.
  Vauban on revocation of, 258.
Edward I.:
  ambition of, 92—100.
  appearances studied by, 82.
  appointed umpire at a duel, 55.
  arbitration by, 84.
  Baliol and, 83—8.
  bigotry of, 97.
  Boniface I. and, 57.
  Boniface VIII. and, 60.
  bribery by, 87.
  Bruce and, 82—4.
  burial of, 99.
  caging of women by, 98.
  child caged by, 98.
  chivalry and, 80.
  Christendom and, 99.
  contraband under, 169.
  cruelty of, 97.
  conquest of Scotland by, 90. [by, 98.
  Countess of Buchan exposed in cage
  David and, 82.

Edward I.:
  death of, 99.
  detestable cruelty of, 82.
  devoutness of, 97.
  foresight of, 87.
  French only language spoken by, 87.
  gauntlet thrown down to, 89.
  inconsistency of, 100.
  judgment pronounced by, 88.
  law of Christendom and, 99.
  Llewellyn and, 81.
  Magna Charta and, 100.
  Parliament called by, 90.
  Parliament summoned by, 82.
  Philip the Fair and, 99.
  vengeance of, 97.
  victims of, 97—8.
  Wallace defeated by, 92.
Edward III.:
  Amiens reached by, 109.
  Benedict XII. and, 102.
  condemnation to death by, 105.
  Count d'Artois and, 102.
  disguised in battle, 107.
  dissimulation of, 105—6.
  does homage to Philip of Valois, 102.
  Eustace de Ribeaumont and, 106—8.
  Eustace de St. Pierre and, 105—6.
  experience in France of, 103.
  French crown claimed by, 101—2.
  French disasters to, 113.
  generosity of, 104.
  Guienne ceded to, 112.
  Henry V. compared with, 126.
  humanity of, 105.
  Jacques d'Arteveld and, 102.
  John of France and, 109.
  licence of followers of, 109.
  magnanimity of, 107.
  Normandy ravaged by, 109. [102.
  proclaims himself King of France,
  Queen Philippa persuades, 105.
  relents, 105.
  renounces crown of France, 111.
  Scotland and, 100.
  Sir Walter Manny and, 107.
  struck down, 107.
  surrender to, 107.
Egra, Count Wallenstein retires to, 213.
Egypt:
  Amasis, King of, 2.
  conquest of, 5.
  invasion of, 4.
Egyptian army, Jerusalem and an, 68.
Egyptians put to death, 5.
Eleanor, Celestine and, 38—9.
Elector of Brandenburg, crown of Prussia assigned to, 277.
Elector of Saxony:
  Baner defeats the, 217.
  condemned as a traitor, 149. [212.
  Count Wallenstein corresponds with,
  dispossession of, 149.
  Oxenstiern thwarted by, 210.

2 B

INDEX.

Electors of Germany invited to elect successor to Frederick II., 49.
Elizabeth of Bavaria, mother of Conradino, 52.
Elizabeth of England: [156—9.
  ambassadors' rights at court of, Bishop of Ross and, 156.
  Cecil and, 155.
  conspiracy against life of, 157.
  contraband under, 169.
  Duke of Norfolk and, 156.
  Earl of Murray and, 155.
  Earl of Northumberland and, 156.
  France and, 153.
  Huguenots and, 153.
  indefeasible policy of, 155.
  imperfect information of, 152.
  James and, 155.
  Mendoza and, 157.
  murder plotted against, 154.
  Netherlands and, 153.
  piratical warfare by, 153.
  policy of, 153.
  public morality in time of, 154.
  Queen of Scots and, 155—6.
  Scotland and, 155.
  slave trade promoted by, 171—2.
  Spain and, 153.
Emperor of Germany, Pope and, 62.
Emperors of the East, Popes and, 64.
Empire, Church and, 44.
Enemy's country, humanity disregarded in, 185.
England:
  Allied Powers make treaty with, 285.
  ambassadors of, 47.
  ambassadorial law in, 229—32.
  anti-Gallican prejudices of, 300.
  arbitration between Holland and, 238—9.
  Castile advanced into by, 294.
  Commons of, 60.
  Count Mansfeld befriended by, 187.
  Cromwell makes a Power of, 227.
  disbanded army of, 278.
  fleet reduced by Government of, 238.
  France friendly with, 242.
  France negotiates with, 307.
  Frederick II. and, 49.
  French disasters to, 113.
  Godolphin ministry in, 305.
  Gustavus Adolphus approved by, 191.
  Henry of Guise and, 153.
  Holland at war with, 237—9.
  Holland combined against by France and, 246—7.
  Holland makes peace with, 248.
  Holland's rivalry with, 237.
  invasion prepared for against, 154.
  Irish victories in, 263.
  Jacobite plots in, 262.
  James I. restrains, 186.
  Leopold makes treaty with, 279.
  Leopold not encouraged by, 277.

England:
  Louis XIV. alarms, 278.
  New York acquired by, 239.
  Peter the Great and, 297—9.
  Philip II. and, 153.
  powerlessness of, 278.
  Prince Eugene visits, 311, 313.
  Prince of Parma and, 154.
  Protestant sympathies of, 186.
  pugnacity of people of, 311.
  Romanus III. and, 67.
  Scotland united with, 293.
  slavery opposed in, 26.
  slavery prohibited in, 26.
  slave trade and, 171.
  Tourville disperses fleet of, 265.
  Wars of the Roses in, 131.
  William III. acknowledged by, 262.
  see also London. [218, 219.
English Channel, naval contest in the,
Enterprise of man, 1.
Ernest Count Mansfeld, Protestant military commander, 180. See also Count Mansfeld.
Euphrates to the Danube, 66.
Europe:
  balance of power in, 319.
  Charles XII. amazes, 277.
  Church and, 61.
  contraband and, 169.
  Cromwell's fame in, 229.
  modern public law of, 23.
  maritime law of, 165.
  revolutions in, 64.
  standing armies and, 319.
  three epochs of, 319.
  wars in, 64.
European princes, Church and, 60.
Eustace de Ribeaumont, Edward III. and, 106—8. [105—6.
Eustace de St. Pierre, Edward III. and,
Excommunication:
  France sentenced to, 57.
  Frederick II. suffers, 45.
  Innocent III. threatens, 41.
  Popes and, 62.
Extradition:
  Earl of Suffolk suffers from, 118.
  Roman, 17.

Falkenberg killed in defending Magdeburg, 197.
Falkirk, battle of, 92.
Fealty, Baliol swears, 88.
Fecian College, order of the, 16, 17.
Fénélon, Marlborough and, 306.
Ferdinand and Isabella, Moors and, 131.
Ferdinand of Austria, success of, 144.
Ferdinand II. of Austria, otherwise Ferdinand of Styria:
  amnesty granted by, 216.
  army equipped by, 182.
  Bavaria disposed of by, 185.
  bigotry of, 189.

INDEX. 371

Ferdinand II. of Austria :
  Bohemia ceded to, 177.
  brightening prospects of, 188.
  Catholic proclivities in favour of, 201.
  Catholic restoration by, 180.
  compromise refused by, 183.
  constancy of, 201.
  Count Tilly military commander under, 182.
  Count Wallenstein hated by, 212.
  Count Wallenstein humiliates, 202.
  Count Wallenstein volunteers to serve, 187—8.
  crown of Germany assumed by, 180.
  death of, 217.
  deposition of, 181.
  Diet summoned and opened by, 185.
  disasters to, 201.
  edict of restitution by, 180. [216.
  edict of restitution abandoned by,
  elected Emperor of Austria, 181.
  Elector of Saxony gained over by, 185.
  Frederick V. declared a rebel by, 185.
  Gustavus Adolphus encouraged by zeal of, 191.
  heresy hated by, 183. [212.
  hope of recovering supremacy by,
  hostilities commenced between Gustavus Adolphus and, 193.
  Jesuit advisers of, 212.
  Jesuits in league with, 177.
  John George makes treaty with, 215.
  Lusitania disposed of by, 185.
  Maximilian of Bavaria in alliance with, 182.
  Maximilian of Bavaria received with friendliness by, 204. [185.
  Maximilian of Bavaria rewarded by, murderers of Count Wallenstein rewarded by, 214.
  Palatinate disposed of by, 185.
  Protestant dread of, 177.
  Protestantism defied by, 180.
  religious liberty recalled by, 183.
  religious tendencies of, 183.
  resistance resolved upon by, 182.
  Spain in alliance with, 182. [211.
  toleration regarded as a deadly sin by,
  Vienna defended by, 180.
  war encouraged by, 212.
Ferdinand III. of Austria :
  Bavaria deserts, 220.
  Calvinist commander of, 220.
  Melander and, 220.
  peace forced upon, 224.
  resolute character of, 218.
  Spain can no longer support, 220.
Ferdinand V. of Spain, surnamed the Catholic :
  acquisitions of, 136.
  Africa and, 136.
  Columbus and, 136.
  Henry VIII. and, 137.

Ferdinand V. of Spain:
  intrigues of, 136.
  most remarkable monarch, 133.
  ports claimed by, 134.
Feudalism, growth of, 23.
Feudal system :
  character of the, 100.
  pretext of the, 101.
Feudal tyranny, Papal power and, 60.
Flanders :
  France acquires towns in, 253.
  religious wars in, 150.
  Spain and, 227.
  Spanish acquisitions in, 267.
  suzerainty of, 99.
  William III. invades, 264.
Florence, surrender of, 132.
France : [236—7.
  affront at Rome to ambassador of,
  Allied Powers declare war against,
  Alsace annexed to, 224. [283.
  Alsace ceded to, 215.
  ambassador of Spain disputes with ambassador of, 236.
  ambition of, 70.
  annexations by, 150.
  Artois retained by, 233.
  attempted conquest of, 101.
  Austria and, 176.
  Austria co-operated against by, 210.
  Austrian rivalry with, 139.
  Bar acquired by, 234.
  Bavaria makes treaty with, 278.
  Blenheim fatal to ascendency of, 290.
  Boniface VIII. and, 58.
  Burgundy commands for, 294.
  cardinal infante invades, 217.
  Castile victory of, 294.
  Catholics respected by, 215.
  Charles of Austria invades, 146—8.
  Charles of Austria visits, 146.
  Charles I. at war with, 189.
  chivalric cruelty in, 119.
  Church and, 57.
  citizens abandon, 257.
  civil war in, 227.
  claim to crown of, 101.
  clergy and, 57.
  Clermont acquired by, 234.
  Cromwell's influence upon, 234.
  commerce destroyed by, 265.
  Condé fights against, 227.
  Count of Evreux and, 101.
  Cromwell augments strength of, 223.
  dangerous ascendency acquired by, 234.
  daughter of Louis X. and, 101.
  defensive attitude of, 291.
  De Ruyter fights the fleet of, 251.
  Duke of Anjou and, 314.
  Duke of Brunswick and, 249.
  Duke of Burgundy and, 314.
  Edward III. renounces crown of, 111.
  England friendly with, 242.

INDEX.

France:
England negotiates with, 307.
English losses in, 113.
Elizabeth and, 153.
escape from persecution in, 257.
excommunication of, 57.
failure of male line of, 101.
famine imminent in, 299.
famine in, 301.
females excluded from crown of, 101.
feudal sovereignty of kings of, 99.
first English victory in, 104.
Flanders towns ceded to, 253.
Franche-Comté restored by, 241.
Franche-Comté wholly ceded to, 253.
free passage conceded to armies of, 234.
Germany expels subjects of, 261.
Germany subject to intrigues of, 226.
Gustavus Adolphus makes treaty with, 101—2.
Gustavus Adolphus regarded with jealousy by, 210.
heiress of, 210.
heirship of, 314.
Henry VIII. invades, 138, 148.
Henry the Great of, 153.
Holland combined against by England and, 246—7.
Holland makes peace with, 267.
Holland negotiates with, 251.
Huguenot conspiracy in, 152.
humiliation prepared for, 235.
impoverishment of, 110.
intercourse prohibited with, 261.
Italy favourable to, 277.
James I. and, 186.
James I. correctly predicts about, 215.
John Churchill in army of, 250.
John of, see John.
La Fronde in, 227.
Leopold declares war against, 249.
Lorraine in part acquired by, 234.
Louis XV. becomes the absolute master of, 235. [295.
Marlborough defeats armies of, 289.
Marlborough totally defeats, 302.
marriage contracted between Maria Theresa and the King of, 234.
Mazarin plenipotentiary of, 233.
Medici influence in, 176.
Medici misgovernment of, 152.
meeting of plenipotentiaries of Spain and, 233.
Messina and, 251.
Metz annexed to, 224.
misery of people of, 301—2.
modern civilisation of, 27.
National Council of, 57.
Netherlands campaign of, 294.
Netherlands cities abandoned by, 289.
Netherlands conquests of, 241. [240.
Netherlands war between Spain and, nobles support the King of, 58.

France:
Oxenstiern appeals to, 215.
Palatinate retired from by, 260.
paralysed by murder of Henry IV., people of, 301. [176.
Philip IV. makes offers to, 232.
Philip V. and heirship of, 314.
Pignerol annexed to, 224.
Popes and, 59.
preparation for war in, 286.
Prince Eugene defeats army of, 278.
Protestantism and, 145.
Protestants co-operated with by, 210.
Pyrenees made the boundary between Spain and, 233.
ravage of, 104.
recovery of, 131.
religious discord let loose on, 257.
religious liberty in, 153.
religious wars in, 150.
representatives of first families of, 233.
resources of, 301.
retreat of army of, 250.
Roman Pontiffs and, 59.
Roussillon acquired by, 233.
Rhine fortresses forbidden by, 224.
Richelieu and, 176.
Richelieu resolute in favour of, 217.
rural population of, 301—2.
Saracens in, 30.
sailors abandon, 258.
Salic law of, 101.
Sicily and, 251.
slavery in, 27.
soldiers abandon, 258.
Spain at war with, 215.
Spain continues war with, 227.
Spain forbidden to unite with, 309.
Spanish alliance disastrous to, 234.
Spanish infantry defeated by, 219.
Spanish treaty with, 151.
States-General of, 57.
Strasburg annexed to, 224.
Strasburg formally ceded to, 268.
subsidy granted to Oxenstiern by, 215.
sufferings of people of, 301—2.
Sweden and, 224.
Sweden in alliance with, 202.
Torstenson in alliance with, 220.
Toul annexed to, 224.
towns ceded to, 268. [233.
towns in Luxembourg acquired by, unsuccessful against Germany, 217.
Vendome commands for, 291.
Vendome recalled to, 289.
Vendome saves, 290.
Verdun annexed to, 224.
war of Burgundy and Orleans in, 122.
William III. defeated by army of, 264.
Franche-Comté:
France wholly acquires, 253.
France restores, 241.
Francis I.:
Alps crossed by, 139.

INDEX.

Francis I.:
　ambition of, 139.
　capture of, 141.
　Charles of Austria challenges, 143.
　Charles of Austria entertained by, 147.
　Charles of Austria makes final treaty of peace with, 148.
　Constable Bourbon and, 141.
　death of, 149.
　defeat of, 140, 141.
　hard terms imposed upon, 141.
　Henry VIII. and, 145.
　new rivalry between Charles of Austria and, 145.
　proposals of marriage by, 145. [145.
　Protestant princes make treaty with,
　ransom of sons of, 144.
　renunciation by, 143—4.
　repudiation of treaty by, 142.
　Savoy invaded by, 146.
　Solyman the Magnificent makes treaty with, 146.
　treaties disregarded by, 146.
　war again breaks out between Charles and, 147.

Frankfort:
　Council of, 140.
　Gustavus Adolphus enters, 200.

Franks, Greeks and, 69—70.

Frederick, Duke of Holstein:
　elected King of Denmark, 160.
　Lutheran religion and, 161.

Frederick I. of Austria:
　commerce and, 36.
　cruelty of, 36—7.
　discipline of, 36.
　good faith of, 36.
　humanity of, 36.
　Lodi merchants and, 33.
　Lombardy and, 34—6.
　merchants and, 36.
　merciful treatment by, 35.
　Milanese people and, 34.
　Popes and, 53.
　warfare by, 36.

Frederick II. of Austria:
　accusation against, 46.
　adultery of, 46.
　atrocity of, 45.
　barbarity of, 44.
　Bishop of Carniola accuses, 46.
　cardinals made prisoners by, 45.
　Church struggle with, 45.
　churches plundered by, 45.
　concubines of, 46.
　Conradino, grandson of, 50, 52. [49.
　Count of Holland claims to succeed,
　crusade promised by, 45.
　death of, 50.
　defiance of Pope by, 47—8.
　denial on behalf of, 47.　　[47.
　denunciation of Church revenues by,
　deposition of, 47.

Frederick II. of Austria:
　disasters to descendants of, 50.
　electors invited to supersede, 49.
　England and, 49.
　English ambassadors defend, 47.
　eventual ruin of, 45.
　excommunication of, 45.
　French ambassadors defend, 47.
　grandson of, 50.
　Gregory the Ninth and, 45.
　hatred towards, 44.
　Henry III. and, 49.
　Honorius and, 45.
　infidels favoured by, 46.
　Innocent III. and, 42.
　Innocent IV. and, 45.
　invasion of Papal States by, 45.
　Italian prospects of, 49.
　Italy and, 44.
　Jesus Christ and, 46.
　Landgrave of Thuringia claims to succeed, 49.
　Mahomet and, 46.
　Manfred, illegitimate son of, 50.
　Moses and, 46.　　[age, 50.
　most conspicuous personage of his
　most powerful monarch of the age, 47.
　no evidence against, 47.
　occupation of Papal cities by, 45.
　Pagan associates of, 46.
　pirates imprisoned by, 47.
　plunder of churches by, 45.
　prelates made prisoners by, 45.
　refuses to attend Council of Lyons, 47.
　restrained by no laws, 46.
　retirement to Apulia of, 50.
　ridicule of the Church by, 45.
　Saracen associates of, 46.
　sentence thundered forth against, 48.
　Soldan of Babylon and, 46.
　sons of, 50.
　Thaddeus de Suessa defends, 47.
　threat of ecclesiastics by, 47.
　total defeat of, 50.
　unbelief alleged against, 46.

Frederick I. of Prussia:
　Innocent XII. protests against elevation of, 278.
　Marlborough and, 285.　　[277.
　Prussian monarchy commenced by,

Frederick V. of Bohemia:
　Bethlem Gabor allied with, 182.
　Calvinistic prejudices of, 182.
　Catholics offended by, 182.
　Christian sects dismayed at, 182.
　church pictures stripped down by, 182.
　coronation of, 181.
　crown left behind by, 182.
　defeat of army of, 182.
　denunciation as a rebel of, 183—185.
　flight of, 182.
　Gustavus Adolphus joined by, 200.
　Gustavus Adolphus writes reply to letter of, 193.

374   INDEX.

Frederick V. of Bohemia:
  head of German Calvinists, 181.
  Holland affords a refuge for, 183.
  James I. opposed to, 181.
  Lutherans offended by, 182.
  Maurice of Nassau a kinsman of, 181.
  misgivings of, 181.
  pusillanimity of, 182.
  Rupert, son of, 182.
  unfitness of, 182.
French:
  Bajazet and the, 73.
  Constantinople attacked by, 70.
  language spoken by Edward I., 87.
French ambassadors, Frederick II. and, 47. [114.
Froissart on the massacre at Limoges,

Galway, surrender of, 263.
Gaul, Julius Cæsar and, 21.
Gauls:
  regarded as barbarians, 4.
  Romans and, 3.
Gelon:
  admiration for, 6.
  treaty with, 5.
Genoa, war between Pisa and, 43.
Germanic Empire, Treaty of Westphalia constituted by, 226.
Germans:
  marauding charged against, 205.
  massacre of, 115.
Germany:
  atrocities of the army of, 197.
  Charles XII. watched with alarm by princes of, 277.
  chivalry and, 79.
  Christianity in, 27.
  civil war in, 49. [184.
  Count Mansfeld marches into North, desolation of, 183.
  Diet of, 177. [of, 180.
  Ferdinand of Styria elected Emperor
  France unsuccessful against, 217.
  French advantages over, 226.
  French expelled from, 261.
  Jesuits in, 177.
  Louis XIV. hated by, 261.
  Richelieu and, 215.
  slavery in, 27.
  unsettled state of, 176—7.
  weakening of, 226.
Ghibelline faction, Sicily and the, 52.
Gibbon on Mohammedan generosity, 67.
Gibraltar, Sir George Rooke captures,
Godolphin: [289.
  Marlborough dissuaded by, 286.
  Peace of Utrecht and, 306.
  resignation of ministry of, 305.
Gods, appeal to the, 19.
Gordon:
  Count Wallenstein deserted by, 213.
  Count Wallenstein murdered by contrivance of, 214.

Gordon:
  Piccolomini conspires against Count Wallenstein with, 213.
Goths:
  Christianity respected by, 21.
  Rome invaded by, 29.
Grand Duke of Tuscany, Philip V. disputes with, 234.
Great Britain:
  Holland makes treaty with, 241.
  maritime law of, 165.
  Sweden makes treaty with, 241.
  United States make treaty with, 257.
  see also England.
Greece:
  alliances of, 13.
  arbitrations in, 12.
  coalitions with, 13.
  invasion of, 6.
  literature of, 65.
  slavery and, 25.
  war with States of, 11.
Greeks:
  characteristics of, 15.
  Franks and, 69.
  indifference to human life of, 15.
  international appeal and, 13.
  Italian dominions lost by the, 66.
  Mahommedans and, 65.
  promise tribute, 74.
Greek Church:
  attitude of the, 66.
  Constantinople and, 65.
  dependency of the, 66.
  Mahomet II. protects the, 78.
Gregory the Great:
  humane example of, 26.
  liberation of slaves by, 25.
  subjection of, 29.
Gregory II., Martel and, 39.
Gregory III., Leo III. attempts seizure of, 64.
Gregory VII., Hildebrand, see Hildebrand. [45.
Gregory IX., Frederick the Second and,
Grotius on the right to injure, 192—3.
Guienne:
  Black Prince made governor of, 112.
  Edward III. obtains sovereignty of,
Guinea, slave trade with, 170. [112.
Gustavus Adolphus:
  advantageous consequences of humanity of, 196.
  armour not worn by, 210.
  asserted ambition of, 209.
  Augsburg taken by, 203.
  Austria and, 191.
  Austria beaten by, 209.
  Baltic crossed by, 191.
  battle of Leipsic won by, 199—200.
  Bavaria entered by, 203.
  Bernhard of Saxe-Weimar joins, 198.
  Brandenburg refuses passage to army of, 197.

INDEX. 375

Gustavus Adolphus :
bridge constructed by, 203.
character of, 195.
charge in person by, 209.
Christina, only child of, 210.
complete victory of, 200. [195.
Count Wallenstein contrasted with,
Count Wallenstein declines to attack, 204.
Count Wallenstein followed by, 208.
Count Wallenstein pitted against, 202.
Count Wallenstein resisted by, 188.
Count Wallenstein resumes hostilities against, 203. [204.
Count Wallenstein seriously menaces,
Danube marched to by, 203.
death of, 209.
Donauwerth stormed by, 203.
Elector of Brandenburg stands aloof from, 191. [191.
Elector of Saxony stands aloof from,
Electors stand aloof from, 198.
enforced inactivity of, 195.
England approved of, 191.
Ferdinand of Styria commences hostilities with, 193.
Ferdinand of Styria writes letter of remonstrance to, 193.
Ferdinand's zeal encourages, 191.
fortress after fortress surrenders to,
forty tons of gold sent to, 206. [200.
France makes treaty with, 191—2.
Frankfort entered by, 200.
Frederick V. joins, 200.
French jealousy of, 210. [205.
Germans accused of marauding by,
gold entrusted to, 206.
Grotius and, 192—3.
hanging of a lieutenant by, 207. [196.
hanging of Scottish volunteer by,
Huguenots said to be in correspondence with, 201.
humanity of, 196.
imperial crown said to be the object of, 209.
invincibility denied to, 207.
irritable temper of, 209.
James I. and, 187.
John George joins, 199.
King of Poland kinsman of, 210.
Landgrave of Hesse joins, 198.
last march of, 208.
limit of operations of, 195. [201.
Louis XIII. uneasy at success of,
magistrates take oath of allegiance to, 203.
marauding earnestly discountenanced by, 205—6.
Marlborough compared with, 238.
Mecklenburg and, 195.
Metz winter quarters of, 201.
mortally wounded, 209.
most immaculate of conquerors, 209.
motives declared by, 193—4.

Gustavus Adolphus :
motives of, 191.
Munich entered in triumph by, 203.
Naumburg ovation to, 208.
Nuremberg head-quarters of, 204.
Nuremberg retired from by, 208.
orderly conduct of army of, 195.
outrages vehemently denounced by, ovation to, 208. [206.
Oxenstiern reinforces, 204.
Palatinate occupied by, 200.
Pappenheim repulsed by, 199.
Paris said to be in peril of, 201.
payment for provisions by, 195.
peasantry well treated army of, 193.
Poland at war with, 187.
Pomerania and, 195.
Pomerania invaded by, 190. [206.
proclamation against his officers by,
protection of invaded people by, 195.
Protestantism re-established by, 203.
Protestant princes and, 191. [194.
Protestant princes emboldened by,
Protestants make alliance with, 198.
Protestants rescued by, 209.
Providence said to have interposed to encompass death of, 210.
prowess of, 210.
Richelieu's sympathies with, 201.
rights on the Baltic claimed by, 194.
Scottish volunteers in army of, 196.
sincere religion of, 195.
Spain beaten by, 209.
Spanish troops retire before, 209.
Stettin taken by, 190.
Stockholm address of, 192.
Stralsund assisted by, 195.
subsidy payable to, 191—2.
successes of, 190.
Swedes exonerated from the charge of marauding by, 205.
temporary discomfiture of, 199.
Tilly advanced upon by, 203.
Tilly approached by, 199.
Tilly finally defeated by, 203.
Tilly prepares to resist, 202.
work accomplished by, 209.
Gustavus Vasa :
Christian II. and, 160.
Lutheran religion accepted by, 160.
Sweden and, 160.

Halle, Pappenheim ordered to seize, 203.
Hannibal :
career of, 13.
character of, 20.
Scipio and brother of, 7.
Hanseatic League :
contraband and, 169.
maritime law under the, 166.
Hanse Towns, maritime law and the,
Hapsburgs : [167—8.
ambition of the, 300.
Bourbon duel with, 278.

376 INDEX.

Hapsburgs:
  Bourbons and, 272.
  Louis XIV. makes offers to the, 290.
Harbours, neutral, 7.
Harfleur, surrender of, 125.
Harley:
  Peace of Utrecht and, 310.
  Swift and, 313.
Haroun al Raschid, Irene and, 65. [113.
Hearth-tax, the Black Prince imposes a,
Heidelberg Castle, Louis XIV. burns, 260.
Heinsius, Marlborough dissuaded by,
Hellespont, march to the, 3. [286.
Henry of Guise, England and, 154.
Henry II. of France:
  Calais and, 151.
  Lorraine invaded by, 150. [150.
  Maurice of Saxony makes treaty with,
  Metz captured by, 150.
  Toul captured by, 150.
  Verdun captured by, 150.
Henry III. of England:
  arbitration appealed to by, 83.
  Frederick II. and, 49.
  Louis IX. and, 83.
  Simon de Montfort and, 83.
Henry IV. the Emperor, 32—3.
Henry IV. of France:
  army of, 176.
  assassination of, 176.
  Austria humbled by, 226.
  Austria opposed by, 175—6.
  Edict of Nantes and, 257.
  Edict of Nantes promulgated by, 153.
  peace under, 153.
  Ravaillac assassinates, 176.
Henry V., popes and the Emperor, 33.
Henry V. of England:
  barbarity of, 126.
  Calais marched on by, 125.
  cold-blooded murders of, 128.
  crown of France ceded to, 124.
  death of, 124.
  degeneracy of, 125—6.
  devastation forbidden by, 125.
  Duke of Burgundy and, 124.
  Duke of Orleans and, 127.
  Earl of Buchan and, 128.
  Earl of March and, 124, 126.
  Edward III. compared with, 126.
  enormous ambition of, 127.
  exasperation of, 128.
  France during reign of, 122.
  gentlemen prisoners hanged by, 128.
  hanging of Scots by, 129. [125.
  hanging of soldiers for sacrilege by,
  King of Scots and, 126—8.
  premature death of, 129.
  religious zealotism of, 124—5.
  revengeful disposition of, 127.
  Scots treated as rebels by, 129.
  starvation of non-combatants by, 127.
  transformation of, 127.
  wanton execution by, 127.

Henry VII.:
  David of Israel compared to, 118.
  Earl of Suffolk imprisoned by, 118.
  Philip of Castile detained by, 117—
Henry VIII.: [18.
  Charles of Austria makes and breaks
    treaty with, 188.
  death of, 149.
  Earl of Suffolk murdered by, 118.
  Ferdinand V. and, 137.
  France invaded by, 138, 148.
  Francis I. and, 145.
  inactivity of, 140.
  Julius II. and, 137.
  Louis XII. and, 137.
  maritime law of, 168.
  Scotland invaded by, 148.
  Solomon compared with, 118.
Heralds, privileges of, 4.
Heresy, Ferdinand's hatred of, 183.
Heretical opinions, Innocent III. and,
  43.
Heretics, Louis XIV. hunts, 258.
Herodotus informs us, 1, 2, 6, 8.
Hildebrand:
  afterwards Gregory VII., 32.
  besieged, 33.
  Countess Matilda and, 33.
  dream of, realised, 43.
  exile of, 33.
  founder of Papal power, 31.
  marriage of clergy forbidden by, 31.
  moderation not a virtue of, 33.
  Robert Guiscard and, 33.
Holland:
  Charles II. and, 237—9.
  debt of, 253.
  digue threatened in, 284.
  England at war with, 237—9.
  England makes peace with, 248.
  England makes treaty with, 251.
  fortune favours, 249.
  France and England combined against,
    246—7.
  France makes peace with, 267.
  Frederick V. takes refuge in, 183.
  Great Britain makes treaty with, 241.
  Louis XIV. alarms, 278.
  neglect of defences of, 244.
  Parliament reluctant to vote supplies
    for war with, 248. [247.
  Shaftesbury in favour of war with,
  Spain and, 224.
  Spain without sympathy with, 241.
  Sweden makes treaty with, 241.
  Surinam acquired by, 239.
  William III. ruler of, 272.
Holy places, plunder of, 45.
Holy Sepulchre, Popes and the, 69.
Homage, Scotch, 86.
Homeric age, chivalry and the, 79.
Honorius, Frederick II. and, 45.
Hospitality, violation of laws of, 8.
Hostility, see Warfare.

INDEX. 377

House of Commons:
  Louis XIV. and the, 252—3.
  Peace of Utrecht and, 311.
  William III. mortified by, 272.
House of Lords, Peace of Utrecht and, 306, 311.
Huguenot rebellion, Sir Nicolas Throgmorton and, 158.
Huguenots:
  conspiracy of, 152.
  Elizabeth and the, 153.
  Gustavus Adolphus said to be in correspondence with, 201.
  Louis XIV. persecutes, 258.
Human life, Greek indifference to, 15.
Hume on Crusaders and Saracens, 69.
Hungary:
  Austria absorbs, 144.
  Bajazet and, 73.
  Bethlem Gabor acquires part of, 182.
  insurrections in, 254.
  rebellion in, 286.
  serfs in, 27.
  Turks abandon, 269.
Huss, see John Huss.

Images, dispute about, 64.
Indians, slave trade and, 170. [ing, 46.
Infidels, Frederick II. accused of favour-
Innocent III.:
  Albigenses and, 42—3, 61.
  Armenian king and, 42.
  Bohemian king and, 42.
  Bulgarian king and, 42.
  Castile and, 41.
  Count of Thoulouse and, 42.
  Crusaders and, 71.
  death of, 43.
  debased coin condemned by, 42.
  Denmark and, 60.
  deposition of kings by, 42.
  despotic character of, 43.
  Duke of Austria and, 40.
  excommunication threatened by, 41.
  fever of, 43.
  Fourth Lateran Council and, 42.
  Frederick II. and, 42.
  heretical opinions and, 43.
  Inquisition introduced by, 43.
  interdict by, 41.
  Isemburga and, 41.
  justice of, 43.
  King of Aragon and, 42.
  kings created by, 42.
  last incident in life of, 43.
  noble birth of, 41.
  Otho IV. and, 42.
  Papal power of, 41.
  Peter II. and, 41.
  Philip Augustus and, 41.
  Portugal and, 41.
  princes of Christendom and, 41.
  supreme court of, 42.
  supreme reign of, 43.

Innocent IV.:
  Baldwin the Second and, 46.
  cardinals in scarlet hats and, 46.
  council held by, 45—6.
  council opened by, 46.
  departure from Rome of, 46.
  Frederick II. and, 45.
  pirates said to be kinsmen of, 47.
Innocent VI., John of France and, 109.
Innocent XII.:
  Charles II. of Spain appeals to, 273.
  Prussia and, 278.
  Spanish succession settled by, 275.
Innspruck, Maurice of Saxony advances upon, 150.
Inquisition, introduction of the, 43.
Interdict:
  Innocent III. and, 41.
  Popes and, 62.
International amity, feudalism and, 23.
International appeal, first court of, 12.
International comity, 1.
International justice:
  recognition of, 11.
  Romans and, 17.
International morality in the twelfth century, 37—8.
International obligations, 1, 2.
  religious character of, 5.
Ireland:
  English victories in, 263.
  James II. repairs to, 262.
  Louis XIV. and, 262.
  Parliament of, 262.
  William III. opposed in, 262.
Irene and Haroun Al Raschid, 65. [101.
Isabella, daughter of Philip the Fair,
Isemburga, Queen of France, Innocent III. and, 41.
Italy:
  Charles VIII. and, 132.
  contest in, 13.
  distracted state of, 44.
  France favoured by, 276.
  Frederick II. and, 44.
  Frederick II. in, 49.
  maritime law of, 164.
  Normans invade, 66.
  Philip V. visits, 284.
  Sicily extended over south of, 51.
  Sicily separated from, 56.
  slavery in, 26.
  Vendome recalled from, 289.
  weakness of, 133.

Jacques d'Arteveld and, 102,
Jamaica, conquest of, 227.
James I:
  Christian of Denmark and, 187.
  Count Mansfeld befriended by, 187.
  death of, 187.
  Denmark and, 187.
  England restrained by, 186.
  Frederick V. opposed by, 181.

378   INDEX.

James I.:
French negotiations of, 186.
Gustavus Adolphus and, 187.
prediction of, 215.
Protestant contest and, 186.
slavery till time of, 27.
Spanish negotiations of, 186.
Swedes and, 187.

James II.:
death of, 279.   [262.
Dublin Parliament summoned by,
flight of, 263.
Ireland repaired to by, 262.
Louis XIV. abandons, 267.
Louis XIV. acknowledges the son of, 279.
Louis XIV. befriends, 261—2.
Louis XIV. sustains, 264.
Marlborough deserts, 279.
plots in favour of, 262.
Prince of Orange deposes, 259.
William III. defeats, 263.

James VI., Elizabeth's treaties with, 155.

Jean Bart:
Louis XIV. grants letters of marque to, 266.
terror of the North Sea, 266.

Jerusalem:
capture of, 68.
Christians surrender at, 69.
Egyptian army at, 68.
frightful carnage at, 68.
retaking of, 68.
storming of, 69.

Jesuits:
Expulsion from Bohemia of, 180.
Ferdinand of Styria advised by, 212
Ferdinand of Styria and, 177.
German, 177.
intrigues of the, 173.
Prince Eugene dogged by a spy of the, 313.

Jesus Christ, Frederick II. and, 46.

Jews:
Banishment from France of, 111.
burning alive of, 68.
persecutors of the, 80.
return to France of, 111.

John Churchill:
French army includes, 250.
see also Marlborough.

John of France:
Black Prince and, 110.
Burgundy and, 111.
David II. and, 111.
death of, 111.
defeat of, 110.
humiliation of, 111.
Jews and, 111.
Philip, son of, 111.
prisoner in London, 110.
three millions of gold crowns levied upon, 110.
Visconti and, 111.

John George:
Ferdinand of Styria makes treaty with, 215.
Gustavus Adolphus joined by, 199.
Protestants led by, 194.

John the Handsome, 65.

John Hawkins, slave trade by, 171—2.

John Huss:
burning of, 119.
treachery towards, 119.

John, son of Philip VI.:
Constable d'Eu beheaded by, 109.
Edward III. and, 109.
Innocent VI. and, 109.
King of Navarre prisoner of, 109.
outrage perpetrated by, 109.
succession of, 109.
violent temper of, 109.

John Petit justifies murder, 121.
John, Richard I. and, 37, 80.

John VI., prisoners' freedom purchased by, 26.

Joseph, successor of Leopold of Austria:
Charles XII. and, 291—2.
death of, 305.
Law of Nations and, 291.
Louis XIV. makes secret overtures to, 290—1.

Judas Maccabæus, time of, 9.
Juliers, occupation of, 175.
Julius Cæsar, violence of, 21.

Julius II.:
ambition of, 133.
fatal error of, 136.
Henry VIII. and, 137.
Romagna claimed by, 134.

Justinian:
codes of, 63.
Rome and, 29.

Justiniani, Constantinople defended and deserted by, 76.

Kaminieck, Turks abandon, 269.

King of Aragon:
Constantina, wife of, 54.
duel accepted by, 55.
Innocent III. and, 42.

King of Sweden, arbitrator between England and Holland, 238—9.

King of Hungary, son and heir of Ferdinand of Styria:
Count Wallenstein succeeded in command by, 214.
Nordlingen besieged by, 214.
Oxenstiern defeated by, 214.
Ratisbon surrenders to, 214.
Swedish army defeated by, 214.

King of Navarre, imprisonment of, 109.

King of Poland, kinsman of Gustavus Adolphus, 210.
Leopold allied with, 254.   [254.
Mohammedan invasion repelled by,

King of Portugal, Allied Powers joined by, 285.

INDEX. 379

King of Scots, Henry V. and the, 126—8.
Kinsky, murder attempted by, 180.
Knowledge, Church domination incompatible with, 62.

Lacedæmonians, fine of, 11.
La Fronde, France and, 227.
La Hogue, French defeat at, 264.
Landen, battle of, 264.
Landgrave of Hesse:
  Gustavus Adolphus joined by, 198.
  imprisonment of, 149.
Landgrave of Thuringia claims to succeed Frederick II., 49.
Languedoc:
  heretics hunted from, 258.
  Protestant insurrection in, 285.
Las Casas, slave trade and, 170.
Lateran Council (Third), 26.
Latin League, political character of the, 16.
Latins:
  boundless insolence of the, 72.
  Reformation rejected by, 160.
Law of Nations:
  ancient, 1—22.
  antiquity of principles of, 21.
  armed intervention in the, 193.
  Christianity affected the, 28.
  elementary rules of the, 157.
  Joseph of Austria appeals to the, 201.
  maritime, 163—172.
  Middle Age, 23—62.
  modern, 2.
  origin of, 1.
  Papal power and, 28.
  St. Peter's successors and, 23.
Laws of war, Louis XIV. and the, 231.
League of Cambray, 133—7.
League, Hanseatic, 166.
League of Smalkalde, 144.
Legnano, battle of, 35.
Leibnitz, Church and, 62.
Leipsic:
  Charles XII. quarters near, 201.
  Diet of, 194.
  surrender to Tilly of, 199.
Leo III. (Emperor):
  Byzantine Empire and, 63.
  images denounced by, 64.
Leopold of Austria:
  England declines to encourage, 277.
  England makes treaty with, 279.
  flight of, 254.
  France resisted by, 249.
  Joseph, son and successor of, 290.
  King of Poland allied with, 254.
  Louis XIV. opposed by, 259.
  Louis XIV. resisted by, 278.
  Spanish succession disputed by, 277.
  Turks defeated by, 263.
  Turks threaten war with, 253.
Liberties, defence of, 14.
Liège, &c., Marlborough captures, 234.

Limerick, surrender of, 263.
Limoges:
  Black Prince carried into, 114.
  Froissart on the siege of, 114.
  massacre at, 114.
  siege of, 113.
Literature:
  Grecian, 65.
  Louis XIV. patronises, 255.
Livy, information from, 7, 29.
Llewellyn:
  Anglesea and, 81.
  capture of bride of, 81.
  David, brother of, 81.
  death of, 81.
  head of on Tower, 81.
Lodi, two merchants of, 31, 33.
Lombard League, 35.
Lombardy:
  discord in, 44.
  Frederick the First and, 34.
  independence of, 35, 44.
  Popes supported, 60.
  Prince Eugene winters in, 279.
  suzerains of, 99.
London:
  ambassadors' dispute in, 236.
  John of France prisoner in, 110.
  marine losses of, 265.
  Plague of, 238.
  projected advance upon, 154.
  riot concerning a brother of the Portuguese ambassador in, 229—32.
  Russian ambassador arrested for debt in, 297.
  see also England.
Long bow of yeomen, battle of Creci and, 104. [157—9.
Lord Burghley, Bishop of Ross and,
Lorraine:
  Count Mansfeld takes refuge in, 184.
  France acquires part of, 234.
  Henry II. invades, 150.
  Louis XIV. seizes whole of, 245.
Louis II. of Bohemia slain in battle, 144.
Louis X., daughter of, 101.
Louis XI.:
  execution of 50 prisoners by, 115.
  feudal abuses and, 131.
  iron despotism of, 131.
  standing army of, 132.
Louis XII.
  Cardinal d'Amboise and, 134.
  death of, 139.
  excommunication of, 137. [of. 200.
  Gustavus Adolphus excites uneasiness
  hanging of prisoners by, 115.
  Henry VIII. and, 137.
  Mary of England betrothed to, 138.
  private virtues of, 136.
  Venetian Lombardy claimed by, 134.
Louis XIV.
  absolute master of France, 235.
  Allied Powers make peace with, 301.

Louis XIV.:
  Amsterdam threatened by, 245.
  art patronised by, 255.
  atrocities in the Palatinate by, 260.
  Austrian war with, 278.
  bad faith of, 235.
  barbarity of, 255.
  Catholic fears of, 259.
  courteous reception by, 256.
  Charles II. a pensioner of, 255.
  Charles II. makes secret treaty with, 242—3.
  Charles II. forces peace on, 252.
  Charles II. of Spain opposes, 259
  Charles XII. and, 291.
  cities given to the flames by, 260.
  Colbert, admiral of fleet of, 254.
  consummate skill of, 276.
  crown of Spain renounced by, 234.
  dead not spared by, 260.
  death of, 318.
  defeat of fleet of, 264.
  Denmark opposes, 259.
  designs of, 286.
  De Witt and, 238.
  De Witt held in enmity by, 244. [256.
  Doge of Genoa required to come to,
  Duke of Savoy appealed to by, 266.
  Duke of Savoy opposes, 259.
  England alarmed by, 278.
  flatterers of, 258.
  generals of, 254.
  Genoa bombarded by, 256.
  German hatred of, 261.
  hatred against, 258, 261.
  Hapsburgs receive offers from, 230.
  Heidelberg Castle burned by, 260.
  heretics hunted by, 258.
  Holland alarmed by, 278.
  House of Commons and, 252—3.
  Huguenots persecuted by, 258.
  impossibilities demanded of, 304.
  infernal mandate of, 261.
  Ireland and, 262.
  James II. abandoned by, 277.
  James II. befriended by, 261—2.
  James II.'s son acknowledged by, 279.
  James II. sustained by, 264.
  jealousy against, 237. [266.
  Jean Bart gets letters of marque from,
  Joseph receives secret overtures from,
  laws of war and, 261. [290—1.
  Leopold commences war upon, 278.
  Leopold opposes, 259.
  letters of marque granted by, 266.
  literature patronised by, 255.
  Lorraine wholly seized by, 245.
  Louvais checked by, 261.
  Louvais, war minister of, 256, 260.
  Luxembourg ceded to, 253.
  Luxembourg invaded by, 255. [280.
  Madame de Maintenon prevails with,
  Madame Scarron married to, 258.
  Maria Theresa betrothed to, 234.

Louis XIV.:
  Marlborough regrets, 300.
  Mary of Modena prevails with, 280.
  Mazarin tutelage of, 235—6.
  Mazarin under, 227.
  Mons captured by, 263.
  navy of, 262. [278.
  Netherlands fortresses garrisoned by,
  Netherlands partly claimed by, 230
  overtures of peace by, 299. [—40.
  Palatinate claims of, 258—9.
  Palatinate invaded by, 259.
  Palatinate laid waste by, 260.
  peace concluded by, 253.
  peace proposals of, 245—6.
  peace sought by, 266, 304.
  people appealed to by, 301.
  Pondicherry ceded to, 267.
  Pope unfriendly to, 256.
  Philip IV. apologises to, 236.
  preponderance of, 253.
  Prince of Orange continues opposition to, 259.
  Prince of Orange enemy of, 255. [252.
  Prince of Orange forces peace on,
  Prince of Orange invited to make peace with, 251.
  Prince of Orange resists, 246—7.
  professed desire for peace by, 279.
  Protestant fears of, 259.
  red-hot shot employed by, 255.
  retrospect of, 318.
  sanction of atrocities by, 261.
  Spanish fortresses garrisoned by, 278.
  Spanish succession renounced by, 271.
  Spanish succession secured to grandson of, 276.
  Strasbourg ceded to, 253.
  Sweden opposes, 259.
  tombs rifled by, 260.
  treaty of United Provinces with, 236.
  Treves saved, 261.
  Triple Alliance and, 241.
  turn of tide against, 266.
  United Provinces invaded by, 245.
  unrivalled urbanity of, 256.
  Utrecht court of, 245.
  victory of fleet of, 263.
  villages burnt by, 255.
  Voltaire on, 281.
  William III. acknowledged by, 267.
  William III. coalesces against, 260.
  William III. compared with, 281.
  William III. makes concessions to, 271.
  William III. renews resistance to, zenith of power of, 254. [281.
Louvais, war minister of Louis XIV.:
  atrocities of, 260.
  Louis XIV. checks, 261.
Low Countries, Spain and the, 236.
Lubeck, treaty of, 189.
Lusitania, Ferdinand of Styria disposes of, 185.

INDEX. 381

Lutheranism, Protestantism distinguished from, 216.
Lutheran religion:
  Denmark and, 160.
  Duke of Holstein and, 160.
  Gustavus Vasa embraces, 160.
Lutherans:
  Calvinists distinguished from, 173.
  Calvinists placed on equality with, 225.
  Frederick V. offends, 182.
  Protestants distinguished from, 173.
Lutter, battle of, 188.
Lutzen:
  battle of, 209.
  Count Wallenstein posted at, 208.
  Gustavus Adolphus killed at, 209.
Luxembourg (Duchy of):
  Louis XIV. acquires, 253.
  Louis XIV. invades, 255.
Luxembourg (General):
  Genoa bombarded by, 256.
  humanity of, 265.
  nickname of, 265.
  Prince of Orange defeated by, 250.
  Ruvigny allowed to escape by, 265.
  standards captured by, 265. [265.
  William III. never succeeded against,
  William III. surprises, 264. [264—5.
  William III. twice defeated by,
Lyons, Council of, 46, 56.

Macedon:
  alliance with King of, 12.
  defeat of King of, 8.
Macedonian monarchy, power and end of, 13.
Machiavelli:
  Aristotle compared with, 161—2.
  Catherine de Medici and, 161.
  Charles V. and, 161.
  influence of, 161.
  Philip II. and, 161.
Madame de Maintenon, Louis XIV. yields to, 280. [258.
Madame Scarron, Louis XIV. marries,
Madrid:
  allied army enters, 303.
  Archduke Charles rejected by, 303.
  Philip V. enters, 276.
  treaty of, 141.
Magdeburg:
  burning of, 197. [197.
  Count Pappenheim leads storm of,
  Falkenberg killed at, 197.
  outrages upon men, women, and children at, 197. [198.
  Protestants aroused by atrocities at,
  reasons for besieging, 196.
  religious liberty arose out of the ashes of, 198.
  storming of, 197.
  Te Deum sung for victory over, 198.
  terrible sack of, 197.
Magdeburg:
  thirty thousand lives wantonly sacrificed at, 198.
  Tilly besieges, 196.
  vengeance on defenceless inhabitants of, 197.
Magna Charta, Edward I. and, 100.
Mahomet II.:
  Charlemagne compared with, 27.
  Constantinople captured by, 76—7.
  Frederick II. and, 46.
  freedom proclaimed by, 78.
  Greek Church protected by, 78.
  massacre by, 77.
  patriarch installed by, 78.
  see also Mohammedans.
Maid of Orleans, infamous treatment and doom of the, 129—30.
Malplaquet:
  battle of, 302.
  Waterloo compared with, 302.
Manfred:
  body of, thrown to the dogs, 52.
  Constantina, daughter of, 52.
  crowned King of Sicily, 50.
  defeat and death of, 51.
  illegitimate son of Frederick II., 50.
  monument to, 51.
  Pope never acknowledged, 51.
  resistance of, 51.
Mansfeld, see Count Mansfeld.
Marauding, Gustavus Adolphus very earnestly denounces, 205—6. [289.
Margrave of Baden, Marlborough and,
Maria Eleonora of Cleves, 174—5.
Maria Theresa:
  crown of Spain renounced by, 234.
  dowry of, 234.
  Louis XIV. agrees to marry, 234.
Marie of Savoy, death of, 314.
Maritime law of nations, 163—172.
  Admiralty Courts and, 165.
  alteration of, 164—5.
  America and, 165.
  Amsterdam and, 166.
  belligerent shipping and, 164—5.
  binding, 164.
  Bremen and, 166.
  captures under, 165.
  conflicts of, 167.
  consolato del mare, 164—5.
  contraband and, 169.
  costumbres maritimos, 164.
  Crusades as affecting, 164.
  disputes about, 164—5. [165.
  enemy's goods in neutral ships and,
  enemy's ships with neutral goods and, 165—6, 170.
  Europe and, 165.
  first germs of, 164.
  flag protection under, 167, 170.
  fourteenth century, 166.
  free ships, free goods, and, 167—170.
  Great Britain and, 165.

382 INDEX.

Maritime law of nations:
  Hanseatic League and, 166.
  Hanse Towns and, 167—8.
  Henry VIII. and, 168.
  innovation in, 169—70.
  Italy and, 164.
  lawful prizes under, 165.
  Mediterranean and, 164.
  neutral shipping and, 164—5, 170.
  new doctrines concerning, 164.
  Peace of Utrecht and, 316.
  recaptures under, 166.
  right of search and, 168.
  Sartorins on, 168.
  slave trade and, 170—2.
  Spain and, 164.
  Treaty of Paris and, 165.
  United States and, 165.
  warfare and, 21.
Marius, massacres by, 21.
Marlborough (Duke of):
  allied army under, 283.
  always won, 283.
  Archbishop of Cambray and, 306.
  attacking policy of, 288. [288.
  battle of Blenheim personally led by,
  Blenheim victory of, 289.
  Bonfflers declines to meet, 284.
  bribery attempted of, 299.
  bribery by, 292.
  charges against, 300.
  Charles XII. sided with by, 291.
  Charles XII. visits, 292—3.
  Coblentz moved upon by, 287.
  deprivation of, 306.
  diplomatic success of, 291.
  Donanwerth advanced upon by, 287.
  Duke of Berwick, nephew of, 294.
  Duke of Ormond succeeds, 311.
  embezzlement imputed to, 312.
  Fénélon and, 306.
  flattery by, 292. [289.
  Franco-Bavarian army defeated by,
  Frederick I. and, 285.
  French sufferings referred to by, 301—2.
  French totally defeated by, 302.
  Godolphin dissuades, 286. [288.
  Gustavus Adolphus compared with,
  Heinsius dissuades, 286.
  humanity of, 287—8.
  imperturbable temper of, 283.
  inaction forced upon, 289.
  James II. deserted by, 279.
  jealousy against, 286.
  last battle of, 303.
  Liège recaptured by, 284.
  Louis XIV. regretted by, 300.
  luxuries despised by, 292.
  made commander-in-chief in the Netherlands, 283.
  Margrave of Baden refuses co-operation with, 289.
  Moselle valley ascended by, 289.

Marlborough (Duke of):
  never lost, 283.
  Peace of Utrecht and, 306.
  peace vainly expected by, 300.
  Prince Eugene concerts with, 287.
  Prince Eugene joins, 288.
  Prince Eugene recalled from, 289.
  Prince of Orange with, 302.
  reply refused by, 299.
  Schellenberg stormed by, 287.
  Swift libels, 312.
  tactics of, 288.
  Tallard taken prisoner by, 289.
  testimony in favour of, 282.
  thousands taken prisoner by, 289.
  Torcy negotiates with, 299—300.
  Tory opponents of, 312.
  Tournay captured by, 301—2.
  Turenne the tutor of, 300.
  Vendome defeated by, 295.
  Villars battled with by, 289.
  Villeroi totally defeated by, 289.
  William III. commissions, 279.
  William III. succeeded by, 282.
  wounded enemy cared for by, 303.
Marriage of clergy first forbidden, 31.
Marshal Boucicault, death in captivity of, 127.
Marsin, Prince Eugene defeats, 289.
Martel:
  champion of Christianity, 30.
  Gregory II. and, 30.
  victory at Tours by, 30.
Martin I., heresy and treason of, 29.
Martin IV. prevents a duel, 55.
Martinitz:
  attempted murder of, 178—9.
  hostility to Protestants of, 178.
Mary of England betrothed to Louis XII., 138.
Mary of Modena:
  Louis XIV. yields to, 289.
  son of James II. and, 279.
Mary of Scotland, see Queen of Scots.
Maurice of Nassau, Frederick V. a kinsman of, 181.
Maurice of Saxony:
  Charles of Austria befriends, 149.
  Charles of Austria defeated by, 150.
  Henry II. makes treaty with, 150.
  Innspruck advanced upon by, 150.
  Protestants make treaty with, 150.
Maximilian of Austria:
  Adriatic provinces claimed by, 134.
  treacherous execution by, 115.
  weakness of, 135.
Maximilian of Bavaria:
  Count Wallenstein protested against by, 202.
  Count Wallenstein resisted by, 190.
  Ferdinand of Styria allied with, 182.
  Ferdinand of Styria appears friendly with, 204.
  Ferdinand of Styria rewards, 185.

INDEX. 383

Maximilian of Bavaria:
  humiliation of, 204.
  Palatinate and, 224—5.
Mazarin:
  alliance effected by, 227.
  ambition of, 234.
  Austria humbled by, 226.
  avarice of, 234.
  Condé and, 233.
  Cromwell listens to, 228.
  death of, 234, 236.
  Louis XIV. and, 227.
  Louis XIV. emancipated from tutelage of, 235.
  Louis XIV. under tutelage of, 236.
  plenipotentiary of France, 233.
  Richelieu and, 220.
  splendid appointments of, 233.
Mecklenburg:
  Count Wallenstein is promised, 203.
  Count Wallenstein takes, 188.
  Gustavus Adolphus and, 195.
Medici, France under influence of, 176.
  see also Catherine de Medici.
Mediterranean:
  De Ruyter enters the, 251.
  English fleet dispersed in the, 265.
  maritime law in the, 164.
  naval battles in the, 251.
Melander:
  Ferdinand III. and, 220.
  Turenne totally defeats, 220.
Memphis, siege and capture of, 4, 5.
Mendoza, ambassador of Philip II., 157.
Merchants of Lodi, 33.
Messina, insurrection at, 251.
Metz: [150.
  Charles of Austria advances upon,
  Duke of Guise defends, 150.
  France acquires, 224.
  Gustavus Adolphus winters at, 201.
  Henry II. captures, 150.
Middle Ages:
  battles of the, 116.
  chivalry and the, 79.
  distinguished names of the, 31.
  pernicious influence of warfare in the, piracy of the, 163. [127.
  strangers in the, 118.
Migratory habits of man, 1.
Milan:
  Charles VIII. resisted by, 132.
  tyranny of people of, 34.
  Visconti, the wealthy tyrants of, 111.
Milanese, total defeat of, 44. [of, 110.
Military success, irresistible fascination
Mohacz, battle of, 144.
Mohammedans:
  Byzantine Empire and, 70.
  generous treatment by, 67.
  Gibbon on the, 67.
  Greeks and, 65. [254.
  King of Poland resists invasion of,
  see also Mahomet.

Mons:
  Allied Powers invest, 301.
  Louis XIV. captures, 263.
Montague, Spain and, 228.
Montereau:
  meeting at, 123.
  siege of, 127.
Montesquieu, opinion of, 6. [146.
Montmorency, resistance of Austria by,
Moors, Ferdinand and Isabella and, 131.
Morea, Turks abandon the, 269. [154.
Morecambe Bay, landing projected in,
Moselle, Marlborough ascends valley of the, 289
Moses, Frederick II. and, 46.
Munich, Gustavus Adolphus triumphantly enters, 203.
Munster:
  Treaty of, 220—224.
  wrangles at, 220.
Murad II., father of Mahomet II., 75.
Muratori on slavery, 26.
Muscovy, Charles XII. in, 203.

Najarra, battle of, 112.
Namur, William III. captures, 266.
Nanci, siege of, 115.
Nancy, razing of fortifications of, 263.
Naples:
  Charles VIII. and, 133.
  Charles VIII. seizes, 132.
  ravage of coasts of, 146.
  revolt against Spain of, 223.
  sea-fight in Bay of, 54. [24—5.
Narses, achievements and humanity of,
Narva, battle of, 277. [of, 57.
National Council of France, summoning
Naumburg, Gustavus Adolphus receives an ovation at, 208.
Navarre:
  conquest of, 137—8.
  war commenced at, 141.
Necessities of man, 1.
Negroes, slave trade in, 170.
Negro slaves, Peace of Utrecht and, 316.
Netherlands:
  aggressive policy of, 240.
  Count Mansfeld in the, 184.
  Elizabeth and the, 153.
  French campaign in, 294.
  French conquests in the, 241.
  Louis XIV. claims part of, 240.
  Louis XIV. garrisons fortresses of, resistance to, 241. [278.
  Spain and the, 153.
  success of, 241.
Neuburg, Cleves and, 175.
Neutral harbours, 7.
Neutral territory, inviolability of, 7.
Neutral waters, 7.
Neutrals:
  belligerents and, 257.
  maritime law as to, 164—5.
  ships of war by, 257.

Nevil's Cross, battle of, 111. [239.
New Amsterdam, New York first called,
New York:
  England acquires, 239.
  New Amsterdam changed to, 239.
Nice, siege of, 146.
Nicholas IV., vassalage and, 86.
Nicopolis, battle of, 73.
Nimeguen, treaty of, 253.
Nordlingen, King of Hungary defeats Swedish army at, 214.
Normandy:
  Edward III. lands in, 104.
  ravage of, 109.
Norman Conquest, humanity obsolete at, 26.
Norman kings, commons under the, 60.
Normans:
  barbarity of, 67.
  claims of, 87.
  Italy invaded by, 66.
  rapacity of, 67.
  Turks contrasted with, 67.
Northampton, Treaty of, 100.
North Foreland, battle off, 237.
Northumberland, invasion of, 91.
Nuremberg:
  Gustavus Adolphus makes head-quarters at, 204.
  Gustavus Adolphus retires from, 208.
  marauding around, 205.

Oaths:
  Middle Age, 37—8.
  twelfth century, 37.
Oleron, laws of, 163.
Oracle, appeal to an, 8.
Orleans: [119—24.
  House of Burgundy and House of, Maid of, 129.
  siege of, 129.
Othman, founder of the Ottoman Empire, 73.
Otho the Fourth, Innocent the Third and, 42.
Oudenarde, battle of, 295.
Oxenstiern (Chancellor):
  allies summoned to a meeting by, 210.
  ascendency of, 211.
  Count Wallenstein makes vain overtures to, 212.
  diplomatic triumphs of, 211.
  Elector of Saxony thwarts, 210.
  France appealed to by, 215. [204
  Gustavus Adolphus reinforced by, King of Hungary defeats, 214.
  meeting summoned by, 210,
  military operations entrusted to, 210.
  Palatinate restored by, 210.
  war continued under influence of, 210.

Pactyas, adventures of, 8.
Pagans, Frederick II. and, 46.
Palestine, ferocity of Crusaders in, 67.

Palatinate:
  Charles Louis and the, 224.
  Charles Louis restored to the, 210
  Ferdinand of Styria disposes of the, France retires from the, 260. [185.
  Gustavus Adolphus decides about the, 200.
  Louis XIV.'s claims on the, 258—9.
  Louis XIV. invades the, 259.
  Louis XIV. lays waste the, 260-1.
  Maximilian of Bavaria and, 224—5.
  Oxenstiern restores the, 210.
  Spain seizes the, 183.
  William III. and the, 260.
Papacy, jurisdiction of the, 29.
Papal power:
  abuses of the, 60.
  advantages of the, 60.
  Alexander III. and, 35.
  feudal tyranny and, 60.
  growth of, 61.
  Hildebrand, founder of, 31.
  Innocent III. and, 41.
  invaded by Frederick the Second, 45.
  law of nations affected by, 28.
  meridian height of, 30, 41.
  strengthening of the, 35.
Pappenheim:
  Count Wallenstein instructs, 208.
  furious religious zeal of, 198.
  Gustavus Adolphus repulses and defeats, 199.
  slain, 209.
Paris:
  advance upon, 104.
  Gustavus Adolphus said to meditate marching on, 201.
  massacre of Orleanists at, 122.
  violence and bloodshed in, 122.
  see also France.
Parliament:
  Berwick, 90.
  Charles of Anjou summons a, 52.
  Edward I. calls, 90.
  Shrewsbury, 82. [248.
  supplies for war reluctantly voted by,
Parma, attack upon, 44.
Passau, treaty of, 173.
Patriarch, Rome and the, 42.
Patriarchs:
  Mahomet II. instals one of the, 78.
  modesty of the, 66.
  prostitute on throne of the, 71.
Paul III., truce arranged by, 146.
Pavia, battle of, 141.
Peace, atrocities during, 22.
Peace of Utrecht:
  Allied Powers and, 309.
  armistice preliminary to, 313.
  Bolingbroke arranges terms of, 315.
  Catalans and the, 318.
  conferences to arrange, 314.
  congress to arrange, 311.
  Count Gallas and, 309—10.

Peace of Utrecht:
  Godolphin and, 306.
  Harley and, 310.
  House of Commons and, 311.
  House of Lords and, 306, 311.
  maritime law and the, 316.
  Marlborough and, 306.
  negro slaves and the, 316.
  pamphlets about the, 311.
  preliminaries of the, 308—18.
  St. John and, 310.
  Torcy arranges terms of, 315.
  treaty confirming the, 319.
Peasantry, army of Gustavus Adolphus befriended by, 196.
Pedro the Cruel:
  bad faith of, 113.
  Black Prince and, 112.
Pekin, Tamerlane and, 75.
Peloponnesian war:
  causes of, 13.
  outrage during, 3.
People, privileges denied to the, 60.
Perseus, surrender of, 8.
Persians:
  defeat of, 6.
  neutral rights and, 8.
  regarded as barbarians, 4. [171.
Postilence, slave trade compared with,
Peter the Great:
  England and, 297—9.
  Queen Anne seeks to conciliate, 297.
Peter II. of Aragon, Innocent III. and,
Philip III. of Austria, policy of, 14. [41.
Philip of Castilo, Henry VII. detains, 117—18.
Philip the Fair of France:
  Baliol and, 88.
  Boniface VIII. and, 56.
  daughter of, 101.
  death of, 101.
  defeat of Boniface by, 59.
  Edward I. and, 99.
  excommunication of, 59.
  imperious and headstrong, 57.
  Isabella, daughter of, 101.
  resists Boniface VIII., 57.
  Scotland abandoned by, 96.
  sons of, 101.
  successors of, 101.
Philip VI. of France:
  death of, 109.
  John, son of, 109.
Philip II. of Spain:
  England menaced by, 153.
  Machiavelli and, 161.
  war with France continued by, 151.
Philip IV. of Spain:
  Condé pleaded for by, 232.
  Cromwell receives offers from, 227.
  death of, 240.
  France receives offers from, 232.
  Maria Theresa, daughter of, 234.
  matrimonial projects of, 233.

Philip V. of Spain: [285.
  Archduke Charles pitted against,
  Castile devoted to, 303.
  ceremonial ideas of, 284—5.
  Duke of Savoy and, 285.
  Grand Duke of Tuscany disputes with, 284.
  Italy visited by, 284.
  Madrid entered by, 276.
  Spain preferred, 304.
  Stanhope defeats, 303.
Philip Augustus:
  Innocent III. and, 41.
  Richard I. and, 37.
Philip, Duke of Burgundy, 124.
Philip of Valois:
  acknowledged King of France, 102.
  conspiracies against, 102.
  Edward III. does homage to, 102.
  Salic law interpreted by, 103.
Philippa persuades Edward III., 105.
Phocians, fine of, 11.
Phœnicians, good faith of, 5.
Piccolomini (Octavio):
  Count Wallenstein betrayed by, 213.
  Count Wallenstein murdered at suggestion of, 214.
  Gordon conspires against Count Wallenstein with, 213. [182.
Pictures, Frederick V. tears down church,
Pietro Tiepolo, hanging of, 44.
Piety, slave trade and, 171—2.
Pignerol, France acquires, 224.
Pillage forbidden, 4.
Pilsen, Count Wallenstein quits, 213.
Piracy:
  Alfred the Great put down, 28.
  Elizabeth's, 153.
  Middle Ages and, 163.
  Saracens practised, 163.
  Scandinavians practised, 163.
Pirates related to Innocent IV., 47.
Pisa, surrender of, 132.
Plague of London, 238.
Plutarch informs us, 9.
Plutarch on Coriolanus, 16.
Podolia, Turks abandon, 269.
Poitou, heretics hunted from, 258.
Poland:
  Charles XII. invades, 277.
  Charles XII. makes conquest of, 291.
  Count Wallenstein aids, 193.
  Gustavus Adolphus at war with, 189.
  James I. and, 187.
  war between Sweden and, 193.
Political communities, 1.
Polybius the historian, 2.
  passage of, 9.
Pomerania:
  Count Wallenstein takes, 188.
  Gustavus Adolphus and, 195.
  Gustavus Adolphus invades, 190.
  Sweden acquires, 224.
Pondicherry, Louis XIV. acquires, 267.

2 c

Pontoise, taking of, 116.
Pope:
  defiance of the, 47—8.
  disregard of the, 52.
  Emperor of Germany and the, 62.
  ferocity of legate of the, 68.
  Louis XIV. not friendly with the, 256.
  temporal jurisdiction of, 49.
  white palfrey presented to the, 51.
Popes:
  ascendency of the, 61.
  Barbarossa and the, 33.
  Crusade sanctioned by, 69.
  distinguished, 61.
  emperors and, 33, 64.
  end of ambitious era of the, 59.
  excommunication by, 62.
  France and the, 59.
  Frederick I. and the, 33.
  Henry V. and the, 33.
  Holy Sepulchre and the, 69.
  interdicts by, 62.
  jurisdiction of the, 61.
  leading part of the, 59.
  Lombardy and the, 60.
  obedience compelled by, 62.
  Saracens and, 30.
  sided with the weak against the strong, 60.
  slavery opposed by the, 26.
  temporal power subjected to spiritual power of, 33.
  vices not conspicuous in, 61.
  virtues of the, 61.
  West allies of, 64.
  see also Rome, Church, &c.
Portocarrero, Spanish succession and, 273.
Ports, blockade of 8, 9.
Portugal:
  Allied Powers and, 305.
  Castile advanced into by, 294.
  Innocent III. and, 41.
  riot in London concerning brother of an ambassador of, 229—32.
  slave trade and, 171.
  Spain revolted against by, 219.
Prague:
  attempted murder by flinging from windows of the castle of, 178—80.
  battle of, 182. [201.
  Count Wallenstein builds a palace at,
  Count Wallenstein winters at, 211.
  treaty of, 216.
Prelates imprisoned, 45.
Prerogative, Edward I.'s notions of, 88.
Priesthood, Fecial order of, 16.
Prince of Arabia, permission by, 6.
Prince Christian of Brunswick:
  arm lost in battle by, 184.
  childhood of, 184.
  churches plundered by, 184.
  Count Mansfeld imitated by, 184.
  Count Mansfeld joined by, 184.
  created a bishop, 184.

Prince Christian of Brunswick:
  death of, 188.
  defeat of, 184.
  "enemy of priests," 184.
  "friend of God," 184.
  marauding army of, 184.
  palaces dismantled by, 184.
  peasants' dwellings wrecked by, 184.
  proclamation of, 184.
  Protestantism and, 184.
Prince Eugene of Austria:
  Alps crossed by, 278.
  Catinat defeated by, 278.
  Duke of Savoy joins, 291.
  English reception of, 311, 313.
  French defeated by, 278.
  Jesuit spy dogs, 313.
  Lombardy wintered in by, 279.
  Marlborough concerts with, 287.
  Marlborough joined by, 288.
  Marlborough left by, 287.
  Marsin defeated by, 280.
  Sultan defeated by, 268.
  Toulon vainly attacked by, 291.
  Villars defeats, 315.
  Villeroi repulsed by, 279.
Prince of Orange:
  Charles II. admired, 251.
  Charles II. assisted by, 246—7.
  Condé defeats, 250. [—60.
  crown of England acquired by, 259
  invincible spirit of, 250.
  Louis XIV. forced to peace by, 252.
  Louis XIV. made greatest enemy of,
  Louis XIV. opposed by, 250. [255.
  Louis XIV. resisted by, 246—7.
  Louis XIV. seeks peace with, 251.
  Luxembourg defeats, 250.
  Princess Mary betrothed to, 251.
  restoration of, 246.
Prince of Parma, England menaced by the, 154.
Prince of Salerno:
  defeat and imprisonment of, 54.
  son of Charles of Anjou, 52.
Princes:
  criminal enterprises of, 61.
  dissolute lives of, 61. [251.
Princess Mary, Prince of Orange and,
Prisoners:
  banquet given in honour of, 107.
  beheading of, 73.
  burning alive of, 52.
  cast in the Seine, 116.
  chivalry and barbarous treatment of, 114—15.
  Count Wallenstein returns, 207.
  courtesy towards, 110.
  exchange of, 20, 65.
  exposure in chains of English, 116.
  generosity towards, 104.
  humanity to, 289.
  Marlborough takes thousands of, 289.
  presents given to, 104—5.

INDEX. 387

Prisoners:
  purchase of freedom of, 26.
  put to death, 73.
  ransom of noble, 73.
  roasting of, 68.
  Saladin and, 69.
  starvation of, 127.
  sumptuous entertainment of, 105, 107.
  sureties first accepted for, 74.
  treatment of, 19, 37.
Protestantism:
  Bethlem Gabor and, 184.
  champions of, 184.
  Charles of Austria resists, 149.
  Christian II. and, 160.
  Count Mansfeld and, 184.
  disastrous year for, 188.
  Duke of Alva and, 149.
  English sympathies with, 186.
  Ferdinand of Styria defies, 189. [203.
  Gustavus Adolphus re-establishes, James I. and, 186. [216.
  Lutheranism distinguished from, measures for suppression of, 149.
  Prince Christian and, 184.
  princes who supported, 149.
  rapacity of princes of, 173.
  Richelieu embarrassed by, 186—7.
  Sweden and, 160.
Protestant princes:
  France and, 145.
  Francis I. makes treaty with, 145.
  League of Smalkalde by, 144.
  Maurice of Saxony makes treaties with, 150.
  rapacity of, 173.
Protestant rebellion:
  Ernest Count Mansfeld, commander of, 180.
  Thurn, leader of, 180.
Protestants:
  acknowledged leaders of, 191.
  annexation of, 174.
  challenge and threat to, 178.
  challenge to European, 185. [291.
  Charles XII. intervenes on behalf of, churches forbidden to, 291.
  closing of churches of, 177.
  confiscation of estates of, 183.
  Count Thurn prominent amongst, 178.
  Count Wallenstein levies upon, 189.
  Count Wallenstein recommends fair terms to, 211.
  demands of, 194.
  destruction of church of, 177.
  Diet summoned by, 181.
  emboldenment of, 194.
  execution of noble, 183.
  execution without trial of, 183.
  Frederick V. elected by, 181.
  Ferdinand of Styria deposed by, 181.
  Ferdinand of Styria dreaded by, 177.
  French co-operation with, 210.
  Gustavus Adolphus and, 191.

Protestants:
  Gustavus Adolphus makes alliance with, 198.
  Gustavus Adolphus rescues, 209.
  Huguenot persecutions and European, humanity disregarded by, 185. [258.
  indignation of, 174.
  John George one of the leading, 191.
  Kinsky one of the, 180.
  Leipsic Diet of, 194.
  Louis XIV. excites fears of, 259.
  Lutherans distinguished from, 173.
  Magdeburg atrocities aroused, 198.
  Martinitz hostile to, 178.
  murder attempted by, 178—80.
  pledges of, 194.
  remonstrance and reply to, 177—8.
  retreat from Vienna by, 180.
  Silesian, 291—2.
  Slawata hostile to, 178.
  Vienna marched upon by, 180.
Provence, invasion of, 146.
Providence, slave trade and, 171—2.
Prussia: [277.
  Frederick I. founds the monarchy of,
  Innocent XII. protests against creation of, 278.
Punic War, First, 20.
Punic War, Second, 7, 20.
Pyrenees: [233.
  boundary between France and Spain,
  Treaty of the, 232—5.

Queen Anne:
  accession of, 283.
  amiable qualities of, 318.
  death of, 318.
  failing health of, 311.
  Peter the Great and, 297.
  Scotland and, 283.
  William III. eulogised by, 283.
Queen of Scots:
  Conradino compared with, 159—60.
  Elizabeth and, 155—6.
  execution of, 160.
  imprisonment at Tutbury of, 154.
  proceedings against, 159.
Quintus Fabius, challenge by, 4.

Ramillies, battle of, 289.
Randolph, Earl of Murray and, 158.
Ransom of prisoners, 19, 115—16.
Ratisbon:
  Bernhard of Weimar overruns, 212.
  Diet of, 185, 190. [of, 214.
  King of Hungary accepts surrender truce of, 253. [176.
Ravaillac, Henry IV. assassinated by,
Rebels, massacre of, 114.
Recaptures, maritime law on, 166.
Reciprocity, 1.
Reformation:
  Celtic races and the, 160.
  Church lands and the, 173.

Reformation:
    establishment of the, 160.
    Latin races and the, 160.
    proceedings against the, 149.
    progress in Germany of the, 144.
    quiet progress of the, 149.
    rival creeds of the, 173.
    Scandinavian proclivities for the, 160.
    Slavonic races and the, 160.
    Teutonic proclivities for the, 160.
Religious discord, France abandoned to demon of, 257.
Religious equality, Thirty Years' War resulted in establishment of, 225.
Religious liberty:
    arose out of ashes of Magdeburg, 198.
    Bohemian, 177.
    Ferdinand of Styria recalls, 183.
    first concession of, 151.   [177.
    freedom of worship excluded from, French, 153.
Religious regard for treaties, 5.
Religious wars:
    Flanders subject to, 150.
    France subject to, 150.
    moral progress suspended by, 151.
    stimulation of worst passions by, 150.
Revocation of the Edict of Nantes, 257.
Rhine:
    Count Mansfeld advances on the, 183.
    Dauphin crosses the, 259.
    France forbids fortresses on the, 224.
    navigation of the, 268.
Rhodes, earthquake at, 2.
Richard I.:
    barbarity of, 69.
    Bishop of Beauvais and, 40.
    Celestine and, 37, 39.
    chained like a slave, 40.
    Chaluz besieged by, 80.
    chivalry and, 80.
    Duke of Austria and, 38.
    Eleanor and, 38—9.
    ferocity of, 40.
    generosity of, 40.
    generous at times, 80.
    Henry the Sixth and, 38.
    imprisonment by, 40.
    imprisonment of, 38.
    international morality in time of, 37—8.
    John and, 37, 80.
    King of Scotland and, 37.
    oaths in time of, 37—8.
    Oleron laws and, 163.
    Philip Augustus and, 37.
    Siege of Acre by, 69.
    slaughter of Saracens by, 37.
    William the Lion and, 37.
Richelieu:
    Alsace and, 217.
    Austria humbled by, 226.
    Condé and, 220.
    Count Wallenstein opposed by, 190.

Richelieu:
    death of, 220.
    France and, 176.
    France resolutely defended by, 217.
    Germany and, 215.
    Gustavus Adolphus defended by, 201.
    influence of, 198.
    Mazarin and, 220.
    Oxenstiern in alliance with, 215.
    Protestantism an embarrassment to, Turenne and, 220.   [186—7.
Right of asylum, 7.
Right of search, maritime, 168.
Robert II., first of the Stewarts of Scotland, 111.
Robert III., capture and captivity of son of, 117.
Robert Guiscard, Hildebrand and, 33.
Romagna, Julius II. claims, 134.
Roman Pontiffs:
    commanding influence of, 66.
    France and the, 59.
    see also Popes.
Romans:
    ambassadors and the, 157.
    defeat of army of, 4.
    extradition by, 17.
    Gauls and, 3.
    generosity of, 9.
    high morality of, 15.
    insatiable ambition of, 18.
    institutions of, 16.
    Jews and, 9.
    repudiation of treaty by, 19.
    Samnites and, 17.
    security attained by, 7.
    surrender of army of, 17.
    war with, 4.
Romanus III.:
    battle of Hastings and, 67.
    defeat of, 67.
    England during reign of, 67.
    generous treatment of, 67.
    invades Asia Minor, 67.
Rome:
    ambassadors from, 3.
    Bajazet threatens, 73.
    Belisarius' victories over, 29.
    bishops of, 29.
    breaking up of Empire of, 23.
    Charles of Anjou progresses to, 51.
    chivalry and, 79.
    Christian pillage of, 24.
    Conradino enters, 52.
    Constantine and, 29.
    Constantinople and, 64.
    council at, 58.
    decline of, 21.
    deposition of Pope Sylverius of, 29.
    election of new Pope of, 29.
    early history of, 15.   [—7.
    French ambassador insulted at, 236
    Goths invade, 29.
    Justinian and, 29.

INDEX. 389

Rome:
  march upon, 4.
  military discipline of, 65.
  moral state of, 20.
  origin of temporal power of, 30.
  Patriarch and, 42.
  ruthless pillage of, 24.
  siege and sack of, 24.
  subjection of bishops of, 29.
  surrender of, 132.
  taking by assault of, 142.
  unexampled horrors at, 142.
  Zachary and, 30.
Rongemont, taking of, 128.
Ronssillon retained by France, 233. [56.
Rudolph of Hapsburg, confirmation of,
Rudolph II., religious liberty proclaimed
  by, 177.
Rugen, Sweden acquires, 224.
Rupert, son of Frederick V., 182.
Russia: [299.
  arrest for debt of an ambassador of,
  Charles XII. advances upon, 277.
  Charles XII. and fugitives of, 291.
  serfs in, 27.
Ruvigny, a Huguenot, Luxembourg
  allows escape of, 265.
Ryswick, Treaty of, 266—9.

Sacrifice of children, 6.
St. Germains, James II. dies at, 279.
St. John:
  Peace of Utrecht and, 310.
  Swift and, 313.
St. Omer, battle of, 250.
St. Peter's:
  Bajazet threatens, 73.
  law of nations affected by, 28.
Saladin:
  generosity of, 68.
  prisoners put to death by, 69.
Salamis, defeat at, 6.
Salic law:
  Count de Montfort on the, 103.
  France subject to the, 101.
  Philip of Valois on the, 103.
Samnites:
  Romans and, 17.
  slaughter of, 21.
Saracens:
  Constantine and, 63.
  Crusaders and, 69.
  France and the, 30.
  Frederick II. and, 46.
  piracy of the, 163.
  Popes and, 30.
  Sicily and the, 30.
  slaughter of thousands of, 37.
  Spain and the, 30.
Saragossa, battle of, 303.
Sartorius, maritime law by, 168.
Saturn, sacrifice of children to, 6.
Savoy:
  Allied Powers and, 305.

Savoy:
  invasion of, 146.
  Spanish succession and, 276.
Saxons:
  Charlemagne beheads, 27.
  Charles XII. beats the, 277.
Saxony:
  Baner advances into, 217.
  Count Wallenstein invades, 208.
  Elector of, see Elector.
  Gustavus Adolphus and the Elector
    of, 191.
  persistent neutrality of, 195.
Scandinavia, Reformation accepted by,
Scandinavians, piracy by the, 163. [160.
Scarlet hats first worn by cardinals, 46.
Scarron, see Madame Scarron.
Schellenberg, Marlborough storms, 287.
Scholars, burning alive of, 89.
Scipio, adventures of, 7.
Scotland:
  attempt to annex, 101.
  Boniface VIII. and, 60.
  conquest of, 90.
  contest for crown of, 83.
  Elizabeth and, 155.
  England united with, 203. [196.
  hanging for outrage of a native of,
  Henry VIII. invades, 148.
  homage and, 86.
  Jacobite plots in, 262.
  laws guaranteed to, 296.
  new claim to crown of, 97.
  Philip the Fair and, 96.
  prosperity of earlier, 101.
  Queen Anne and, 283.
  Stewarts of, 111.
  war of independence in, 100.
  William the Lion of, 37.
  William III. acknowledged by, 262.
  William and, 283.
Scottish Covenanters, Charles I. and
  the, 218.
Seine, prisoners cast in the, 116.
Senef, battle of, 250.
Servia subdued by Bajazet, 73.
Shaftesbury speaks in favour of and acts
  against war, 247—8.
Sheffield Castle, Queen of Scots' im-
  prisonment in, 157. [118.
Shimei, Earl of Suffolk compared to,
Ships of war, neutrals supplying, 257.
Shipwreck, Oleron laws as to, 163.
Shrewsbury, Parliament at, 82.
Sicilian Vespers, massacre of the, 54.
Sicily:
  arbitration on crown of, 56.
  atrocities in, 53.
  attack upon, 6.
  Clement X. vainly pleads for, 53.
  decision of fate of, 52.
  extended over South of Italy, 51.
  Ghibelline faction in, 52.
  heir to crown of, 52.

Sicily:
  Italy separated from, 56.
  kingdom of, 51.
  Louis XIV. and, 251.
  Saracens in, 30.
  throne of, 40.
Sigismund:
  Bajazet and, 73.
  treachery of, 119.
Silesia, Protestant churches forbidden in, 291.
Sir John Chandos, Brittany and, 108.
Sir John Pennington, Van Tromp writes to, 219.
Sir Nicolas Throgmorton, Huguenot rebellion and, 158. [107.
Sir Walter Manny, Edward III. and,
Sir William Temple seeks to make peace,
Sixteenth century: [250.
  artifice of the, 161.
  duplicity of the, 161.
  Machiavellian influence upon the, 161.
  political changes of the, 161.
  religious changes of the, 161.
Slavery:
  Alexander III. and, 26.
  ancient and modern, 22.
  Anglo-Saxon, 25.
  Anglo-Saxon kings and, 26.
  antiquity of, 171.
  Aristotle and. 25.
  Bristol and, 26, 27.
  Christianity and, 25.
  Conqueror and, 26.
  England and, 26.
  France and, 27.
  Germany and, 27.
  Greece and, 25,
  Gregory the Great and, 25.
  Hungary and, 27.
  Italian, 26.
  James the First and, 27.
  Norman Conquest and, 26.
  Popes and, 26.
  Russia and, 27.
  slave trade distinguished from, 171.
  Wulfstan and, 26.
Slaves, liberation of, 25.
Slave trade:
  aborigines and the, 170.
  Africans and the, 170—2.
  America and the, 170—1.
  Elizabeth and the, 171—2.
  English adventurers in the, 171.
  European taskmasters and the, 170.
  first cargo in the, 171.
  Guinea and the, 170.
  Indians and the, 170.
  John Hawkins and the, 171—2.
  Las Casas and the, 170.
  negroes and the, 170.
  Peace of Utrecht secured to England the, 316.
  pestilence compared with, 171.

Slave trade:
  pious justification of the, 171—2.
  Portuguese adventurers in the, 171.
  Providence appealed to in support of the, 171—2.
  slavery as distinguished from the, 171.
  Spain and the, 171.
  Spanish adventurers in the, 171.
  Spanish colonies and the, 170.
  war compared with, 171.
Slavonians, Constantine and, 63.
Slavonic races, Reformation rejected by,
Slawata: [160.
  attempted murder of, 178—80.
  hostility to Protestants of, 178.
Smalkalde, League of, 144.
Smithfield, Wallace executed in, 97.
Social nature of man, 1.
Soissons, surrender of, 115.
Soldan of Babylon, Frederick II. and the, 46.
Solyman the Magnificent:
  decisive victory of, 144.
  Francis I. makes treaty with, 146.
Spain:
  Allied Powers declare war against, 283.
  Archduke Charles and, 276.
  Archduke Charles rejected by, 303—4.
  Austria and, 176.
  Barcelona restored to, 267.
  Bishop of Toledo and, 273.
  Blake and, 228.
  Black Prince invades, 112.
  Bourbon claims to, 272.
  Bourbons confirmed in, 301.
  Castile law of, 270.
  Catalonia recovered by, 227.
  Catalonian restorations to, 267.
  Catalans revolt against, 219.
  Charles I. at war with, 189.
  Charles I. bribed by, 218.
  Charles V. and the succession to, 271.
  Charles VI. and, 305.
  Condé annihilates flower of, 219.
  Condé fights for, 227.
  Count Mansfeld defies, 183.
  Cromwell attacks colonies of, 227.
  danger of uniting France with, 275.
  dauphin declared successor to crown of, 275.
  dauphin's claims to, 270.
  decline of, 228.
  Don Louis de Haro, plenipotentiary of, 233.
  Duke of Anjou declared heir to, 275.
  Duke of Anjou proclaimed as Philip V., King of, 276.
  Duke of Berri aud, 276.
  Dunkirk recovered by, 227.
  Dutch destroy fleet of, 218—19.
  Earl of Peterborough and, 293.
  Elizabeth and, 153.
  end of Dutch truce with, 184.

INDEX. 391

Spain
  Ferdinand of Styria allied with, 182.
  Ferdinand III. deserted by, 220.
  Flanders and, 227.
  Flanders restorations to, 267.
  France continues war with, 227.
  France declares war with, 215.
  France forbidden to unite with, 309.
  French treaty with, 151.
  French victory over, 220.
  Gustavus Adolphus beats, 209.
  Gustavus Adolphus compels retirement of the troops of, 200.
  heir to the crown of, 270—1.
  Holland and, 224.
  Holland without sympathy with, 241.
  Innocent XII. decides upon succession to, 275.
  James I. and, 186.
  Leopold disputes title to crown of, 277.
  Leopold's grandson and the succession of, 270—1.
  Louis XIV. proposes the partition of, 270—1. [270.
  Louis XIV. renounces claim to, 234.
  Low Countries and, 236.
  Margaret Theresa and the succession to, 270.
  Maria Theresa renounces crown of, 234, 270.
  maritime law of, 164.
  meeting of plenipotentiaries of France and, 233.
  Mendoza, ambassador of, 157.
  Montague and, 228.
  Netherlands and, 153. [240.
  Netherlands war between France and,
  Palatinate seized by, 183.
  peace forced upon, 223.
  Peterborough, see Earl of Peterborough.
  Philip V. preferred by, 304.
  Portocarrero and, 273.
  Portugal revolts against, 219.
  proposed partition of, 270—1.
  Saracens in, 30.
  Savoy and, 276.
  Scipio conquers, 7.
  secret treaty for partition of, 270.
  slave trade and, 170—1. [192.
  squadron threatened in the Baltic by,
  succession to crown of, 270.
  troops furnished for Bohemian war by, 183. [219.
  Van Tromp destroys fleet of, 218,
  war drags on in, 303.
  war encouraged by, 212. [270—1.
  William III. agrees to partition of,
Sparta, aggressive spirit of, 13.
Spartan Commissioners, judicial murder by, 15.
Spartans:
  charge against, 10.
  crime by, 3.

Spies, severity towards, 5.
Spinola, siege and retreat by, 184.
Stadtholders, attempted murder of, 179—80.
Standing army of France, 132.
Stanhope, Philip V. defeated by, 303.
States-General of France, summoning of, 57.
Steinkirk, battle of, 264.
Stettin, Gustavus Adolphus takes, 190.
Stewarts of Scotland, Robert II. first of the, 111.
Stirling, battle of, 90.
Stockholm, Gustavus Adolphus's farewell address at, 192.
Stralsund: [188.
  Count Wallenstein vainly besieges,
  Gustavus Adolphus assists, 193.
Strangers:
  Middle Ages and, 118.
  rules towards, 1.
Strasburg:
  France acquires, 224.
  France formally acquires, 268.
  Louis XIV. acquires, 253.
Sultan:
  Austria threatened by the, 254.
  captive entertained by the, 67.
  Count Wallenstein threatens the, 190.
  first, 73.
  Prince Eugene defeats the, 268.
  Tekeli retained prisoner by the, 269.
Supremacy:
  English claim to, 86.
  Scotland and, 86.
Surinam, Holland acquires, 239.
Susa, expiation at, 3.
Sweden:
  Denmark and, 160.
  exhaustion of, 224.
  France and, 224.
  France in alliance with, 202.
  Great Britain makes treaty with, 241.
  Gustavus Vasa of, 160.
  Holland makes treaty with, 241.
  independence of, 160.
  James I. and, 187.
  Louis XIV. opposed by, 259.
  Pomerania annexed to, 224.
  Protestantism in, 160.
  Rugen annexed to, 224.
  subsidy accorded to, 224.
  war between Poland and, 193.
Swedes exonerated, 205.
Swift:
  Harley and, 313.
  Marlborough libelled by, 312.
  punishment of, 313.
  St. John and, 313.
Swiss cantons, independence conceded to, 225.
Sylla:
  slaughter by, 21.
  unfavourably compared, 21.

Sylverius, deposition of, 29.
Syracuse, treaty with Prince of, 5.

Tagliacozza, battle of, 52.
Tallard, Marlborough makes prisoner of, 289.
Tamerlane:
    approach of, 75.
    China and, 75.
    death of, 75.
    Pekin and, 75.
    Voltaire on, 75.
Tamworth, Earl of Murray and, 158.
Tancred, vain resistance of, 68.
Tartars, Turks and, 75.
Taxes, exemption of ecclesiatics from, 51.
Tekeli, Hungarian refugee, Sultan refuses to give up, 269.
Temple, Triple Alliance and, 241.
Temple of Delphi:
    burning of, 1.
    engraving on column of, 11.
Teutons, Reformation accepted by, 160.
Thaddeus de Suessa defends Frederick II., 47.
Thames, De Ruyter enters the, 239.
Thebans:
    alliance, with, 12.
    success of, 11.
Thebes:
    aggressive spirit of, 13.
    seizure of citadel of, 10.
Theodosius (Emperor):
    barbarous massacre by, 23.
    tears of, 24.
Thessalonica, murder of Governor of, 23.
Thirty Years' War, 173—226.
    barbarous treatment during, 115.
    commencement of, 178.
    end of the, 220.
    prelude to the, 176.
    religious equality established by, 225.
    religious settlements effected by the, 225.
    two greatest armies of the, 205.
Thomas à Becket, Alexander III. and, 35.
Thrasymene, battle of, 14.
Thucydides informs us, 3.
Thurn, Protestant rebellion led by, 180.
Tilly (Count):
    attempt to shield, 198.
    Bavarian force of, 202. [188.
    Christian of Denmark defeated by, death of, 203.
    Ferdinand of Styria and, 182.
    flight of, 190. [203.
    Gustavus Adolphus advances upon,
    Gustavus Adolphus finally defeats, 203.
    Gustavus Adolphus guarded against by, 202.
    Gustavus Adolphus totally defeats, 199.
    irreproachable character of, 185.

Tilly (Count):
    Magdeburg besieged and sacked by, mortally wounded, 203. [196—8.
    promotion of, 195.
    Te Deum ordered by, 198.
    total defeat of, 199—200.
    unbounded outrage permitted by, 197.
Torcy: [—300.
    Marlborough negotiates with, 299
    Peace of Utrecht arranged by, 315.
Torstenson, France in alliance with, 220.
Tory opponents, Marlborough and his,
Toul: [312.
    capture of, 150.
    France acquires, 224. [291.
Toulon, Prince Eugene vainly attacks,
Toulouse, Black Prince marches upon, 110.
Tournay, Allied Powers capture, 301.
Tours, victory of Martel at, 30.
Tourville, English fleet dispersed by, 265.
Transylvania:
    Bethlem Gabor usurps, 182.
    Turks abandon, 269.
Travellers, inhospitable treatment of, 117.
Treaties:
    noblest of, 6.
    rarely observed, 5.
    repudiation of, 19.
    sanctity of, 6.
    sixteenth century, 131.
Treaty of
    Aix-la-Chapelle, 241.
    Breda, 239.
    Carlowitz, 269.
    Cateau Cambresis, 151—2.
    Heilbron, 215.
    Munster, 220—224.
    Nimeguen, 253.
    Passau, 173, 225.
    Prague, 216.
    Paris, 165.
    Ryswick, 266—9, 270.
    the Pyrenees, 232—5, 276.
    Utrecht, 319; see also Peace of Utrecht.
    Westminster, 248.
    Westphalia, 173—226.
Treves, Louis XIV. saves, 261.
Triple Alliance, 241.
    De Witt and the, 241. [241.
    Louis XIV. tries to dissolve the,
    Temple and the, 241.
Turenne:
    Austria and, 220.
    Condé opposed by, 227.
    death of, 249, 254.
    Marlborough tutored by, 300.
    Melander totally defeated by, 220.
    Richelieu and, 220.
Turin, battle of, 290.
Turks:
    Adrianople captured by, 73.
    Asia Minor invaded by, 66.

INDEX.   393

Turks:
  Asiatic provinces recovered by, 75.
  Azoff surrendered by, 269.
  Bethlem Gabor in alliance with, 182.
  Byzantine Empire and, 66.
  Dalmatia surrendered by, 269.
  defeat before Vienna of, 254.
  enormous loss of the, 269.
  Hungary abandoned by, 269.
  Kaminieck surrendered by, 269.
  Leopold defeats, 268.
  Leopold threatened by, 253.
  Morea surrendered by, 269.
  Normans contrasted with, 67.
  Ottoman, 73.
  surrenders by, 269.
  Tartars and, 75.
  total defeat of, 75.
  Transylvania abandoned by, 269.
  Vienna advanced upon by, 254.
Tutbury, Queen of Scots imprisoned at, 154.
Tyre, respect for treaties by, 5.

Unbelief, Frederick II. accused of, 46.
United Provinces:
  France makes treaty with, 236.
  Louis XIV. invades the, 245.
United States:
  Great Britain makes treaty with, 257.
  maritime law and the, 165.
Urban II., speech of, 69.
Usages of mankind, Xerxes and, 3.
Utrecht:
  Louis XIV. holds court at, 245.
  Peace of, see Peace of Utrecht.
  Treaty of, 319.

Valencia, Peterborough masters, 293.
Valentine Visconti, Duke of Burgundy and, 122.
Vandals, humanity of the, 24.
Van Tromp, exploits of, 218—19.
Vassalage:
  English kings claim, 85.
  Nicholas IV. upon, 86.
Vattel, opinion of, 7.
Vauban on Revocation of Edict of Nantes, 258.
Vendome:
  Allied Powers defeated by, 304.
  Burgundy thwarts, 294.
  France saved by, 290.
Venetians:
  Ancona and the, 56.
  Constantinople attacked by, 70.
  jealousy of, 70.
  massacre at Padua by, 115.
Venice:
  assailed, 135.
  Charles VIII. resisted by, 132.
  despoiled, 136.
  excommunication of, 136—7.
  Louis XII. and, 134.

Venice:
  Papal conspiracy against, 133—4.
  restoration of, 136.
  zenith of power of, 133.
Verdun:
  capture of, 150.
  France acquires, 224.
Verneuil, battle of, 117, 129.
Versailles:
  building of, 256.
  Doge of Genoa visits, 256.
  domestic calamities at, 314.
  splendid ceremonials at, 258.
Vienna:
  defeat of Turks before, 254.
  Duke of Lorraine defends, 254.
  Ferdinand of Styria defends, 180.
  Leopold's flight from, 254.
  Protestants march upon and retreat from, 180.
  Turks defeated before, 254.
Villars:
  Marlborough battles with, 289.
  Prince Eugene defeated by, 315.
  wounding of, 303.
Villeroi:
  Marlborough totally defeats, 289.
  Prince Eugene repulses, 279.
Visconti (The) of Milan, 111.
Voltaire on:
  Louis XIV. and William III., 281.
  Tamerlane, 75.

Wager of battle in Brittany, 108.
Wales, conquerors of, 80.
Wallace:
  achievements of, 92.
  Alnwick monastery saved by, 91.
  atrocities of, 91.
  chosen guardian, 92.
  defeat of, 92.
  example of, 92.
  execution of, 97.
  exhibition of limbs of, 97.
  magnanimity of, 91.
  retires to France, 92.
  rising of, 90.
  taken prisoner, 96.
Wallenstein, see Count Wallenstein.
Walloon soldiers, merciless cruelty of,
War: [197.
  Peloponnesian, 3.
  slave trade compared with, 171.
  superior humanity during, 22.
  Thirty Years', 173—226.
Warfare:
  Alfred the Great and, 28.
  Christinnity and, 21, 23.
  commerce and, 21.   [183.
  Count Mansfeld introduced lawless,
  Count Wallenstein observes the courtesies of, 207.
  dark spots of, 21.
  foraging during, 36.

2 D

Warfare:
  Frederick I. and, 36.
  intercourse during, 21.
  maritime laws of, 21.
  marked improvement in usages of, 21.
  prisoners in, 37; see also Prisoners.
  rapine during, 36.
  twelfth century, 36.
Wars of the Roses, English, 31. [302.
Waterloo, Malplaquet compared with,
Waters, neutral, 7.
Westminster:
  stone of destiny removed to, 90.
  Treaty of, 248.
Westphalia:
  history of Treaty of, 173—226.
  signing of Treaty of, 235—6.
William III.:
  Boufflers opposed to, 266.
  Charles II. contrasted with, 282.
  constitutional monarchy made practicable by, 282.
  critical position of, 263.
  Cromwell compared to, 281.
  death of, 281.
  driving back of, 264.
  Duke de Chartres opposed to, 264.
  England acknowledges, 262.
  Flanders invaded by, 264.
  French army defeats, 264.
  Holland ruled by, 272.
  House of Commons mortifies, 272.
  Ireland opposes, 262.
  James II. defeated by, 263.
  James II. deposed by, 259.
  Louis XIV. acknowledges, 267.
  Louis XIV. coalesced against by, 260.

William III.:
  Louis XIV. compared with, 281.
  Louis XIV. continues to resist, 281.
  Louis XIV. obtains concessions from, 271.
  Luxembourg never defeated by, 265.
  Luxembourg twice defeats, 264—5.
  Marlborough commissioned by, 279.
  Marlborough succeeds, 283.
  motives of, 272.
  Namur captured by, 266.
  painful submission of, 282.
  Palatinate and, 260.
  Prince of Orange becomes, 259—60.
  prominence of, 283.
  Queen Anne eulogises, 283.
  Scotland and, 283.
  Scotland acknowledges, 262.
  20,000 men lost by, 265.
  unpopularity of, 282.
  Voltaire on, 281.
William the Lion, 37.
Winchester, pirates executed at, 28.
Women, chivalry and, 79.
Wulfstan, slavery opposed by, 26.

Xerxes:
  invasion of Greece by, 6.
  magnanimity of, 3.
  march of, 3.

Yeomen, Battle of Creci won by, 104.

Zachary:
  freeing of prisoners by, 26.
  Rome and, 30.
Zanta, battle of, 268.

www.ingramcontent.com/pod-product-compliance
Lightning Source LLC
Chambersburg PA
CBHW022120290426
44112CB00008B/751